Human Aspects of Computer-Aided Design

Human Aspects of Computer-Aided Design

Ann Majchrzak, Tien-Chien Chang
Woodrow Barfield, Ray Eberts
and Gavriel Salvendy

Purdue University, West Lafayette, Indiana

Taylor & Francis
Philadelphia and London
1987

USA Taylor & Francis Inc., 242 Cherry St., Philadelphia, PA 19106–1906

UK Taylor & Francis Ltd, 4 John St., London WC1N 2ET

British Library Cataloguing in Publication Data

Human aspects of computer-aided design
1. Engineering design—Data processing
I. Majchrzak, Ann
620′.00425′0285 TA174

ISBN 0-85066-364-4

Library of Congress Cataloging in Publication Data

Human aspects of computer-aided design
Bibliography: p.
Includes index.
1. Computer-aided design. 2. Man-machine systems — Psychological aspects. 3. Work environment.
I. Majchrzak, Ann.
TA174.H87 1987 620′.00425′02854019 86-14489

The screen image on the front cover was produced using the SAMMIE computer-aided design system. SAMMIE originated at the University of Nottingham, England, and the pictures were produced by Professor Maurice Bonney of the University of Nottingham, and Dr Keith Case and Dr Mark Porter of Loughborough University of Technology, who are also directors of SAMMIE CAD Ltd. SAMMIE allows one to model and construct possible workplace arrangements using a computerized man model and computer models of the workplace.

Cover design by Russell Beach.
Typeset by Alresford Typesetting & Design, Alresford, Hants.
Printed and bound in Great Britain by Taylor & Francis (Printers) Ltd, Basingstoke, Hants.

Preface

The purpose of this book is to provide information about technical, management and human-computer aspects of computer-aided design (CAD) systems. This information is intended to enhance the effective design and use of CAD systems. Ideally the book should provide comprehensive guidelines for the effective design and use of CAD systems. Due to the relatively immature nature of the CAD discipline, however, it is not possible at this stage of development to present this information. Instead, the book presents theoretically-based and practically-oriented information, which when integrated into the design and operation of CAD systems could enhance the effective and wider use of CAD systems. It is also envisioned that the reading of this book will stimulate additional research into the human aspects of designing and operating CAD systems. Thus this book should be of use to managers, CAD users, designers of CAD systems and human factors professionals.

Estimates suggest that in 1985 there were only about 100 000 CAD workstations worldwide with annual sales of over US $3 billion. This represents less than one-tenth of one per cent of the areas where CAD systems could be applied worldwide. In the United States this percentage is about 2·5 per cent. It is estimated that by the year 2010, CAD will be an over US $10 billion annual business with over 2 million CAD systems in use worldwide.

Because of the existence of this current demand and the potential for rapid accelerated future growth of CAD use, the content of this book is presented with the notion that it can make a positive contribution towards more effective design and use of CAD systems. Although computer-aided design is frequently linked to computer-aided manufacturing, this book addresses only the first part (CAD) of this integrated function.

The authors are grateful for the excellent cooperation of Michael Dawes and David Grist of Taylor & Francis, as well as the kind cooperation of the organizations who so willingly allowed us to use their material in the illustrations. Each of these sources is acknowledged in the text. The writing of this book was made possible through the support of the National Science Foundation (Grant No. ISI-8641482) and the NEC Corporation.

The authors would like to thank Joe Mickel and Jim Fleming for making some of the research cited in Part III possible; Pat Mosher for identifying material for this Part; Jim Jacobs and Robert Newton for carefully reviewing an earlier version of Part III; and Janet Yoakum, Debbie Hulsey and Diana Huffer for their patience in typing and retyping major parts of this book.

Purdue University, Indiana
June 1986

Ann Majchrzak
Tien-Chien Chang
Woodrow Barfield
Ray Eberts
Gavriel Salvendy

Contents

Chapter 1
Introduction

1.1. What is CAD?

Computer-Aided Design (CAD) can refer to any kind of activity which utilizes a computer to assist in the creation, modification, presentation and analysis of a design. In any design process the three major functions are: synthesis, analysis and presentation. Figure 1.1 illustrates a typical design process in which the synthesis stage of design includes mental processes such as decision making and creativity. The synthesized object is represented in a generally accepted format, such as an engineering drawing or a physical model. After synthesis, the object is then analyzed, evaluated and modified. After several iterations, the final design can be prepared for presentation and approval. In a traditional design process or non-CAD system, all three functions are carried out manually with the aid of drafting instruments, calculators, handbooks, tables, charts, etc. A computer-aided system uses a computer and I/O (input/output) devices to substitute for these traditional aids.

The term CAD is also used to refer to any of the sub-functions of the computer-aided design system, e.g. a design drafting package, a finite element analysis program, a structure analysis program, etc. However, CAD has also been associated only with the utilization of interactive computer graphics with design functions. Although some design functions do not necessarily have to use interactive computer graphics, it is generally accepted that the graphics interface is part of a CAD system. Therefore, a CAD system is defined in this book as a design software/hardware package which utilizes interactive computer graphics.

1.2. A brief history

The development of CAD can be dated back to the early 1960s when researchers at the Massachusetts Institute of Technology (MIT) started their work on the Sage system (CRT display and operating system). Figure 1.2 shows the historical development of CAD as well as some related technologies. The pioneer work of Ivan Sutherland on developing the Sketchpad interactive computer graphics system at MIT (Sutherland, 1963) allowed the use of the CRT system as an elec-

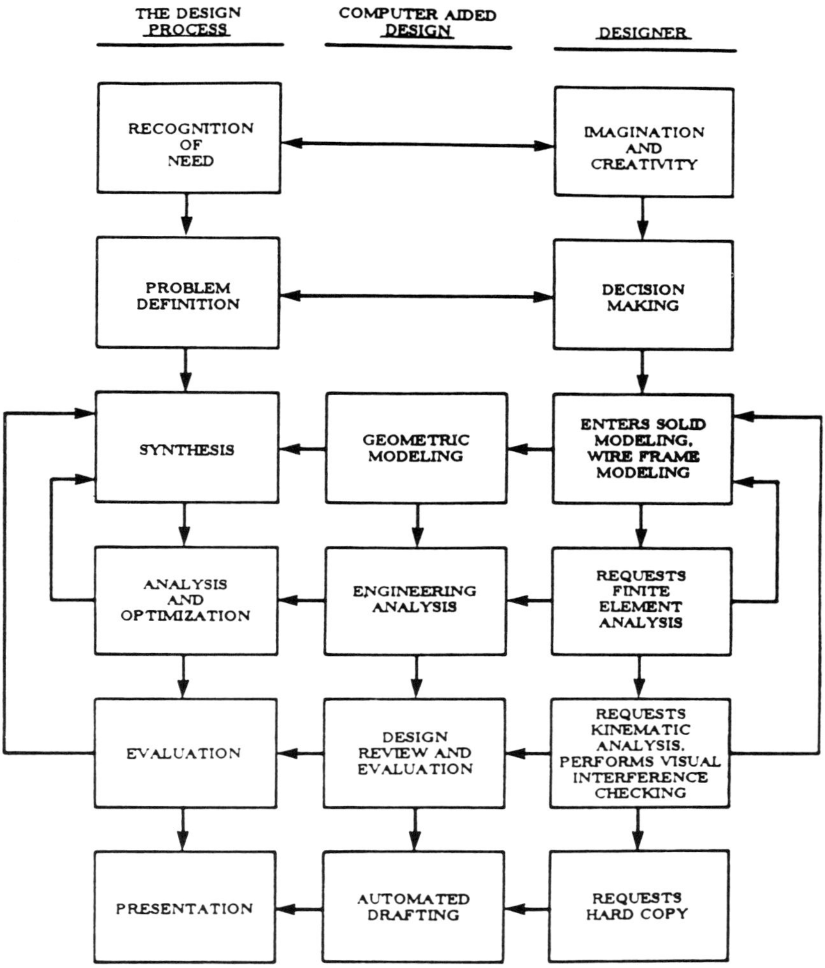

Figure 1.1. The design process.

tronic drafting board. In the early 1960s there were also systems using APT-like (APT is a part programming language used in the control of numerical control machine tools) commands to control a plotter to draw two-dimensional (2-D) engineering diagrams.

Two-dimensional drafting, three-dimensional (3-D) drafting, wireframe CAD systems and Unisurf sculpture surface (Bezier, 1968, 1972) were developed in the 1960s shortly after interactive computer graphics devices became available. However, in these early years, due to the high cost of computers and peripheral devices, CAD was considered a luxury. In the 1970s, with the drastic drop in computer software and hardware costs, increases in their capability, and the

1955	MIT started APT development
	AI, Dartmouth Conference
	LISP language
	APT language
1960	
	CRT display
	Sketchpad interactive computer graphics
	Coon's patch, sculptured surfaces
	Ferguson's patch, sculptured surfaces
1965	Unisurf, Bezier's patch, sculptured surfaces
	CAD drafting
	Mini-computers
1970	
	Solid modelling development started
	Build-1 Solid modeller
	Micro-computers
1975	
	3-D CAD systems
	Super-mini computers
	PADL-1·0 solid modeller
1980	Super-computers
	Micro-based workstations
	Solid modeller became commercialized
	PC based CAD
1985	
	MAP, TOP LAN standards
	Expert CAD systems

Figure 1.2. The history of CAD.

development of user-friendly software, CAD became more widely accepted. During this period, software for 3-D solid modelling and shaded color graphics were developed. Many software programs for engineering analysis applications were also integrated into CAD systems. At this time CAD was moving from computer-aided drafting to computer-aided design and modelling.

In the 1980s, developmental work in CAD has moved toward interfacing standards and powerful and specialized hardware and software. The development of super-minicomputers in the late 1970s and super-microcomputers in the early 1980s has added a new dimension to CAD. CAD has become an affordable tool for nearly every company. The development of CAD software for personal computers now enables everyone to use CAD and has spawned interest in the development of expert CAD systems.

1.3. The design process

An engineering design can be represented in one of the several ways:

1. Language description
2. 3-D projection drawings or sketches
3. 2-D three-view drawing
4. Special code, i.e. group technology (GT) code
5. Physical model, i.e. clay model

A language description or special code is not accurate because each method of representation only approximates the definition of an object. A physical model is difficult to make and to modify. The most effective way to convey the designer's idea is through a drawing. Since a designer is limited to working on two dimensions, engineers have developed drafting rules which represent details of three-dimensional objects on paper by presenting three projected views. A trained engineer/designer can reconstruct the lines and curves on a drawing precisely into a three-dimensional object in his or her mind. Sections and auxiliary views are used to provide more details. 3-D projection drawing, such as an orthographic projection and a perspective projection, are widely used to show the finished product and assembly drawing. Due to its inability to show details on the inner and opposite side of the object, a 3-D projection drawing is used only as a supplement to engineering drawing.

Before the computer era, all drawings were done with pencil and paper. It is a painstaking process to prepare a drawing and modify it. Engineers were trained to be extra-cautious when handling drawings; and draftspersons were trained to convert rough sketches into a final engineering drawing. Long lead times for drawing preparation were an accepted fact when designing manually. Inevitably there were always the potential human errors in conveying and interpretating not only the sketches but also the final drawings.

One of the main advantages of a CAD system is to shorten the lead time of drafting. The drafting function of a CAD system is the substitution of a drafting board and instrument. In a computer-aided drafting system, standard drafting symbols and rules are used. Although the entire design/drafting process is still the same, it is much faster and easier for a draftsperson to enter, modify, and plot a drawing with CAD. Design updates can be done easily and the final paper drawing (hardcopy) is always neatly prepared. It is also possible to merge two drawings and/or to rescale a drawing. Frequently used symbols and parts can be saved in the system, and retrieved when needed. Thus, design productivity is greatly increased.

A further improvement of computer-aided drafting is computer-aided design/modelling. Three-dimensional objects can be "modeled" in a computer. The frame of an object is modeled by a series of enclosed curves called wire-frames. Coordinate transformation is used to rotate the object in space. One can not only view the object from different angles, but also view a cut-off of the object. Standard three-view drawing can also be prepared automatically. Instead of reconstructing an image in one's mind, a realistic picture can be displayed on the graphics terminal. Human interpretation errors are reduced. Using the new tool, a draftsperson has to re-orient his or her thinking in three-dimensional geometry. Points, lines, circles, curves and surfaces are entered as 3-D objects. Dimensions can be added interactively or semi-automatically. Additional texts can also be attached.

Complex surfaces which are defined by mathematical equations can be represented in a 3-D CAD system. Their shape can be plotted on the screen or on paper. Combined with machine control part programming languages such as APT and Compact II, design and manufacturing processes can be integrated. CAD systems which also have NC (numerical control) part programming capabilities are usually called CAD/CAM systems. However, as mentioned in the Preface, the focus in this book will be on CAD and not CAD/CAM.

It has always been a problem for engineers to represent free form surfaces such as the body of an automobile, ship or aircraft. It is extremely difficult to find a mathematically exact description of a free form surface. Unfortunately many objects have free form surfaces. Since they are difficult to represent on paper, such surfaces were represented with manual drafting by using their sections. In a conventional design studio, a clay mould is first made, then sectional measurements are taken. The measurements are plotted on either paper or wooden templets—one for each section. In ship-building this operation is also called lofting, and it is a very difficult and tedious task with a final manufactured surface compared with those templets. Sculpture surface programs such as Unisurf developed by Bezier (1968, 1972) solved this problem. A free form surface can not only be modeled on a CAD system but the numerical control part program for machine tools can also be produced from the model.

For an engineering analysis such as calculating volume, mass, stress, etc., a wireframe model does not provide enough information. A wireframe model does not possess information on the content of an object. There is no way of telling whether a point is inside or outside the body of a wireframe object. In the 1970s solid modelling techniques were developed. In solid modelling, objects are represented using solid primitives or boundary faces. The inside or outside of an object can be determined, thus an engineering analysis can be performed on the model. Since it is relatively easy to translate a solid model into a wireframe, the display of a solid model in the traditional representation can be made. One can also display any cut-off views of an object. Intricate details of any object or objects can be displayed. Popular engineering analysis methods, such as finite element analysis, can be performed on a solid model, and the results displayed for the original model. A new dimension of Computer-Aided Design has emerged.

The development of Artificial Intelligence (AI) and Expert Systems (ES) technology in recent years brings the possibility of automating the design process. Although the creativity of the human can not be substituted for, at least in the near future, AI can assist human designers in improving the design and can ease the modelling task. One can expect to see more and more involvement of computers in the design process.

1.4. Effective use of CAD

In order for CAD to be effectively utilized it must result in improved performance (Salvendy, 1982), improved human interactive system design (Salvendy, 1984, 1987), improved organizational factors (Dunnette, 1976) and reduced stress (Salvendy, 1981). In addition, a report of the National Research Council (NRC, 1986) shows that it has become evident, based on effective practices in industry, that for the effective implementation of computer-automated technologies such as CAD the existing organizational context in which the technology is implemented must be considered. Such organizational factors include:

- Organizational culture
- Organization design
- Information systems
- Job design
- Compensation and appraisal
- Personnel selection, training and education
- Employee–employer relations

It could also be argued that before CAD systems can be effectively implemented, the design process must first be fully understood so that an effective interactive mode between the designer and the CAD system can be achieved. This mode should maximize the designer's creativity and thus encourage the design engineer to interact directly with the CAD system. By so doing, the need to have a specialized CAD operator to interface with the CAD designer is eliminated.

Finally, advanced technology such as CAD is frequently being introduced into an organization progressively resulting in 'islands of automation': at the outset of such an introduction emphasis must be placed on the end goal of total information integration and exchange with other sections of the organization. For example, it is well known that the link between CAD and computer-aided manufacturing (CAM) is not as close as we may wish it to be. It is also evident that the link between CAD and other parts of the organization is even weaker. Furthermore, the communication between CAD systems and design operators is not as good as it could be.

A framework for CAD systems design and use is illustrated in Figure 1.3. This figure also illustrates the content of this book. The rationale for this figure and for the sequence of the subject presentations in the book is based on the notion that first the equipment characteristics and functions must be understood. Hence, the technical information about CAD is presented first in Part I. In order for the equipment to be well designed, to be most acceptable by users and result in increased quality and productivity of design, the interaction between the human and the equipment must be considered. Part II discusses how best to design both the software and hardware interface for comfortable and productive performance. In this part, the human factors issues address only the interaction between CAD operators and equipment. Part III addresses the management issues associated with the job design of CAD operators, the interaction among CAD users, and the interaction between CAD users and other sectors of the organization. Although Parts I, II and III address distinctly different issues associated with CAD, and hence are presented separately, they are both conceptually and operationally integrated in Part IV into one unified objective of easy and productive CAD design and use. Therefore, Part IV is presented to integrate the conclusions from the different parts of the book into a unified conceptual framework for effective design and use of CAD systems.

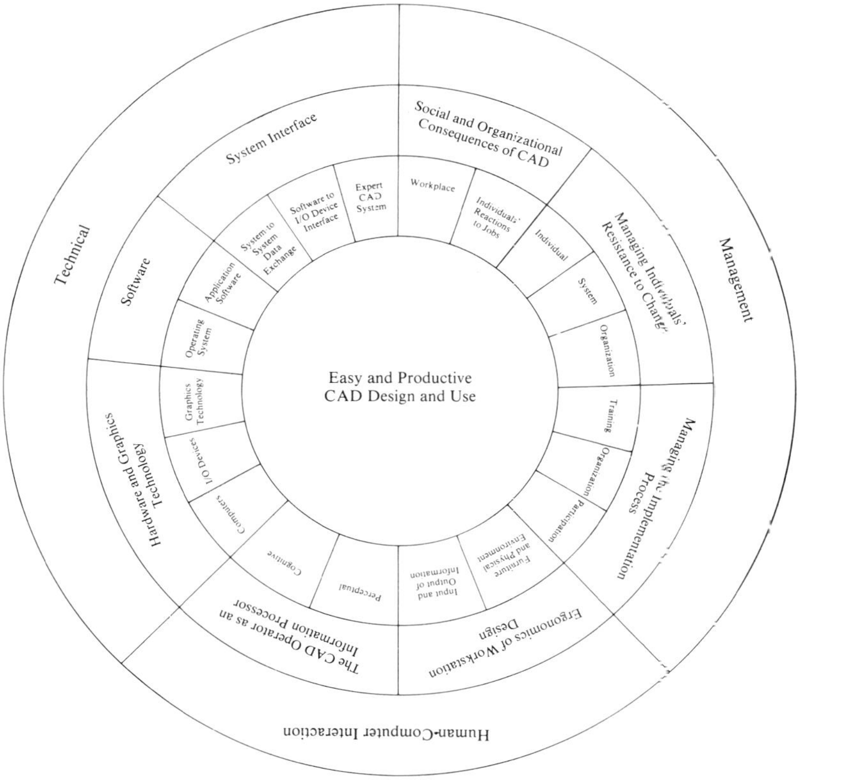

Figure 1.3. A framework for CAD systems design and operation.

Part I

TECHNICAL ASPECTS OF CAD

Computer-aided design is a technology which includes geometric modelling, drafting, and engineering analysis. It is implemented by computer software and hardware. The hardware provides the physical interface with the human user, while the software directs the logic operations of applications. In order to know CAD and its capabilities and limitations one has to be familiar with both the hardware and the software of CAD. It is the purpose of this Part to familiarize readers with the fundamentals of CAD technology. There are three chapters included in this Part: CAD Hardware and Graphics Technology, CAD Software, and CAD System Integration and Future Development.

The chapter on CAD hardware and graphics technology introduces the commonly used hardware and fundamentals of computer graphics. The chapter on CAD software introduces the operation system and application software, with the emphasis placed on the different types of application softwares. These are classified first by their complexity, such as 2-D, 3-D, sculptured surface, and solid modelling, then by their application areas. Chapter 4 discusses the system integration and future development issues; CAD interface standards are briefly introduced, expert CAD systems development is discussed, and the future trend of CAD development is predicted.

Chapter 2
CAD hardware and graphics technology

The basic CAD hardware consists of three parts: computer, input devices and output devices (Figure 2.1). The computer does data storage and retrieval, data manipulation, and peripheral control. The input devices are used to input design information and system command, the output devices display design representations, either on a video display or on a hardcopy medium. Due to the heavy data processing demands and massive data storage requirements for CAD, the computer used in CAD must run fast and have large amounts of memory. In the 1970s, computers used in CAD were either mainframe computers or dedicated minicomputers. In recent years, the advances of computer technology to increase

Figure 2.1. A CAD workstation (courtesy G E Calma)

computing power have made it possible to have the mainframe computing power and memory in a desk top computer. The increased speed and storage as well as networking capability have made CAD faster, performing larger tasks while remaining affordable. In this chapter, CAD hardware and graphics technology is described. Computers used in CAD are introduced first in Section 2.1; Section 2.2 discusses input and output devices; and Section 2.3 covers basic graphics technologies which are related to hardware.

2.1. Computers used in CAD

The computer is the brain of a CAD system. It stores, retrieves and manipulates design data. Data entered from the input devices are temporarily kept in the RAM (Random Access Memory) of a computer. RAM is the active memory of a computer; as soon as the computer is powered off, the information in the RAM is lost. For permanent storage, hard disk and magnetic tape are used. A hard disk can provide from several million to several billion bytes of data storage. A byte is a computer memory measurement unit, equivalent to eight bits. Each bit can store either a 1 or 0. Normally one byte can store one character of information. Information stored on a hard disk can be retrieved randomly and quickly (several million bytes per second). Therefore, hard disks are used to store frequently used design data as well as the CAD software package itself. Magnetic tapes are sequential devices. Data on the tape are stored and retrieved sequentially. The read/write to and from the magnetic tape is relatively slow. However, tapes are much cheaper and removable and thus are used for data archiving.

CAD is both storage and computation demanding. For each picture, thousands of data points have to be processed and stored. Usually fast processing speed and large storage capability are required. Therefore, both fast hard disk and mass storage back-up tapes are needed for CAD systems. Hard disks are used for storing the operating system, CAD software, frequently used design symbols, and files of the current designs. Old design files are dumped onto tapes for archiving.

CAD has been implemented on all types of digital computers. Digital computers can be classified as super-computer, mainframe computer, minicomputer, and microcomputer. Due to the rapid technological advances in the micro-electronic and computer fields, the lines dividing computer classes become vague. Sometimes the major distinction is based on the physical size, especially for minicomputers and microcomputers. The computer speed is also no longer a good measure to separate micros from minis, and even mainframes.

Within minicomputer and microcomputer classes there are also super-minicomputers and super-microcomputers. Most of the super-microcomputers are packaged as engineering workstations. They are powerful yet relatively inexpensive compared to minicomputers. In recent years they have become very popular for CAD. In the following sections, different types of computers are introduced.

Super-computer

Super-computers are a special breed of computers. They have special architectures (e.g., pipelining, parallel processors, vector processors, densely packed VLSIs, etc.) to enable them to run fast and to access massive amounts of memory. Super-computers can run at the speed of tens of Million Instructions Per Second (MIPS), and have tens of million bytes of RAM memory. They can solve very large scale problems at a fast speed. Examples of super-computers are Cray computers and CDC Cyber 205, etc. They usually cost several million dollars each. They are able to display complex shaded pictures with extreme high resolution. Animation of realistic pictures is also made possible by using super-computers: the cinema and commercial industry use super-computers for animation works. Super-computers are also being used to assist in the design of other computers. Although they are powerful for CAD applications, due to the cost of such computers they are not commonly used in CAD.

Mainframe computer

Mainframe computers are large-scale computer systems. Mainframe refers to the cabinet or rack which holds the Central Processing Unit (CPU) of the computer. In a mainframe computer system, there may be several cabinets full of electronic circuits containing CPU, memory and I/O interfaces. Mainframe computers are built for general computing. They can access much more memory than minicomputers and microcomputers. They also run fast (more than 10 MIPS), can access several megabytes of RAM memory, and have a wide variety of peripheral devices. They can handle very large databases, and solve large-scale business as well as engineering problems. A mainframe computer usually costs from a quarter million to several million dollars.

Mainframe computers have been used in CAD applications and, although expensive, 20 to 100+ users can use them at the same time. Both graphics and analysis programs can be installed in a mainframe computer, and in addition, such computers can support large databases of design and analysis information. Multiple users can share the system and information. Example mainframe computers are IBM 370, 30xx, and CDC 6xxx.

When mainframe computers are used in CAD, a centralized computing center houses all the hardware and provides software support. While such a system relieves individual users from the burden of maintaining the system, it removes their flexibility to select system components and to change the operating environment. For example, decisions for selecting terminal, peripherals, operating schedules, and priorities must be made by a centralized computing staff when a mainframe computer is used. In addition to centralizing operations, a mainframe necessitates the use of special graphics workstations/terminals. Such graphics workstations/terminals must conform with the specification of the CAD vendor.

Minicomputer

Minicomputers were invented in the 1960s, the results of electronic miniaturization. Using LSIs, the circuit of a computer is reduced to microchips, thus the size of the computer is miniaturized. They were designed to be small departmental or dedicated process control computers. Early 16-bit models can only run at a speed of one MIPS and have 64 K (1 K equal to 1024) bytes of RAM memory. Now super minicomputers usually have 32-bit architecture, run at several MIPS and have several megabytes of RAM memory. Due to the advances in technology, the minicomputers in the early 1980s are as fast as those mainframe computers used ten years ago. Minicomputers cost from tens of thousands to several hundred thousand dollars each.

In the 1960s, minicomputers used to be the workhorse of CAD. They were used to perform the lower level graphics calculation and manipulation for CAD displays, while the data processing functions were performed on mainframe computers. Gradually, those lower level display-related functions were built into the terminals themselves. Minicomputers have also been made powerful enough to substitute mainframes for all of CAD's data processing needs. Although they still can not support as many users as mainframe computers do, the speeds of some super minicomputers are comparable to those of mainframes, and they virtually provide all the functionalities of mainframe computers. Examples of minicomputers are DEC PDP 11, VAX 11, HP 2100, HP 3000, Prime computers, etc.

Due to their low cost and high performance, minicomputers have become the major computer type used in multiple-user CAD. The majority of turnkey CAD/CAM systems are based on super-minicomputers. They can usually support from 5 to 20 users. However, when there are several users doing heavy computation on the system, the performance of the system deteriorates drastically. The system response time (the time it takes the system to respond to a user's request) may become so bad that it upsets users. Minicomputer-based CAD systems are usually operated by a department. A company may have several of such systems. Thus data exchange between those systems is an important issue.

Microcomputer

Microcomputers are characterized by their single chip Control Processing Unit (CPU or Micro-Processing Unit, MPU). Since the invention of microcomputers in the early 1970s, they have gone through several revolutions, moving from the initial 4-bit architecture to today's 32-bit architecture.

Earlier microcomputers were used mostly for home computing and dedicated process control. Their data processing capacity was very limited: most microcomputers in those days had less than 64 Kbytes of memory, and ran at a fraction of 1 MIPS. Floppy diskettes were the major permanent storage media. Such microcomputers included Apple II, TRS 80, and Atari 800. Home computers cost a few hundred dollars each.

In recent years, advances in microelectronics technology have improved the capabilities of microcomputers. Functionalities such as fast data processing speed, unlimited RAM memory, large mass storage, multiprocessing, multiprogramming, sophisticated operating systems, languages, etc. are all available on microcomputers. IBM PC, XT, and AT and compatible PCs are representatives of these later advances. Millions of microcomputers have been installed in homes, offices and factory floors.

Modern microcomputers can be further classified as home computers, personal computers, multi-user computers and engineering workstations. Home computers are designed for household use. Due to their limited memory, slow data processing speed, and poor graphics resolution, they are not powerful enough for CAD. Personal computers are those used in offices for single users. Examples of personal computers are IBM PC, XT, AT, and Apple Macintosh. Due to the advantages of low cost (as low as $1 000) and availability, many PC CAD software packages have been developed. Limited by their storage and speed, those PC CAD software are mostly design drafting systems rather than fully-fledged CAD design and analysis systems. Usually PCs do not have high-resolution graphics (320×200 pixels; 4 color); unless enhanced with high-resolution graphics cards (a functional printed circuit board is called a card), PC CAD cannot be used for high quality work. Analysis packages are usually not available on those PCs. Multi-user microcomputers usually employ powerful microprocessors as their central processing unit, while several other microprocessors are used for I/O control. They are much more expensive than single-user PCs. Except for multi-user microcomputers, all microcomputers have a built-in graphics display, and no additional graphics terminal is needed. Multi-user microcomputers share the same limitations as PCs.

Engineering workstation

Engineering workstations are much more powerful than home computers and personal computers. Their usage is becoming popular in CAD systems, thus only engineering workstations will be discussed in more detail below.

Engineering workstations are actually powerful microcomputers with high-resolution graphics and interface capabilities. (A CAD graphics workstation refers to a high-resolution graphics terminal and associated input and output devices, without the local computer.) Workstations usually use one or several of the most powerful microprocessors in the system to provide the power needed for engineering computing. Figure 2.2 shows an engineering workstation. They have 32-bit CPU architectures and provide the power of minicomputers on the desk top at a fraction of the cost, costing from several thousand to 100 000 dollars. A typical engineering workstation provides 1–16 megabytes of RAM memory, 40–300 megabytes of disk space, 1000×1000 bit mapped color display, thousands of colors and full communication (local area network) capability. The majority of minicomputer software is supported on workstations. Workstations

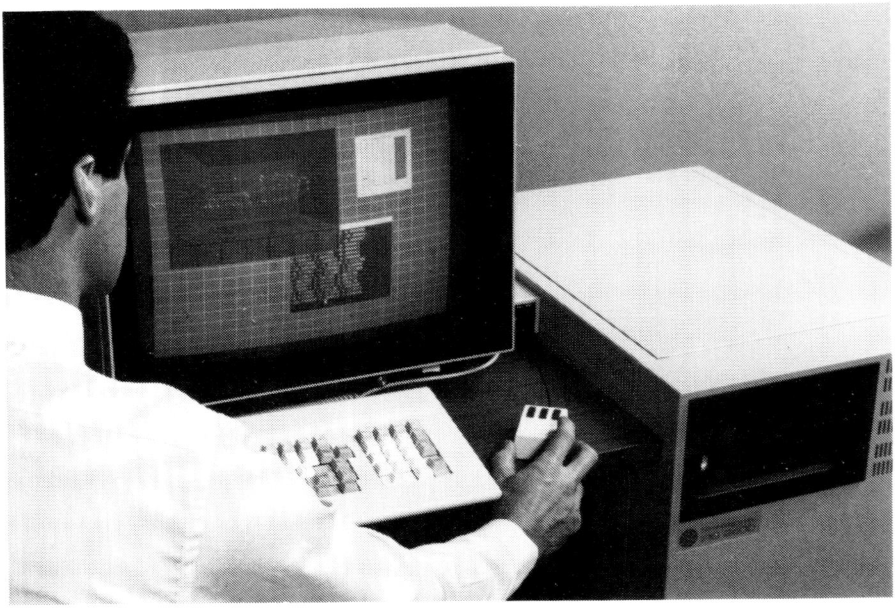

Figure 2.2. An engineering workstation (courtesy Silicon Graphics).

are single-user systems, and they provide better performance than super-mini-computer systems with many users working on them. Engineering workstations can be networked together to share resources such as hard disk drive, printers, plotters, etc., and software, data and resources can be shared. Most CAD vendors supply their software for engineering workstations.

There is a trend of using networks of engineering workstations as the major computing environment for engineering functions. Mainframe computers are used for general business applications and very large-scale problem-solving tasks. Minicomputers are used to handle departmental databases. Individual engineers can use their own engineering workstations to design products, exchange information, and conduct analyses. Design information can be sent to related personnel on the network, thus reducing lead time and eliminate the paper associated with physically drawing the part. Engineering workstation-based CAD systems will play a very important role in the future.

2.2. *Input/output devices*

CAD requires that the user be able to interact with the system. A computer alone will not be able to do much. Input devices such as keyboard, light pen, tablet, etc. are used to input the design information into the computer. Design information includes geometry of the object, dimension of the object, text and CAD system commands. Output devices can be categorized into two types: those which produce hardcopy, and those which produce images. Hardcopy devices such as plotters and slide recorders are used to output permanent (hardcopy) records. CRT and semiconductor displays are image-producing devices, used for operator interaction. In this section commonly used input and output devices are introduced.

Terminals

A terminal is a device which can both input information to a computer or display the output from a computer. A CAD workstation usually uses one or two terminals. It is the basic unit for humans to communicate with a computer system. A terminal consists of a CRT or non-CRT display, a keyboard, and associated electronics. There are alphanumeric terminals and graphics terminals: alphanumeric terminals can only display texts, and graphics terminals can display graphics and texts. Alphanumeric terminals use a built-in character generator to generate character patterns on the CRT. In addition to character generators, graphics terminals have circuits to display points, lines, circles and curves. Some other graphics manipulation functions may also be built in. Graphics terminals can be classified into color graphics terminals and monochrome terminals: monochrome terminals display only two colors, black/white or black/another color, and color terminals can display multiple colors. The more colors a terminal can display the more expensive it is.

CAD systems either use a graphics terminal or use a graphics display (no keyboard) and an alphanumeric terminal. In the latter case, command and system response are displayed on the alphanumeric terminal, and graphics terminal pictures are displayed on the graphics display. In the following sections, CRT, non-CRT, and keyboards and function keys are discussed.

CRT

The cathode ray tube (CRT) is a device to display data and graphics. It is the standard CAD image output device. CRT is the major part of a terminal. The CRT uses electric fields to generate and deflect a finely focused beam of electrons to various parts of a phosphor coated screen. The phosphor when excited by the electron beam glows to produce a visible spot or trace for a short moment.

A fundamental characteristic of the basic CRT is that the glow produced by the electron beam dies soon after the beam has moved away, depending on the persistence of the phosphor. This presents a problem for preserving an image on the screen for any duration, but it also provides the opportunity to generate fast moving dynamic displays.

Various display techniques combining different deflection schemes and methods of preserving or re-writing the image have developed over the years. The three basic schemes are: Direct View Storage Tube (DVST), Vector Refresh, and Raster Scan. Although for a lay person it is not always obvious to tell which scheme is used, each scheme does have its own advantages and limitations.

DIRECT VIEW STORAGE TUBES (DVST)

The DVST is an adaptation of the CRT with an extremely persistent screen. The electron beam is designed not to write directly on the phosphor, but on a storage grid, which is a fine-mesh wire grid coated with a dielectric and mounted behind the face of the tube. Figure 2.3 illustrates a DVST. This produces an image pattern of the charges on the grid which is transferred to the phosphor viewing surface by a continuous flood of electrons issuing from a separate cathode. The electrons not repelled by the storage mesh pass right through it and strike the phosphor, maintaining the image generated by the writing beam. The DVST provides a flicker-free image, regardless of image size. The resolution depends on the density of storage grid's mesh and associated software to control the beam. Usually it can provide very high resolution. The main disadvantage is that it cannot erase parts of the picture selectively. Although color DVSTs are available, they are not very popular. The majority of DVSTs are monochrome.

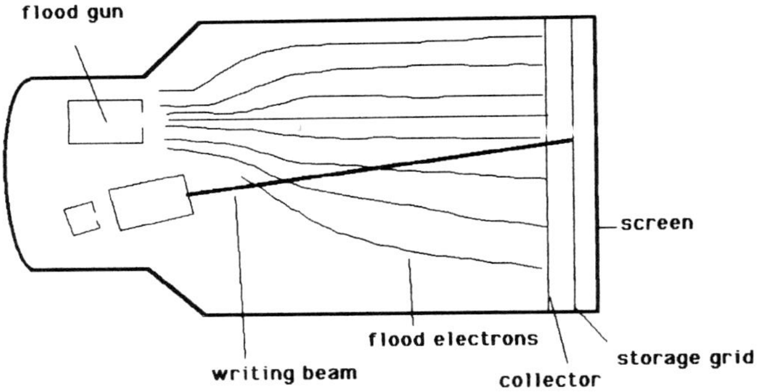

Figure 2.3. A direct view storage tube.

VECTOR REFRESH DISPLAYS

In vector refresh displays (Figure 2.4) the image is vectorized and stored in display lists. Each element in the display list is a vector (pair of points). To overcome the fading of the phosphor the picture is maintained on the screen by repeated regeneration or 'refreshing' from the stored display list. In order for the image to appear steady, the rate at which the image is refreshed must be faster than the flicker-fusion rate of the eye (at least 30 times/s). Complex images (in excess of 4000 vector inches, or 10 000 vector cm) may require a refresh cycle longer than the phosphor can stay ignited, thus causing flicker. By changing the contents of the display list, an image can be partially altered. The advantage is a

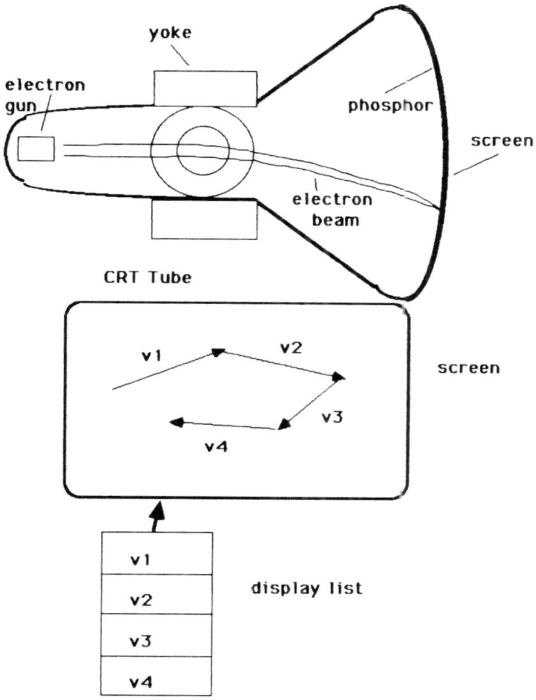

Figure 2.4. A vector refresh display.

high degree of dynamics, high resolution, good image brightness and high speed of interaction. A disadvantage is the extra hardware and/or memory for refresh cycles, which in turn increases cost and system complexity; and it cannot handle very complex images. Color can be easily implemented. Color shading has to be simulated by filling in lines in the shaded area.

RASTER SCAN DISPLAYS

Raster scan displays (Figure 2.5) differ from vector refresh displays in the way they refresh the screen. They display non-flickering pictures, yet allow partial altering. Raster scan implies that the image is scanned onto the screen in a raster sequence, i.e., as a succession of equidistant scan lines. Scan lines are composed of pixels (smallest addressable dot on the display). Pictures are drawn to the display from memory (frame buffer). Each pixel has a corresponding memory location in the frame buffer, specifying its on/off condition, color and brightness. The beam scans across the lines and energizes pixels in accordance with the pattern stored in memory.

The picture is refreshed constantly at a fixed scanning rate and is not

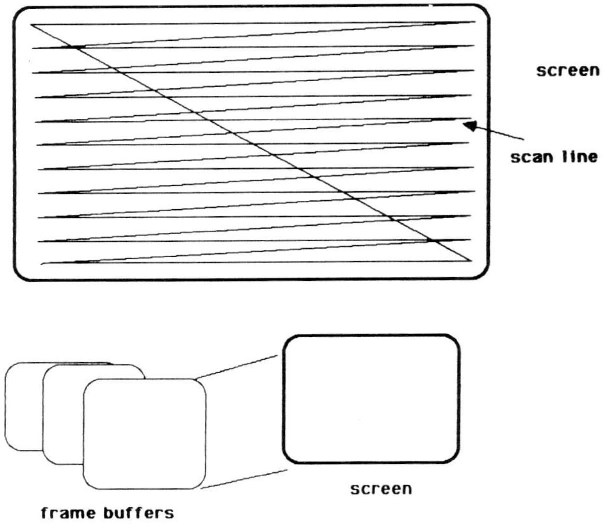

Figure 2.5. A raster scan display.

dependent on the complexity of the image. The resolution is determined by the number of pixels, and each pixel requires a separate memory element. A high resolution (1000×1000 pixels) color display requires more than 1 Mbyte of memory. Reducing costs of memory no longer limit improved resolution. Raster scan displays have good brightness, accuracy and opportunity for unlimited color. Cost is directly proportional to the resolution and number of colors available. All built-in microcomputer displays are low-resolution raster scan displays, and raster scan displays are becoming more popular in CAD systems due to their versatility. However, since vector refresh displays are cheaper they are still used in some graphics systems, but DVSTs are less common and are used in applications which require very high resolution and static display.

Non-CRT displays

Non-CRT displays such as Plasma Panel, Laser, LED, LCD, etc. are less popular than CRT displays. At the time of writing, in terms of display quality and cost, they are still not as good as CRTs, yet some of them provide unique characteristics which in some cases can better satisfy the desired applications.

PLASMA PANEL DISPLAYS

Plasma panel displays use a panel with a raster of gas discharge channels, with one for each representable point. Two grids, one on each side of the panel, act as the electrodes. By applying voltages between the electrodes, the gas within the panel is made to glow to produce the picture. With such displays, there is the ability to write and erase whole rectangular arrays or each point separately. The screen is flat, unlike the CRT. This flatness is the major advantage of the plasma panel. CRTs require a depth to allow the electron beam to deflect, and the electron gun also takes some detph; the bigger the CRT screen, the bigger the electron gun and the longer the tube. However, the depth of the plasma panel is not affected by its screen size. Plasma panels also consume a fraction of the power consumed by CRTs. The main disadvantage of plasma panels is their poor resolution and complex addressing and wiring requirements, and as a result they are not popular for CAD use; nevertheless, in recent years they have been used in many lap-top portable computers.

LASER DISPLAYS
Laser displays are one of the few high-resolution, large screen display devices. Instead of using electron beams on phosphor, coated screen laser beams and a large screen are used. A laser display is capable of displaying an image 3×4 feet (90×120 cm) while maintaining a relatively small dot size. CRT technology cannot achieve this quality. Because of these advantages, laser displays have been used in displaying maps, high quality text and elaborate circuit diagrams.

OTHER NON-CRT DISPLAYS
Some other physical effects for developing displays that are in early stages of development include Liquid Crystals (LCD), Light Emitting Diodes (LED) and electro luminescent powder layers. These technologies promise large flat-screen displays and lower power consumption rate; however, the quality (resolution, color, etc.) of these displays has yet to reach acceptable levels for CAD applications.

Keyboard and function keys

An alphanumeric keyboard is part of a terminal. It is the standard device for input of commands and numbers used in communicating with the operating system and utilities. Keyboards may sometimes be extended by function keys and numerical key pads. Numerical key pads are especially handy when there are a lot of numeral inputs. Function keys are used to simplify the input of commands. They can also be used to select menu items and move a cursor; for example, F1 key may be defined as redraw picture, and instead of typing the command 'redraw picture', a user can press F1 key only. Some of the function keys may be programmable with respect to their effect, while some may have a fixed meaning.

Input devices

Input devices are used to input data or graphics into the computer. Some of the input devices must be used in conjunction with a terminal, such as a light pen, digitizer tablet, etc. Some others can be used independently of the terminal, such as an optical scanner. Input devices are used by users to interact with graphics, draw pictures and select elements of a displayed picture on the screen. Different input devices are discussed in the following paragraphs. These devices include tablets, light pens, mice, touch panels, joysticks, tracking balls, thumbwheels, optical scanning systems and audio input devices.

Tablet

A tablet is a graphical input device for inputting point coordinates. It consists of a flat writing surface and a stylus or crosshair (for aiming) and buttons (for action selection) which the user moves over the tablet. The tablet is placed flat on the table top (see Figure 2.6). The tablet surface has either a matrix of touch sensitive squares or an electronically detectable grid. Location on the tablet can be tied to user-defined symbols or functions. The symbols or patterns associated with each square can be selected using a stylus and a menu overlaid on the tablet surface. By means of a cross-hair cursor on the CRT which moves in relation to the stylus on the tablet surface, the selected symbol can be positioned. Some systems use pull-down menus displayed on the CRT. When a menu item is pointed and selected, submenu items are displayed beside it. A user can move the stylus or crosshair to submenu items and select one of them. The tablet surface can be mapped to the CRT surface, so a menu can be selected by using the stylus.

Some tablets have a z-axis input, which allows the stylus tip to be moved through some pre-defined 3-D volume. The stylus is attached at the end of a mechanical linkage (arm), and through the transducers attached on each joint of the stylus arm, x, y and z coordinates can be found.

Most tablets in CAD systems are used to set up a menu of commands to make the user's task easier. Tablet menus typically include standard geometric construction and editing commands but may also include special commands

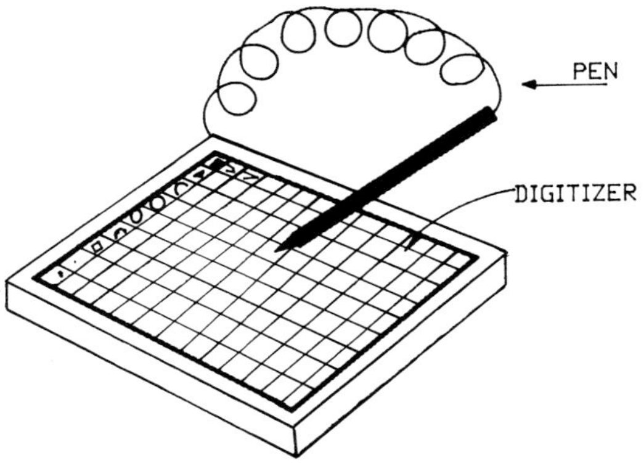

Figure 2.6. A digitizer tablet.

created by the user for a particular application. Since a tablet is analogous to pencil and paper, it is easily adoptable by users, and it is more popular in CAD systems than other types of input devices (except the keyboard). Tablets cost from several hundred to several thousand dollars.

Light pen

Light pens (Figure 2.7) are photo-optical devices capable of interacting directly with the picture on a CRT. A user can use a light pen to 'pick up' a graphics element from the CRT by pointing the light pen at the picture and clicking a button. Through firmware (programs built in the hardware), the coordinates of the location where the light pen is pointed are returned to the computer and compared with reference locations of the graphics elements. The light pen can also be used as a tracing or sketching instrument that permits direct drawing of lines and points and curves on a CRT screen.

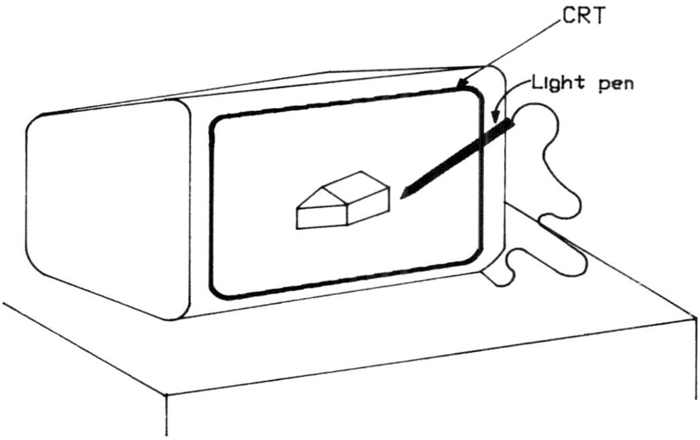

Figure 2.7. A light pen.

Light pens were widely used in the early interactive computer graphics systems, although there is a declining trend of use. They are very inexpensive (about $100). Most light pens are not easily used for fast, accurate graphics element picking. They are also not natural for freehand input: the operator has to hold the pen in an elevated position at the CRT and this can be tiring after an extended period of time.

Mouse

A mouse (Figure 2.8) is used for applications that need to locate the relative position of the cursor on the screen. It has a small ball rolling on two orthogonal

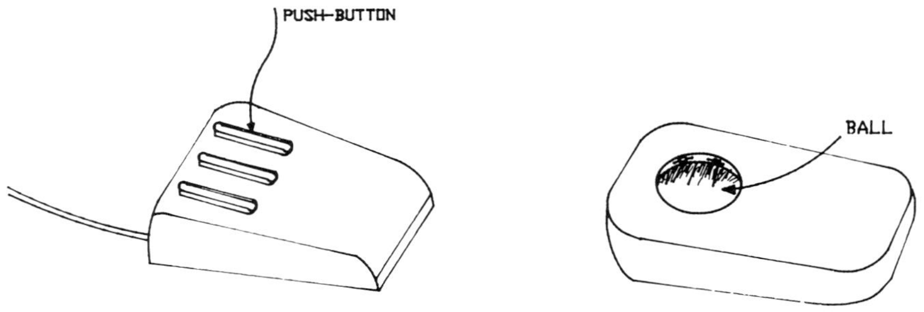

Figure 2.8. A mouse.

wheels attached to an encoder to convert it to coordinates on the screen. Push buttons may be mounted on the top of the mouse to enable a user to select commands. It can be rolled on any flat surface.

The mouse is inexpensive (about $100) and simple. Since a user need not pick it up in order to use it, and it can roll on any flat surface, it is quite easy to use. The mouse has other unique properties as well: if the mouse is picked up and put down somewhere else the cursor position will not change; and the coordinates delivered by the mouse wrap around when overflow occurs. However it cannot be used for tracing data from paper, since a small rotation or a slight loss of contact will cause cumulative error; and it is very difficult to hand print characters for recognition by computer. For such applications a tablet is essential. Finally, it is easier to implement pull-down menus using a mouse.

Touch panel

Touch panels (Figure 2.9) are similar to tablets except that they are sensitive to the touch of a finger, and usually have poorer resolution. Touch panels can be incorporated and overlaid on the CRT screen or may be in the form of digitizing tablets. Since touch panels have no stylus or crosshair, the selection is done by the finger tip. Touch panels are suited for menued symbols and commands. Their resolution is much lower than tablets and they are not suitable for digitizing line work. Some touch panels are built in with graphics terminals and some are separate units.

Joystick

The joystick (Figure 2.10) is a manual input device for graphics display consoles which allows the user to input the x and y coordinates of a point simultaneously. Typically, the current coordinate values specified by the joystick are indicated on the screen with a point or a cursor. By providing a button the joystick can also be used for selecting.

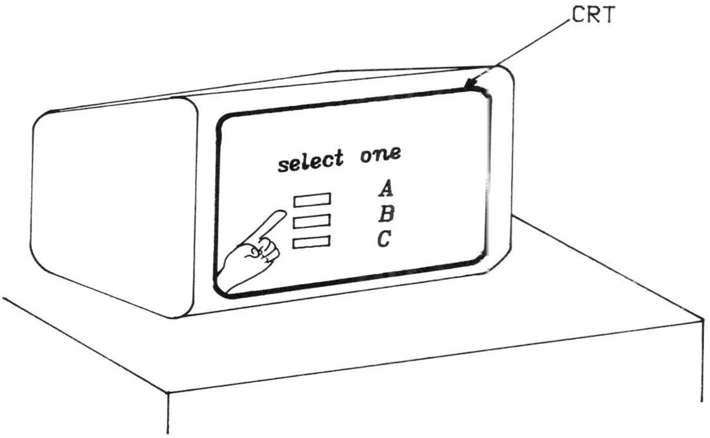

Figure 2.9. A touch panel.

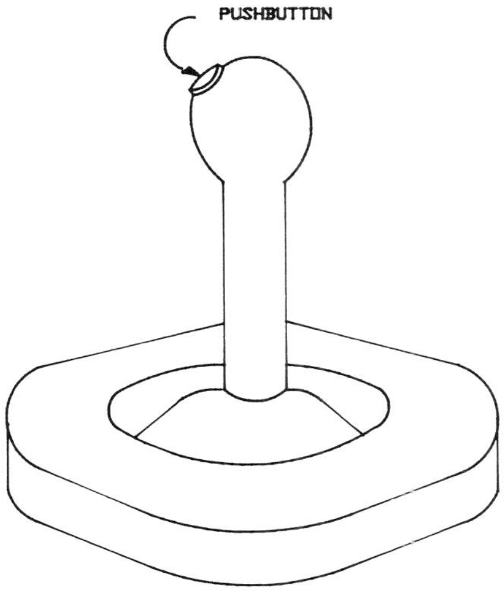

Figure 2.10. A joystick.

Physically the device consists of a lever that rotates freely in two axes for positioning the cursor. The angular displacements of the lever are converted into x and y coordinate values. Although they are widely used in remote control and video games, joysticks are not popular in CAD systems because of the difficulty in reaching an accurate position, yet many graphics terminals have a built-in joystick. A joystick may cost as little as a few dollars.

Tracking ball

The tracking ball (Figure 2.11) operates in the same manner as a mouse, but its position is fixed. In fact it can be considered as an inverted mouse. The operator rotates the ball with his hand to move the cursor on the screen. It is useful for locating a cursor on the screen. Since the tracking ball is stationary, it does not need any additional desk space for operation, and a few terminals have tracking balls built-in. The disadvantage of the tracking ball is that it does not have such good control as a mouse.

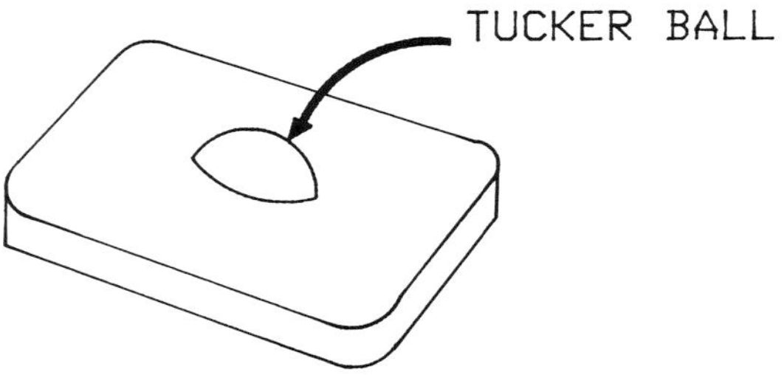

Figure 2.11. A tracking ball.

Thumbwheels

Thumbwheels (Figure 2.12) physically consist of two wheels which provide separate control of the x and y coordinates of a crosshair on the display. Each wheel is controlled by a finger, and in order to follow a path two fingers have to be perfectly coordinated. It is difficult to follow a path using thumbwheels and they are slow to use, yet they are very inexpensive to include in a terminal and many graphics terminals have built-in thumbwheels.

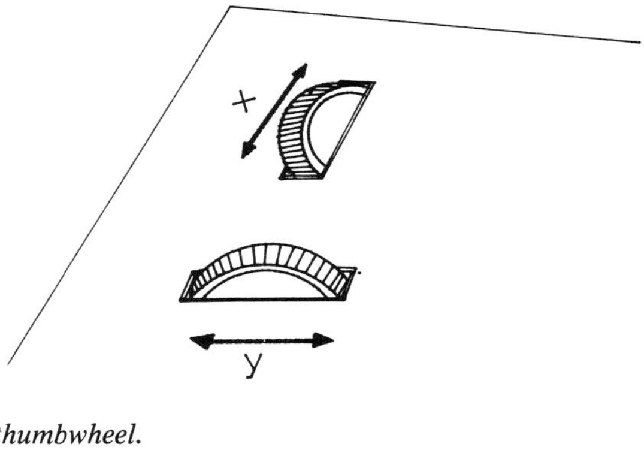

Figure 2.12. A thumbwheel.

The optical scanning system

This is a high-speed process of recognizing and translating machine-printed or hand-printed words, letters, symbols and numbers into computer-processable information. It can be used for automated capture of large databases and eliminates the need for keyboard entry. For example, pages of typed materials can be quickly input into a word processor by an optical scanning system. There are commercial products which will read existing drawings into a CAD system using an optical scanning system.

Audio input devices

An audio input device consists of a microphone and a voice recognition device. Current systems can recognize several hundred spoken words; however, the user has to teach the system to understand the words—the system understands a person's commands only after it is taught by the person and other users' voices are not understood. Audio input devices provide the user with hand-free operation of the system. They are relatively expensive and not widely used.

Output devices

There are two kinds of output devices: those that generate only pictures and those that generate hardcopy. A CAD system terminal can only temporarily display pictures. Hardcopy devices are used to:

1. Create check plots for offline editing.
2. Make permanent copies of CRT displays.
3. Produce final drawings and documentation on paper, film or microfilm.

Two basic methods of plotting are vector plotting and dot matrix or raster plotting.

Vector plotting

This is similar to displaying vectors on a vector refresh CRT. Plotting can be done using incremental or absolute coordinates and high-resolution line drawings can be produced on either paper or transparencies. There are two types of vector plotters: drum plotters and flat-bed plotters. Due to their quality to cost ratio, vector plotters are most popular in CAD systems.

Drum plotters (Figure 2.13) are used to generate two-dimensional plots on paper. One dimension is produced by rotary motion of the drum and the other by the lateral motion of the pen carriage. Either ball-point or liquid-ink pens may be used. The drum-type plotter uses special chart-paper rolls and can produce continuous plots up to 120 feet (36 m) in length. Several pens can be mounted in the carriage to obtain color and different line widths.

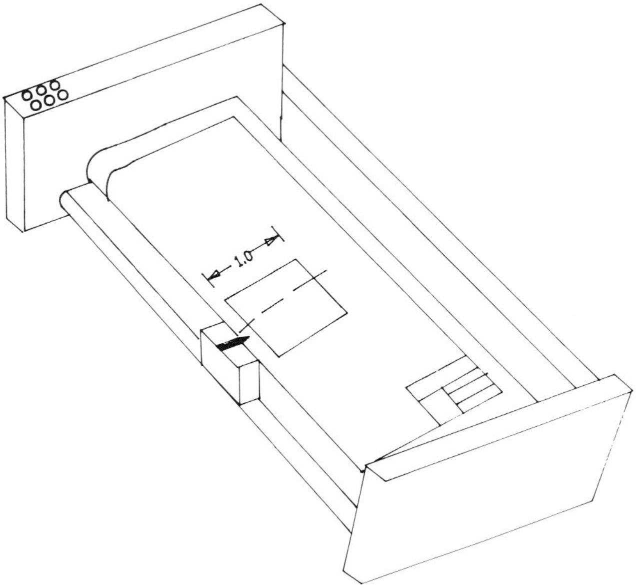

Figure 2.13. *A drum plotter.*

With flat-bed plotters (Figure 2.14), the paper is mounted on a flat bed and the pen movement is in both x and y directions. Flat-bed plotters do not require special paper and can handle a large variety of pre-printed forms. Paper is held by electrostatic attraction, vacuum, or mechanical means. Flat-bed plotters generally provide higher resolution and a continuous display during plotting as opposed to drum plotters and an accuracy of 0·001 inch (0·025 mm) can be achieved.

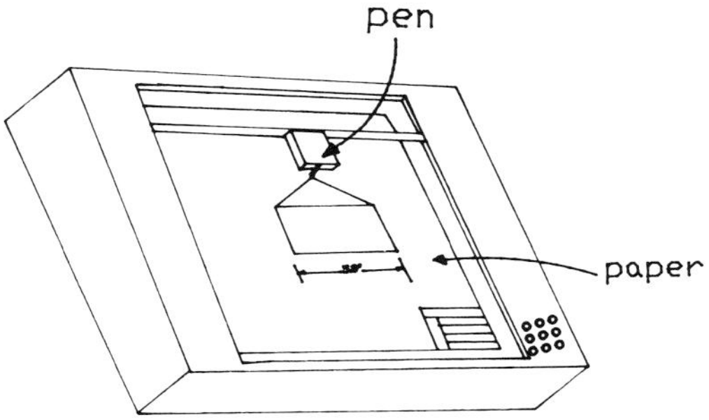

Figure 2.14. *A flat-bed plotter.*

However, they take a larger space for installation. Vector plotters cost between one and several thousand dollars.

Dot matrix or raster plotting

This method of plotting is analogous to displaying information on a raster CRT. The presence or absence of dots is used to formulate the information present on the document. There are four types of dot matrix plotters: electrostatic plotters, laser plotters, ink-jet plotters, and impact plotters.

With electrostatic plotters, all the information constituting one picture has to be buffered and processed into a sequence of dots. The sequence of dots is electrostatically transferred to a conductive paper substrate coated with an insulating layer, and the printed image is then placed in contact with a toner. Despite the additional processing time required, these plotters are fast compared to line drawing plotters, since there is no physical travel time of the pen. Although the preprocessing time is dependent upon the complexity of the picture, time to output a picture is independent of that complexity. Color cannot be produced but area shading is possible. Very high resolution (up to 400 dots per inch, dpi) can be obtained, and special paper is needed. They cost from \$50 000 to more than \$100 000 each.

Laser plotters are similar to electrostatic plotters, except that writing is done by a laser element, which works the same way as xerographic machines. They are very fast and best suited for combining alphanumeric and graphic output. Regular paper can be used. Currently only black/white pictures or text can be printed, but with the advances in color xerography, one can expect color laser plotters in the near future. Laser plotters can achieve more than 1 200 dpi resolution. Cheap models which have 300 dpi resolution cost only a few thousand dollars, while a high quality laser film plotter for CAD may cost as much as \$300 000.

Ink-jet plotters make use of electrically charged droplets of ink to produce the output. They are used particularly for graphics output of colored areas rather than lines. However, this is not a limitation of ink-jet plotters—line drawings and texts can be printed as effectively. Ink-jet plotters can get from 100 to 400 dpi resolution, and cost from several thousand dollars to \$200 000 each.

Impact plotters/printers operate on a mechanical basis. A matrix of needles or flexible character types are hit against ribbons of different colors while being moved along a line to be printed. They are slow, and not popular in CAD environments for plotting. However, for low cost PC CAD systems they can be used to print the draft. They usually have a resolution of 100 dpi, and the cost ranges from a few hundred to several thousand dollars.

Other plotters

Two other types of plotters, photo-plotters and microfilm plotters, are also frequently used in CAD systems. They are special purpose plotters and are used only for particular applications.

Photo-plotters operate in a manner similar to pen plotters except that a light source replaces the pen and film replaces the paper. Light beams with different apertures and speeds can be used to control line width and grey scales. Larger apertures result in wider lines and faster speeds cause underexposure of the film and thus a lighter line. Photo-plotters are used mainly for integrated circuit layout or for printed circuit board applications, such as preparing a photo-mask for Printed Circuit Board (PCB) etching.

The picture lines on microfilm plotters are either drawn directly on the film by electron or laser beam, or are projected onto the film. Combined alphanumeric output is possible. Most of the computer microfilm generating devices have the disadvantage of making positive microfilm which is not so easily read on screen as negative microfilm. Microfilm plotters are particularly suited for preparing presentation and space saving archival storage.

2.3. Graphics technology

In this Section, technologies used in computer graphics are introduced. These technologies include those associated with the display, manipulation and storage of the graphics.

Picture display

To display a picture on a CRT screen, several steps have to be taken. To illustrate, assume that a line drawing is to be displayed. Assume further that the drawing consists of six line segments, *a*, *b*, *c*, *d*, *e* and *f* (Figure 2.15(*a*)). To draw this, several steps are needed. First, the coordinates of each line segment have to be stored in a display file in the memory of a graphics terminal (Figure 2.15(*b*)). Depending on the types of graphics terminal used, different operations have to be performed. When a vector drawing refresh tube is used, data in the display file is

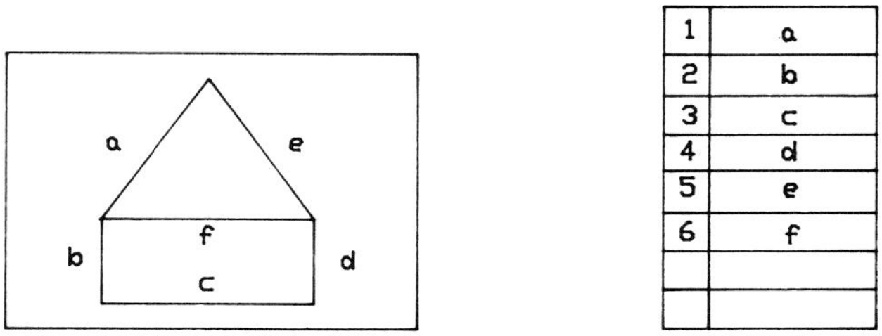

(*a*) (*b*)

Figure 2.15. (a) A picture and (b) a display list.

used directly. A display controller in the graphics terminal takes vector data sequentially from the display file and uses the data to move an electronic beam on the CRT. The result is the finished drawing in Figure 2.15(*a*). As discussed on p. 18, such an operation is repeated 30 times or more each second. By deleting one of the vectors from the display file, a line can be deleted from the CRT display immediately.

Raster graphics terminals display the same picture quite differently. A raster graphics terminal is a point drawing device. A frame buffer which is the display memory corresponds to the physical CRT screen. Each pixel (picture element, which is a dot on the screen) is represented in the frame buffer. Each frame buffer location records the color and intensity of the pixel. The entire picture is drawn to the frame buffer first, then a display controller takes the information stored in each pixel and dumps it on the CRT. At a fixed cycle, the entire frame buffer and screen are scanned. The speed is not affected by the quantity of information in the frame buffer; however, any line or curve has to be approximated by points before it can be saved in the frame buffer. Conversion algorithms are used to convert lines and curves. Figure 2.16 illustrates a picture and its enlargement. The pattern, a letter 'A' and a line are shown in enlarged pixels. A conversion algorithm converts the line definition into the pixels. These conversion algorithms are generally implemented in the graphics terminal in such a way that the user does not need to be concerned with this level.

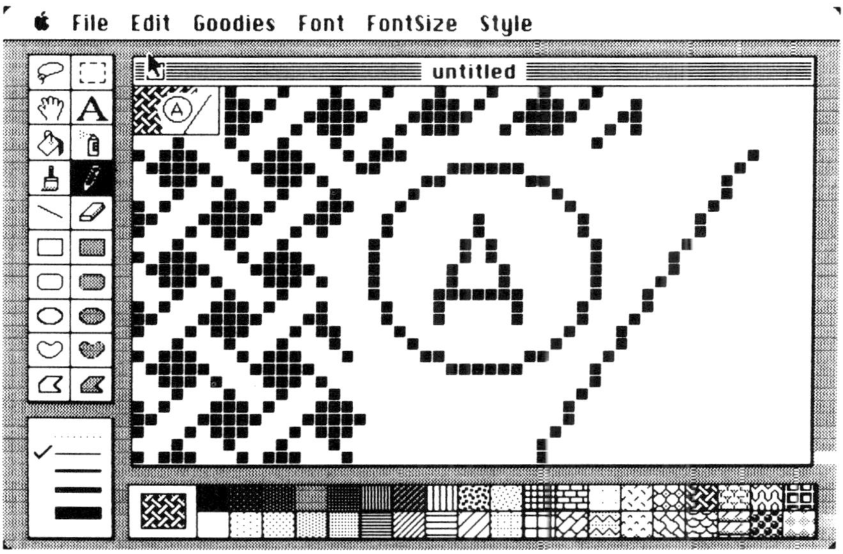

Figure 2.16. A raster display outline, circle, letter and pattern. The upper left corner of the display shows what the picture looks like.

Picture manipulation

In order to get more information from the display, one may want to manipulate the entire or part of a picture on the CRT screen. In general, there are rotating, zooming and panning operations in manipulating pictures. In the case of three-dimensional objects, view transformation, which transforms a three-dimensional model onto the two-dimensional CRT screen, is also required. View transformations include perspective view and isometric view transformations. Although in some of the sophisticated graphics terminals such manipulations can be done on the terminal level through firmware, they are usually performed through software in the computer. Some important picture manipulation functions—window, picture transformation, three-dimensional projection, and hidden line/surface removal—are introduced below.

Window

Pictures are defined in an imaginary world coordinate system. For example, a line may be defined by two ending points (1,1) and (3,4). Both (1,1) and (3,4) are defined in a Cartesian world coordinate system. Since it is not possible to display the entire world (from $-\infty$ to $+\infty$), windows are used to limit the portion of a picture displayed. There are two types of window: virtual window (window) and screen window (viewport). Virtual window is an imaginary window in the world coordinate system. It limits the portion of the world that will be displayed. The screen window defines the part of a screen to be displayed and the virtual window is mapped to the screen window (Figure 2.17). Several screen windows may be opened at the same time, in which each displays a different picture. They are defined in terms of the screen coordinates. In some systems, several screen windows can be opened overlapping each other, and the user is able to move the

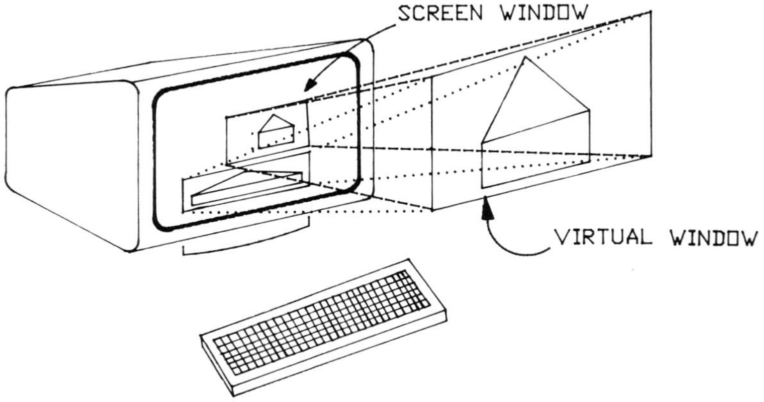

Figure 2.17. A screen window and a virtual window.

window dynamically; thus more information can be displayed in a well organized manner.

A clipping operation is used to clip off anything outside the window. Without clipping, lines outside the window will be displayed. When a line is outside the screen boundary it will be wrapped around and produce unreadable pictures. For example, any given line segment in a picture can either be entirely in a window, entirely outside a window, or partially inside a window and partially outside a window. In the first two cases, the line is either drawn or discarded; in the third case, the portion which is outside the window must not be discarded and the intersection of the line with the window boundary has to be found. There are several efficient clipping algorithms available.

Picture transformations

Picture transformations, such as rotation, zooming, panning and mirror imaging, are performed within each window. Rotation enables a viewer to see a picture from different angles. Rotation is achieved by applying a homogeneous transformation matrix to every data point in a picture. A homogeneous transformation matrix is a 4 × 4 matrix in which each of the first three rows and columns corresponds to the x, y and z coordinates and an additional row and column is used to consider translation. Figure 2.18 shows some homogeneous transformation matrices for rotation, translation (panning), scaling (zooming) and mirror imaging.

For example, in a simple 2-D case, a line [(1,1), (2,2)] is rotated about the origin (0,0) by 30°. Represented in homogeneous coordinates, point 1 is $(1,1,0,1)^T$ and point 2 is $(2,2,0,1)^T$. (z coordinate is zero and always add a 1 at the fourth position.) The transformation matrix T on the x, y plane, $T_{r_z}(\theta)$, is (rotate the line 30° = rotate the coordinate frame −30°, therefore $\theta = 30°$):

$$T_{r_z}(\theta) = \begin{pmatrix} \cos\theta & \sin\theta & 0 & 0 \\ -\sin\theta & \cos\theta & 0 & 0 \\ 0 & 0 & 1 & 0 \\ 0 & 0 & 0 & 1 \end{pmatrix}$$

So, for point 1:

$$V_1' = \begin{pmatrix} 0{\cdot}866 & -0{\cdot}5 & 0 & 0 \\ 0{\cdot}5 & 0{\cdot}866 & 0 & 0 \\ 0 & 0 & 1 & 0 \\ 0 & 0 & 0 & 1 \end{pmatrix} \begin{pmatrix} 1 \\ 1 \\ 0 \\ 1 \end{pmatrix}$$

and for point 2:

$$V_2' = \begin{pmatrix} 0{\cdot}866 & -0{\cdot}5 & 0 & 0 \\ 0{\cdot}5 & 0{\cdot}866 & 0 & 0 \\ 0 & 0 & 1 & 0 \\ 0 & 0 & 0 & 1 \end{pmatrix} \begin{pmatrix} 2 \\ 2 \\ 0 \\ 1 \end{pmatrix}$$

$$V_1' = (0{\cdot}366 \quad 1{\cdot}366 \quad 0 \quad 1)^T$$

$$V_2' = (0{\cdot}732 \quad 2{\cdot}732 \quad 0 \quad 1)^T$$

The new line is therefore [(0·366, 1·366), (0·732, 2·732)].

Zooming is used to enlarge a portion of a picture display, and is useful to obtain details of a picture. Zooming usually involves a scaling operation. It is equivalent to redefining the size of the virtual window.

When a picture is too large to be completely displayed on the screen, the display window covers only part of the picture. Panning is the operation of scanning the picture. It is obtained by translating the display window.

3-D view projection

In addition to rotation, translation, zooming and panning, another feature of the manipulation of CAD graphics is that a three-dimensional picture has to be projected onto a two-dimensional screen. CAD pictures are either projected using isometric projection or perspective projection. Figure 2.19 illustrates the procedure of performing a perspective transformation. (0,0,0) of frame (x_e, y_e, z_e) is the eye position. The screen position is defined by frame (x_s, y_s, z_s). Let (x, y, z) be the coordinates of a point in the world, and d the distance between the eye and the screen. Using the relationship shown in Figure 2.19(*b*), x_p and y_p on the screen can be found:

$$x_p = \frac{x}{z/d}$$

$$y_p = \frac{y}{z/d}$$

By using the above equations, any point in the real-world frame can be transformed onto the screen frame (CRT screen window). Changing the eye and the screen positions will change the display. Before a picture is displayed, every vertex of a picture has to be transformed onto the screen, a process which can usually be done quite quickly.

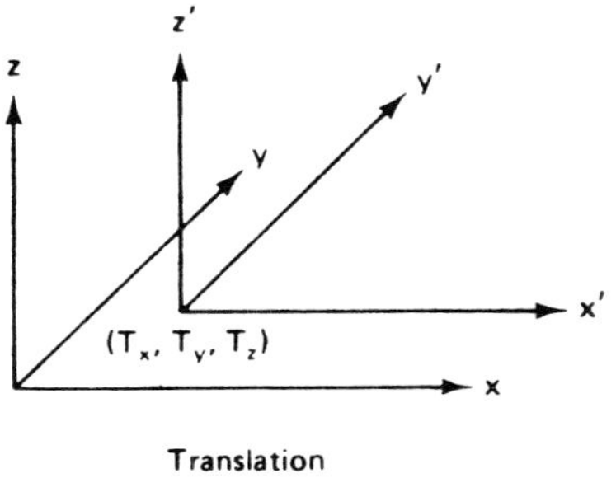

$$T_t = \begin{bmatrix} 1 & 0 & 0 & 0 \\ 0 & 1 & 0 & 0 \\ 0 & 0 & 1 & 0 \\ -T_x & -T_y & -T_z & 1 \end{bmatrix}$$

$$V' = V\,T_t$$
$$V = [x \;\; y \;\; z \;\; 1]$$

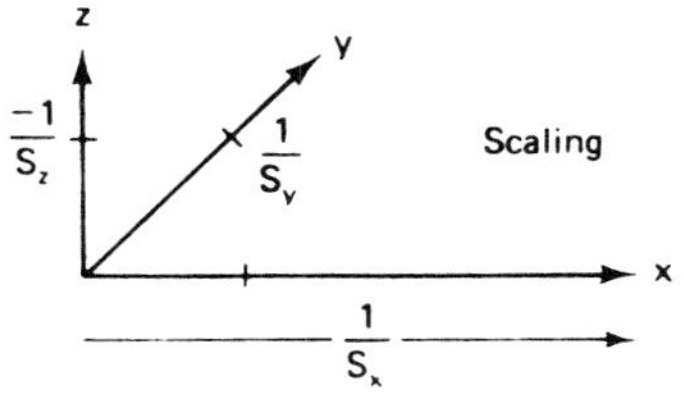

$$T_s = \begin{bmatrix} S_x & 0 & 0 & 0 \\ 0 & S_y & 0 & 0 \\ 0 & 0 & S_z & 0 \\ 0 & 0 & 0 & 0 \end{bmatrix}$$

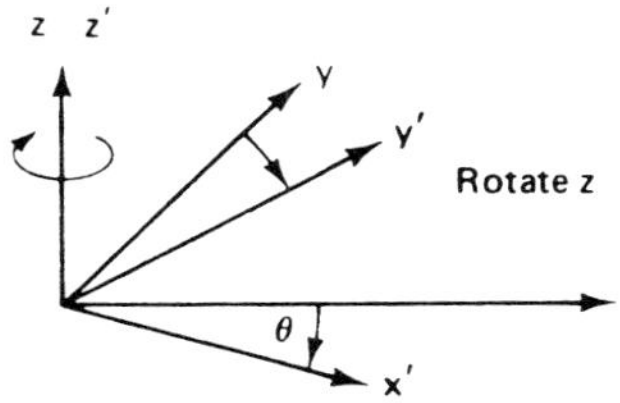

$$T_{r_z} = \begin{bmatrix} \cos\theta & +\sin\theta & 0 & 0 \\ -\sin\theta & \cos\theta & 0 & 0 \\ 0 & 0 & 1 & 0 \\ 0 & 0 & 0 & 1 \end{bmatrix}$$

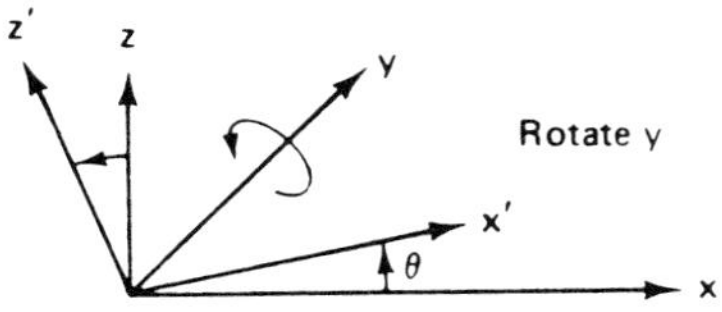

$$T_{r_y} = \begin{bmatrix} \cos\theta & 0 & -\sin\theta & 0 \\ 0 & 1 & 0 & 0 \\ \sin\theta & 0 & \cos\theta & 0 \\ 0 & 0 & 0 & 1 \end{bmatrix}$$

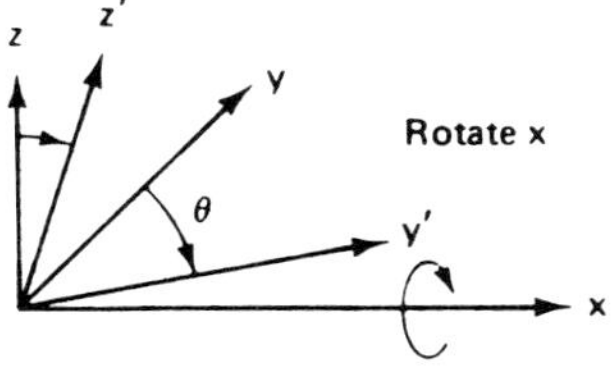

$$T_{r_x} = \begin{bmatrix} 1 & 0 & 0 & 0 \\ 0 & \cos\theta & \sin\theta & 0 \\ 0 & -\sin\theta & \cos\theta & 0 \\ 0 & 0 & 0 & 1 \end{bmatrix}$$

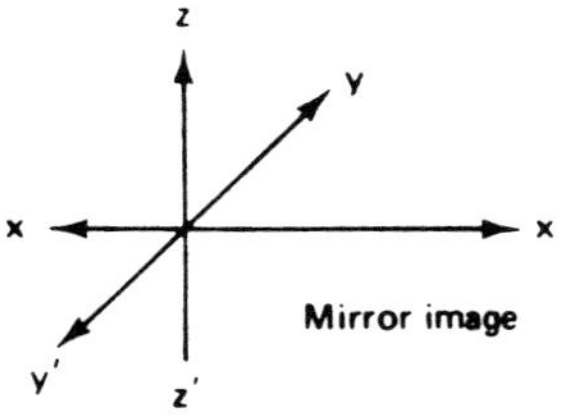

$$T_m = \begin{bmatrix} -1 & 0 & 0 & 0 \\ 0 & -1 & 0 & 0 \\ 0 & 0 & -1 & 0 \\ 0 & 0 & 0 & 1 \end{bmatrix}$$

Figure 2.18. Transformations (from Chang and Wysk (1985), courtesy Prentice-Hall).

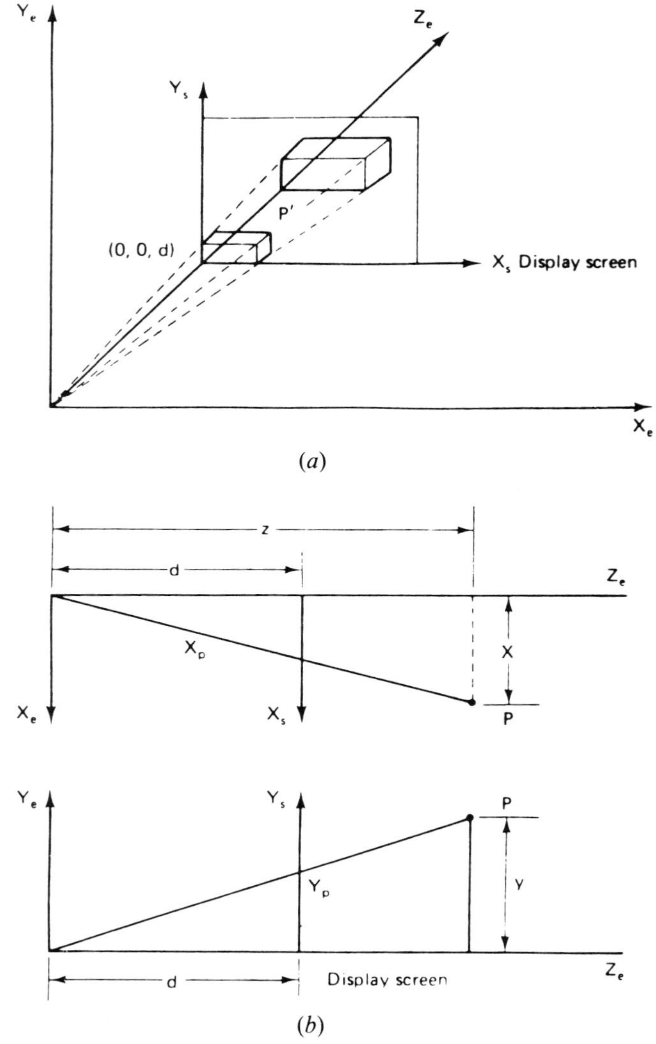

Figure 2.19. Perspective projections (a) of an object on a display screen, and (b) of a point (x, y, z) *(from Chang and Wysk (1985), courtesy Prentice-Hall).*

Hidden line/surface removal

When a 3-D object is displayed, unless the object is transparent, only part of the object can be seen. The hidden parts of the picture must be removed from the picture so a more realistic picture is displayed. For example, in Figure 2.20, a wireframe box consists of 12 boundary edges. If the box is a solid box, the three

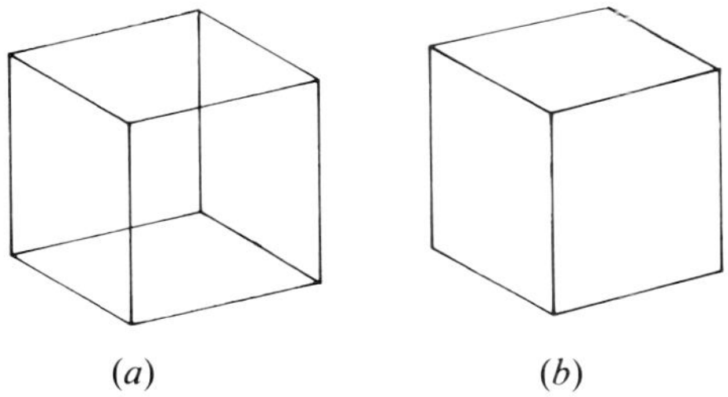

Figure 2.20. Hidden line removal. (a) A box without the hidden lines removal, and (b) the same box with the hidden lines removed.

edges at the back should not be seen. By applying hidden line algorithms, those hidden lines can be removed. These algorithms use some form of geometric sorting to distinguish visible parts of an object from those that are hidden, and work either in object space (in the world model) or image space (on the display screen/frame buffer) (Newman and Sproull, 1979). An object-space algorithm concentrates on the geometric relationship among the objects in the scene in order to determine which parts are visible. An image-space algorithm concentrates on the final image and determines what is visible with each raster pixel.

Picture storage and editing

If one is only interested in the display of a completed picture, the above mentioned techniques are sufficient. However, in a CAD system one is also interested in the creation and modification as well as display of engineering pictures. A picture must be stored in a proper way in order to ensure efficient retrieval, and modification. Depending on the application for engineering pictures, special data structures and data manipulation primitives must be designed. For example, Figure 2.21 shows a typical data structure. The data structure is built in a way so that picture primitives can be added and deleted, attributes can be changed, and calculations can be performed. Data structures must also be flexible enough to include all the design information including both geometric and technological data.

The data structure is independent of the hardware used. A data structure manipulation language is needed to manipulate the data. Such a language (or subroutine calls) consists of commands such as "add primitive (a picture primitive can be a point, a line, a symbol, or even a picture) before current primitive", "delete current primitive", "change parameters of the current primitive", "update data linkage", etc. The data structure also needs to accommodate dimensions and text strings, etc. When users use a CAD system to input or edit a picture (design), the CAD graphics editor uses a data structure manipulation language to store data in the design data base or to change the data base.

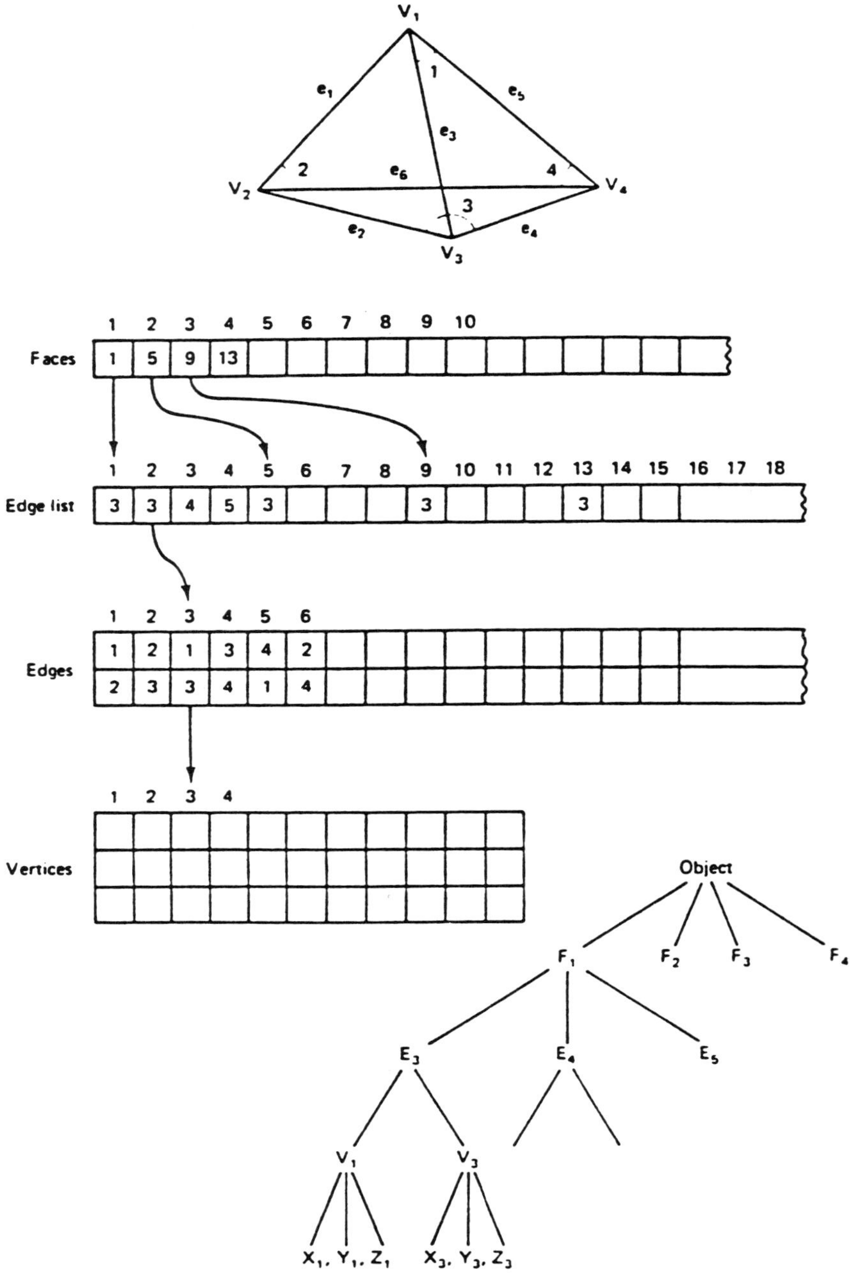

Figure 2.21. Simple data structure (from Chang and Wysk (1985), courtesy Prentice-Hall).

2.4. Concluding remarks

In this chapter, hardware and basic graphics technology used in CAD have been introduced. They provide readers with some information on the available devices as well as basic graphics manipulation knowledge. However, due to the rapid advances of computer hardware technology, many characteristics of hardware may change. It has not been the intention of the authors to present precise data in this chapter; rather the intention has been to provide information on current technology.

As computers are made more powerful and their costs drop, one can expect that computing power will not become a major issue in future CAD systems. However, the costs of peripheral devices (I/O devices) are not dropping as fast as computers; printers, plotters, etc. have many mechanical components and the benefits of electronic miniaturization do not help in improving the costs of mechanical manufacturing as much as they have done to electronics devices, so the overall CAD hardware will still be relatively expensive. What makes CAD systems different will not be the hardware, it will be the software. In the next chapter CAD software is introduced.

Chapter 3
CAD software

In the previous chapter, CAD hardware and graphics technology were introduced. Although they are essential for CAD applications, the most important part of a CAD system is the software which supports CAD functions. Software used in CAD usually consists of two general types:

1. Operating system software
2. Application software

Operating system software is the interface between CAD application software and the hardware. The application software are programs which do 2-D and 3-D modelling, drafting, and engineering analysis. Their functions are discussed in the following sections.

3.1. The operating system

The operating system is the supervisor of a computer system. It performs basic functions such as creating and removing operating tasks (i.e., programs or sub-programs in execution), controlling the progress of tasks, allocating hardware resources among tasks, and providing access to software resources such as files, editors, compilers, and utility programs. Figure 3.1 shows the relationship of the operating system with other software/hardware. The operating system also provides protection, access control, and security for information. Users seldom perform a computation without assistance from the operating system. Unix, VMS, VM/CMS, MS-DOS/PC-DOS, CPM, etc. are examples of some of the popular operating systems. Any CAD system, be it large or small, networked or stand-alone, needs an operating system (or a limited subset of the operating system) to control the communication between the operator and CAD system hardware and software.

All operating systems (OS) provide batch and/or interactive processing. Under batch processing, the user submits the program and data of the task together with the control information describing what the system is to do with the task. In an interactive system, the control information is replaced by a set of commands interpreted by a command system which receives control information

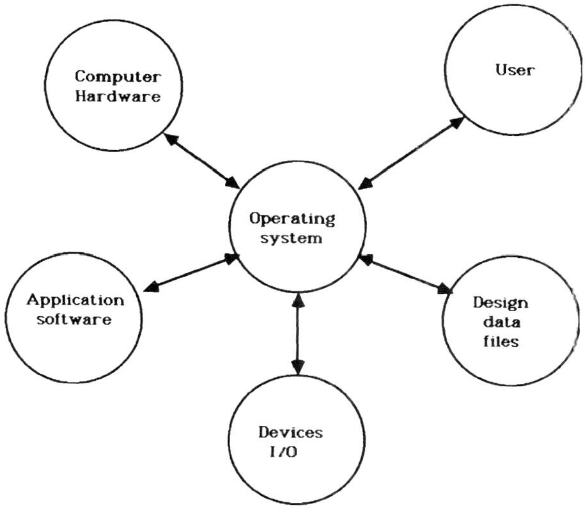

Figure 3.1. Operating system functions.

directly from the user at a terminal. Each command issued by the user causes a task to be executed. It is possible in some systems for the user to interact with the task, modifying it or its behavior as the user sees fit. Most CAD systems provide the user with both batch and interactive processing. A typical design session needs to be done interactively. Analysis, on the other hand, takes a much longer time to perform and thus can be processed through batch. Plotting, which also takes a considerable amount of time, can also be submitted to the batch processor.

Most modern operating systems except those used in home computers and personal computers (e.g., PC-DOS) are multi-user, multi-task OSs. For example, Unix, VMS and VM/CMS can support tens of users simultaneously, and each user can run several programs at the same time. This means that several users can share the same data base of design files and application software. Users can also run an analysis package in the background or batch while working on an interactive design session.

Some modern operating systems also provide windowing capability. (The window mentioned here is different to the graphics windows discussed in Chapter 2.) Several application and/or system windows can be opened at the same time on the screen. Each window is associated with an application or task, and the message from the application is displayed in the corresponding window, providing the user with information on concurrently executing tasks. A task running in one window can also interact with another task in another window. A CAD software package designed to run under one operating system may not run under another operating system. Users usually need to learn some essential instructions of the operating system in order to use a CAD package: instructions such as copy file and delete file are most common. Most CAD systems also have built-in functions which allow users to submit operating system commands within the CAD software.

3.2. Applications software

Applications software performs specific tasks for users rather than for the computer. Some of the applications software available in CAD systems are:

1. 2-D drawing
2. Basic 3-D drawing
3. Sculptured surfaces
4. 3-D solid modelling
5. Analysis software

2-D drawing software includes 2-D drafting and other drawing applications which only need two-dimensional representation. Basic 3-D models as defined here include every 3-D CAD software which is neither sculptured surface software nor solid modelling software, including, for example, both 3-D wireframe software and $2\frac{1}{2}$-D software. Sculptured surface implies free-form surface, such as those surfaces on an automobile body. 3-D solid modelling is a method which models an object as a solid. Engineering properties can be calculated and analysis performed on them. In the following sections each of the above software types and their application areas will be discussed in detail.

2-D drawing

Traditionally engineering designs were presented in two-dimensional drawings. Figure 3.2 shows an engineering drawing produced by a CAD system. 2-D drawing software is designed to substitute manual drawing, and since it is done on an electronic sheet, it is easier to create and much easier to modify. 2-D drawing software is one of the essentials of a CAD system. Applications of two-dimensional drawings include:

1. Mechanical part drawing
2. Wiring diagram
3. Printed circuit board layout
4. Pattern nesting (garment and sheet metal)
5. Facilities layout
6. Architectural design
7. Graphics art, technical publication

Most of the above applications can be done by drafting; however, in order to add additional intelligence to the system, in some applications more than drafting is required. For example, in pattern nesting other than drafting, the system has to

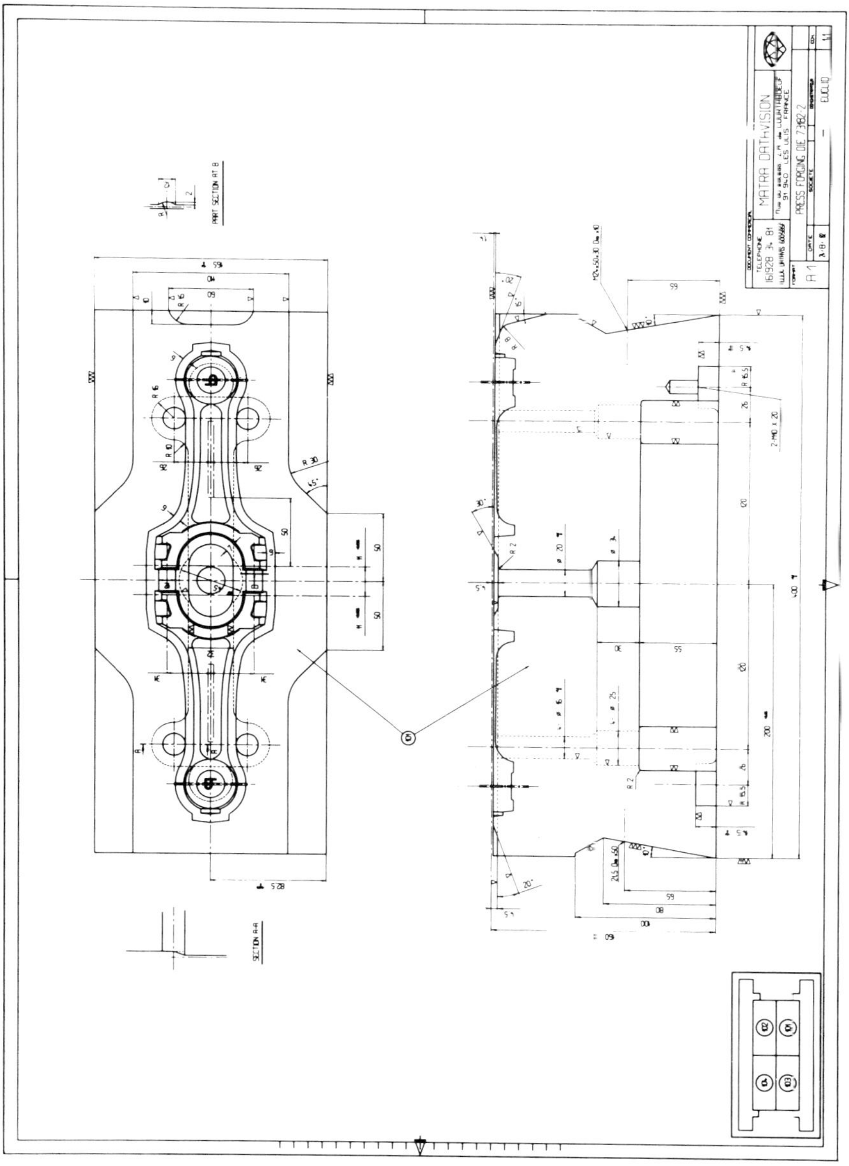

Figure 3.2. An engineering drawing (courtesy Matra Datavision).

be able to calculate area and material utilization, and to perform automated nesting. However, drafting is the most popular and most fundamental method for many engineering applications. Below, CAD drafting is introduced, printed circuit board layout application is discussed, and other applications are briefiy mentioned.

Application of CAD to general drafting

Drafting is the act of producing a 2-D engineering drawing. The result of the drafting process is an engineering drawing which basically consists of a geometric description of an object in the form of one or more planar projections. The graphic representation of the object using drafting is not a complete description and in itself is not sufficient for all engineering purposes, such as volume and area calculations. Drafting software is available in all CAD systems.

Two-dimensional CAD drafting applications are a substitute for conventional drafting methods, with the CAD system used as a graphics editor. In mechanical engineering applications, basic geometries such as points, lines, circles, arcs, cones, polygons and spline curves can be defined interactively. Other drafting symbols such as tolerancing, cross hatching, dimensioning lines, standard threads, chamfers, etc. are also available to the operator. Those symbols must conform with the national/international standards, such as ANSI-Y14. For other applications, such as wiring diagrams (Figure 3.3), printed circuit board layouts, etc., a CAD system provides drafting symbols for the specific application. Many symbol libraries from either the CAD software vendor or a third party can be installed. For example, in an architectural library, standard doors, windows, stoves, tables, etc. are available. Users can select a symbol from the library scale and then place it in their drawing. Text can also be added easily. Usually several letter sizes and fonts are provided.

In practice, a CAD drafting system is much more flexible in terms of geometry definition than conventional drafting methods. For example, the basic geometry of drafting, points, lines and circles, can be defined in several ways with CAD, such as the following:

Points

a. coordinates, (x, y)
b. relative position to another point
c. selecting by cursor on the screen
d. intersection of two elements (lines, circles, curves)
e. center of a circle

Lines

a. coordinates of two points, $(x_1, y_1),(x_2, y_2)$
b. two points (selected by cursor)
c. bisector of an angle
d. a point and an angle
e. parallel, perpendicular or median to a line

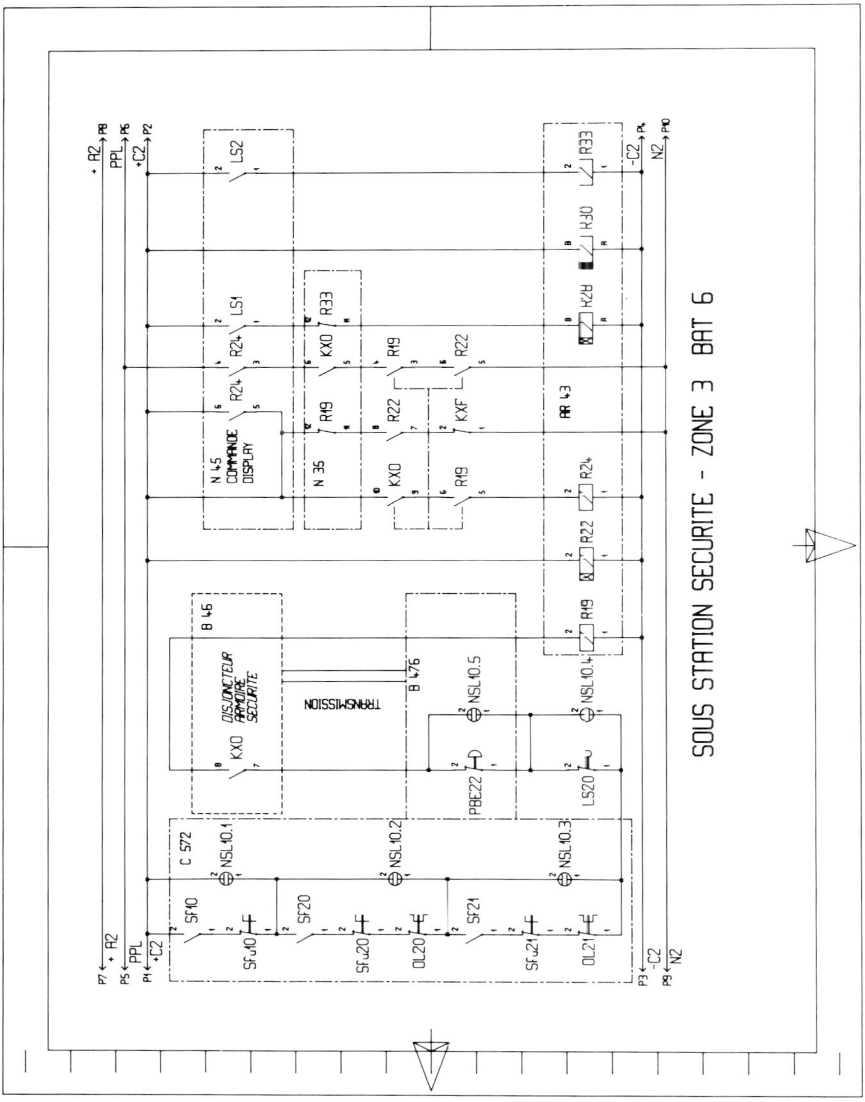

Figure 3.3. *A wiring diagram (courtesy Matra Datavision).*

f. tangent to two circles
g. a point tangent to a circle

Circles and arcs of circles
a. three points
b. center and radius
c. center and tangent line
d. tangent to two lines

Usually these alternatives are graphically shown on an overlay menu on the digitizer tablet or a help menu (Figure 3.4) on the CRT screen so that the user does not have to memorize all the acceptable methods. Moreover, the menu is usually user-definable, which means the user can design his or her own customized menu layouts. With customized menus, symbols and commands more commonly used by the company can be placed. However, for standardization purposes, a customized menu for an individual drafter is not encouraged. There are also menus prepared and marketed by third party vendors for special applications.

Deletion of a geometrical element is even easier on a CAD system than doing it by hand. A geometrical element can be 'picked' using a graphics cursor (with the cursor being controlled by one of the input devices discussed in Chapter 2);

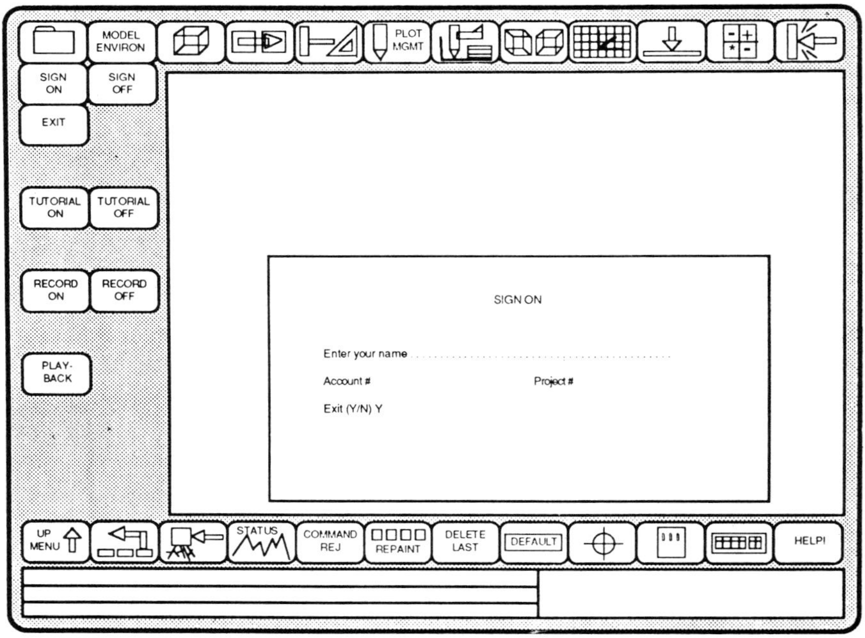

Figure 3.4. A screen menu (courtesy UniCAD).

standard drafting symbols can be defined as geometrical elements (shapes). The user can pick up a symbol, scale it, then put it at the appropriate position. A geometric element on the screen can be picked, then deleted, or be dragged to another location.

To aid correction, some systems allow the user to retrace and restore steps taken in the creation of a drawing. Some systems can also support automatic or semi-automatic dimensioning; users tell where and what kind of dimension is needed and the system automatically places the dimension lines and text. Zooming or panning functions are generally available.

Using 2-D drafting systems has its limitations. The solid object cannot be represented as a solid, hence engineering analysis cannot be performed; the user cannot see the 3-D image on a display; and there is difficulty in representing objects which are smoothly curved in two directions, e.g., a sphere—section and auxiliary views are needed for those objects. However, those are also limitations of traditional manual drafting.

Application of CAD to printed circuit board layout

Printed Circuit Board (PCB) layout is the task of laying out the components and interconnecting wires on the board according to the circuit schematics. Figure 3.5 shows a PCB layout drawing produced by a CAD system. There are single-layered boards and multi-layered boards. The application of single-layered boards requires 2-D. 3-D software is needed for multi-layered boards. The interconnecting wires are produced by chemically etching out the unwanted portion from a copper covered board. IC chips are usually packaged in DIPs (Dual-In-line Package) with 12–40 pins. Some IC chips consist of several identical logic elements which may be used in different parts of the circuit. Some PCB layout systems provide automated routing, logic element swapping, and pin swapping capabilities. Design rule checking software is also available on some systems. PCB layout systems can generate bills of materials, final artwork of the board layout, printed circuit masks, and NC part programs for PCB hole drilling. Using a CAD system for PCB layouts, not only can one speed up the design/manufacturing lead time, but also reduce the potential errors (through design rule checking).

Other applications

Several applications cannot be satisfied by simple drawing functions and special functions are needed. For example, in pattern layout (or pattern nesting) for garment cutting and sheet metal cutting, it is necessary to optimize the utilization of material. Figure 3.6 shows a pattern nesting drawing produced by a CAD system. Such systems allow operators to interactively place the patterns on the raw material, and the system then calculates the areas of used and unused

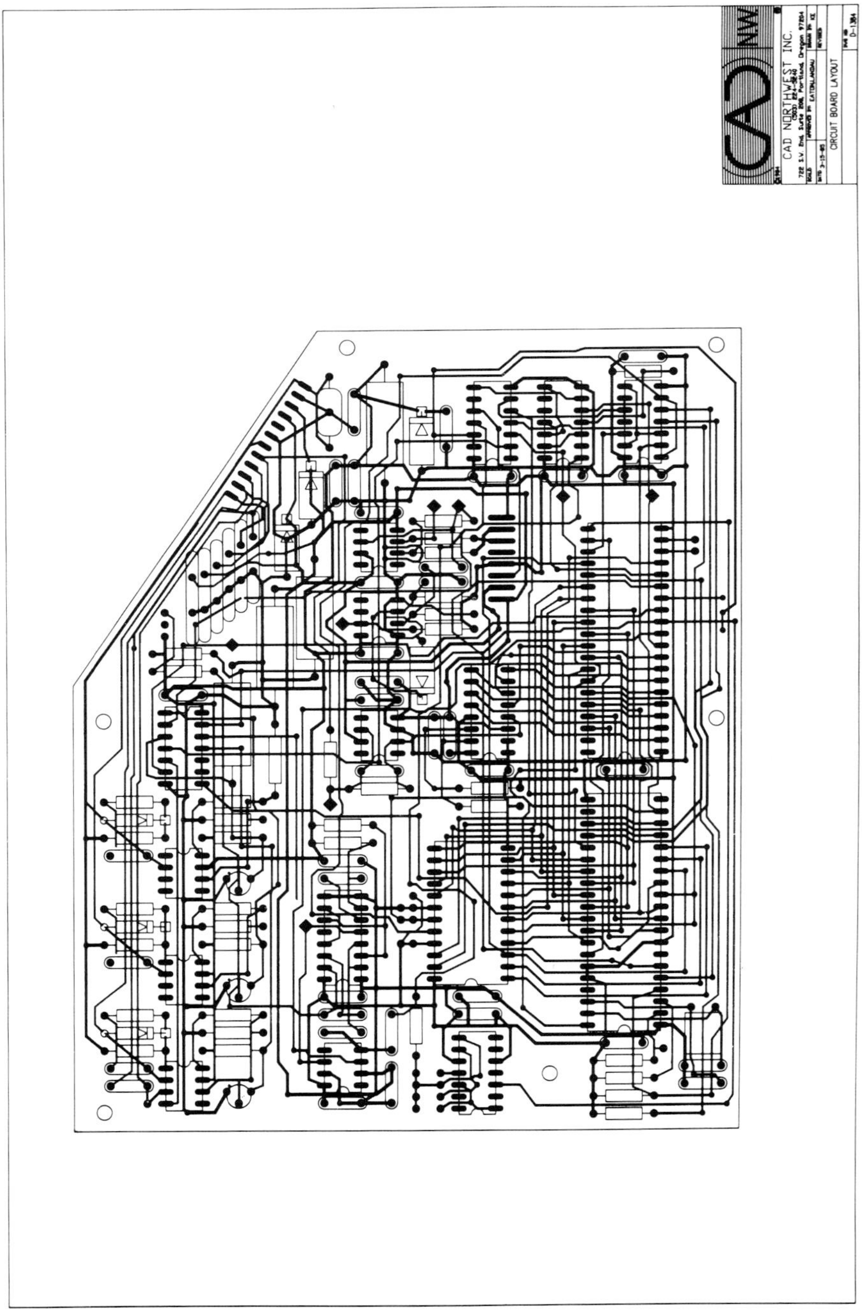

Figure 3.5. A PCB layout. Darkened lines represent interconnections. Components are shown in thin lines (courtesy AutoDesk).

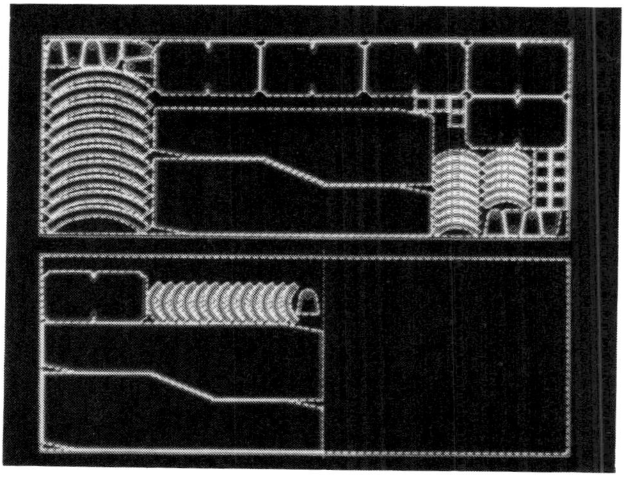

Figure 3.6. A pattern layout (courtesy Intergraph). Interactive nesting software enables the operator to plan pattern layouts which optimize material usage. Material grain direction, kerf width and clearances.

material. Therefore, operators can optimize the utilization of material interactively. The final layout is used to generate numerical control instructions automatically.

Basic 3-D models

In this section, 3-D wireframe, $2\frac{1}{2}$-D drawing and mapping models are discussed. A 3-D wireframe model describes the edges and outlines of curves (Figure 3.7). A two-and-a-half dimensional model is a 2-D model with a constant *z* axis dimension, such as a shaft, and a simple box. Mapping models are different to others: digitized terrain data are processed to produce contour and/or 3-D drawings.

Basic 3-D models such as wireframe models are a direct extension to 3-D space of the concept of edges used in 2-D drafting. 2-D drafting can be easily generated from the 3-D wireframe model. The additional dimension enables users to display the drawing in different views. An object can be viewed from different angles, and final drawings can be a combination of 3-view engineering plus an isometric view of the object. Complete numerical control part programs can be generated. It is a level above the 2-D drafting systems.

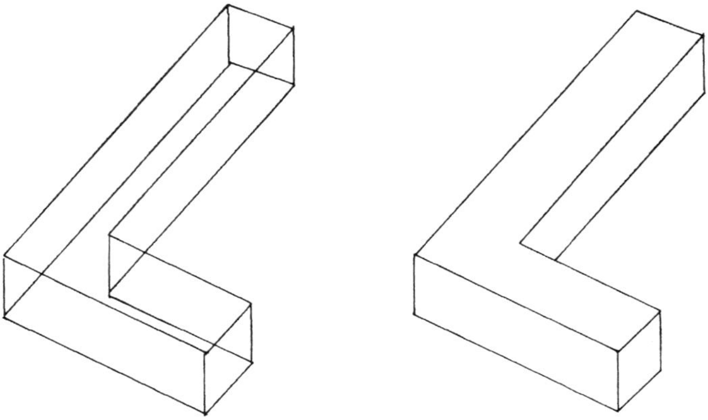

(*a*) (*b*)

Figure 3.7. A wireframe model (a) with hidden lines and (b) without hidden lines.

Wireframe models are easy to generate and work with, are simple to store and manipulate in computers and are useful as visual aids. However, since there is no information on the surfaces nor the inside or outside of the object, the notion of solidity is not conveyed.

Despite these limitations on modelling 3-D objects, 3-D wireframe models are useful for many applications. So far it is the most popular form of CAD/CAM modelling methods. Some of the applications are:

Mechanical engineering
1. Part design
2. Assembly design
3. NC tool path
4. Robot programming

Architectural engineering and construction
1. Building design
2. Structural analysis
3. Piping layout and analysis
4. Site planning
5. Interior design

Electrical and electronic engineering
1. IC chip layout
2. PCB layout

Cartography
1. Map preparation

In a pure wireframe model there is no concept of surface. Surfaces are undefined entities whose intersections form edges which are explicitly represented as space curves. The shape of surfaces whose boundary edges are defined by such curves are left to be determined by the user's imagination.

Since surfaces are defined by their edges, curved surfaces cannot be dealt with in a pure wireframe model. For example, the only 'wires' that can be associated with a finite cylinder are two parallel circles, which is the same representation for two hemispheres. In the case of a sphere, there are no edges to represent it at all. To remedy this situation, 'wires' are added where there are no real edges in order to approximate shape of curved surfaces. These unreal or fake edges can be thought of as contours resulting from hypothetical planar sections of objects.

Another consequence of the absence of surface in wireframe models is that the notion of 'inside' and 'outside' is lost. Certain wireframe models are ambiguous, i.e., the same representation corresponds to more than one solid. In Figure 3.8, wireframe '*a*' can be interpreted as object '*b*', '*c*', or '*d*'; there is no unique interpretation. Absence of surfaces also makes it difficult to support a fully automatic elimination of hidden lines or computation of sectional views in a pure wireframe model. For example, in Figure 3.8 it is unclear whether there is a top surface. Drawings *c* and *d* show top surfaces, yet *b* does not have a top surface. Hence, 3-D wireframe models are not sufficient for engineering applications that require calculation of mass properties (e.g., volume, weight, center of gravity, moment of inertia, etc.).

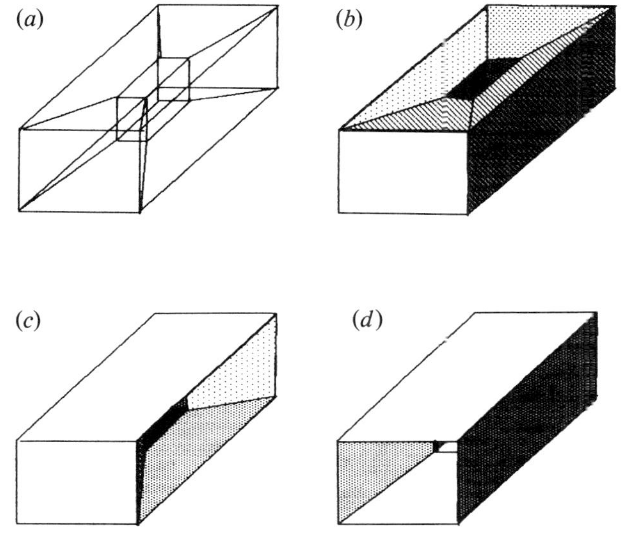

Figure 3.8. The ambiguity of a wireframe model: various possible interpretations, (*b*), (*c*) *and* (*d*), *of the original wireframe* (*a*).

In CAD systems, wireframe models are often augmented by relatively simple surface definition facilities to provide a more complete geometric model (see Figure 3.9), with or without extensive drafting functions extended to 3-D. By using such surfaces, hidden lines/surfaces algorithms can be applied, and surface shading is also made possible.

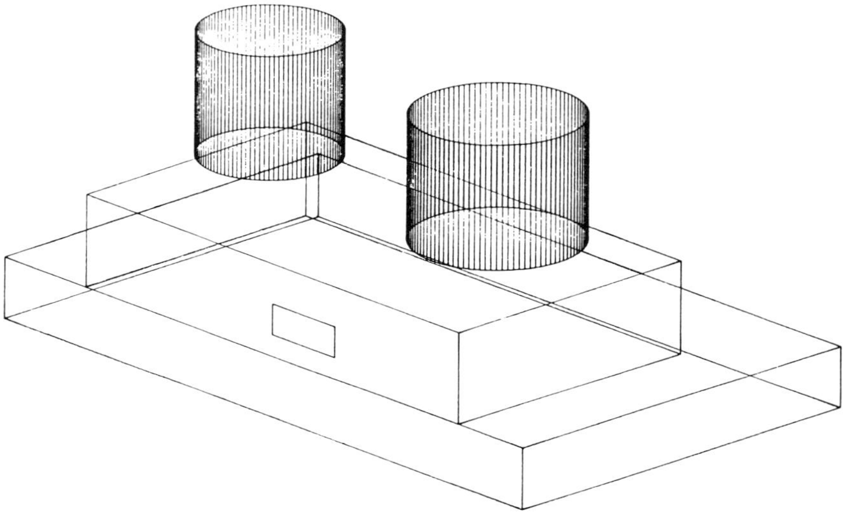

Figure 3.9. A wireframe with a rule surface.

Wireframes are used frequently as a CAD tool to generate projection views of an object for drafting. There are also certain applications such as semi-automatic generation of finite element models where wireframes provide reasonably sufficient representations.

Similar to their 2-D counterpart, 3-D CAD systems usually provide a menu of often-used geometries. A model is built by choosing the appropriate geometries and placing them on the right position. However, since the screen is 2-D, the third dimension cannot be entered directly. Extending 2-D drafting to 3-D is done in many ways. One way to enter 3-D objects is to work directly with 3-D coordinate values, instead of 2-D. For example, to define a point, x, y and z coordinates are typed in. For a line, two sets of point coordinates are typed in. However this is not always convenient since data have to be entered through the keyboard. It is more desirable to have users interact with the system by directly working on the picture on the screen.

Another way to enter 3-D objects is to provide a mode of operation where one coordinate can be factored out dynamically from the user–system communication. This is done by introducing the concept of a 'current work plane (layer)' which permits users to carry on a 2-D dialogue with the system relative to a local coordinate system on the work plane. After a user defines a work plane, all subsequent geometries defined are placed on that plane until the work plane is redefined. 2-D geometries are used on the plane, and the coordinates are converted to 3-D automatically. Either isometric or perspective views of the object can be displayed on the CRT screen.

Many 3-D systems provide split screen displays. The screen is split into four parts, each displaying front, top, side, and isometric views of the design. By constructing the design on one view, the other views are changed automatically. Users can work on 2-D views (front, top and side) and have the 3-D view (isometric view) displayed simultaneously.

Characteristics of 3-D and $2\frac{1}{2}$-D models directly related to their applications are discussed below.

Mechanical engineering applications

2-D drafting can be generated from 3-D wireframe models. Although it may be difficult to represent curved surfaces, edges can be easily projected to three projection planes. Usually two separate data layers are used for each 3-D model: the first layer consists of the geometry and the second layer contains the dimensions and tolerance information. They overlay each other on the display and the final plot, and although they are separately stored and displayed, changing the geometry affects the dimension. Most CAD systems have built-in capabilities to change both when there is a change in one.

Individual parts can be put together to form an assembly drawing. Each part can be displayed in different colors. Explosion drawing can be generated to show the relationships of parts, for example, in Figure 3.10 the explosion drawing of a differential gearbox produced by a CAD system is shown. Another useful feature is to generate a parts list and BOM (Bill of Materials) for assemblies. Since both the engineering drawing and the technical illustration can be generated from the same set of CAD models, time is saved and error reduced. As discussed before, simple surfaces can be added on the 3-D wireframe model; thus realistic shading and hidden line/surface removal can be applied.

By adding on further information on the kinematics of the assembly, simulation can be done using the model. For example, the kinematics of a robot arm (Figure 3.11) can be simulated on screen. There are special software packages which combine the modelling and display power of a CAD system and its own analysis capability to study the mechanism of a product. Interactively, a user can set up the motion of each element of the product and the coordinated motion of the entire product can be played back: before the final design is made, a designer can visualize the operation of the product.

There are also special software packages for robotic cell design and simulation. Using either robots from an existing library of CAD models or a user defined robot, the systems allow users to place each robot in a manufacturing cell.

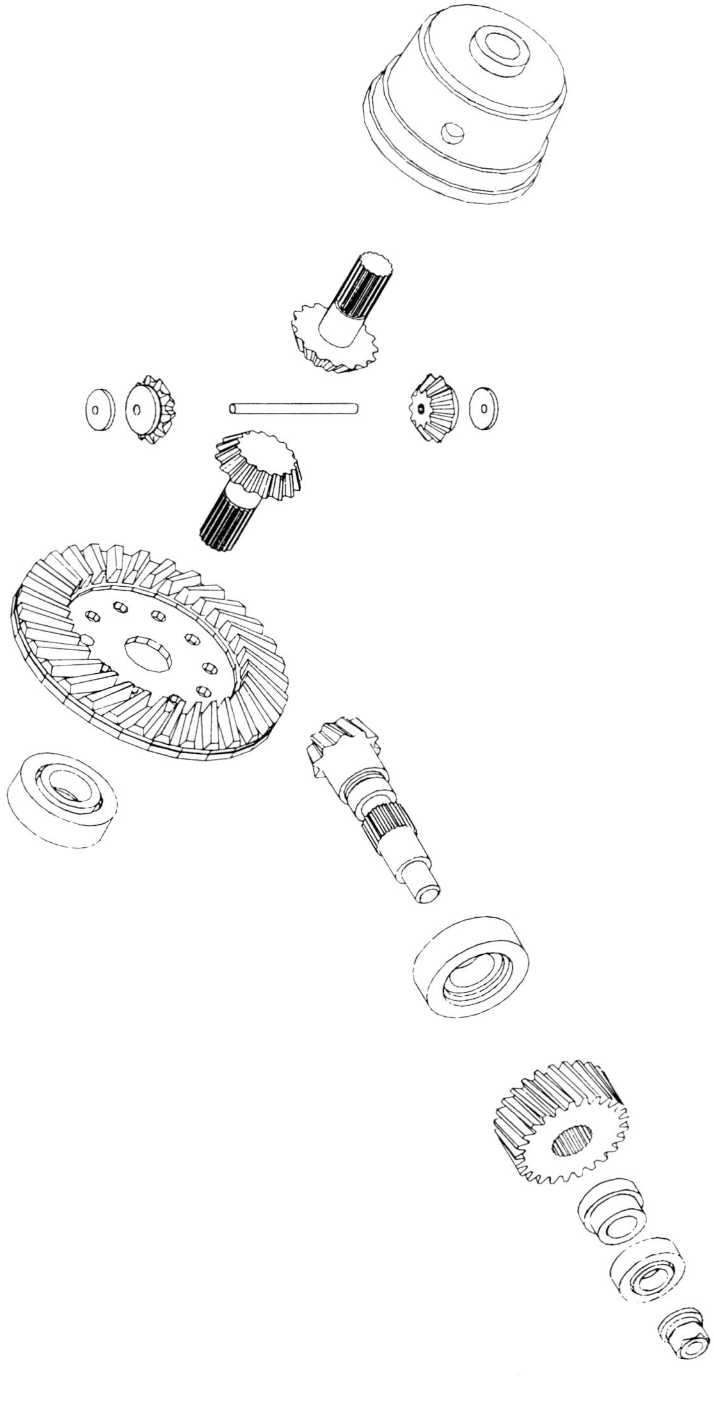

Figure 3.10. An assembly drawing of a differential gearbox (courtesy Matra Datavision).

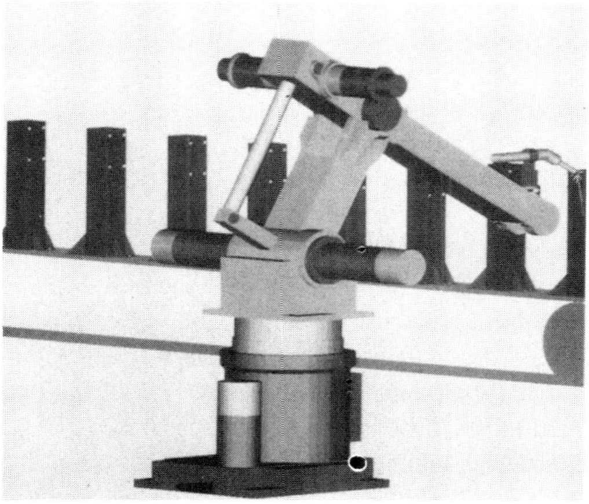

Intergraph robotic capabilities include graphics display of robotic action as well as work cell planning and layout.

Figure 3.11. *Robotic cell design and simulation (courtesy Intergraph).*

Peripheral devices such as part feeders, conveyor belts, work benches, etc. can be added into the design through ordinary CAD functions. After a robotic cell is designed and robot programs are interactively entered, the entire system can be simulated graphically on the screen. Such a package allows a design engineer to test the design concept and final design and make improvements. It reduces the physical testing needed and thereby decreases the cost and lead time of building a robotic application. The finished layout can also be plotted for system installation, and the robot programs can be downloaded to each robot directly. This off-line programming capability allows users to develop applications while the system is uninterrupted from its normal operation. Thus the lead time for product change is minimized.

Numerical control (NC) part programs can be generated interactively from a 3-D model. (Since a 2-D model does not have *z* coordinate information, it is not possible to generate an NC part program directly.) By selecting from menus, tools, cutting parameters and commands, a user can interactively locate the geometry and direction of motion. For example, a user selects a motion statement such as GO, the system prompts the user for TO, ON and PAST options (minor words). After the minor word is chosen, the user points a line on the screen. A cutter path with the image of a cutter is drawn from the current cutter position to the newly defined position. The appropriate part programming language statement is written to a file. Usually pocketing (machining a pocket), cycle (a fixed sequence of operations such as drill cycle, and mill cycle), etc. functions are supported. The end result is either an APT or Compact II source program file, or a CL (Cutter Location) data file.

For NC part programming application, dimension lines and texts are not needed, only the geometry layer is displayed. However, the geometry has to be on a scale of 1:1. Since the system has to calculate the cutter offset and geometry intersections, all pockets must be closed. Many minute errors which do not show on the drawing will cause computer calculation errors. For example, a line is supposed to tangent to a circle, but due to definition error there is a small gap between the line and the circle, and since the gap is small it is not detectable on the screen—during the NC part programming stage, an instruction for the cutter to go to the tangent point will result in calculation error in the computer. Therefore, part programming systems have to check the design before a satisfactory part program can be generated.

Not every CAD system is designed to have the ability to perform the design check, many of them do not have an easy user interface for part program generation. For this reason, some of the CAD systems are not appropriate for NC application. A company may use one CAD system for design and a different system for NC application.

Most systems also support the NC cutter path simulation capability. Figure 3.12 shows a cutter path generated by a CAD system. 3-D cutter paths can be displayed over the part drawing on the screen. Programming errors can be detected visually. The final program can be downloaded to another part programming computer for processing, or directly post-processed and downloaded to a CNC machine. A CAD system which possesses NC programming capability is usually called a CAD/CAM system.

Architectural engineering and construction

Most engineering designs are reviewed by engineers only and engineers are trained to interpret 2-D drawings. With conventional drafting, there is little difficulty in

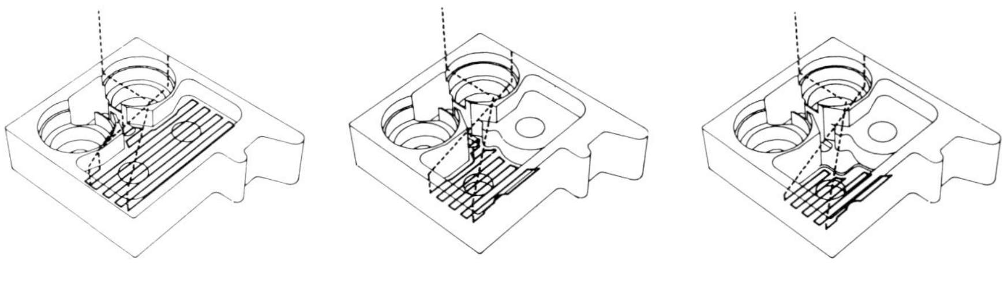

Figure 3.12. NC tool path generation and simulation. The dashed lines show the cutter travel in the air, the heavy solid lines show the cutting (courtesy Matra Datavision).

conveying one engineer's idea to another. However, architects always need to convey their ideas to ordinary people, so conceptual designs are normally done using perspective projections. For each view, an entire new drawing has to be prepared nearly from scratch. After the design is accepted, detailed design drawings have to be prepared. Using 3-D models, all the drawing can be prepared from the same data base. By selecting the viewpoint interactively, the best projection can be made. It is also possible to add background and other finishing touches to the drawing before it is presented for approval.

Although architectural designs can still be done using 2-D systems, 3-D systems offer many more features than 2-D systems. Realistic 3-D layouts give both the architect and the customer a better idea about the finished building. Figure 3.13 shows a layout of an office produced by a CAD system. Basic office equipment can be modelled separately and stored as menu items and the designer can select equipment and drag it to the location, as if the real furniture is being placed. The finished drawing with the hidden lines removed presents a clear view of the office layout.

Another important area for architectural application is in structure design and analysis. Structural members such as beams and trusses must be placed within the existing building design and engineering analysis needs to be performed in order to ensure the safety of the building. One of the applications of 3-D CAD systems is the integration of structure engineering design and analysis.

Piping is another important part of construction engineering. One can find piping in buildings, automobiles, ships, aircraft and chemical plants. Piping in buildings and automobiles is relatively simple and less critical; piping in ships, aircraft and chemical plants is complex and critical, especially in the latter two. How to fit curved pipes in a limited space without interfering with each other is a difficult task. Using the feedback on interference provided by CAD systems, it is easier to fit pipes than to do it by hand. Figure 3.14 illustrates a piping design for a chemical plant generated by a CAD system.

Several CAD systems allow users to perform 3-D piping design and interference checking. There are also packages which will output NC part programs for pipe bending on NC bending machines. Those packages are used mostly in the aerospace industry.

Another important application in architectural and construction engineering is with maintenance. Especially in the petrochemical industry, replacement of pipes, valves and pumps, etc. occurs very frequently and it is impossible to maintain an up-to-date drawing of the physical plant manually. With a CAD system, it is made much easier, and indeed there are companies which use CAD systems primarily for maintenance.

Electrical and electronic engineering

There are two major applications of 3-D CAD for electrical and electronic engineering: IC layout and design and PCB layout and design. IC (Integral

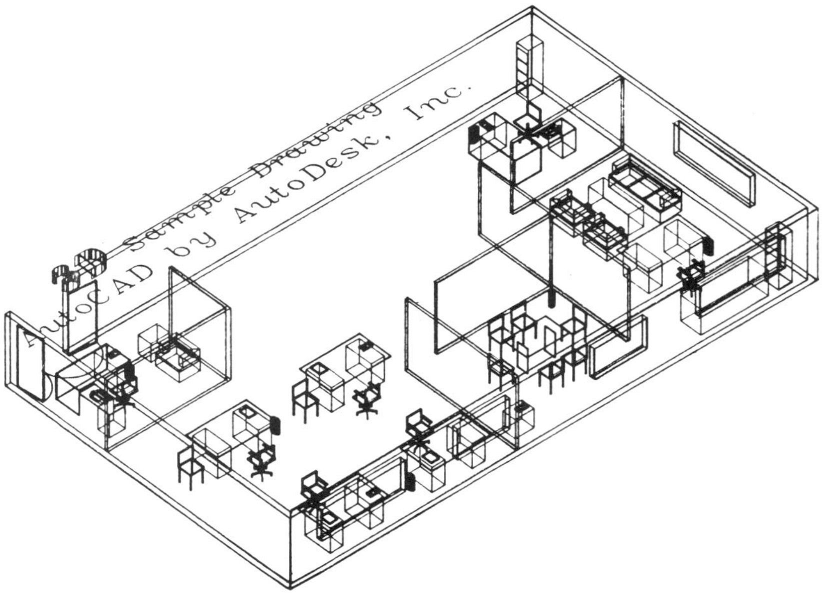

(a)

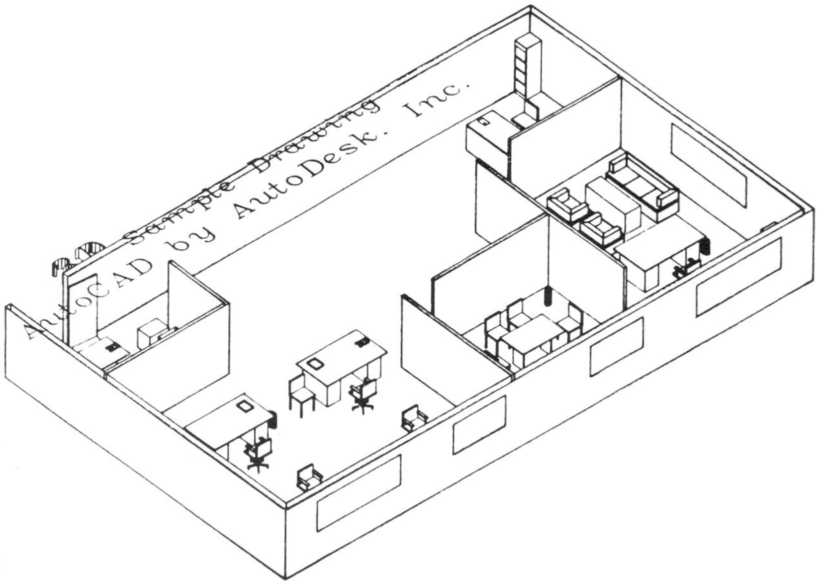

(b)

Figure 3.13. An office layout (a) with hidden lines, and (b) without hidden lines (courtesy AutoDesk).

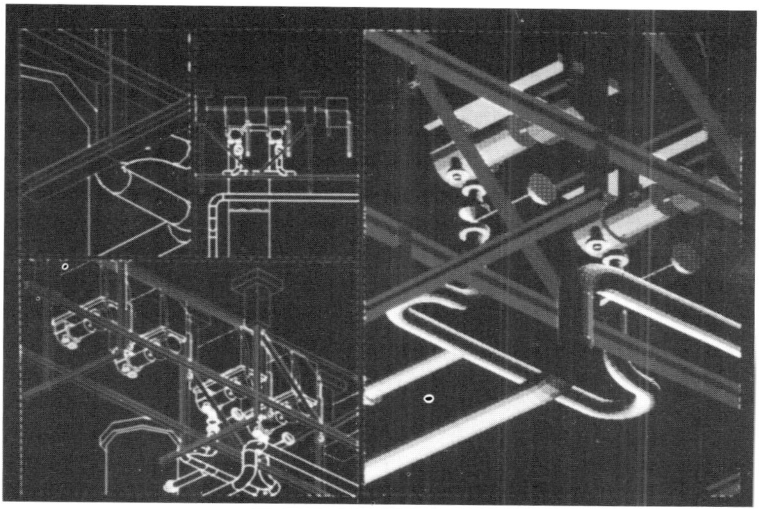

Figure 3.14. A steel piping and equipment model (photographs courtesy GE Calma).

Circuit) layout and design is the application of laying out circuits and analyzing the circuits for the production of IC chips. 2-D line drawings can be used to lay out individual layers, but since IC chips are of multi-layer construction, 3-D systems are needed. Although standard drafting can be used to provide assistance to a designer, a special design package is necessary. During the layout phase, an engineer uses logic gate symbols to layout an IC chip or VLSI (Very Large Scale Integral circuit). Logic gates are the building blocks of digital circuitry, and each symbol represents a logic gate in which the details of the circuit are stored in the systems library. Considering the hundreds of thousands of gates which can be placed in a chip by modern manufacturing technology, the process of laying out those gates is extremely complex.

Design analysis functions are necessary for speeding the design process and reducing error. IC layout and design systems use design rules to check the correctness of the design, and there are also programs which can lay out the standard circuits automatically. Masks (the layout pattern on the film) used during each stage of IC chip manufacturing can be produced through an optical plotter. Using such a CAD system, the design and the manufacturing of IC chips can be integrated.

Multi-layered printed circuit boards also need 3-D CAD systems for their design. Components may be placed on both sides of the PC board, and inside the PC board there are several layers of interconnecting wires; thus the system needs the capabilities of those discussed in the 2-D section as well.

Cartography

Cartography is the process of producing maps. Most maps are 2-D maps showing river, roads, cities, landmarks, etc. but for many engineering, mining, taxation and military applications, more elaborate maps are needed. Those maps usually also show the terrain. Terrain is either shown as contours on 2-D or plotted in 3-D projected views. Figure 3.15 shows a 3-D terrain model generated by a CAD system.

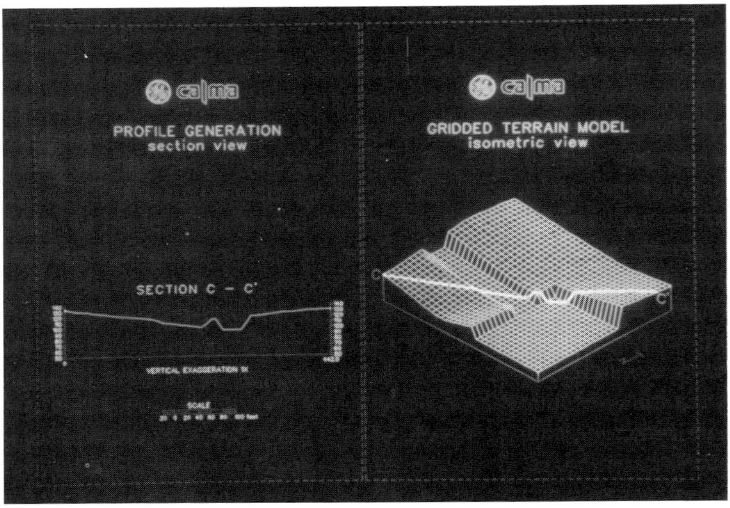

Figure 3.15. *A CAD mapping output (photographs courtesy GE Calma).*

Cartographic data are collected either by physical survey or from imagery scanning devices. The digital data are fed into a special package for processing, which includes contour fitting, polygon closing, coordinate rectification, traverse adjustment, bearing and distance calculations, etc. Coloring and text font selection are also provided.

Sculptured surfaces software

In the previous section 3-D software was discussed. The 3-D geometries were limited to those of simple geometries such as points, lines and circles, as well as analytical surfaces. Another class of surfaces which is not analytical is the sculptured surfaces. Many applications such as vehicle body design and design of aircraft and ships require modelling of surfaces. Some of the applications of sculptured surface software are:

1. Die design and manufacturing

2. Automobile, ship and aircraft body design
3. Commercial and art work

In traditional design practice the design of 'free form' curves (i.e., the design of curves and surfaces by non-analytical means such as using physical splines or clay models) consists of two distinct phases: the 'generation' phase, which results in preliminary shape description; and the 'fairing' phase, which leads to final shape definition of appropriate quality. In the automotive industry, for example, a clay model of the car body shape is produced from a draft of the shape design, modified according to the stylist's instructions until the form can be digitized and faired to tool-making tolerances.

The current trend in most industries is to use the computer to assist in the fairing phase as well as the generation phase. The two methods used for representing a surface in the computer are: (*a*) polygon mesh; and (*b*) parametric representation.

Polygon mesh is a set of planar surfaces each of which is bounded by a polygon and defined by a plane equation. The plane must be small enough to accurately represent the actual curved surface. The amount of storage required is very large and the resolution is fixed, independent of the eventual display. Furthermore, even with the most sophisticated continuous-shading models, polygonal techniques generally result in visually objectionable images (Barsky, 1984). For some applications, polygonal representation may be quite sufficient and an exact surface description not needed.

The parametric representation of sculptured surfaces was pioneered by Coons (1967) and Bezier (1968), who introduced the use of non-linear parametric equations for representing segments and patches to form surfaces (Faux and Pratt, 1979). The points on the curved surface are defined by three equations; one each for x, y and z; and each equation has two parameters u and v, up to the third order. The patches defined in this way can be made to satisfy the desired order of continuity. When creating joints the designer often wants to control the order of continuity at the joint. Zero-order continuity means that the two curves meet; first-order continuity requires the curves to be tangent at the point of intersection; second-order continuity requires that the curvatures be the same.

Two methods which are widely used in commercial CAD systems are: (*a*) Bezier surfaces; and (*b*) B-spline surfaces.

When a large surface is designed using the Bezier surface method, it is divided into small surface patches, with each patch defined by 16 points. The surface is under a 'characteristic polyhedron' which is specified in terms of the position vectors of its 16 vertices (Figure 3.16).

Those 16 points form a 4 × 4 matrix.

$$\begin{matrix} P(1,1) & P(1,2) & P(1,3) & P(1,4) \\ P(2,1) & P(2,2) & P(2,3) & P(2,4) \\ P(3,1) & P(3,2) & P(3,3) & P(3,4) \\ P(4,1) & P(4,2) & P(4,3) & P(4,4) \end{matrix}$$

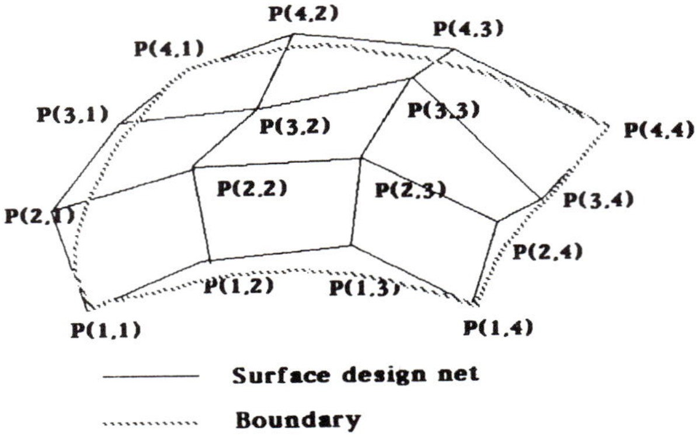

Figure 3.16. A Bezier surface (one patch).

Each row and column define a curve (Bezier curve) on the surface (each one consists of 4 points). For example on row one, there are four points, P(1,1), P(1,2), P(1,3) and P(1,4). The curve starts at point P(1,1) and ends at P(1,4), P(1,1) and P(1,2) define a tangent vector at P(1,1), P(1,3) and P(1,4) define a tangent vector at P(1,4), and the curve is enclosed by the polygon formed by those four points. Users first place four corner points on the screen and then adjust the other 12 points. In order to make the final large surface continuous and smooth, a few rules need to be followed. First, the adjacent boundary curve of two patches P and Q must be identical to both patches, which means $P(i,4) = Q(i,1)$, where $i = 1,4$. This will ensure the continuity of two adjacent patches. For the surface to be smooth, tangents at the boundary must be identical for both patches. To make tangents identical, $P(i,3)$, $P(i,4)$ and $Q(i,2)$ must be co-linear.

The patch is in a sense a smoothly blended approximation to the control polyhedron, with only the corner points lying on the curve. The configuration of the polyhedron gives the designer a good indication of the general shape of the corresponding patch and modification of the points alters the patch in a predictable way.

Bezier curves and surfaces exhibit global control, thus the movement of a single vertex affects the entire curve or surface. Pieces of separate Bezier surfaces can be put together to form a composite surface. The method chosen depends on the degree of continuity desired (for details see Faux and Pratt, 1979).

B-spline curves and surfaces are another popular sculptured surface method. Splines are named after the devices used by draftsmen and ship-builders to draw curves. A physical spline is used like a French curve to fair a smooth curve between specified data points, and can be mathematically defined as a set of polynomials over a knot vector (for details see Faux and Pratt, 1979). When B-spline is used, $n \times n$ points are used to define the surface. Since n is a variable, by increasing n a large surface can be defined. There is no need to use several smaller patches and B-splines therefore have the advantage of local control and have greater flexibility for controlling continuity.

The user of a sculpture surface system interactively defines the control point on the screen, the curve or surface is drawn immediately and the user can play with the system to generate the final design. Since a sculptured surface can not be represented by its boundary, rule curves are added automatically to the plot in order to show the surface. Since both Bezier and B-spline surfaces are represented by parametric equations, NC tool paths for 3- or 5-axis milling machines can be generated from the equations. Since a sculptured surface is always used in conjunction with other analytical surfaces, sculptured surface packages are usually offered as part of a CAD system.

3-D solid modelling

A final software package is 3-D solid modelling. Several methods exist for constructing 3-D objects within a CAD modelling system (Baer, 1979; Requicha, 1980). The 3-D objects are used in CAD systems to build a model, modify a model, generate a projective display for line drawings, generate projective displays for hidden line removal, evaluate collisions between separate solids, and compute geometrical and internal properties.

Representation schemes for 3-D objects should satisfy the following criteria (Requicha, 1980): validity, completeness, uniqueness, conciseness, ease of creation and modification, and efficiency of storage and manipulation.

The commonly used internal representations in solid modelling systems are:

1. Constructive solid geometry (CSG)
2. Boundary representation (BREP)
3. Sweeping
4. Pure primitive instancing
5. Spatial occupancy enumeration
6. Cell decomposition

A CAD system may implement one or several of the internal representations. Figure 3.17 illustrates each of the above internal representations. Their advantages and limitations are discussed below.

Constructive Solid Geometry (CSG)

The method of constructing the intersection, or difference of simple solids called primitives is CSG. The primitives may be blocks, cones, cylinder, spheres, etc. (Figure 3.18). Operators such as union, difference, glue, etc. are used to construct primitives into the final part. The construction procedure is represented internally as a tree. Figure 3.19 illustrates the procedure of building a 3-D model using CSG. In the figure the part is represented in the computer in a CSG tree. The instructions used to create the CSG tree are illustrated in (*c*). The CSG scheme is

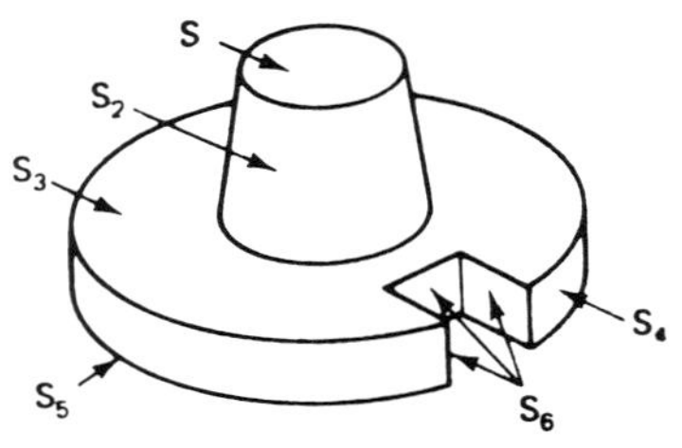

(a) CSG: (Δ · dif · Δ) · un · (· dif ·)

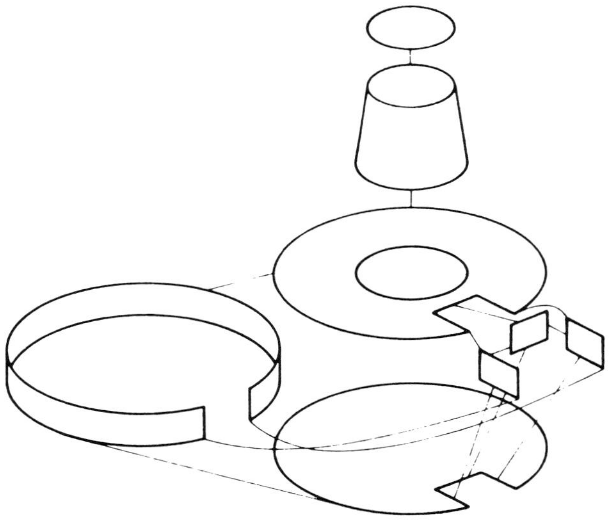

(b) Boundary

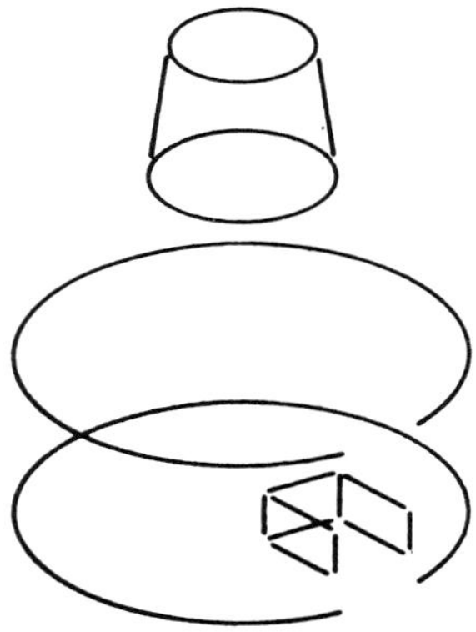

(c) Wire frame

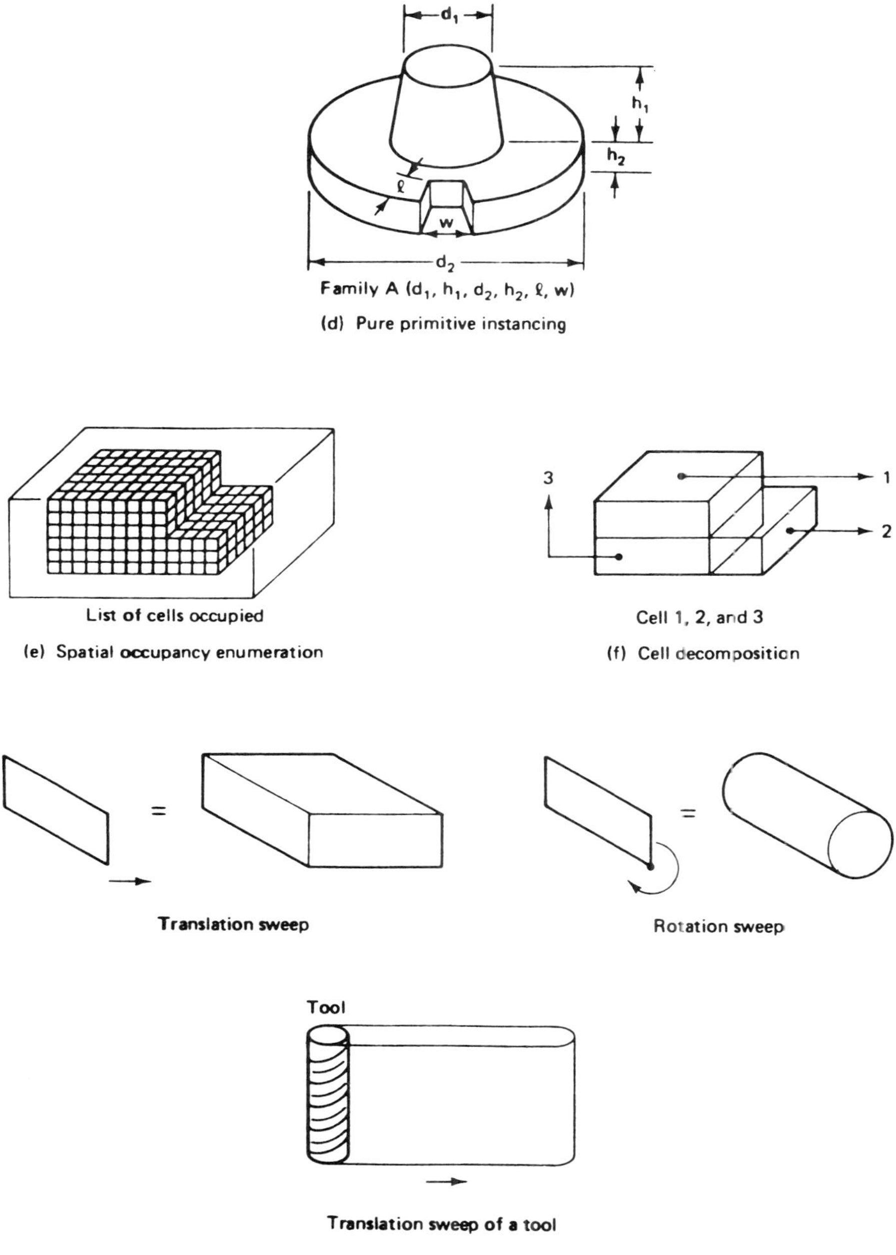

Figure 3.17. Three-dimensional representation schemes (from Chang and Wysk (1985), courtesy Prentice-Hall).

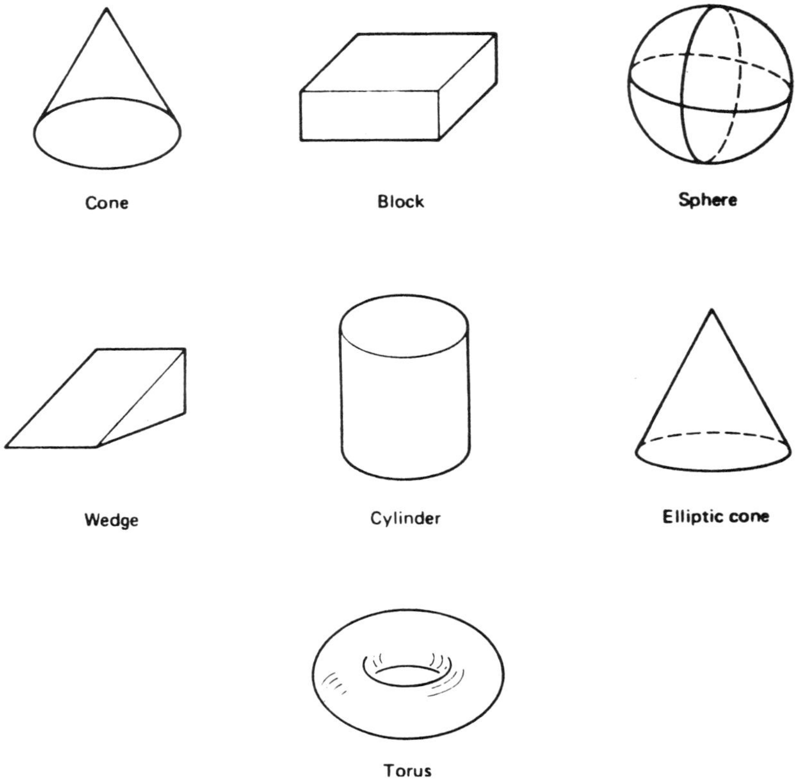

Figure 3.18. An illustration of some primitives (from Chang and Wysk (1985), courtesy Prentice-Hall).

unambiguous but not unique and the validity of CSG trees can be easily ensured. It is concise and very easy to create a representation of unsculptured mechanical parts, but CSG representation is not suitable for producing line drawings and graphic interactions such as 'pick an edge' are difficult to support directly. Current trends indicate that CSG will be of considerable importance for manufacturing automation.

Boundary Representation (BREP)

This is a method of representing a solid object using its boundary surfaces (Figure 3.17(*b*)). The 'faces' of the solid are represented by its boundary, edges and vertices. Boundary representation schemes are unambiguous (if faces are represented unambiguously) but generally not unique, so the validity of BREP has to be established both by geometry and topology. BREP requires considerably more

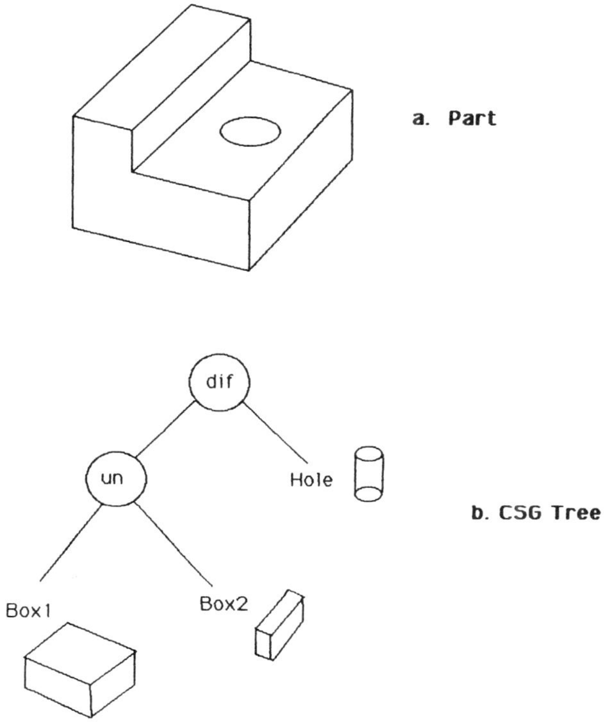


```
Hole = CYL(...) AT(. . .)
Box1 = BLO (. . .) AT(. . . )
Box2 = BLO(. . .) AT(. . .)
Box = Box1 UN Box2
Part = Box DIF Hole
```

c. Instructions to construct part

Figure 3.19. A CSG example.

storage than CSG, and the volume of required data and validity complexity make it difficult to construct without the help of computers. Usually a BREP model is converted from other representations, for example, users input a part design using the format in Figure 3.19(*c*), and the system then evaluates the input and generates a BREP, illustrated in Figure 3.20. The object is represented by faces f1, f2, ..., f9, and each face is represented by an ordered list of edges, for example, f1 is represented by e1, e2, ..., e6, with each edge having two vertices. Even for the simple example part, a large BREP tree is needed. The main advantage of BREP is that the information between faces, edges and relations between them is easily available and makes it suitable for generating line drawings, graphic displays, and graphic interaction. Users can also apply Euler's operators to manipulate faces, edges and vertices (which cannot be done on CSG tree).

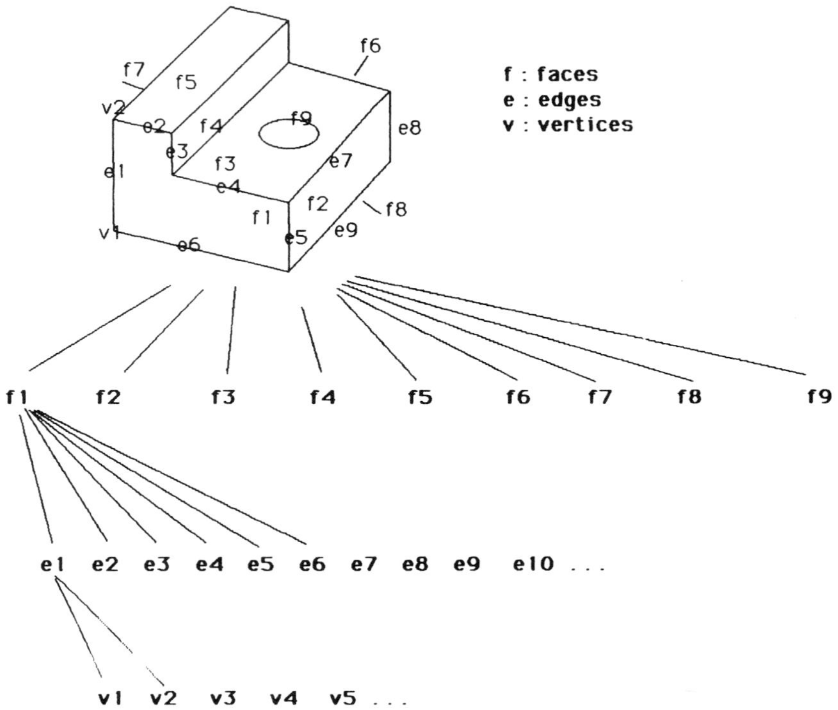

Figure 3.20. BREP of the part in Figure 3.19.

Sweeping

Sweeping is a technique for forming a solid object by moving a 2-D shape along a trajectory, and is of two types, translation and rotation (Figure 3.17(*g*)). By translating a plane, a block can result, while rotating a rectangular plane around an axis produces a cylinder. More complex shapes can also be swept. These schemes are unambiguous but not unique and are limited to objects which have rotational or translational symmetry. Sweeping is used as a means for entering object descriptions in geometric solid modellers.

Pure primitive instancing

This representation scheme is based on the notion of families of objects with each family being distinguished by a few parameters (Figure 3.17(*d*)). Individual objects within a family are called primitive instances and objects can be designed using a combination of instances. These schemes are unambiguous, easy to validate, concise and easy to use, but limited to very small domains. The main problem is the difficulty of writing algorithms for computing properties of such objects.

Spatial occupancy enumeration

Representation using a sequenced list of spatial cells (spatial arrays) occupied by the solid is called spatial occupancy enumeration. On this representation the cells are of fixed size and lie in a fixed grid (Figure 3.17(*e*)). Spatial arrays are unambiguous, easy to validate and unique, but require large storage and are not very well suited for modelling of mechanical objects, such as that used in finite element analysis.

Cell decompositions

More general cases of spatial occupancy enumeration are referred to as cell decompositions. The cells are tetrahedra and must be either disjointed or meet at a common face (Figure 3.17(*f*)). Cell decompositions are unambiguous but non-unique, and validity is difficult to establish. They are used primarily in finite element methods.

The different representation schemes along with their properties and applications are summarized in Table 3.1 (Requicha, 1980). The table shows the properties and applications of each of the six solid representation methods. In the table, G means the method is good for the properties and applications; P means it is promising but more work is needed; ? means it is not clear at this time whether the method is applicable; and a blank entry means either unpromising or poor for the applications or properties.

3-D solid modelling is a very powerful tool for modelling engineering objects. Since solid models are complete, design drafting as well as design analysis can be performed directly on them. Users need to enter the design only once, and the same design data base can be shared by all design, analysis, drafting, and manufacturing modules. Much time can be saved by re-inputting the same design data for different modules using different formats. 3-D solid modelling also eliminates potential errors during data re-input. Colored, realistic, 3-D pictures of models can be displayed on the CRT screen, as can accurate cut-off views. However, solid modelling systems do not come without some disadvantages: they are very complex systems; many internal operations have to be performed in order to evaluate the model and to generate the display; they run much slower than 3-D wireframe systems; and generally they need more powerful computers and larger storage spaces. The way a solid model is constructed is very different than those of traditional drafting, it is similar to playing 3-D puzzles. In the case of CSG modelling, users cannot modify the design directly on the display, but have to trace the changes back to the original CSG tree and locate the primitive or primitives which need to be modified. Due to the difficulty of using solid modellers, they have not been widely used in engineering design. Much research and development work still needs to be completed.

Currently solid modelling is most popular in the making of movies and TV commercials. Movies and TV commercials require realistic and colorful pictures

Table 3.1. *A summary of representation scheme properties and their applicability* (*courtesy* Computing Surveys).

		Properties						Applications											
		Domain	Validity	Completeness	Uniqueness	Conciseness	Ease of creation	Null object	Object equality	Line drawings	Graphic interaction	Shaded drawings	Mass properties	Homological properties	Finite element analysis	Interference analysis	Rough machining	Finish machining	MC tape verification
Primitive instancing			G	G	G	G	G	G	G	G		?	G	G	?		G	G	G
Spatial enumeration			G	G	G			G	G	?	?	?	G	G	G	G			
Cell decomposition		G		G				G		?	?	?	P	G	P	?	?	?	?
CSG	General 1/2 spaces	G		G				?	?		P	?	?			P	P	?	P
CSG	Bounded primitives	G	G	G		G	G	?	?		P	?	?			P	P	?	P
Sweep	Translational & rotational		G	G	?	G	G	G	?	G	G	?	G	?	P				
Sweep	General	G		G				G											
Boundary		G		G		?		G	?	G	G	P	?	P			P		

Key: G = good; P = promising; ? = unclear; Blank = unpromising or poor.

which can only be satisfied by solid modelling. They also do not need the precision as engineering design does. Teamed with super-computers, movie and TV industries can create very realistic animations.

Since in engineering design there are needs for drafting, surface modelling and solid modelling, many CAD vendors have integrated solid modellers into their existing systems—3-D wireframe, sculptured surface and solids can be used to define a part or product and drafting symbols and dimensions can be added on prior to the plotting. This integration enables users to take advantage of features of each system.

In the past designers were constrained by 2-D paper drawings. They were familiar with thinking in the 2-D representation of 3-D objects. It was most natural for them to express their design ideas in two dimensions (anything drawn on the paper is limited by two dimensions). Although 3-D wireframe systems can model 3-D objects, they still use the concept of 2-D design with an added *z* dimension as it is not too difficult for designers to adapt 3-D wireframe software.

However, solid modelling methods are based on an entirely different concept which is no longer compatible with the old way of thinking. In order to take advantage of the 3-D solid modelling technology, one has to re-orient one's thinking. Instead of thinking of a part in terms of edges, one should think in terms of its surfaces and/or primitive elements.

Analysis software

Engineering analyses commonly conducted on a design include: finite element analysis, volume and weight calculation, kinematics simulation, circuit analysis and simulation, etc. The most widely used group of methods for analysis are Finite Element Methods (FEM) (Pao, 1984) which are widely used in:

1. Static and dynamic analysis of complex structures such as aircraft, bridges, buildings, cars, dams, etc.
2. Fluid flow, diffusion and consolidation problems
3. Lubrication problems
4. Heat conduction and thermal stresses

Practical designs inevitably involve complicated geometric shapes and different materials. In order to quantitatively assess a design it is necessary to decompose a complicated structure into basic elements, each being of geometric shape and made of a single material. Figure 3.21 shows a part with finite elements. The physical characteristics of each of these basic elements can be determined by classical theories. Thus the problem is solved by solving the set of simultaneous equations for all the elements. The elements are connected at nodes that form a network known as a mesh. For critical areas on the part, finer mesh is needed, and unimportant areas can have coarse mesh. The finer the mesh the more accurate the result and the more expensive it is to run. Usually it requires an experienced user to set up the mesh.

Prior to the analysis of a structure by FEM, the structure must be preprocessed so that it is partitioned into discrete elements. The common shape of a discrete element called the shape function is a triangle for a 2-D structure and a tetrahedron for a 3-D one; however, other shape functions can be used. CAD systems can be used to design the structure and help in automatic mesh generation. The ability of CAD systems to assist in mesh refining and adding geometric details is best done in an interactive graphics environment. Presentation of results, interpretation and evaluation of results is aided by computer graphics, for example Figure 3.22 shows the steps of using graphics aids for conducting finite element analysis. Models of the part as well as FEM are built interactively on the CRT and the output is displayed on the screen graphically to permit the visual interpretation of analysis results.

Another analysis program, in addition to FEM, included in CAD systems is the simulation of dynamic processes. Such capabilities provide the user with the ability to check the interference of mating parts, collision between moving objects, and other dynamic processes. It can also be used for the automatic verification of

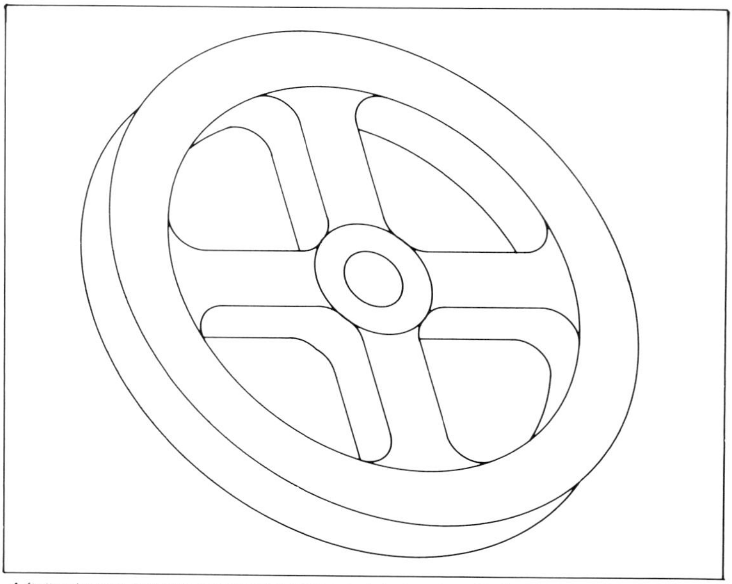

A finite element model is constructed from a part design stored in the data base (in this case, a wheel)

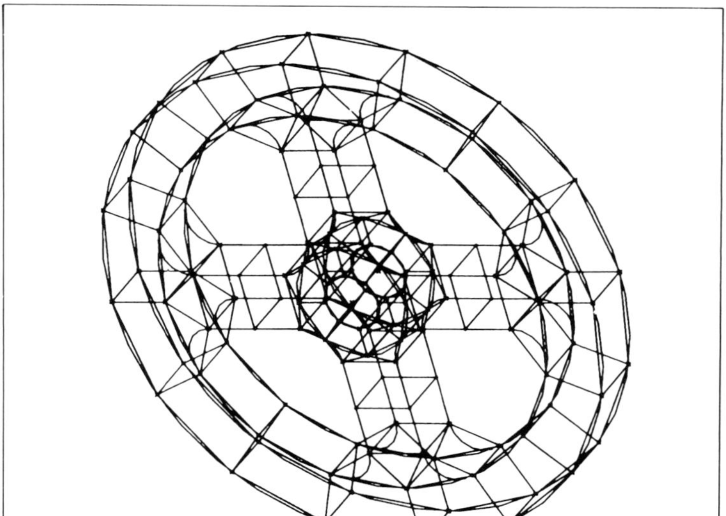

The nodes and elements are interactively constructed from the part design geometry

Figure 3.21. FEM (courtesy Auto-Trol).

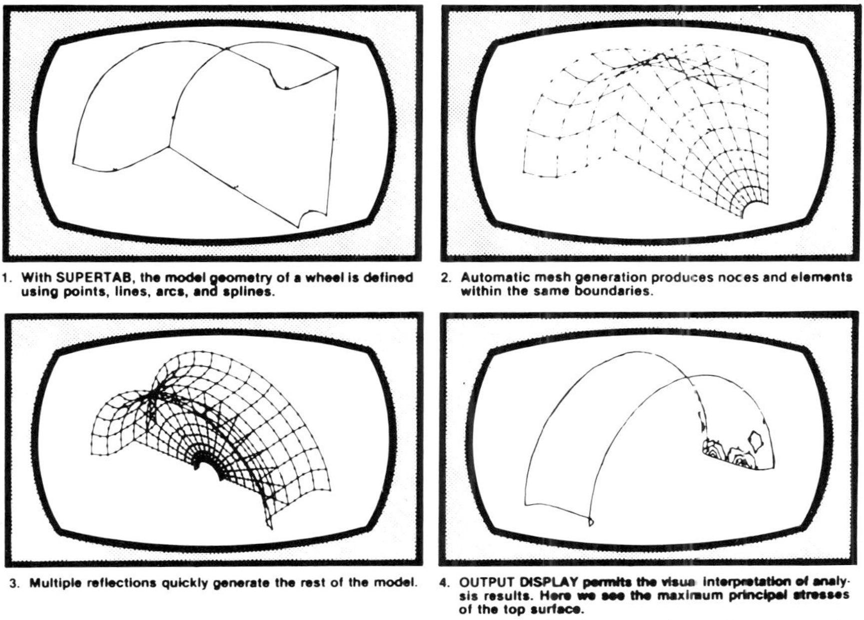

Figure 3.22. Preprocessing and postprocessing of a wheel rim in finite element analysis (courtesy Structural Dynamics Research Corp.).

NC tapes and simulation of the machining process (Hunt and Voelcker, 1982).

Optimization methods can be used in analysis to replace human judgment in the synthesis evaluation loop. Optimization techniques when applied to design need a formal statement of the problem, including the design parameters and all dependent quantities used in the evaluation of constraints and functions of merit.

When CAD design modelling, drafting, part programming, simulation and analysis functions are integrated such an approach is commonly referred to as Computer-Aided Engineering (CAE). A CAE system allows users to perform design, analysis and manufacturing tasks on the same workstation and data base, and this is the direction in which CAD is developing.

3.3. Concluding remarks

In this chapter, CAD softwares and their applications were introduced. CAD is still an evolving technology and the capabilities and limitations discussed in this chapter are changing every day, with many applications softwares being developed by the CAD vendors as well as researchers at universities and industry. This chapter provides a general introduction to the state-of-art technology of CAD and is intended to give readers an overall concept of what CAD is and what it can do. Issues related to systems integration, standards and future development are discussed in the following chapter.

Chapter 4
CAD systems interface and future development

In this chapter CAD systems interface and future development are discussed. In the systems interface sections, system-to-system data exchange methods will be discussed and the data exchange standard—Initial Graphics Exchange Standard (IGES)—which allows CAD systems to exchange data freely will be introduced. Data standards for the CAD software-to-I/O-devices interface will be discussed in the following section. In the third section of this chapter expert CAD systems will be described. Artificial Intelligence (AI) has regained its popularity in recent years, one of the major reasons being the development of Expert Systems (ES). Expert systems are computer programs which can perform compatibly with human experts. Design is one of the problems which fall into the domain of ES applications. Some of the existing research will be introduced and the future development of CAD will be discussed in the last section of this chapter.

4.1. System-to-system data exchange

CAD systems have a number of hardware and software components which must exchange data. There are basically two levels of interfaces: CAD system-to-CAD system and CAD software-to-I/O-devices. Several interface standards have been developed for both levels, as shown in Figure 4.1.

The need for standards for system-to-system data exchange stems from the fact that CAD systems from different vendors do not communicate directly. Many companies install several CAD systems for different functions. For example, a CAD system which is the best for one function (e.g., drafting) may not be as productive for another function (e.g., NC part programming). This creates the need to install each system for one specific function. Thus, a situation arises where the design department uses system A (for product design), the engineering analysis department operates system B (for product analysis), and the manufacturing department uses system C (for part programming).

Because different CAD systems in an organization are noncompatible, information is transferred from one system to another through conventional engineering drawings. A design produced by the design department is plotted on paper and

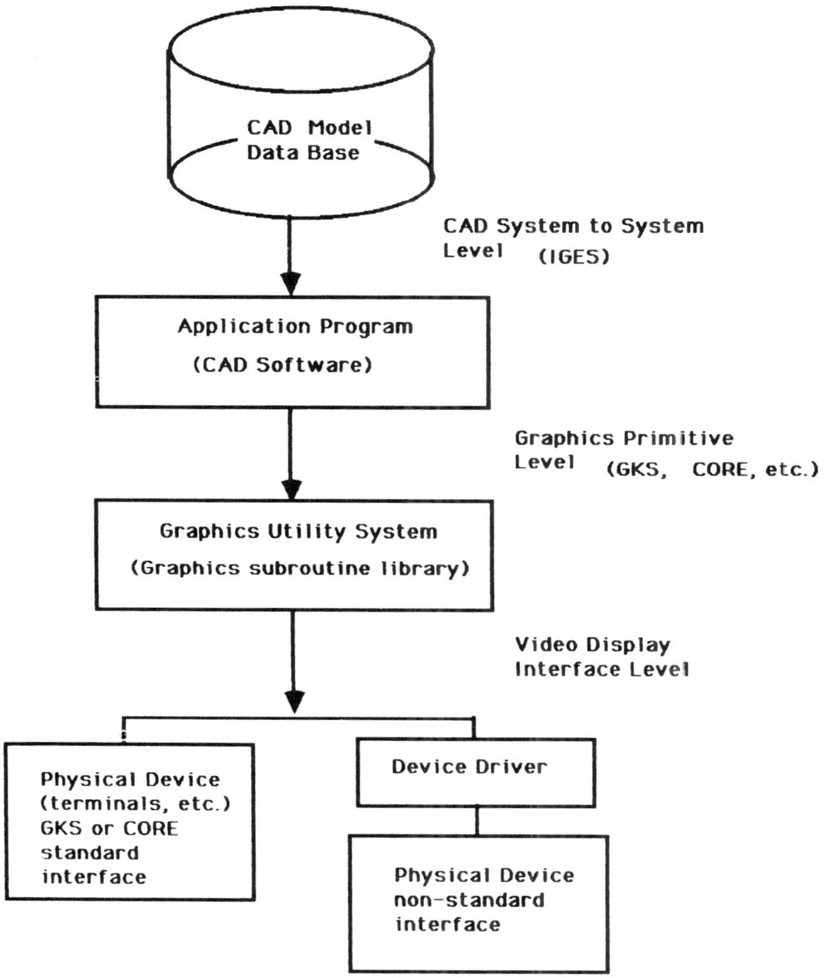

Figure 4.1. Standards levels.

then sent to the engineering analysis department. The engineering analysis department re-enters the appropriate part of the design in system B for analysis. The analysis results are sent back to the design department on paper. If it is approved, another drawing is plotted and sent to the manufacturing department. When the design arrives at the manufacturing department, the geometry is input into system C on a 1:1 scale. Dimension, tolerances and other drafting symbols are left out, since they are not used for NC programming. NC programs are prepared using the data in system C. This process requires several data re-entries, which takes time and is prone to error.

To solve the above-mentioned problem, a translator may be written to translate the data from one system to another. The internal design data in system A is translated into the internal data format of system B then sent to system B. Operators of system B can display and edit the design data right away without reinput. The translation is unidirectional which means another translator is needed for translating data from system B to system A. In this point-to-point translation scheme, 2^n translators are needed for *n* CAD systems.

In addition to the large number of translations needed, such point-to-point translators also have to be rewritten every time there is a vendor system update, which occurs very frequently. Thus, it is impossible for the end users to maintain the system. Considering the number of different CAD systems, it is impractical to implement such a scheme.

The second approach to the noncompatibility problem is to use an intermediate data format. The intermediate data format has to accommodate all the necessary features of CAD systems. Using this approach, each CAD system will need only two translators: a preprocessor and a postprocessor. The preprocessor is used to translate from the intermediate data format to the system's internal data format. The postprocessor is used to output the internal data format to the intermediate data format. For *n* CAD systems, only $2 \times n$ translators are needed. Such translators can also be provided as part of the CAD package from the vendors.

The Initial Graphics Exchange Specification (IGES) format is such an intermediate data format (Smith, 1983). Figure 4.2 shows the concept of IGES data file exchange. Through IGES, users can exchange data among CAD systems without developing custom translators.

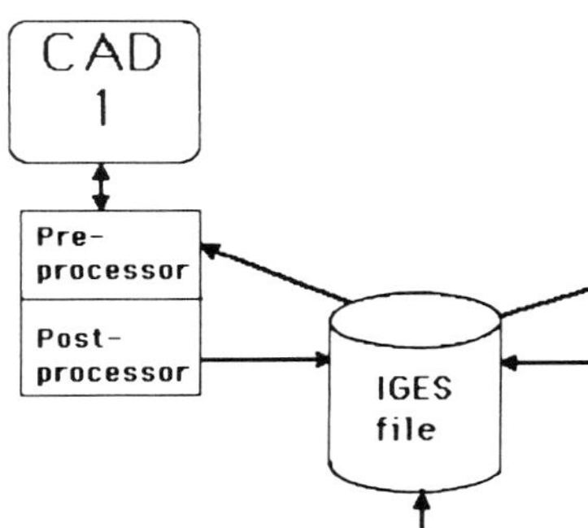

Figure 4.2. The IGES data transfer concept.

IGES is the result of a joint effort funded by the US Air Force and co-ordinated by the National Bureau of Standards (NBS). Task team members from NBS and some aerospace industry users began the initial development in 1979. By 1980, IGES 1.0 data format was published. It was approved as part of American National Standards Institute (ANSI) specification Y14.26M for communication of products definition data in 1981. Since then, the majority of CAD vendors have provided IGES product in their systems. Currently IGES supports basic wireframe mechanical part data, drawing attributes (dimensions, text), rational B-spline curves and surfaces, geometric arrays, surfaces of revolution, finite-element modelling, electrical geometry, piping diagrams, architecture, mapping, etc. Solid modelling data are to be included in the future.

IGES file structure

CAD systems usually store data in files that consist of entities and attributes. Entities are primary data elements, such as points, lines, circles, dimensions, etc. Attributes are information associated with the entities, such as coordinates, width, color, style, etc. for a line segment, or text string for a title, etc. A data structure exists which links all the entities. The inter-relationships are defined in the data structure, so related entities can be identified together. In the data file, each entity is designated by a unique code or number to be distinguished. Each vendor may use a different kind of coding scheme and data structure. When they upgrade their product they may add new entities, or change the data structure. Those changes are all unique to their system.

IGES is modelled following the products of major CAD vendors. Basic entities are: geometry entities, annotation entities, and structure entities. An IGES file is written on 80 column records, using the ASCII character set. The file is commonly readable to most systems. An IGES file consists of five major sections:

1. Start section
Man readable data, such as designer i.d., name, design time, company name, etc. It can contain an arbitrary number of records.

2. Global section
Information for pre/postprocessor, such as data file i.d., bit precision, field delimiter character, etc.

3. Directory entry section
Data common to all entities in the file. There is a pointer linking it to a parameter data record. Other data included are: line font, pattern, label, line weight, etc.

4. Parameter data section
Parameters for each entity, such as, coordinates. These vary from entity to entity.

5. Terminate section
It has exactly one record.

Although efforts have been made to ensure the success of data transfer using IGES, there are still cases when some entities cannot be properly translated. IGES is still an ongoing project.

4.2. CAD software-to-I/O devices interface

Each I/O device has its unique characteristics as well as coding format. Due to the fact that users may have their preference for one device over another, different CAD installations with the same CAD software may have different configurations of I/O devices. A CAD software package must be able to interface with a large number of different I/O devices and devices of different manufacturers. In order to accommodate the variations, device-independent graphics are used. Such graphics split the CAD system into a device-independent part and a device-dependent part. The device-dependent portion of the graphics is a collection of device drivers, which are a set of device-dependent software routines that generate output to, and receive input from, a specific physical graphics device. For example, if two different input/output devices such as a plotter and a CRT display are used, then the device-dependent portion would consist of two device drivers, one for the plotter and one for the CRT. If the CRT is changed to another display, then the device driver would be changed, and the device-independent part would stay the same.

Most CAD software comes with a configuration program. The configuration program allows the user to define the hardware devices used in the system. Each device driver is loaded into the system automatically. Therefore, users can select devices they need. As far as the user is concerned, the operation of the CAD system is unchanged.

The need for device drivers partially stems from the fact that there is no universally accepted graphics I/O standard. To draw a line on terminal A, a computer needs to send code A. When the same function is performed on terminal B, a different code is needed. If a front-end interface is accepted by every device manufacturer, then the problem is solved. There are a few such interface standards proposed, such as GKS, Core, etc.; however, so far none of them have been accepted by every manufacturer.

GKS (Graphic Kernal System) provides a functional interface between an application program and graphical I/O devices (Encarnacao and Schlechtendahl, 1983). The functional interface contains all the basic functions for interactive and non-interactive graphics and provides for a device-independent graphics capability. It is on an abstract level and shields the hardware peculiarities from the application program. To offer different levels of graphics support, a GKS level structure has been defined which offers different levels of capabilities. Nine levels have been defined to support the full set of functions though not every GKS implemented has to support the full set. GKS has been adopted as a standard by the International Standards Organization (ISO), and ANSI is also considering it.

4.3. Expert CAD systems

In recent years there have been many studies in the field of AI and expert systems as well as many successful implementations of expert systems in industry. Research on expert systems is the most interested research area in the field of computer sciences for the 1980s. Expert systems are defined by Waterman and Hayes-Roth (Hayes-Roth *et al.*, 1983) as "a computer program that embodies the expertise of one or more experts in some domain and applies this knowledge to make useful inferences for the user of the system" (p. 169), i.e., expert systems are domain-specific. For example, expert systems like Dendral can identify candidate molecular structures from mass spectral and nuclear magnetic resonance data; Mycin can diagnose certain classes of infectious blood diseases; and Xcon can configurate VAX computers of Digital Equipment Corp. (Hayes-Roth *et al.*, 1983). The types of problems expert systems address are: interpretation, prediction, diagnosis, design, planning, monitoring, debugging, repair, instruction and control. In expert systems, knowledge of human experts is captured and stored. The knowledge is stored as facts, procedures and rules. To build an expert CAD system, designers' knowledge of design rules, drawing understanding, and domain-related problem-solving methods are encoded into a knowledge base.

According to Rasdorf (1985), design knowledges can be classified into:

1. Facts
2. Procedures (algorithms, operations)
3. Judgments (heuristics, beliefs)
4. Control

Factual knowledge consists of information found in handbooks, including: standard material specifications, engineering properties, equipment specifications, engineering data and standard parts lists. They are most easily implementable into an expert system.

Procedural knowledge includes both algorithmic and operative knowledge. Algorithmic knowledge in engineering design is mostly numeric formulae. For example, engineering analysis algorithms and programs and optimization methods belong to algorithmic knowledge. Operative knowledge creates, deletes, modifies and transports facts. Together, operative knowledge and algorithmic knowledge determine how to transform data.

Judgmental knowledge consists of rules-of-thumb. It is the kind of knowledge which is difficult to encode in conventional programs. It is based on human experiences or educated guesses. Judgmental knowledge is involved in all phases of the design process, from conceptualization and planning to testing and revision. It is the most difficult type of design knowledge to capture on an expert system.

Finally, control knowledge directs the way reasoning is applied. It decides which facts, procedures and rules to apply. It controls and coordinates other knowledge in an expert system. Since it is knowledge about knowledge, it has been referred to as 'metaknowledge'.

As discussed in Chapter 1, a design process consists of synthesis, analysis, evaluation and representation. Design synthesis depends on the creativity and experience of humans. Analysis is a more established area than synthesis with many engineering analysis methods already developed (e.g., finite element analysis, kinematics, etc.). Evaluation is based on certain criteria such that while several evaluation procedures exist (such as simulation, project evaluation, etc.), the interpretation of evaluation results requires human experience. Finally, representation can be either performed using graphics (in CAD) or non-graphics (in non-CAD). To represent a design, established methods such as engineering drafting can be used. Representation is a problem of converting within the computer from one format to another. Although methods for representing designs are well developed, the interpretation or understanding of representations requires human experience.

Ideally, an expert CAD system can automate the entire design process. To date several expert design systems have been developed in research laboratories, but none of these have automated the entire design process. Moreover, the majority of the design expert systems developed to date are not linked with commercial CAD systems. Many of them do not even use computer graphics. All of the current expert design systems deal with very specific domains and have very limited scope for problem solving. Some of the approaches and existing systems are introduced below.

Brown and Chandrasekaran (1983) foresee an expert CAD system that will have the capabilities to refine an engineer's design. Such a system will support routine design work by maintaining a data base for manufacturing criteria, functional constraints, material factors, evaluation criteria, and redesign rules for part geometry. It will evaluate initial designs produced by a human designer and provide redesign recommendations.

Tirupatikumara (1985) developed an expert plant layout system called Iflaps. Iflaps takes as input the departments to be placed in a plant, layout objectives, and requirements of each department, such as the need for an outside door or the need for compressed air, and designs the layout automatically from these inputs. In addition, the system considers materials flow and other criteria like safety and employee convenience. The system can also explain its reasoning through a user interface and acquires new knowledge through rule-based learning. Iflaps does not have graphics interface and it is currently still a prototype system: no real factory layout has been designed and implemented by it.

Xcon (R1) (McDermott, 1981) is a highly successful expert system used in industry daily for computer configuration. It has been used at Digital Equipment Corporation (DEC) to configurate orders for DEC VAX super-minicomputers since 1980. Users (DEC computer sales persons) type in functional specifications according to customers' needs, and Xcon automatically selects system components and configuration. An accuracy rate of over 95 per cent has been reported (Mishkoff, 1985). Configurating a computer involves putting many computer system components such as CPU, memory boards, disk drives, power supplies, etc. together to satisfy the need of a user. Because of the number of options available and complex restrictions on the interconnections, configurating a computer is a difficult design task for humans. Xcon does not have a computer graphics interface.

Vaghul *et al.* (1985) reported a prototype system called Impard which assists in evaluating designs of subclasses of injection molded parts. Impard evaluates simple manufacturability criteria such as wall thicknesses, corner radii, boss dimensions, melt flow length, etc. Using a GeoMod solid modeller as the graphics interface, designs can be displayed graphically, and feature primitives are used to build parts. During each stage of the design, compatibility and manufacturability are evaluated and fed back to the designer. As such, Impard acts as a designer's assistant.

Sacon (Bennet and Englemore, 1980) was developed to solve structural engineering problems. It helps users to work with a finite element software package called Marc for structural analysis and to interact with Sacon to generate a finite element model.

A system called Pearl developed at Digital Equipment Corporation can assist in the design of power supply Printed Wiring Board (PWB) layouts (DeJesus and Callan, 1985). Pearl acts as an advisor to the layout designer, providing expert assistance with the selection and placement of components on PWBs, either semi-automatically or automatically. It uses an interactive computer graphics interface and it has been used in real design environments since 1985. There are also several Large Scale Integrated circuit (LSI) and Very Large Scale Integrated circuit (VLSI) design expert systems (Mori *et al.*, 1984; Birmingham and Siewiorek, 1984; Brown *et al.*, 1983). These systems can assist in the lay out of logic elements in an LSI or VLSI.

The expert CAD systems described above are only some of the research efforts to date. Many AI and expert system research results will eventually benefit the development of expert CAD systems. Geometry understanding systems such as Ortho (Lafue, 1978; Choi *et al.*, 1984) and Features (Henderson, 1984; Yoshiura *et al.*, 1984) provide a mechanism for computers to obtain information from drawings or solid models. The study in natural language understanding will provide an English interface to users, so people unfamiliar with CAD can more easily use CAD. The studies in knowledge representation and expert system architecture will enable more powerful expert CAD systems to be built. It is a field that requires much research and development.

4.4. The future of CAD technology

CAD is a powerful tool for design. In the past 20 years it has evolved from simple 2-D drafting to today's 3-D solid modelling. CAD uses every type of computer from dedicated minicomputers to super-computers. Figure 4.3 shows the trend of the cost of CAD systems. The drastic reduction of workstation-based CAD systems and the introduction of expert CAD systems will have a major impact on the users. In the paragraphs below the future of CAD technology in both hardware and software is discussed.

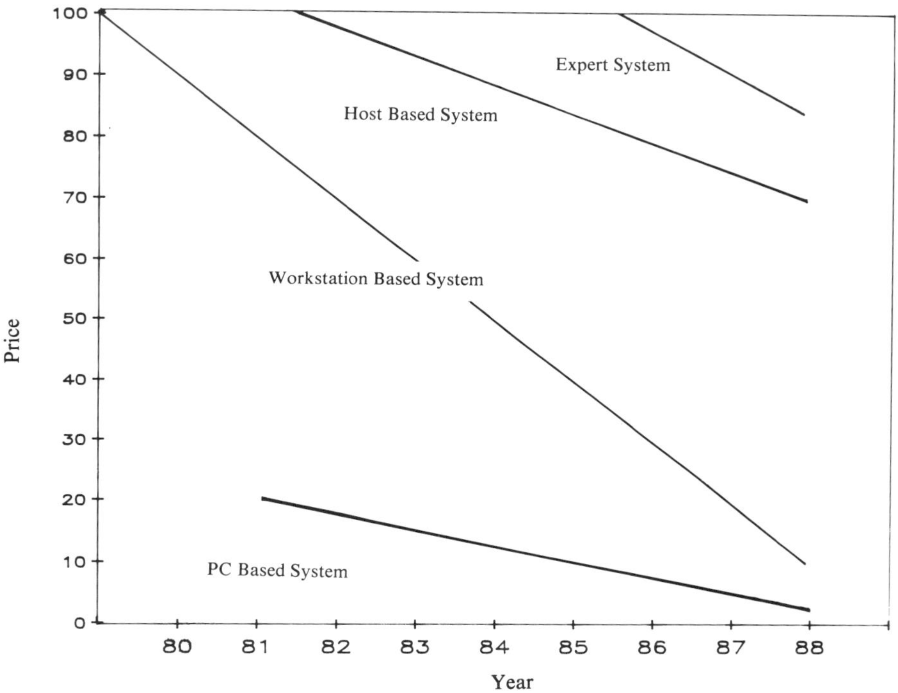

Figure 4.3. The trend of the cost of CAD systems (source Datatech).

For CAD hardware, most past development work has been focused on both the development of computers and I/O devices. The development of computers is not unique to CAD. As general-purpose computers become more powerful, CAD software can be larger and run faster. The display terminal technology also benefits from the advances of microelectronics: since computer graphics is a very storage and computation demanding task, massive RAM memory and a fast processor are needed in a terminal. The development of large capacity (256K or 1 Mega) RAM chips and VLSI technology makes it possible to build cost-effective high-quality color terminals. 1024 × 1024 resolution is usually regarded as standard resolution, and today, 1024 × 1024 resolution multi-color graphics terminals cost only a few thousand dollars. Although higher-resolution terminals are desirable for many applications, they are at present very expensive. Very high resolution terminals such as 4k × 4k pixels will be available at a reasonable price in the near future, allowing very fine design work. Although there are also improvements in other I/O devices, they are not as critical as those in the terminal and computer.

The most significant development in hardware is probably the development of high-speed, user-friendly engineering workstations, offering practically unlimited expansion capability. Millions of bytes of RAM memories can be added. Local Area Network (LAN), a communication network that is confined to a small area, such as a single building or a small cluster of buildings, allows workstations to access large databases. Users can perform design, analysis, word processing, electronic mail, etc. with their personal workstations. The proposed MAP (Manufacturing Automation Protocol) and TOP (Technical Office Protocol) LAN standards will enable all the computer devices in a company to communicate. MAP is a broad-band token bus computer network standard proposed by General Motors. The transmission medium is a copper coaxial cable similar to those used by the cable TV industry. TOP is an office automation network protocol proposed by Boeing Computer Service, and is a base-band token ring computer network standard. Copper coaxial cable is also used in TOP. Using such LAN standards as MAP and TOP, design data can be transferred from a design workstation to a manufacturing engineering workstation. With such an integrated system, CAD will become a paperless design process.

For more sophisticated CAD works, such as very large system graphic simulation and extra fine graphics display generation, mainframe and super-computers can speed up the process. For simple drafting work, every person who has access to a personal computer can perform 2-D and 3-D design drafting. PC CAD systems are affordable at less than $10 000, and such an outlay can obtain a system complete with computer, software, plotter, printer and tablet. The same PC can be used for many other non-graphics applications, such as spread-sheet calculation, accounting and word-processing. At the time of writing, there are already more PC CAD installations than CAD workstations. As the performance of today's personal computer reaches that of yesterday's super-minicomputer, the limitation of PC CAD is definitely reduced. One can expect to see workstation-based and PC-based CAD systems installed all over.

In terms of the future of CAD software, other than the development in 3-D solid modelling, integration is the most important issue. Both design graphics and design analysis functions have been partially integrated. To date, there are still many interface problems yet to be resolved, and although it has been improved, the user interface has not yet reached the perfect stage. A considerable amount of user learning is involved before a user can master a CAD system. User errors occur when there are ambiguities in the command language or the design procedure. How to relieve users from error prone tasks and tedious details is a problem that needs to be addressed.

A future CAD system should have the ability to perform solid modelling, sculptured surface, wireframe modelling and drafting functions—all in one package. Users should be able to select whatever is most convenient to design the product. NC programming, process planning and engineering analysis functions need to be part of the system, or interfaced through a design and manufacturing data base. Automated programming should be introduced. The human should be relieved from working on routine works. NC simulations which compare the simulation result with the design model have not yet been developed.

One will also see more solid modelling software being used in product design. Solid modelling is a promising modelling method; however, the way a model is built is not most natural to human operators. Users have to use limited primitives to construct a model instead of working on the outline of a model. To design a product is like putting a jig-saw puzzle together. Intelligent design interfaces which will assist a user to model a product are necessary. Expert CAD systems which consist of design rules for a specific type of application need to be developed, and such systems need to be able to perform all design functions and generate final drawings.

In an article entitled, "Fourth Generation CAD/CAM", Hanratty and Lowman (1985) claimed that fourth generation CAD/CAM systems will be achieved when "mathematical inconsistencies are resolved with a new solid modelling system that generates a geometrically true solid. Features of these solids include creation of skin or surface and also Boolean operations of union, intersection, and difference." Drafting, wireframe modelling and solid modelling will then be integrated. The design, analysis and NC functions will then be properly connected to the solid modelling data structure. While the fourth generation systems are based on software, the fifth generation systems which is yet to come will be in hardware. CAD programs will first be burned into PROMs (Programmable Read Only Memory, a kind of memory IC chip which is programmable by high electric current—burning), the PROM with the programs is called the firmware. Using firmware eliminates the need to load the programs from disks, thus saving time, and the system will run faster. Special logic circuits will eventually be designed to execute the CAD programs, an operation that could be optimized by building the programs into the silicon IC chips. The technology will make powerful CAD available to every user who needs it.

Part II

THE HUMAN–COMPUTER INTERFACE

Human–computer interaction is concerned with the design of the interface so that the CAD operator can interact with the computer as easily and efficiently as possible. Since the operator's main task is to design, the mental processes should be focussed on that task instead of, as an example, which command will carry out a particular function. In other words, the overall goal of human–computer interaction is to make the computerized task as comfortable and easy as possible. Much of the work in this area has been conducted on many kinds of computer tasks and not necessarily CAD workstations. Chapters 5 and 6 will refer to this work and, since in many cases comparable studies do not exist for CAD, the implications for CAD tasks will be discussed. Any analysis of human–computer interaction as applied to CAD would not be complete without a consideration of what can be done in the future in terms of the optimal human factors design of CAD. This involves a detailed study of information capabilities of the CAD operator from a perceptual and cognitive viewpoint. This basic analysis in Chapter 6 should be the starting point to help answer design questions about CAD workstations.

Chapter 5 begins with a discussion of a problem which confronts any computer user. Because of the nature of the computerized task, health problems, such as eyestrain, neck- and back-aches, and stress, have been observed. The rest of the chapter considers guidelines which can help to alleviate these problems. The guidelines can be divided into two groups: the physical design of the workstation and the design of the input and output devices and displays. For the physical design, illumination levels, glare problems and chair and table design will be discussed. For the input and output considerations, possible interface modes, input devices, the visual display of information, and the choice of command names will be discussed.

Chapter 6 concentrates on the perceptual and cognitive analysis of CAD tasks. It begins with a human information processing model which provides a framework for discussing the remaining material in the chapter. A CAD operator will process information through a series of stages and subsystems: perception, cognition and response. In the perceptual stage, the operator receives information from the senses and starts to manipulate that information. In the cognitive stage, the operator encodes the spatial information, manipulates it (e.g., rotates figures), makes decisions and solves problems. The result of this stage is a specification of a response which will change the environment in some way so that the operator begins the process again by perceiving this new information. Having a basic understanding of the CAD operator's processing of information will help in the design of effective workstations, will be useful in choosing the best design, and will suggest possible training methods so that the information provided can be easily processed by the operator.

Chapter 5
Workstation and interface design for CAD

When working on a CAD system, the operator should be able to concentrate on the creative design aspects of the CAD task instead of paying attention to the interaction with the computer. Several factors can divert attention away from the creative design process. In particular, a possible problem with the CAD task and other computerized tasks is that the operator is required to sit in front of a visual display terminal (VDT) for a long number of hours. If the physical comfort of the workstation design is not optimized, then health problems, such as back pains, and stress problems may occur. Such problems can result in low productivity, absenteeism on the job, and low morale which would all divert attention away from the important CAD tasks. Another problem could occur in the interaction with the computer system. The CAD operator is required to input commands to the computer and interpret displayed information. This input and output of information has been studied extensively in human–computer interaction research. The goal is to design this interaction to be natural, easy and user-friendly so that interaction with the computer can occur with the least amount of training problems and errors. Although the use of CAD systems has not been studied in as much detail as other VDT tasks (e.g., for tasks such as word processing), the problems could be similar and thus the solutions could also be similar. These issues will be considered in this Chapter. The first sections are concerned with the ergonomics of the workstation design to alleviate visual and health problems. The later sections are devoted to the human factors of human–computer interaction to suggest methods to make the interaction easy, fast and efficient.

5.1. Health problems associated with computerized work

On the surface, computerized tasks would seem to have few health problems associated with them, especially compared to higher risk jobs such as on the shop floor or in the construction industry. Yet, early and rather informal studies indicated that workers reported many complaints in terms of vision and musculo-skeletal problems due to difficulties in seeing the displays used for computerized tasks and they were tasks in which the operator would remain seated for long periods of time. As an example of this early work, Gunnarsson and Ostberg (1977) investigated airline reservation clerks and found that 76% of the VDT operators reported visual complaints, 47% indicated the visual problems persisted after work, and 65% indicated some form of muscular discomfort.

A problem with this study and others like it was that comparisons with non-computerized tasks were not evaluated. A possibility is that all workers may have these kinds of problems and the computer may have little to do with it. Subsequent studies compared VDT users to other similar groups. Grandjean (1979) established a relationship between reported health problems and the use of the computer. He and his associates found that 72% of the VDT operators reported visual complaints while 55% of non-VDT typists and 50% of non-VDT office workers reported these problems. In terms of sore shoulders, 60% of the VDT operators reported they had sore shoulders due to their work while only 25% of non-VDT typists and 25% of non-VDT office workers reported this problem. A group of investigators in Germany (Cakir *et al.*, 1978, 1979) studied over 1000 VDT operators and were interested in how these and similar kinds of complaints depended on the type of computerized task. They looked at the incidence of neckaches and headaches (see Table 5.1). Copy typists reported large incidences of these problems with 70% reporting neckaches and 45% reporting headaches. In all cases, other workers using VDTs reported smaller incidences of these problems with the higher paid and higher prestige jobs reporting the fewest.

Table 5.1. Percent of workers reporting neckaches and headaches (from Cakir et al., *1978, 1979).*

Worker group	Neckaches	Headaches
Copy typists	70%	45%
Other clerical VDT operators	45%	23%
Information typist	40%	23%
Editors	39%	8%
Programmers	22%	6%

Smith *et al.* (1981) carried out one of the most comprehensive investigations of this problem by increasing the number of health issues studied and comparing the computerized tasks and jobs. In this study, health complaints for workers at four newspapers and one insurance company were investigated by comparing clerical VDT workers to professional VDT workers and control subjects. The clerical VDT workers (102 were tested) were data entry clerks, data retrieval clerks, classified advertising clerks and circulation and distribution clerks. The professional workers (125 were tested) were reporters, editors, copy editors and printers. The control subjects (93 were tested) had similar working conditions to the clerical VDT operators but did not work on a computer. When the results for clerical VDT workers were analyzed statistically for differences between their health complaints and those of the non-VDT control group of clerical workers, differences were found for 25 of the 59 health complaints investigated (see Table 5.2). The differences found fell into three general classes: visual complaints (e.g., 91% of the clerical VDT users reported eye strain compared to 60% of the non-VDT users); musculoskeletal pains (e.g., 70% of the clerical VDT workers reported sore shoulders compared to 38% of the non-VDT users); and emotional problems (e.g., 50% of the clerical VDT workers reported nervousness compared to 31% of the non-VDT users). For professional VDT users, the differences between them and the control group were fewer (see Table 5.3) than that seen in the earlier comparison for clerical workers. Only 6 of the 59 health complaints tested achieved a statistically significant difference between the two groups and only three of those indicated more problems for the VDT users than for the non-VDT users. The main problem was in terms of eye strain for the VDT users. In addition, the VDT users reported being more irritable than the non-VDT control group.

Table 5.2. Significant differences in the health complaints between clerical VDT workers and clerical non-VDT workers (from Smith et al., *1981).*

Health complaint	Clerical VDT (%)	Clerical non-VDT (%)
Skin rash	57	31
Irritability	80	63
Fainting	36	17
Nervousness	50	31
Fatigue	74	57
Pain down arms	37	20
Stomach pains	51	35
Change in color perception	40	9
Irritated eyes	74	47
Burning eyes	80	44
Blurred vision	71	35
Eye strain	91	60
Swollen muscles and joints	50	25
Back pain	78	56
Painful or stiff arms or legs	62	35
Painful or stiff neck or shoulders	81	55
Numbness	47	18
Neck pressure	57	34
Difficulty with feet	49	35
Sore shoulder	70	38
Loss of feeling in wrists or fingers	33	11
Neck pain into shoulder	56	19
Hand cramps	49	16
Loss of strength in arms or hands	36	14
Stiff or sore wrists	47	7

Table 5.3. Significant differences in the health complaints between the professional VDT workers and clerical non-VDT workers (from Smith et al., *1981).*

Health complaint	Professional VDT (%)	Clerical non-VDT (%)
Burning eyes	60	44
Eye strain	78	60
Irritability	76	63
Fainting	8	17
Pain down arms	11	20
Colds and sore throat	49	63

This work was not performed on CAD operators so we have no way of knowing how well these results would generalize to CAD systems. CAD operators are included in Grandjean's (1986) compilation of survey questionnaire data from several sources (van der Helden *et al.*, 1984; Hünting *et al.*, 1981; Läubli and Hünting, in press; Maeda *et al.*, 1980). Since all of this work was done in the same laboratory, the questions asked were similar although the workers had different jobs, falling into eight categories (see Table 5.4) which differ not only in the kind of work performed (the task—computerized or non-computerized—and the number of hours on the task) but they also differ in the characteristics of the workers in the samples tested (sample size, age and sex). The eight categories of workers are:

1. Data-entry terminal—the operators enter numeric data with the right hand, gazing mainly at documents and not the VDT.
2. Conversational terminal—the operators enter payment transactions at banks in which they usually gaze at the screen 50% of the time and the source document 50%.
3. CAD operating—mechanical design, printed circuit board and electrical schematics design were tested in which the operators gaze at the screen 60% of the time.
4. Mechanical and wiring board design—this is the same job as the CAD operator but without the VDT.
5. Space control for an airline—the operators look at the screen the whole time they are performing the task.
6. Accounting machine operating—this is similar to the data entry terminal except a VDT is not used.
7. Full-time typing—use a typewriter to copy from documents or a dictating machine.
8. Payment transaction in a bank branch office—this task is done without a VDT and keyboards are used only occasionally.

In the surveys used in the data compilation of Table 5.4, the workers were asked if they had almost daily pains in the neck, shoulder, right arm or left arm.

Table 5.4. The eight groups of the surveys of Maeda et al. *(1980), Hünting* et al. *(1981), van der Heiden* et al. *(1984) and Läubli and Hünting (in press) (from Grandjean, 1986).*

	n	Age $x \pm$ S.D.	Women (%)	>6 h/day at keyboard or terminal (%)
Data-entry terminal	53	30 ± 8	94	81
Conversational terminal	109	34 ± 12	50	73
CAD operators	69	33 ± 8	23	20
Mechanical and wiring board design	52	34 ± 12	31	—
Space control in airline	45	29 ± 7	58	100
Accounting operators	119	21 ± 3	100	80
Full-time typists	78	34 ± 13	95	65
Traditional office work	55	28 ± 11	60	30

Table 5.5 contains the percentages which reported these pains for the eight classes of worker. The percentages for the CAD operators were quite low (3% across all categories). When compared to a non-VDT control group (the mechanical and wiring board design group), incidences of these pains are always greater for the VDT users. In this report of the data, no statistical analyses are performed on the data so we have no idea of how reliable these differences are. The percentages reported are much lower than those seen in the articles reviewed previously. This is probably due to the wording of the questionnaires (they used the wording "almost daily pain" in the questionnaire whereas the data reported in Tables 5.2 and 5.3 asked only if these pains occurred) and the amount of VDT use during a day was probably lower than in this other work. As an example of this latter point, only 20% of the CAD operators reported using the VDT for more than six

Table 5.5. Incidence of "almost daily" pains reported from the four surveys (from Grandjean, 1986).

	Subjects with almost daily pains in			
Group	Neck (%)	Shoulder (%)	Right arm (%)	Right hand (%)
Data-entry terminal	11	15	15	6
Conversational terminal	4	5	7	11
CAD operators	3	3	3	3
Mechanical etc. design	2	1	2	0
Space control in airline	7	11	4	5
Accounting operators	3	4	8	3
Full-time typists	5	5	4	5
Traditional office work	1	1	1	0

hours a day whereas a higher percentage of the clerical VDT users in Tables 5.2 and 5.3 would spend more hours at the VDT. This would tend to indicate that the CAD operators sampled in the Grandjean (1986) compilation of surveys were professionals instead of technicians and, thus, would have lower health complaints in general. It is possible that health complaints will increase for CAD operators as the number of hours of use per day increases and as more of the tasks are done by technicians instead of professionals.

In comparing the results from Tables 5.2, 5.3 and 5.5, several conclusions can be made. First, jobs requiring the use of a computer can increase the number of health complaints when compared to similar non-computerized jobs (Table 5.2). Second, this problem is greater if the computer operator is a non-professional rather than a professional (seen when comparing Tables 5.2 and 5.3). Third, even though the incidence of complaints on a daily basis for CAD operators is low (Table 5.5), general complaints have a potential to increase if the work of the CAD operators in the future becomes more like clerical VDT work (e.g., the amount of computerized work during the day increases and non-professionals perform more of the work). From these studies and similar research, investigators have concluded that the health complaints are due to two factors: the characteristics of the computer (Grandjean, 1986) and the characteristics of the job design (Smith *et al.*, 1981). Characteristics of the computer design will be evaluated in terms of the ergonomic design of the computerized workplace and the human factors of human–computer interaction. Job design will be discussed in Part III.

5.2. Ergonomics of computerized workstation design

Computerized workstation design includes the design of the characteristics of the display of information on the visual display terminal and the physical design of the chairs, desks and terminals. Information display can cause visual problems due to improper illumination, glare on the screen, improper contrasts in luminance and flicker. The visual display terminal itself has caused some concern due to the possibility of radiation or chemical contaminants. A few years ago, before VDTs were in high use, we were told to not sit close to the color television due to possible radiation problems. Now, CAD operators routinely sit close to color terminals for long periods of time. Many of the musculoskeletal problems that arise could be due to poor physical design of the workstation so that poor posture or positioning of the machinery could be troublesome. For each of these categories, research has indicated the guidelines which should be followed to reduce these problems.

Radiation and chemical contaminants

The issue of radiation and chemical contaminants concerns whether or not these have an effect on computer operator health. The possibility of health problems caused by these factors, especially radiation, has caused considerable concern among VDT operators. As an indication of this concern, in July 1979 three labor unions requested that the National Institute of Occupational Safety and Health (NIOSH) investigate these problems (Murray *et al.*, 1981). Two different kinds of radiation can occur. Ionizing radiation can occur due to the acceleration of negatively charged electrons which impinge on the screen phosphor to form characters or symbols. These X-rays are absorbed by the phosphor and further absorbed by the face plate of the VDT which contains lead. Non-ionizing radiation can occur from the horizontal deflection system which moves the electron beam across the screen. The horizontal output must be pulsed on and off 15 000–20 000 times a second and this creates high voltage radio-frequency fields. In a CAD workstation environment, NIOSH (Murray *et al.*, 1981) indicated that the chemical contaminants could occur due to photographic equipment, photocopiers and other photo-reproduction equipment which may be in close proximity to the CAD systems. Possible chemical contaminants include hydrocarbons, carbon monoxide, acetic acid and formaldehyde.

The NIOSH team (Murray *et al.*, 1981) measured ionizing and non-ionizing radiation on 136 terminals at three different sites. They found that the maximum measured radiation levels for these VDTs were far below current standards, were far below the thresholds for producing biological injury and, in most cases, were not detectable. Similar findings could be expected for other VDTs and for CAD terminals. To place these and similar findings in perspective, Rupp (1984) compared the average personal exposure annually to ionizing radiation and determined that 55·6% is from diagnostic medical tests; 21·6% is from rocks, soil and water; 16·7% comes from cosmic rays; 2·7% is from nuclear fall-out; 0·5% is from nuclear energy; and only 0·5% is from electronic devices including VDTs. Average personal exposure to non-ionizing radiation can be divided into: 65·9% from FM waves; 14·7% from high VHF television waves; 10·6% from UHF television waves; 8·6% from low VHF television waves; 0·14% from land/mobile phones; and 0·04% from VDTs at a distance of 25 cm. In summary, tests have indicated that radiation is not a cause of health problems for VDT operators and, in turn, would not be a source of problems for CAD operators. Radiation from these devices is a very low percentage of the radiation we are exposed to from other sources.

Similar results have been obtained for the levels of chemical contaminants. Again, the concentrations measured were far below any recommended guidelines or standards and the NIOSH study indicated no hazardous chemical exposures for the VDT operators (Murray *et al.*, 1981). The number of samples taken for some of the contaminants were low (only one sample was taken for acetic acid and for formaldehyde) which indicates that more work needs to be done in this area. With the sensitivity of some people to chemicals, especially in terms of watery eyes, and the possibility of formaldehyde emission from new plastic terminals as they become hot, more samples are needed. At this time, the source of the health problems does not seem to be due to increased radiation levels for the CAD terminal but some more work is needed for testing chemical contaminants.

Visual display of information

A survey by NIOSH (Stammerjohn *et al.*, 1981) indicated that the visual display of characters and symbols on VDTs can be bothersome and could, possibly, be the source of the health problems reviewed previously. Grandjean (1982) has established that the quality of screen characters and symbols can influence the level of health complaints. Table 5.6 contains the results of the questionnaire for the percentages of VDT operators rating display design parameters as being bothersome. High percentages of the operators reported glare, flicker, readability and screen and character brightness as being at least occasionally bothersome. Solutions to these problems can be found by using methods to reduce the glare, purchasing equipment designed to reduce flicker, adjusting the illumination levels to optimal values, and choosing proper contrasts in luminance.

Table 5.6. Satisfaction of 69 CAD operators on the legibility of a graphic display (from van der Heiden et al., *1984).*

	Poor image quality (%)	Characters unsharp (%)	Poor resolution (%)
Raster scan displays (number of users = 53)	25	13	30
Vector storage displays (number of users = 16)	6	6	19
Totals (number of users = 69)	20	12	28

Glare was the largest problem reported from the NIOSH study (Stammerjohn *et al.*, 1981). Läubli *et al.* (1980) established that a correlation between the measured intensity of glare reflections and reported annoyance by the VDT user exists. Reducing the glare may reduce annoyance in the operator. Glare can be caused by reflections of overhead lights, windows, and other light sources. Several solutions to this problem exist with none of them being totally satisfying.

The simplest and most widespread solution to this problem is to purchase a CAD workstation with adjustable contrast. This will allow the operator to increase the contrast as the outside illumination from a window, as an example, increases during the day. If the glare level is high, though, then increasing contrast will not allow the screen to be seen. In addition, reflections will appear at different places on the screen so that changing the contrast may not be enough to fix the problem in all areas of the screen.

A second solution is to reduce the outside light sources such as windows and lights. The CAD workstation could be placed in an area without windows, or curtains could be placed over the windows. Blocking light or views from windows can, however, have adverse psychological effects on the workers. For lights, the level of overhead lighting could be reduced and source lighting could be used to illuminate the source documents or the digitizing tablet. For overhead lights, fixtures which focus the light downward, such as parabolic wedge deflectors, can be purchased. A possible problem with these solutions is that the workplace will not be well-lit which could make the environment more depressing for the workers. Many CAD operators would probably prefer to have the annoyance of glare in order to work in a brighter environment.

A third solution to the glare problem is to change the terminal to reduce the glare. Many CAD workstations can be purchased with non-glare surfaces. In some cases, overlays to reduce the glare can be purchased for particular kinds of terminals. The problem with both of these solutions is that non-glare surfaces and overlays can reduce the contrast and luminance of the characters and symbols making them difficult to read.

A fourth solution is to purchase a CAD terminal with a hood over it if overhead lights are a problem. A good terminal design is to have the display surface of the screen set back some distance to reduce the angle for possible glare from overhead lights and side windows. If this hood is large, other problems can occur. In particular, looking into a large hood could cause tunnel vision which decreases the attentional field; subsequent switching to the larger attentional field of a source document or digitizing tablet would be difficult. Additionally, a large hood would make the contrast between the luminance of the terminal and the illumination of the source document or digitizing table large. Problems due to large contrast ratios will be discussed below.

Glare as a problem will probably continue because all of the solutions can cause other problems. The best solution is to be aware of all of the trade-offs and adjust the contrast, light sources, screen surfaces and hood sizes accordingly.

An issue related to glare is the proper illumination of the screen from outside light sources. Too much illumination can cause glare on the screen or make the characters and symbols difficult to read. Too little illumination can cause the characters and symbols to be too bright and may make reading of source documents or digitizing tablets difficult. In traditional offices, illumination levels between 300 and 700 lux are generally considered suitable (Grandjean, 1986). Studies have indicated that a high majority of the workstation areas are kept within these levels (Stammerjohn *et al.*, 1981, found that 85% of the workstations tested had illumination level in this range). If the operator must read from a source document or work with a digitizing tablet as an entry device, then the illumination level should be 500–700 lux; if the operator only interacts with the VDT and not outside sources the illumination level can be reduced to the 300–500 lux range.

The preferred illumination level for CAD tasks falls at the low end of the suggested ranges. Table 5.7 is taken from a study by van der Heiden *et al.* (1984) for CAD operators when they had some control over the illumination levels at the workstation by switching off some of the lights or closing the blinds in front of windows. These 38 CAD operators had median illumination levels around 125 lux with 90% of the readings falling between 15 and 505 lux. These are on the low

Table 5.7. Illumination levels at 38 CAD workstations (from van der Heiden et al., *1984).*

Workplace element	Illumination levels at the workplace (lux)	
	Median	90% range
Tablet	125	15–440
Keyboard	125	15–505
Reference table	118	15–500

side: 100 lux would be insufficient for reading documents. In fact, 22% of the CAD operators thought that the light level was too low for reading documents.

The third visual display problem, improper contrasts in luminance, is related to the previous two problems of glare and illumination levels. The contrast luminance refers to the ratio between the luminance of the screen and the luminance of the surrounding room surfaces. A large contrast or ratio between these two could tax the pupillary response and visual accommodative processes. As an example, the size of the pupil changes depending on the amount of light. If the operator has to fixate on the screen and then fixate on room surfaces such as the digitizing tablet then eyestrain could occur. The guidelines suggested for this ratio fall between 3:1 as a minimum (surrounding surfaces : screen surface) and 10:1 as a maximum (Grandjean, 1986). Hultgren and Knave (1973) found that most workstation areas had contrast luminance ratios which exceeded 3:1 but that operators seemed to prefer values at the higher end of the recommended levels. Some ratios even exceeded 500:1.

All three of the visual display problems are related and many trade-offs occur. One solution to reducing the glare problems is to reduce the illumination levels of overhead lights and windows and have task lighting for source documents or digitizing tablets. Although it will help with the glare problem, the luminance contrast ratio would increase and possible eyestrain would occur. Placing a hood on the terminal would also reduce the glare but would increase the luminance contrast. Using non-glare surfaces on the screen can reduce the glare problem but the illumination level for the screen surface may have to be decreased so that the characters can be read. The illumination level could possibly fall below the recommended levels.

The fourth visual display problem, the flicker rate, is relatively independent of the other three. Flicker occurs for CRTs in which the screen is refreshed to keep the phosphor excited so that images are displayed. In raster scan displays the screen is refreshed at a certain constant rate. For direct view storage tubes the electron beam travels to excite the phosphor only where the images are displayed. In this latter case, the refresh rate is dependent on the number of vectors or symbols at any one time. Flicker occurs when the rate is so low that the phosphor is allowed to decay to a low level and then when the image is refreshed the operator sees the brightness of the display increase.

Perceiving flicker depends on many things. Some individuals are more sensitive to flicker than others; a large area will appear to flicker before a smaller area; a brighter light will appear to flicker before a dimmer light; and less flicker will occur if lower lighting is used. Generally, flicker will not be perceived if the refresh rate is faster than 65 Hz. Most CRTs have refresh rates of 25 or 30 Hz so that the problem could be quite serious. One way to get around this problem is to use the interlace system. Half the lines on the CRT are refreshed on one pass (i.e., the even numbered lines) and the other half are refreshed on the next path (i.e., the odd numbered lines). Using an interlace system has the effect of making the refresh rate appear to double. These values would then fall closer to the value in which most people under all conditions would not be able to perceive the flicker.

The flicker problem is also dependent on the phosphor used and especially the decay time of the phosphor. VDTs generally use longer decaying phosphors than television sets because the image on the VDT does not change as much as the television image. If the phosphor decays more slowly, seeing the flicker is more difficult. A problem with a slowly decaying phosphor, however, is that the after trace of the image could stay on the screen for relatively long periods of time and distinguishing the displayed items from the recently erased items may be difficult.

The problem of flicker can also interact with the problems of illumination levels, glare and luminance contrasts. If glare occurs, a solution is to increase the contrast on the display. Increasing the contrast by making the characters brighter could increase the chances of perceiving flicker. Less flicker is perceived if lower levels of illumination are used. Therefore, illumination levels must stay above 300 lux and the contrast luminance must not be allowed to go below 3:1.

Physical design of the workstation

Poor physical design of workstation features could be a cause of the musculo-skeletal health problems, such as back and neck pains and hand and wrist fatigue, mentioned in Tables 5.1–5.6. Researchers have provided guidelines for the values of these features, many suggesting that these features should be adjustable because individual differences between CAD operators, such as in overall height and arm length, must be considered. The important features of physical workstation design are height and design of the keyboard, screen position and angle, and height and design of the chair.

The height of the keyboard has an effect on the angle of the arm and wrist which if not properly chosen can cause fatigue. Preferred keyboard heights range from 64 to 84 cm (Brown and Schaum, 1980; Cushman, 1984; Grandjean *et al.*, 1983; Miller and Suther, 1981; Rubin and Marshall, 1982; Weber *et al.*, 1984). Other studies (e.g., Nakaseko *et al.*, 1985) indicate that the preferred height of keyboards is much higher than these guidelines; the 95% confidence range of preferred heights was 74–84 cm for their study. Rupp (1984) argues, therefore, that the height of the keyboard and the arm angles are not very important as long as some kind of arm rest or wrist rest is provided.

Another issue which has been considered for the keyboard is the angle of slope. Keyboards are lower closer to the the operator and angle higher towards the screen. Although European labor unions have strong guidelines on this slope, empirical studies show little or no performance differences when the slope is changed from 5° to 25° (Suther and McTyre, 1982). The participants in this study, however, reported that they were uncomfortable at the 5° and 25° angles. Suther and McTyre recommend a keyboard slope of 10–18° for fixed keyboards. Many of the new keyboards have adjustable slope angles and are detached from the computer screen. For these, Suther and McTyre suggest that the keyboard should be adjustable for a range of 10–25°.

Perhaps a more important issue than the height or forward slope of the keyboard is the slope of the keyboard from the middle to the sides. Nakaseko *et al.* (1985) suggest that the keyboard should be split with the highest part in the middle and lower parts to the sides. In biomechanical studies of hand positions, they argue that a less fatiguing position of the hand is when the hand is at an angle, instead of directly over the top, of the keyboard. Studies using trained typists on the split keyboard, which allowed the hands to be placed at a greater angle over the keyboard, confirmed these predictions. Results indicated that the split keyboard was preferred to the traditional keyboard: it decreased reports of pain in arms and hands and it increased feelings of relaxation. When designing keyboards in the future, the split keyboard design should be seriously considered. Present CAD systems do not have this design feature.

The second consideration of physical workstation design is the height and angle of the screen. A comfortable and preferred line of sight to the screen is 10° or more below the horizontal (Rupp, 1984). In addition, operators seem to prefer a viewing distance between 61 and 93 cm (Grandjean, 1986). To accommodate the preferred line of sight, ideally the table height should be adjustable.

The third consideration for the physical workstation design is the design of the chair. Guidelines suggest that the seated position should not result in any prolonged pressure to the backs of the thighs that might inhibit flow of blood from the legs (Rupp, 1984). The angle formed by the trunk and thighs should be more than 90° and the majority of computer users prefer this angle to be between 100° and 120° (Grandjean, 1986). This recommendation is counter to the upright posture which has been advocated in the past. In fact, the source of the popularized conception of the upright seating position was traced by Mandal (1982) to a German physician, Staffel, in 1884. Mandal claims that in this original source Staffel provided no explanation why the upright posture was better than others but this posture seems to have been accepted uncritically by experts since then.

Seat height is usually adjusted somewhere in the range from 43 to 57 cm (Grandjean, 1986). This range is usually adequate for the operators to be able to adjust the chair so the thighs are horizontal, the legs are vertical, and the feet can be placed firmly on the floor if so desired. Many operators, however, prefer to sit with legs outstretched.

For other chair design issues, the chair should provide support to the lumbar region of the back, the chair seat should be moderately padded and the shape of the chair seat should accommodate frequent changes of position, and being able to adjust the chair while seated is a convenient feature.

Most of the recommendations treated in this section have been for general computer users. The reason for this is that much more work has been done on this larger population of workers than has been performed on CAD operators. In addition, CAD operators in the past have been predominantly male and the preferred settings would apply mainly to this group. More women could become CAD operators in the future and this implies that a larger variability in preferred settings would occur. Studies have been performed on CAD operators for some of the design features mentioned in this section. Table 5.8 contains a summary of the preferred settings for CAD operators (11 females and 4 males) from the van der Heiden and Krueger (1984) study. These ranges are comparable to those found in the recommendations for general computer operators.

Table 5.8. Preferred settings of 15 operators of an adjustable CAD workstation (from Grandjean, 1986).

	Median	Range
Seat height (cm)	54	50–57
Work surface height (cm)	73	70–80
Monitor center above floor (cm)	113	107–115
Monitor visual distance	70	59–78
Work surface tilt (degree)	8·6°	2°–13°
Monitor tilt (degree)[a]	−7·7°	−15°–+1°

[a]Negative tilt = a forward monitor inclination (top of the screen toward the operator).

Following these recommendations for the design of the CAD workplace should help to correct some of the health problems listed in Tables 5.1–5.5. It should be emphasized, however, that an optimal workplace design may not be adequate; the human aspects of management and job design, discussed in Part III, must also be considered. The stress accompanied by poor job design is hypothesized to have an effect on these health problems (Smith *et al*., 1981). As an example, just being able to move around on the job or vary activities can be helpful. Encarnacao and Schlechtendahl (1983) found that a designer can spend up to 50% of the time away from the workplace requesting and verifying information while only 25% of the designer's time may be spent actually drawing the product or part being designed. This variation in the job allows the CAD operator to be more satisfied and complain less.

5.3. The mental model for interacting with the system

The CAD operator must enter information into the CAD system, must perceive the displayed information, and then enter new information. In other words, the CAD operator must interact with the computer to perform the tasks. The interface between the CAD operator and the computer is very important in making these tasks as easy as possible. The CAD operator actually has two tasks: the usual drafting task of creating a design and the task of interacting with the computer to create the design. Chapter 6 discusses how the operator creates designs. The next sections in this Chapter consider how the operator does and should interact with the computer to achieve the designs. If interacting with the computer is too difficult, it may have a negative effect on the design process. The interface, therefore, should be designed to be user-friendly, i.e., natural and easy to use, and take into account the processing of information by the operator.

The overall goal for interface design can be represented pictorially in Figure 5.1 (adapted from Norman, 1983). Three concepts are important. First, the conceptual model is a description of the computer system in engineering terms so it is accurate, consistent and complete. Second, the mental model is the model the user forms of how the computer system works; this mental model guides the user's actions and behaviors. And third, the goal is to try to choose the information to represent on the display to enable the mental model, like the conceptual representation, to be accurate, consistent and complete.

Determining the operator's mental models will help in determining how to design the human–computer interface or help to determine those features which are desirable in a CAD workstation. The mental model is built up through interactions with the system. Everybody has an understanding of how a computer system works. This understanding, or mental model, can be accurate or inaccurate and can operate at several different levels. The mental model can be

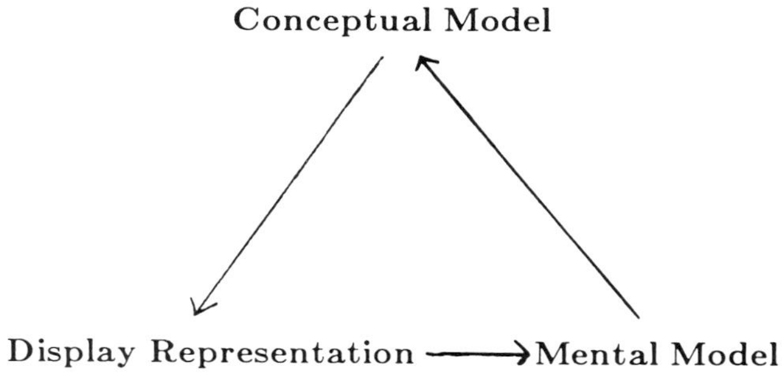

Figure 5.1. Relationship between the conceptual model, the display representation and the mental model. The goal is to choose the display representation so that the mental model can closely correspond to the conceptual model.

manifested in several different ways: in terms of rules, imagery, or mental simulations, as some examples.

Norman (1983) observed the kinds of behaviors associated with calculators as a reflection of a person's underlying mental model. The calculator is a relatively simple device when compared to a CAD workstation yet, even with working on calculators for long periods of times, Norman found the following characteristics of people's mental models:

1. They were incomplete.
2. They were unstable, so the operator can forget how to do things, especially if the function has not been used recently.
3. No firm boundaries exist between machines so that operators often become confused when transferring from one machine to another.
4. They were unscientific in that superstitious behaviour is used.
5. They were parsimonious in that extra physical operations are performed rather than the mental planning needed to avoid these extra actions.

Many of these same observations would probably apply to CAD operators. CAD operators probably only know a small subset of the available commands (the model is incomplete); some of the functions and commands are not used often and would be forgotten (the model is unstable); and the CAD operator would have a tendency to use stereotypical command sequences rather than performing the mental operations needed to use a more efficient command sequence (the model is parsimonious). These points have been verified experimentally by Card *et al.* (1983). They tested an expert CAD operator on a circuit design task and found that the command sequences were very stereotyped: 85% of the command executions utilized only six of the possible command sequences. A very small percentage of the time for this expert was spent in the mental preparation for the command sequence.

Similar to Norman's (1983) observations on mental models, CAD operators would probably have a difficult time transferring from machine to machine. Keeping in memory where the model of one system begins and where the model of the other begins would be difficult (no firm boundaries exist). Counter-intuitively, perhaps, the most problems would probably occur when the old machine and the new machine were similar to each other but slightly different. The CAD operator would confuse the mental models because they are so similar. Less transfer problems could occur if the two systems were completely different.

5.4. CAD operator interactive tasks

The mental model the operator has of the CAD system will determine the methods of interaction with it. It is interesting to determine, for various kinds of tasks on computer systems, the relative importance of each interactive feature. Van der Heiden *et al.* (1984) carried out a study on 38 CAD operators for three different tasks to determine the percentage of time they input information and watch the output on the display. The results of this study are presented in Table 5.9. They found that, depending on the task, CAD operators watch the screen 46–68% of the time, operate the keyboard 14–22% of the time, operate the digitizing tablet 26–48% of the time, and manipulate the document 9–15% of the time. These percentage times indicate the relative importance of each of the interactive tasks for CAD.

Table 5.9. Results of a worksampling study on 38 CAD workstations (from van der Heiden et al., *1984).*

	% of working time spent working interactively at CAD workstation		
Activity	Mechanical design (%)	PWB[a] design (%)	Electrical schematics (%)
Watching screen	52	68	46
Operating keyboard	14	14	22
Operating tablet	48	43	26
Hardcopy manipulation	<1	<1	1
Document manipulation	14	9	15
Number of observations	1681	1670	1177

[a]PWB = Printed wiring board.

Although van der Heiden *et al.* (1984) did not specify the tasks that the CAD operators were performing, assumptions can be made about these tasks. When the CAD operators were watching the screen, they would most likely be looking at the design (viewing displayed information), the menu displays or the visual feedback on performance. When operating the digitizer tablet, the operators would be drawing or pointing to menu items on the display. When operating the keyboard, they would be entering commands. The human factors of each of these issues will be considered in the following sections.

5.5. *Interface modes*

The design of the interface mode determines the other kinds of information which must be displayed and the input devices which can be used. Four different kinds of interface modes are used typically in computer systems: menu, fill-in-the-blank, parametric, and direct manipulation. Each of these has advantages and disadvantages.

Menu displays

Menu displays are becoming more and more popular as the choice for the interface mode. For a menu display, the possible choices for a command are listed on the screen or, in many CAD systems, on the digitizing tablet. In this latter case, an area of the digitizing tablet can be set aside for the menu displays and these can be flexible in that overlays can be placed in this area with different menus for different needs. Figure 5.2 shows an example of such an overlay.

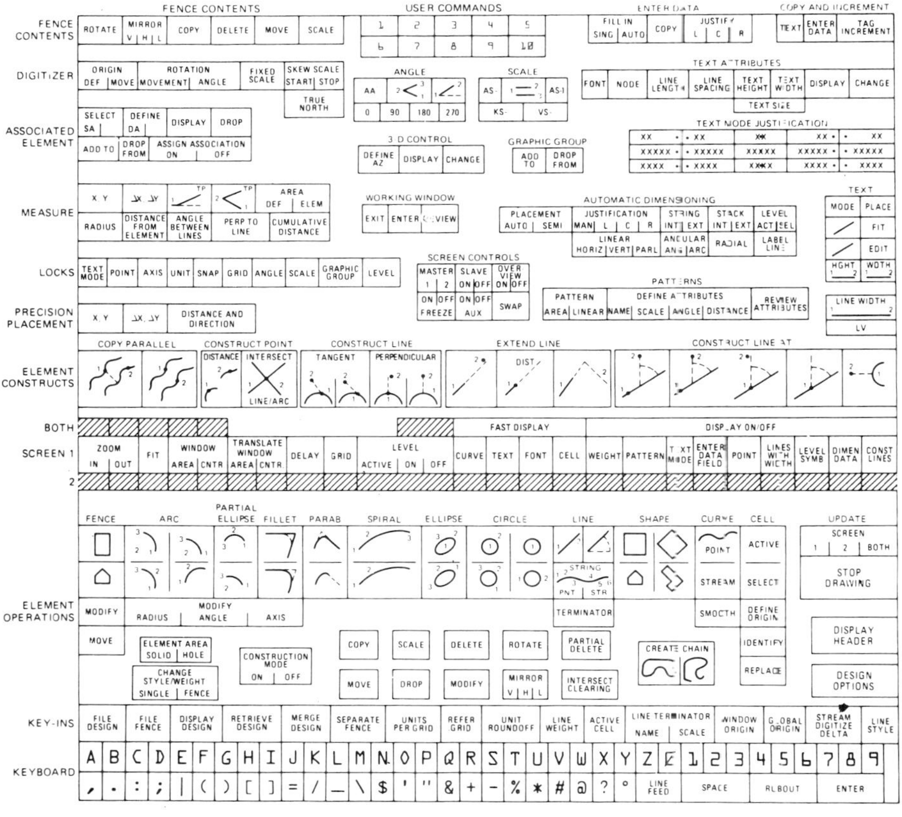

Figure 5.2. A menu overlay for a digitizing tablet (from Artwick, 1984, courtesy Prentice-Hall).

Selecting an item from a menu can occur in four possible ways. In the first method, numbers are displayed next to the word description of the command on the screen. To input the menu item the operator types in the number. In the second method, some kind of pointing device is used for item selection. Several different devices are available: mice, touch screens and light pens. When using these pointing devices, the operator would move the cursor on the screen to the appropriate menu item and register an input by either pushing a button on the mouse, touching the screen for the touch screen, touching the light pen to the screen, or touching the data tablet with the stylus. When a choice is input, the computer will indicate that it has been registered by either providing an auditory tone or video-inverting the chosen menu item on the screen. In the third method, the operator uses arrow keys on the keyboard to choose an item. The display on the screen indicates the current choice of an item by putting an 'x' next to the item or by video-inverting the current item. When the current choice matches the desired choice, the operator pushes the enter or return key on the keyboard. If the current choice is not the one desired, then the operator can push the arrow buttons to move to the item above or below. In the fourth method, with the menu placed on the digitizing tablet the operator uses the input device for the digitizing tablet to point to the appropriate item.

Experiments have not been performed to determine which of the four methods is best in terms of time and errors. Several guidelines, however, can be suggested. Placing the menu on the digitizing tablet can have disadvantages because the operator must divide attention between the tablet and the screen. For large menu displays, however, placing all items from the menu on the screen may not be possible. Entering numbers or using the arrow keys is probably best if many menu items are displayed on the screen. The pointing is probably best if few items are displayed. For the menu displays registered by pointing, experiments have been performed to determine the input device which is fastest and most accurate. These experiments will be considered in a following section.

Menu displays are beneficial because they always display the possible range of commands. Experimental psychologists make a distinction between recognition memory and recall memory (e.g., Anderson, 1980). Research has shown that humans are much better at recognizing a correct choice rather than recalling that choice from memory. Inputting word commands on a keyboard is an example of a recall task. With menu displays, the choices are displayed on the screen and the operator would only have to recognize the correct command and not recall it exactly. Investigators have suggested that menu displays can reduce errors but would probably be slower than other interface modes (Shneiderman, 1980).

Problems occur with menu displays when the number of menu items become large, as they can with CAD systems. In this case, the searching of all the items to find the correct one could be a very time-consuming task and merely displaying all of them on the screen could be impossible due to the screen size. The solution is to arrange the menu items in a hierarchy so that the items displayed on the first screen would branch off into another screen and so on for as many levels as needed. Miller (1981) has found that a trade-off occurs when considering how many items should be included on a screen and how many levels of screens should exist. This has been termed the breadth/depth trade-off and it can be portrayed graphically as an inverted U-shaped curve. The most errors and the slowest performance times occurred when the breadth (1 frame, 64 menu items on the frame) was high and when the depth (6 frames, 2 menu items per frame) was high. Best performance occurred for the intermediate structures (2 frames, 32 items per frame and 3 frames, 11 items per frame).

Additional experimental work has been performed on the structure of menus. The menu items should be arranged on screens according to logical, as opposed to random, groupings (Liebelt *et al.*, 1982). Keeping track of the menu items on multiple screens could, however, be difficult. Billingsley (1982) found that displaying a map of the menu screens increased the ability to use the menus when compared to an index of menu items.

Many CAD operators seem to be content with the menu displays. For example, van der Heiden *et al.* (1984) surveyed 69 CAD operators and reported that 65% of the operators saw no need for improvement in the menus. From the same survey, it is interesting to note that 26% of the operators stated that the menu contained a number of items they never actually used.

Fill-in-the-blank mode

Another popular interface mode for CAD systems has been referred to as fill-in-the-blank (Shneiderman, 1980). For this mode, the computer queries the operator to obtain the appropriate response. As an example, at the beginning of a design session, the computer may ask the operator if he or she wishes to create a new design file (yes or no) and to type in the name of the file. During the design phase, the computer may ask the operator to choose the appropriate symbol to display (the operator could respond with 'line') and then the computer would ask for the length of the line. The computer query could be dependent on answers to previous queries.

A fill-in-the blank mode is often used when the range of possible responses is large (Shneiderman, 1980). This can occur when dealing with numbers for lengths and rotations, for example. Displaying all possible numerical answers in a menu display would not make sense because of the large search times involved and the changing ranges and units. The main problem with this mode, when compared to the menu displays, is that the operator may not be able to remember the possible answers; recall from memory instead of recognition would have to be used. An additional problem is that typing mistakes would be easier to make with this mode than for menu displays which require little or no typing.

Parametric

The third interface mode has been termed the parametric mode (Shneiderman, 1980). The best way to define this mode is through the following example from Shneiderman:

A21AUGJFKLAX

This is an example of a possible input on a keyboard for a travel agent to query the computer about the flight numbers and arrival times for flights on 21 August from J. F. Kennedy Airport, New York to Los Angeles International Airport. An example input like this would not be appropriate for a menu display, because of the large number of airports in the world which would have to be displayed, but could plausibly be used as a fill-in-the-blank mode.

The advantage of the parametric mode is that it can be very fast. If using the fill-in-the-blank, the operator would have to wait for the computer to type out at least three queries and the operator would have to respond to each. Shneiderman (1980) also claims that an advantage is that the operators, after mastering it, have a sense of control over it and enjoy using it. The main problem is that the training time is longer than the other modes. The operator would have to learn the syntax of the command, the abbreviations for each command, and the range of commands. This mode has not been used in CAD systems to a great extent.

Direct manipulation

The final interface mode, direct manipulation, is being used increasingly for newer computer systems and combines some of the features of menu displays. A direct manipulation mode requires some kind of pointing device, such as a mouse, and will use symbols such as icons instead of command names. The icons are pictures which are displayed on the screen. An example of an icon would be a picture of a printer which could be pointed at with the mouse instead of having to enter a command 'print' or choose 'print' from a list of menu items. Many times an icon has one or several pop-down menu lists associated with it. Again, using the print example, if the operator pointed to the print icon a pop-down menu would appear below the icon with menu items for the particular output device and printing style. The operator would then point to the appropriate menu item. Finally, another characteristic of the direct manipulation mode is that items can be moved around on the screen by moving the pointing device. If a symbol needs to be moved to another part of the display, the operator would 'capture' the particular item by moving the cursor with the pointing device such as a mouse, and clicking the button on the mouse would allow the symbol to move as the mouse is moved to the new location, clicking the mouse button again would deposit the symbol in its new location. Bewley *et al.* (1983) describe features of the direct manipulation mode for the Xerox Star computer system which was one of the first to incorporate it.

Direct manipulation has many of the same advantages as menu displays. In particular, display of the icons on the screen allows use of recognition memory instead of recall memory so that the errors can be reduced. Another advantage is that the icons can provide spatial representations of the command names which may help to make abstract concepts more concrete, especially to a novice user. In many cases, the icon also provides an analogy which can help the novice user understand the function of the command by relating new knowledge to old knowledge. An example of an analogy is an icon of a waste paper basket which can be used to indicate deletion of files. Analogies have been useful for explaining concepts to computer novices (Douglas and Moran, 1983; Rumelhart and Norman, 1981; Mayer, 1975). Some researchers argue, however, that icons and the implicit use of analogies hold little advantage over traditional command names (Switchenko, 1985).

The direct manipulation mode shares the same disadvantages of the menu displays. If the number of commands is large, then displaying enough icons on the display would be difficult. The pop-down menu lists, however, can get around some of these problems.

Comparison of the four interface modes

The four interface modes can be compared across several dimensions such as empirical results, ease of use and user-friendliness. Surprisingly, few experiments have been performed to compare the modes directly. Indirect research results can be found by examining some of the theories from cognitive psychology for how people process information. Table 5.10 compares the four modes across several dimensions.

Table 5.10. Summary of the four interface modes over five dimensions of usability.

Dimension	Menu	Fill-in-the-blank	Parametric	Direct manipulation
How fast?	Could be slow	Moderate	Fast	Could be slow
Possibility of error	Error-free	Moderate errors	Many errors	Error-free
Training time	Short	Moderate	Long	Short
Preferences	High	Low	Prefer if trained	High

Theories in cognitive psychology have been invoked previously to justify the use of menu displays and the direct manipulation mode. The superiority of recognition memory over recall memory implies that less errors should occur with menus and direct manipulation modes. Because people find analogies and spatial reasoning useful to solve problems in other domains, the icons of the direct manipulation mode imply that operators would not have to read a description of the icon command to understand what it does. More detailed descriptions would be needed for the commands in the parametric and fill-in-the-blank modes.

Evaluating the interface modes in terms of ease of use and user-friendliness also indicates the advantages of menu and direct manipulation modes to the other two. Bewley *et al.* (1983) argue that pointing is one of the most natural acts humans perform. Since some forms of the menu displays and the direct manipulation make use of pointing to enter commands, this is a natural and easy task for humans to perform. User-friendliness is sometimes evaluated in terms of how forgiving the system is in terms of errors. Since the range of possible inputs is displayed, operators could find menu and direct manipulation modes more friendly.

Computer system designers often provide the operators with a choice of the interface mode to use; the system is adaptable to the individual preferences. Adaptability is another feature of user-friendliness and ease of use. Interface mode choice can be provided by allowing the operator to either enter commands on a keyboard by typing in alphanumeric characters or using the pointing device to choose menu items and point to icons.

The advantage for the fill-in-the-blank mode would be to use it when the number of commands is large or the range of commands is continuous, as it would be when inputting numerical values. The parametric mode is the most useful when training time is not a problem and speed of command entry is a major concern. Shneiderman (1980) argues that operators using the parametric mode like it after training because it gives them a feeling of control over the computer.

One of the few experiments which have compared some of the interface modes experimentally is the Gade *et al.* (1981) experiment. In this experiment, a menu display mode was compared with three other possible input modes: a regular command entry mode using a keyboard; command entry with error correction in which the computer would search for typing mistakes and automatically correct; and command entry with autocompletion in which the computer would complete the command if enough characters were entered to distinguish it from other possible commands. When comparing these four modes in terms of errors and time to complete the task in a data entry task, the experimenters found that the menu display provided a 30% decrease in errors when compared to the normal command entry mode. In addition, a majority (62%) of the operators preferred the menus to the other modes. No differences in time to complete the task were found.

These experimental results confirm the hypotheses about menu displays decreasing the number of errors. The use of menus, unexpectedly, did not slow down the task when compared to a command entry mode. More research needs to be done to determine the point at which the number of menu items is so large that using the fill-in-the-blank mode and parametric mode is more efficient due to excessive search times through the menus. The Miller (1981) experiment on the breadth/depth trade-off only looked at menu displays and did not consider how menus with differing breadth and depths compared to the other interface modes.

5.6. *Human factors of input devices*

For CAD tasks, input devices can perform many different kinds of tasks. The CAD operator must use input devices to draw, to enter commands either through alphanumerics or menus, and to point to items on the screen. Each of these functions will be considered in discussing the human factors of input devices. The technical aspects of these devices were presented in Chapter 2.

Available input devices

Table 5.11 provides a listing from Ohlson (1978) of the possible input devices for graphic input in terms of resolution and accuracy, cost (both hardware and software) and user satisfaction. Other possible input devices, such as keyboards and voice recognition devices, could be used for CAD workstations in tasks other than graphics input, such as entry of commands. These devices will also be discussed.

For CAD tasks, as seen from Table 5.9, the most highly used input device is the digitizing tablet for drawing the graphics designs. It is virtually the only input device which may be used for drafting or hardcopy data entry, free-hand sketching, or producing three-dimensional pictures (Greenstein and Arnaut, 1986). Tablets are also used for tasks in which the operator is required to select or point to an item from an array of menu. Tablets would not be appropriate for data entry tasks which require alphanumeric characters because of the slowness in selecting and pointing to these characters.

The only other input device mentioned for CAD tasks in Table 5.9 was the keyboard. Unlike other computer systems, the keyboard is not the principal input device so it is quite often placed to the side of the digitizing tablet instead of directly in front of the operator. The keyboard is used when large amounts of textual information or large amounts of numerical data must be entered. It is virtually the only input device suitable for these purposes. The keyboard may include a number pad and variable and fixed function keys.

Several other input devices are available for use but are not as widely incorporated in CAD systems as the digitizing tablet and the keyboard. Greenstein and Arnaut (1986) offer the following suggestions for applicability of these input devices. Touch screens are best for working with data already displayed on the screen such as in menu items. They are devices which are relatively easy to use so they are appropriate for novice users or for tasks in which no training is provided. Some low resolution drawing can be done through a touch screen. Mice are best suited for pointing and selection tasks. Some drawing can be done with them. They are not suitable for single character data entry. A trackball is best suited for tasks requiring rapid cursor positioning and is probably not suitable for drawing tasks. It could also be used for moving symbols on a display but it is not suitable for tracing, input of hand-drawn characters, or three-dimension drawings. The joystick is most suited for tracking tasks or pointing tasks which do not require a great deal of precision. It may be used for line drawing if high accuracy and speed are not required and it can be useful in placing and moving symbols. The light pen is well suited to menu selection tasks, can be used for drawing but it is not very accurate, and could be useful for placing and moving items on the screen.

Table 5.11. Graphics input device characteristics (from Ohlson, 1978, courtesy IEEE).

	Functionality		Precision	Cost			User satisfaction		
Input device	Device class	Information classes	Resolution and accuracy	Hardware cost	Software development	Software overhead	Input type	Feedback	Special considerations
Tablet or digitizer	Locator	Position, Vector, Function ID, Object ID	0·05 to 0·001″ up to ±0·006″[a]	Medium to high	Medium	Low	Indirect (sometimes direct) graphical	Digital position readout or independent display	Some units are not suitable for online interactive use.
Touch panel	Locator	Position, Function ID, Object ID	0·25–0·75″[b] accuracy, much higher than resolution	Low to medium	Low	Low	Direct tactile	Independent display	Gross resolution makes use for detail work impossible.
Joystick	Locator	Position, Vector, Object ID	Resolution dependent on A/D converter. ± 10% to ± 0·1%	Low to medium	Low	Low	Indirect tactile	Tactile and/or independent display	Large variety of types to fit most applications.
Mouse and trackball	Locator	Position, Vector, Object ID	As for joystick, 10–1000 accurately differentiable points	Low to medium	Low	Low	Indirect tactile	Tactile and/or independent display	Relative positioning of mouse. Slewing capabilities of trackball.
Potenti-ometers	Valuator	Value 2D possible (if used in pairs)	As for joystick	Low	Low	Low	Indirect tactile	Tactile and/or independent display	Choice of dials, slides, levers, and other styles.
Function switches	Button	Function ID	NA	Low to medium	Medium	Low	Indirect tactile	Visual (switch position)	Possible use of software-programmable buttons.
Light pen	Pick	Object ID, Position, Vector, Function ID	Dependent on display device	Medium	High	Medium to high	Direct graphical	Independent display	Only usable as simple pick on refresh displays, or locators on raster-scan displays.

[a] 0·127–0·00254 cm, up to ±0·0152 cm.
[b] 0·635–1·905 cm.

Comparison of input devices for drawing tasks

Several input devices could potentially be used for graphics drawing in CAD tasks. Because of the correspondence to drawing on paper and the resolution which can be achieved, the device which is usually used for drawing is the digitizing tablet. Keeping the arm in a position to draw on the screen, as would be required for a touch panel display, is very fatiguing. For CAD especially, where 2·5 to 3·5 hours a day are occupied by drawing, the arm would not be able to maintain a position necessary for drawing. Another problem for drawing with these devices is that the arm may obstruct the view of items on the display. Joysticks and trackballs are not appropriate for drawing because they incorporate movements which would not be compatible with drawing movements learnt through drawing on paper.

A problem with the digitizing tablet for drawing is that a translation between the tablet and the screen must be made. Whereas the touch screen and light pen use the screen as both the input and output device, the digitizer tablet has the output in a different physical location from the input. The operator may prefer to look at the arm and hand when drawing. This would be difficult with a digitizing tablet because the output of the drawing, on the screen, may not be in the same visual field as the hand and arm. Care must be taken to provide good visual feedback on the screen of the position of the stylus on the tablet. Usually, crosshairs are used for this visual feedback.

Comparison of input devices for pointing tasks

Pointing must be done when choosing menu items or in some drawing tasks to indicate starting and ending locations for symbols. Touch screens, mice, light pens, data tablets, joysticks and trackballs could all be used potentially for this task. The devices can be compared across empirical results, fatigue and naturalness of device to the task.

Touch screens and light pens have an advantage over the other devices because they interact directly with the output on the screen. With the other devices, a cursor would have to be positioned on the screen as an indication that the operator is pointing at the correct location. This extra translation between input device and cursor position is not as natural as the direct relationship for the touch screen and light pen. Another advantage of the touch screen and light pen is that no extra space is needed; the screen already outputs the items and the operator would input directly on the screen. The joystick and trackball require small spaces. The disadvantage for the light pen and touch screen is the possibility of arm fatigue and obstruction of items on the display by the arm.

Ten experiments have compared positioning accuracy and speed for the possible input devices. Table 5.12, adapted from Greenstein and Arnaut (1986), summarizes the results from these studies. Unfortunately, none of the experiments compared all of the devices at the same time. By looking at which devices were the

Table 5.12. Comparison of ten input devices for positioning tasks (adapted from Greenstein and Arnaut, 1986).

Input device	Number of studies tested	Fastest	Slowest	Most accurate	Least accurate
Mouse	4	2	2	0	1
Data tablet	4	0	0	0	0
Light pen	4	3	1	1	1
Touch screen	2	2	0	0	0
Joystick	4	0	3	0	3
Trackball	3	0	0	3	1
Voice input	2	0	2	0	1

best of those tested for individual experiments, an indication of the speed and accuracy can be determined for all devices together.

Four of the ten studies compared the mouse to other input devices. The comparisons are characterized by widely different results. In two of the four studies which investigated positioning tasks (English *et al.*, 1967; Card *et al.*, 1978), the mouse was the fastest of all the devices tested. For the other two studies, however, the mouse was found to be the slowest device in one (Karat *et al.*, 1984) and the most inaccurate in the other (Haller *et al.*, 1984).

An alternative to the mouse as a possible input device would be the data tablet for positioning a cursor. Overall, performance with a data tablet in terms of both time and errors has been mediocre (Albert, 1982; Gomez *et al.*, 1982; Haller *et al.*, 1984; Whitfield *et al.*, 1983). In none of the experiments was this device the fastest or the slowest; similar results were found for its accuracy.

The touch screen and light pen were found to be surprisingly fast and accurate. The light pen was tested in four experiments; in three of these four (Albert, 1982; Haller *et al.*, 1984; Struckman-Johnson *et al.*, 1984), the light pen was the fastest of all the devices for positioning a cursor. The accuracy was generally mediocre except in the Haller *et al.* study which found that the light pen was the most accurate of the devices. In another study (English *et al.*, 1967), the light pen had the highest error and the slowest times. The touch screen has only been tested in two of the studies. In both of these (Karat *et al.*, 1984; Whitfield *et al.*, 1983) it was the fastest for positioning the cursor.

Joysticks and trackballs are not often used in positioning tasks. For the joystick, three of the four positioning experiments found that the time to position was the slowest and the errors were the highest of all the devices tested (Albert, 1982; Card *et al.*, 1978; English *et al.*, 1967). In the other experiment (Struckman-Johnson *et al.*, 1984), performance was mediocre. Similar mediocre results have been found for trackball positioning speed. In three experiments (Albert, 1982; Gomez *et al.*, 1982; Struckman-Johnson *et al.*, 1984), the trackball was found to be the most accurate. In the other experiment, however, accuracy was the worst for all the devices tested (Haller *et al.*, 1984).

Two experiments have compared voice input devices to other devices. In both studies (Gould and Alfaro, 1983; Haller *et al.*, 1984), the voice input device was the slowest; the Haller *et al.* experiment found the highest error for the voice input device.

Some of the empirical results on the input devices were surprising and counterintuitive in terms of the popularity of some of the devices on the market. It was surprising that the mouse had such widely fluctuating results considering that many new computer systems now use the mouse. Light pens and touch screens, not often incorporated in present computer systems, were very often the fastest and most accurate in the empirical comparisons. The voice input devices would seem to be a device of the future because of its intuitive appeal as a natural response, a response which we use in non-computerized tasks. This device was found to be very poor, however, on the positioning tasks which were studied.

5.7. Information display

In this section, the information displayed to the operator to make interaction easier will be considered. Some of the material in Chapter 6, on cognitive and perceptual aspects of CAD, is similar in that it considers how to display important information for CAD design tasks. The information displayed is quite often the only view the user has of how the computer operates. To make the interaction easy, the information displayed must be chosen carefully so that it provides a clear and consistent picture of the conceptual model of the computer system (refer back to the discussion on mental models and Figure 5.1). Important issues in information display include the use of color and graphics, analog or digital displays, the use of windows, methods to scroll the text, and the size of the display and characters.

Usefulness of color displays

One of the decisions which must be made when purchasing computer equipment, CAD workstations included, is whether or not to purchase color equipment. Color terminals could increase the cost of the total system, decrease the resolution of the display, decrease the data transmission rate, and increase the complexity of programming and interaction with the system. Color can be useful to sell the system to the CAD operator, to highlight information on the display, and to make the drawings easier to see. If color systems are chosen, the number of colors for a system is another decision to be made.

Differences in the perceptibility and speed of response to colors exist. Going from the fastest color to identify to the worst, the search speed order is:

red blue yellow green black white

This order persists across all background colors (Ramsey and Atwood, 1979). Color identification decreases with decrements in illumination although some colors appear to be more resistant to performance decrements than others. Red is superior for distance viewing but will shift markedly in brightness with low illumination. Yellow, on the other hand, has been shown to be the most accurately identified color (Davis and Swezey, 1982).

Experimental results indicate that color is a salient cue to make detection of highlighted areas occur very quickly. Laboratory experiments on human perception of colors at computer terminals have been performed to determine the effectiveness of color coding. A typical experiment will record the time to detect a target in a field of distractors when the target can be distinguished by color differences or by shape differences. Results indicate that color differences were detected faster than shape differences (Schneider and Eberts, 1980; Zwaga and Duijnhouwer, 1984). In the Schneider and Eberts results, color discrimination could occur 2·25 times faster than shape discrimination. The subjects did not have to scan the display to perceive that a color occurred; processing of the display occurred in parallel for all items on the screen. This experiment also indicated that any advantage to color coding would be lost if more than one item on the display had the same color and the operator had to discriminate those items by both color and shape. In this case, discrimination of items on the screen occurred much slower than if the items could be discriminated in terms of shape alone. Color is useful only if it is not over-used and highlights only the important information.

Although the above results indicate that color can be useful if speed is stressed and color is not over-used, other experimental results show little advantage for color over shape coding. As an example, Tullis (1981) tested information display methods to diagnose problems over telephone lines. In two of the conditions, a schematic of the telephone lines was presented. In one of these two conditions, a black-and-white display was used and the operability of each telephone line was shape-coded by having a filled-in box for good, a cross-hatched box for marginal, and an open box for bad. In the other condition, the color condition, everything was the same except that green, yellow and red boxes were used for good, marginal and bad conditions, respectively. The time and errors to make decisions were tested. Tullis found no difference in terms of speed of decision or errors in decision-making when these two conditions were compared. When the operators rank-ordered their preferences, the color display was preferred over the black-and-white display.

A final issue is the choice of colors for information highlighting. People can discriminate about 50 colors (Helander, 1986) so that purchasing CAD systems with more colors than this would not be useful. Investigators suggest that color should be used conservatively to avoid an appearance of clutter on the screen (Brown *et al.*, 1980). The maximum range of colors that should be used in an information display is between 6 and 11 (Barmack and Sinaiko, 1966; Cropper and Evans, 1968; Engel and Granda, 1975). To limit the number of colors used in CAD systems, Frome (1983) suggested that black and white be used for menus, screen divisions and information messages. Color should be reserved to highlight important messages for images which violate design rules.

A consideration with color coding is to design the display so that operators with color weaknesses or color blindness can still perceive the important information. Approximately 8% of males have a problem with color blindness. The largest percentage of this group has trouble distinguishing red from green. Another perceptual problem with color is that various arrangements displayed by a CAD system may under some circumstances lead to visual after-effects. For example, after viewing colored stripes for a few minutes, black and white stripes look tinted and these illusory colors are still seen more than 24 hours after viewing the colored stripes. After viewing black and white stripes, a square could look like a rectangle and this misperception may persist for over 24 hours (Frome *et al.*, 1979).

Color can increase the speed of detecting items on a display if it is not over-used. An experiment in decision-making, however, showed that colors did not increase performance. Perhaps the most important result from this study was the preference among operators for the color display. If a CAD system has to be sold to a customer by a vendor or sold to a drafter by management, color displays could be helpful. Performance-wise, color displays are probably not too useful. Especially if a trade-off of color with resolution or data transmission rate has to be made, color is not worth the cost.

Analog or digital displays

An increasingly relevant question is whether or not to present information to the operator in analog or digital form. Digital watches were very popular at one time but now analog watches seem to have made a comeback. Which kind is easier to read? Does the time 5:50 seem as close to 6:00 as having the minute hand 60° away from 6:00? Digital displays for cars are becoming more popular in the more expensive models. Will these displays also diminish in popularity as the fad wears off? These questions are also relevant to CAD workstations. Dimensions of the drawing can be summarized in terms of textual information or they can be summarized in terms of actual lengths or graphs. A few experiments have addressed the issue of analog or digital display of information.

Three of the experimental conditions from the Tullis (1981) experiment, mentioned in the previous section, are also relevant to this discussion. In one experiment, information about the telephone lines was displayed on the screen in an unstructured manner with the condition of the lines interspersed with irrelevant measured electrical values. In a second experiment, this textual, or digital, information was structured with detailed characteristics presented in a fixed, tabular form. In the third experiment, already mentioned, a schematic, or analog representation, of the telephone lines was displayed with the condition of the line either highlighted by shape or color coding. The results showed no differences in the number of decision-making errors but the times to make decisions were significantly shorter for the analog display. After an hour of practice, however, the structured digital display was just as fast in terms of decision-making as the analog display. Once again, the operators preferred the analog display over the digital display.

This experiment indicates that an analog display is more useful for novice subjects. The results also indicate, perhaps more importantly, that the structure of the display is more important than whether it is analog or digital, at least after a little practice. Analog displays, by their nature, are structured displays. If the digital information is structured in a logical manner, it can be just as useful.

The controversy becomes more complicated when other sensory modalities, besides visual, can be used to display information. In an experiment by Robinson *et al.* (1985), both the visual and auditory modalities were used to display information. In the visual modality, information was presented by using bar graphs (the visual/analog condition) or by using digits (the visual/digital condition). For the auditory condition, information was presented by using tones differing in pitch (the auditory/analog condition) or by using spoken numbers (the auditory/digital condition). In the task, which required that the operator visually monitor a display and make decisions based upon the digital or analog information, the results differed depending on the modality. For the auditory modality, performance was much better if the information displayed was in a digital form than in an analog form. For the visual modality, performance was slightly better if the information displayed was in an analog form rather than the digital form. These results indicate that an analog display is more compatible with the visual modality and the digital display is more compatible with the auditory modality.

In summary, structure of the displayed information is more important than whether the information is analog or digital. Analog displays offer an inherent structure to information; digital displays can be designed with structure in them by grouping items logically in a fixed, tabular form. CAD displays in the future may include auditory information. In this case, it is important that information for that modality be given in a digital form.

Feedback

One of the most enduring results from experimentation on human performance is that performance depends on the feedback and the quality of feedback. An early experiment (Trowbridge and Cason, 1932), obviously not on computer systems but relevant nonetheless, showed that performance improved the most when feedback was quantitative, and that qualitative feedback was better than no feedback. With these results, it is surprising that so little attention is paid to the design of error feedback in computer systems. The classic example is the feedback 'Illegal entry', which occurs in many computer systems yet is very nonspecific about the source of the error. The error could be a typing mistake, a nonexistent command, or a command in the wrong syntax.

Guidelines and experimental results have indicated the best kinds of error feedback. An overall guideline when providing error feedback is to avoid 'computerese' such as 'entry'. The same kinds of words used in everyday speech should be used in error messages. Along these lines, Kennedy (1974) offers the following suggestions and guidelines: a 'social element' to the communication should be maintained, messages should be polite, meaningful and informative, help should be provided when the operator requests it or is having difficulty; and the user should be permitted to control the length of the message. Several design characteristics can be included in the system to satisfy this latter guideline. The length of error message needed for novice and expert operators is different. Novices require long error messages which are very informative. Experts only need to be reminded of the kind of error they made and long error messages would slow them down and become frustrating. A system which based the error message upon the amount of interaction with a system would be useful. A possibility is that at the beginning of the session, the operator could indicate the kind of interaction desired. Along similar lines, Shneiderman (1980) suggests that the operator should be able to ask for help at any time during the interaction and the help messages can occur for various levels of information. Typing a single question mark would provide a minimum of help, typing double question marks would provide more help, and triple question marks would provide a long, detailed help message.

Some experiments have tested various kinds of feedback to determine the most effective kind. One of the strongest effects occurs in terms of the specificity of the error feedback. Shneiderman (1982) looked at the ability to debug computer programs when the specificity of error messages was manipulated. He found that performance improved with increased specificity. In the same set of experiments, Shneiderman manipulated the tone of the error message. It could be either hostile, neutral or courteous. He found that courteous messages allowed for more accurate performance on the task than did neutral messages. Surprisingly, performance with the hostile messages was better than the neutral but slightly worse than the courteous messages.

Although an overall guideline is to provide error messages and feedback which are as much like human feedback as possible, an analysis of feedback occurring between people in natural environments indicates the complexity of the problem. As an example, Pollock *et al.* (1983) analyzed interactions between a radio call-in host and the callers. They found that much of the interaction was spent in defining the questions and callers very seldom had a specific question. Similar things probably occur for computer systems. If the operator could define the question, help probably would not be needed. Help is needed when the operator does not know what the question is. In addition, for human interactions, feedback usually provides more than just answers to questions, people try to look for the source of the problem (McCoy, 1983).

An approach in the attempt to provide more meaningful feedback is to analyze the operator's goal structures for problem solving. Any computer task, such as designing an object on the screen, can be analyzed in terms of the structures of the goals and subgoals needed in the solution (Newell and Simon, 1972). Experimentation has indicated that when operators interact with a computer, they do use goal structures (Robertson and Black, 1983). If the computer could analyze the operator's goal structures, deviations from the structure for a particular problem could be flagged and feedback provided. This has the potential for providing people with meaningful feedback since it could be worded in a way that would fit in with the operator's solution space. It also has the potential for catching the beginning of an error and not just the manifestations of that error at a later time. This could save time and trouble. This kind of error feedback is still in the research stage and could be implemented in future systems. For CAD, more work is needed to determine and classify the goal structures used in design.

Methods to move the objects

An interesting problem is to determine the best relationship between the command and the direction of movement on the screen. This may seem like a trivial problem. After all, if the operator desires that an object move to the right, a command 'right' should cause right-ward movement of the item. The problem is more complicated in that it depends on the frame of reference of the computer operator. Bury *et al.* (1982) provided a good metaphor for the problem which they termed a moving window/scrolling controversy. The moving window is analogous to an astronomer moving the telescope over a stationary star field. If the astronomer wants to see a star to the right, the telescope is commanded to move to the right. In contrast, scrolling is analogous to a biologist moving a slide under a microscope. If the biologist desires to see an organism to the left of that already in view, the slide must be moved to the right.

In a CAD task, the moving window/scrolling controversy can occur when an object appears partly on the screen and partly off (e.g., off to the right). To get the whole object on the screen, the operator could take the perspective that the object is stationary and the computer screen acts like a movable window. In this case, the operator would command that the window move to the right. The operator could alternatively take the perspective that the window on the computer screen is stationary and the object is movable. In this case, the operator would command that the object move to the left. Depending on the perspective, the operator could either command 'right' or 'left'.

No experiment has been performed on CAD operators to determine the perspective that they take in this situation. The perspective would probably be very dependent on their past experience on CAD systems; determining the most natural relationship would be difficult. Bury *et al.* (1982) tested novice operators in a text editing task and found that when given a chance to self define the movement, most chose the moving window. Similar results could occur for novice CAD operators. It would be interesting to try to determine if this perspective changes with practice on the task.

Display size, character size and windowing

Several display considerations not discussed in the above sections have also been tested. Display size is a concern for CAD tasks because in many cases the textual command information appears on one part of the display and the design part of the display is kept separate. An issue is the size of the part of the display for the textual information. For character size, characters can be displayed with a design to indicate various values for parameters, or characters can be displayed for the textual command information. Since CAD displays are high-resolution, much latitude in character size is available. Finally, windowing is a technique to display new information on top of old information. Windows have many potential uses in CAD displays.

A few experiments have been performed on display size and reading time with different results. Duchnicky and Kolers (1983) studied reading time for 80 column displays and 40 column displays. They found that the larger display could be read 40% faster than the smaller display. In the same set of experiments, they also investigated reading time as it related to window size. No reading time differences due to varying window sizes were found. In another experiment, Neal and Darnell (1984) found that the amount of text, either 1 line, 20 lines or 80 lines, had little effect in the reading time.

Guidelines have been established for character sizes. Character sizes are conveyed in terms of visual angle sizes. The visual angle can be determined by measuring the distance from the eye to the item on the screen (call this x) and measuring the size of the item on the screen (call this y). The visual angle, θ, can be calculated as follows.

$$\theta = \tan (y/x)$$

A one degree visual angle is approximately the size of the thumb held out at arm's length. Sixty minutes of arc correspond to one degree of visual angle. Shurtleff (1980) suggests that 10 minutes of visual angle is the minimum acceptable character size. Most recommend about 14 minutes of arc (Helander, 1986). Characters larger than 25 minutes of arc are inappropriate because they disrupt reading time due to excessive eye movements.

5.8. Command names

Most computer systems have the operator input command names from the keyboard to communicate to the computer the functions which should be performed. The choice of command names has been an issue in the interface design. Researchers have investigated the possibility of having the operator choose command names, natural command names have been studied, and command names have been chosen as metaphors of other tasks.

Some command names are chosen as metaphors of non-computerized tasks.

As an example, a text editor could use the command 'CP' representing 'cut-and-paste' for the operation of removing a piece of text and inserting it in another part of the document. This is an operation which would be performed by using scissors and paste for non-computerized tasks. For CAD, many of the tasks which were used in manual drafting could be used as a metaphor for the computerized task. This should make command names easy to remember, especially for a drafter who becomes a CAD operator.

Another issue in the choice of command names, related to the metaphor issue above, is whether to choose command names which are specific to the task or natural to the operator. Dumais and Landauer (1981) had novices choose command names that were the most natural to them. The novices, not being familiar with computer tasks, chose names which were non-specific. As they acquired expertise on the computer, they found that the non-specific command names could be misleading. Specificity of the command name must not be compromised for naturalness.

Scapin (1981) found similar results when investigating the differences between experts and novices. He compared command names that were natural with those which were computer-oriented for both novices and experts. In a free-recall memory task, the novices could more easily recall the functions of the computer-oriented words than the functions of the natural words. The experts were fairly good at the task regardless of the command name. The implication is that natural words may have had other connotations to the novices besides the computer application; moreover, differentiating the computer context from the natural context may have been difficult. An implication for the choice of names based upon metaphors is that the metaphor should be specific to the task, such as drafting, instead of related to other kinds of non-computer tasks.

One of the issues facing the developer/designer of a CAD system is individual differences between operators. One operator may favor one design feature and another may favor a completely opposite design feature. One way to solve this problem is to have the individual operator define the interface and command names. Wixon *et al.* (1983) investigated this possibility in an electronic mail task. In the experiment, novices were given no help, no documentation, and no instruction and told to attempt the task using their own set of commands. If necessary, a hidden operator intercepted the commands, interpreted them, and had the computer carry out the appropriate function. After 67 operators completed the task, 1070 commands were being used and the computer could recognize 76% of them. The investigators claimed that the system was easy to use and the operators could thus define their own command names for performing the task. The results from the Dumais and Landauer (1981) experiment, however, would claim that this method would not be appropriate because novices do not choose specific command names. The Wixon *et al.* (1983) experiment does show how large the individual differences between people could be because they constructed 1070 commands based upon what they perceived would be the best name.

CAD tasks can be assumed to be similar to other computer tasks and therefore the above research should be applicable. CAD tasks are different, though, in that the operator must create, edit and display an image for design purposes. Five commands are useful for this. First, rotation allows the CAD operator to display a different orientation of the object. Some systems allow smooth rotations of a whole image. For example, a whole screen might be rotated about its center, but off-center axes of rotation may be beyond the capabilities of the system. Truly versatile rotations can be performed by CAD software using matrix multiplications of trigonometric functions. Second, scaling and zoom are used to look more closely at an image to see detail or to shrink an image to put it in proper perspective. In addition, one display dimension (the x screen direction for instance) may need to be stretched or compressed to compensate for non-squareness (Artwick, 1984). Scaling is used to perform such operations. When scaling is performed to all elements in the x and y screen directions, the result is 'zoom'. Third, viewports are the areas of the screen used for graphic displays. Viewports can be defined to be square, rectangular, circular or any desired shape. In addition, more than one viewport may be placed on a screen. The operators must be able to command which objects will be placed in the viewport. Fourth, in some systems the operator can call up to 64 windows for different perspectives of the object. Fifth, the translation option allows the CAD operator to move an object from one location to another on the CRT screen. An example to show how these features work together for a specific application is shown in Figure 5.3. An area of the map of the United States (window) is rotated and translated, scaled to new coordinate positions, mapped onto the viewport coordinator, and displayed on the user's screen (viewport) with screen coordinates. Transformations, such as rotation, scaling, translation, etc., can be combined or concatenated as a sequence of transformations (Groover and Zimmers, 1984). The order in which transformations are performed is important for the production of the final design.

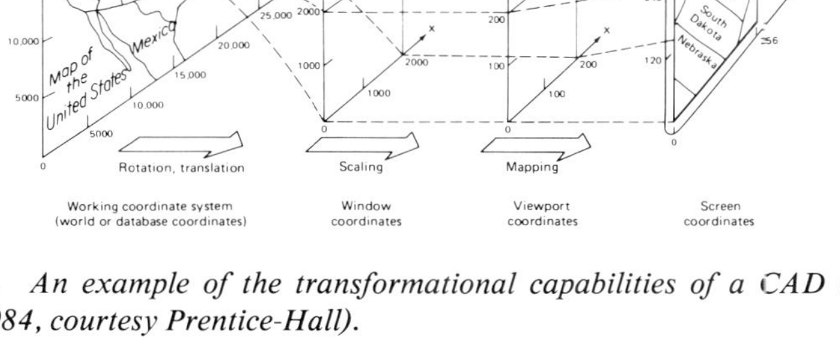

Figure 5.3. An example of the transformational capabilities of a CAD system (from Artwick, 1984, courtesy Prentice-Hall).

Chapter 6
Cognitive and perceptual aspects of CAD

In this chapter, theories of perception, cognitive science, and cognitive psychology are applied to CAD tasks to learn about the operator's cognitive and visual processes when designing and interacting with the CAD system. If the way the designer processes information can be determined, then clues as to how the information should be displayed on the screen can be identified. Furthermore, there is interest in developing expert systems to carry out some functions of the CAD designer. Analyzing the CAD's designer's processing capabilities using the theoretical approaches in perception and cognitive psychology should help to design those expert CAD systems. The following sections provide background information which can be used to help accomplish these objectives.

Separating perception from cognition is difficult. Perceptual theories are concerned with receiving information from the outside world through the senses. Cognitive theories state how humans store information, retrieve information from short- and long-term memory, manipulate that information to make decisions and solve problems, and carry out responses. Processing this information is often described as both a top-down process and a bottom-up process. It is bottom-up because we have to receive information through the senses before it can be manipulated. It is top-down in that the prior information and cognitive processing determines which information sources from the senses will be processed further and where attention should be focused. Perception and cognition interact on many levels.

Cognitive factors, such as human decision-making, creativity, and information processing, are becoming increasingly important for the design of complex systems like CAD. Greater information processing and decision making skills are required of humans who use CAD than those who design manually because a CAD system allows the designer to ask 'what if' questions and receive an immediate answer. A CAD operator can perform kinematic analysis, engineering analysis and finite element analysis at the touch of the fingertips. Of course, the information derived from these analyses requires that the designer process the information and make decisions regarding the different designs.

The way the CAD operator processes information can be summarized as occurring in four steps:

1. Attending to graphic stimuli and alphanumeric information which appears on the screen.
2. Recognizing familiar patterns such as geometrical shapes, and acquiring and integrating new information.
3. Assessing the design with respect to the needed alterations.
4. Deciding on a response such as to change or keep the design.

Theories in perception and cognition exist to explain how people process information, use attention to enhance or filter out sources of information, perform spatial reasoning, make decisions and solve problems. All of these functions can be applied to the CAD designer. Each will be considered in more detail.

6.1. *Information processing*

Information processing underlies all aspects of perception and cognition. Figure 6.1 shows a schematic model of the information processing capabilities of the human. The human is viewed as a channel through which information flows. In

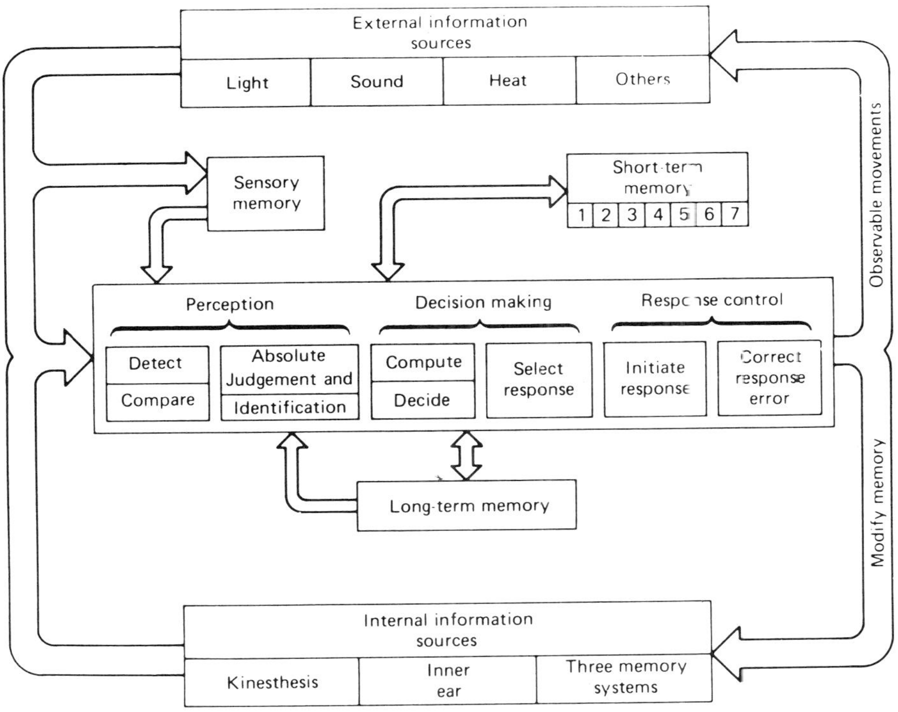

Figure 6.1. A schematic model for the information processing capabilities of the human (from Salvendy and Knight (1982), courtesy John Wiley & Sons).

the model, three information processing stages, or subsystems, are shown: perception, cognition (spatial reasoning, decision making and problem solving) and response control. Also shown are the three memory systems for storing information: sensory, short-term and long-term memories. Human performance, including performance when using a CAD system, depends upon, and is limited by, the information processing capabilities of these three major stages and by the storage characteristics of the memory systems. In addition, the time needed to perform a task on a CAD system is dependent on the time the information needs to pass through each of the stages.

All of the stages and subsystems interact to some extent. Once visual information impinges on the senses, this information is stored in 'raw' form in the visual sensory storage. Because the 'raw' storage requires so much memory and because other visual events always occur simultaneously, the information decays very quickly. Information in short-term memory can indicate to the system which items in the visual sensory store should be considered for further processing. At this time, these items may be transferred from the sensory store to short-term memory. Short-term memory is the working memory for further cognitive processing. Items can also be transferred into short-term memory from the storehouse of knowledge called long-term memory; items in long-term memory cannot be processed without being transferred to short-term memory first. Once a course of action has been decided upon, the response system can carry out that response. A response may be a movement by one of the limbs, speaking, or directing one's attention to a new place on the screen.

Much basic research in perception and cognition has been concerned with identifying and quantifying the parameters of this information processing task. Card *et al.* (1983) reviewed this literature and determined quantities for the parameters of the model. Each of the three subsystems from Figure 6.1 can be described by a few important parameters: the storage capacity in number of items (μ), the decay time of an item (δ), the main code type (κ), and the cycle time (τ). To assign numbers to the three numerically based parameters, Card *et al.* used the research in cognitive psychology to find estimates of the times along with a plausible range. Table 6.1 presents the processors and memories associated with the three subsystems along with the parameters and values for each. In the table, the numbers preceding the brackets are means and the numbers in brackets represent the range of the parameter.

Each of the three processors has a cycle time associated with it. This means that information cannot enter or leave the stage or subsystem until this time period (τ) has been achieved. The cycle time for the perceptual system is 100 ms, for the cognitive system it is 70 ms, and for the motor system it is also 70 ms. Because information passes through stages, new information can start being processed early in the system when the old information is being responded to.

The memories can be described in terms of the decay times of items (δ), the amount of storage available (μ), and the storage code (κ). The visual sensory store

Table 6.1. Parameters for the information processing model.

Processor	Memory
Perceptual	Visual sensory store
$\tau_P = 100\ (50\text{–}200)$ ms	$\delta_{VSS} = 200\ (70\text{–}100)$ ms
	$\mu_{VSS} = 17\ (7\text{–}17)$ letters
	κ_{VSS} = physical
	Auditory sensory store
	$\delta_{ASS} = 1500\ (900\text{–}3500)$ ms
	$\mu_{ASS} = 5\ (4{\cdot}4\text{–}6{\cdot}2)$ letters
	κ_{ASS} = physical
Cognitive	Short-term memory
$\tau_C = 70\ (25\text{–}170)$ ms	$\mu_{STM} = 3\ (2{\cdot}5\text{–}4)$ chunks
	$\mu_{STM} = 7\ (5\text{–}9)$ chunks
	$\delta_{STM} = 7\ (5\text{–}226)$ s
	δ_{STM} (1 chunk) $= 73\ (73\text{–}226)$ s
	δ_{STM} (3 chunks) $= 7\ (5\text{–}34)$ s
	κ_{STM} = acoustic or visual
Motor	Long-term memory
$\tau_M = 70\ (30\text{–}100)$ ms	δ_{LTM} = infinite
	μ_{LTM} = infinite
	κ_{LTM} = semantic

can store from 7 to 17 items for about 200 ms before decaying or further processing occurs. This storage is in a physical form or is a 'raw' image. A corresponding storage occurs for the auditory sense but this is probably not overly important in CAD tasks.

Short term memory, used to make decisions, solve problems, and transfer items from subsystem to subsystem, stores items in chunks. The size of a chunk can depend on many things such as practice, long-term memory and grouping. As an example, the numbers 34990403 would represent eight chunks but the same numbers group differently, 33449900 would only represent four chunks of information. Similarly, the digits 14921776, could be stored as eight chunks for some people but could be stored as two chunks if someone recognizes them as Columbus' discovery of North America and the date of the signing of the American Declaration of Independence. In this case, because of the influence of long-term memory, the eight digits would be two chunks. The three chunk estimate for short-term memory can be considered the 'pure' estimate and the seven chunk estimate occurs when long-term memory can augment short-term memory (this usually occurs in normal tasks outside the laboratory). The decay time for chunks in short-term memory depends on the number of chunks stored and the interference of chunks with each other. If two or more chunks are similar to each other, interference will occur. Taking the interference into account the range of times is quite large, varying from 7 to 226 seconds. This range can be subdivided by considering the number of chunks needed for storage. If one chunk is maintained in storage the decay time is on the average 73 seconds, and if three chunks are maintained the decay time is on the average 7 seconds. Finally, the storage code is acoustic or visual depending on how the information is processed.

Long-term memory, used to store items which are not being currently processed, has no known storage limit and the items probably do not decay from memory at any particular rate. Items may be 'lost' from long-term storage if they are 'misplaced' and cannot be retrieved. The items in long-term memory are stored in a semantic form in terms of meanings instead of physical representations.

Predictions for the amount of time associated with a task can be determined by breaking the task into its components and providing values for the parameters associated with each component. Card *et al.* (1983) present examples of how this information processing model can be applied. In one example, they derive the parameters for Fitts' Law and then estimate times from this model to determine if they correspond to the times found in experimentation. Fitts' Law was formulated to predict the amount of time taken to move a limb from one position to a target and therefore would be quite useful in predicting times to move the stylus to a position on the digitizing tablet as an example for CAD. It can be stated as:

$$\tau_{pos} = I_M \ln (2A/W)$$

where τ_{pos} is the total movement time, I_M corresponds to the time to correct a movement, A is the amplitude of the movement, and W is the width of the target. The human information processing model would state that:

$$\tau_{pos} = n(\tau_P + \tau_C + \tau_M)$$

where n is the number of micromovements required to reach the target and the τ's are those defined in Table 6.1. n can be shown to be:

$$n = -\frac{\ln (A/W)}{\ln \epsilon}$$

where ϵ is the relative accuracy of a movement (it has been found to be around 0·07). Solving for I_M from Fitts' Law produces the following:

$$I_M = \frac{\tau_{pos}}{\ln (2A/W)}$$

$$I_M = -\frac{\ln (2A/W)(\tau_P + \tau_C + \tau_M)}{\ln (2A/W) \ln \epsilon}$$

$$I_M = -\frac{(\tau_P + \tau_C + \tau_M)}{\ln \epsilon}$$

$$I_M = -\frac{100 - 70 - 70}{\ln (0{\cdot}07)}$$

$$I_M = 63 \text{ ms/bit}$$

The numbers for the τ's were taken from the estimates in Table 6.1. Experiments for discrete tasks have shown that I_M is estimated to be somewhere in the range 70–85 ms/bit. Card *et al.* have tested the model on several tasks and the predictions have corresponded closely to the experimental data. As an example, the predicted time in a computer-aided design task was within 16% of the actual times.

6.2. *Models of attention*

When a human processes information, attention is required. Referring back to the information processing model of Figure 6.1, attention can be applied at several places. To transfer items from the visual sensory to short-term memory, the human must attend to the items, otherwise they will decay. Information in short-term memory can be maintained for longer periods of time than that represented by the decay time (δ_{STM}) if the human attends to it. The capacity of STM, however, cannot be increased through attention. Processing information in the cognitive and motor subsystems also requires attention. The concept of attention has implications for the design of CAD systems and the limitations of CAD tasks.

Attention as limited capacity

Early work on attention within an information processing model focused on the ability of people to perform multiple tasks (Broadbent, 1958). In a typical research paradigm, subjects were asked to focus full attention on one signal so that the researcher could observe what happened to other signals arriving at the same time. These experiments revealed that people are limited in their ability to process information and that as the complexity of the task increases, information overload becomes a possibility. A theoretical model by Moray (1967) explained these and similar results by postulating that attention has a limited capacity coming from one general source which can be allocated among tasks. Like a program in a computer, the more complex the plan or action the more capacity it requires and the less capacity remains for other functions. More recently, Kahneman (1973) has postulated that attention can be considered as a resource of limited availability. The human has, therefore, to decide either consciously or unconsciously how these attentional resources will be applied to the various tasks.

A commonplace example of this limited capacity can be seen when driving a car. When traffic is light, the driver can divide attention and perform more than one task such as listening to the radio or talking to another person. When traffic becomes heavy, however, all attention must be placed on the driving task so that the driver cannot hear the radio nor carry on a conversation with another passenger. Similar examples can be constructed for CAD tasks. Working on a design problem requires attention to determine optimal designs and to enter these designs into the system. Interacting with the computer, which may have little or no direct connection with the actual design process, also requires attention. If the interaction with the CAD system has been designed to be complicated, then this part of the task will require the attention and little will be left to be allocated to the creative design process. The design process, therefore, would suffer. The less attention required by the interaction with the computer, the better the design will be because more attention can be allocated to it.

The attentional capacity can be increased effectively in two ways. First, a task can become automatized with practice so that little or no attentional resources are needed to carry out the task (e.g., Schneider and Shiffrin, 1977; Schneider and Fisk, 1982). If certain parts of the computer interaction task became automatized for the CAD operator, then this would free up attentional resources to be applied to the more important design process. Automatization of tasks will occur only with practice. The more one can practice with CAD tasks, the less attentional resources are required for them.

The second method to increase attentional capacity is to design the task so that a compatibility exists between the input and the output. A definition of compatibility has been difficult to formulate. Early experiments on compatibility were rather artificial and not readily applicable to real world tasks. As an example, Simon (1969) had people respond to light stimuli by hitting a response button. Whenever a light on the panel came on, the person hit the button directly below the light (this was a compatible stimulus–response situation). In the incompatible situation, the person would respond with the left button, as an example, if the right light came on. It is doubtful that any CAD manufacturer would design a system which had such an obvious incompatibility between input and output.

CAD design features can be considered in terms of compatibility between input and output. Rotating a figure on a display is one example. A compatible input/output relationship would exist if the operator would turn a dial to move the figure and the figure would rotate the same number of degrees the dial was rotated. This would be more compatible than inputting a number on a number pad or hitting a button several times. Another example would be in moving an object to another location on the screen. A compatible relationship would exist if the operator could 'pick up' the object through a click of a mouse button, move the object correspondingly as the mouse is moved, and then click the mouse button again to 'drop' the object in its desired location. This would be more compatible than entering coordinate locations into the computer system. Both of these examples, because of the expected compatibility between input and output, could reduce the attentional resources required for the task and would, thus, allow these resources to be applied to other parts of the task.

Multiple resource theory

Subsequent research to the Moray (1967) and Kahneman (1973) theories indicated that they could not account for all the data in terms of one limited capacity or one overall 'pool' of resources. Research showed that the capacity did not stay at the same level but could change depending on where the attention was allocated or how tasks interfered with one another. Recently, refinement of this undifferentiated resource theory of attention has resulted in the concept of multiple resource 'pools' explaining task interference as pulling from the same resource pool (e.g., Navon and Gopher, 1979; Wickens, 1980). This multiple resource theory of attention has important implications for the design of CAD tasks, especially those which are complex and require large amounts of attentional resources.

Wickens (1980, 1984) has synthesized the results from this area into a model of the structure of processing resources. He defines this structure as three relatively dichotomous dimensions: two stage-defined resource pools (early versus late processes), two modality-defined resource pools (auditory versus visual encoding), and two resource pools defined by processing codes (spatial versus verbal). The implications of this model for CAD tasks are as follows for each of the dimensions. For the stage-defined resource pools, information is assumed to be processed by the human in stages going from perception through cognition to a response stage as in Figure 6.1. Information in the perceptual and cognitive stages pulls from one resource 'pool' and the response stage pulls from a different resource 'pool'. Thus, the human would be able to perceive or cognitively process information simultaneously with responses to previous information. For the modality-defined resource pools, the human would be able to attend to visual information at the same time that auditory information is attended to. Thus, computer information presentation should be divided between auditory and visual signals to prevent overloading the user. Finally, for the processing code resource pools, information can be presented either spatially (e.g., graphics) or verbally (in textual form). Again, the user would be less likely to be overloaded if both of these resource pools are drawn upon instead of presenting all the information in the form which draws upon one of the pools.

The predictions from the model for human–computer interaction tasks have been validated by experimental work. In particular, manual and vocal responses can be time-shared with a high degree of efficiency. McLeod (1977), Wickens (1980) and Wickens *et al.* (1983) have all shown that a continuous manual task and a discrete verbal task are time-shared more efficiently when the verbal task employs vocal as opposed to manual response mechanisms. In addition, Robinson *et al.* (1985) demonstrated that an auditory verbal display could be perceived more efficiently than visual verbal and visual spatial displays when the operators were required to perform a manual task concurrently. All of these results can be accounted for by the model of attentional resources.

This model has specific implications for the design of CAD systems. Both textual and graphics information can be presented to the operator to reduce the likelihood of drawing attentional resources from just one pool. CAD computer systems should be considered to include both visual and auditory displays. Presenting some of the information, such as verbal feedback of the command, over the auditory channel would reduce the likelihood of overloading the visual channel and using up the limited attentional resources for that pool.

6.3. Perception

Although graphics in CAD systems operate on basic geometric entities such as surfaces (faces), lines (edges) and points (vertices), the CAD operator works at a higher conceptual level dealing with shapes and features (Staley *et al.*, 1983). For example, in three-dimensional mechanical design, holes, slots, and pockets consist of basic entities such as surfaces, lines and points. Perception involves the process of sensing the light patterns on the screen, combining the patterns into basic features, and then organizing the features into objects. Perceiving a CAD screen is a much more difficult task than perceiving physical objects. An obvious problem is that three-dimensional objects must be represented on a two-dimensional screen. Another problem is that physical objects have hidden areas but these areas must be viewed by the CAD operator and this can cause clutter and confusion on how the lines fit together. A not-so-obvious problem is that objects on the screen appear to float in space with little reference to up and down or right and left. For example, Rock (1973) and Rock *et al.* (1972) found that changes in orientation about a horizontal axis perpendicular to the plane of the figure can produce alternations of the up-down and left-right sides of a figure. These transformations produced marked changes in the perception of the figure and its recognition and identification. These findings were explained by proposing that perceivers implicitly assign the directions top, bottom, left and right to a figure on the basis of other information such as gravity or the visual frame of reference. This is missing on most CAD systems.

CAD operators must perform myriad perceptual tasks. The CAD operator must be aware of relationships between or among objects; about the properties of the objects including purpose, context and changes due to time evolution; and about motion both within objects and of objects. Objects may range in complexity from very rigid geometrical forms (such as a screwdriver) to objects that have moving parts (such as a robot).

The CAD operator uses perception as a starting point for making decisions and solving problems. Interference checking is an example of such a task. This task involves the visual analysis of a structure in which there is a risk that components of the figure may occupy the same space. This risk occurs in the design of chemical plants, air-separation cold boxes, and other complicated piping structures and is especially prevalent in wire-frame drawings of complicated figures. Verification through inspection and integration of the model is another task. Important verification questions are: Has the integrity of the model been preserved? Are the tolerances acceptable? Does the model look right in an overall sense? Have local changes resulted in any global anomalies? What is the distance between two braces? To understand these and other CAD tasks, perception of the

CAD operator must be considered. Perception will be discussed in terms of object perception and depth perception which underlie many of the functions performed by CAD operators.

The 'goodness' of forms

One criterion of any drawing system is the perceived 'goodness' of the form. The CAD operator tries to determine how well the drawn form represents physical objects. Several issues can be considered for the 'goodness' of forms. The relationship between 'goodness' and wire-frame or solid modelling techniques will be discussed. Also, important parameters for displaying polygons will be considered.

One indication of the 'goodness' of a form is the ambiguity of it. Information about the surfaces of objects in wire-frame modelling is not conveyed, so the CAD operator may not be able to differentiate between the inside and outside of objects. As a result, wire-frame models may be ambiguous to the CAD user and subject to different interpretations. Further, the inability of wire-frame models to represent the solid nature of the object may also lead to misinterpretation, for example, the same surface model may represent either a solid object or a hollow structure. Considering that the human's perceptual system tries to combine surface, line and point features into meaningful objects, wire-frame modelling provides few of the real-world cues to do this.

The objects created by solid modelling have less of a chance of being misinterpreted and, thus, represent better forms perceptually. As an indication of this 'goodness' of form, Doo and Sabin (1978) list three criteria for solid-modelling objects. First, the object must be valid in that a real three-dimensional object must correspond to any given representation of the object. Second, the object must be unique in that only one three-dimensional object should be representable by the display representation. Third, the object must be concise in that the representation should not contain redundant information. When these three criteria are satisfied for solid modelling, ambiguity of objects will not be possible.

Various graphics techniques can also be used to create images. A concern is to determine which graphics techniques produce the best images. Atherton and Caporeal (1985) investigated people's perceptions of 'goodness' of objects by having them rate objects on form faithfulness and aesthetic appeal. Table 6.2 describes the graphics techniques which were used to construct 27 polygon figures along with the CPU time required to draw the image. Nine polygon models were created using three density and shading techniques: flat shading, shade interpolation and normal interpolation. Examples from the 27 figures are shown in Figure 6.2. The results of the subjective ratings are plotted in Figure 6.3 (a 0 means poor form and a 10 means good form). These results indicate that little was gained by reducing the average polygon areas below 100 pixels per polygon. Also, little is gained in image quality when going from about 256 polygons to about 400 polygons to represent the same sphere. Furthermore, in terms of polygon size, little is gained by decreasing the average polygon area in image space from about

Table 6.2. Number of polygons and the average number of pixels per visible polygon across several techniques for creating polygon models (from Atherton and Caporeal, 1985, courtesy P. R. Atherton).

	Number of polygons	Average number of pixels per visible polygon	CPU seconds required to generate image (VAX 11/780)		
			Flat shading	Shade interpolation	Normal interpolation
1	16	1513	34·0	36·3	75·9
2	36	766	34·4	36·9	76·9
3	64	442	35·5	37·2	77·2
4	100	283	35·8	37·3	78·0
5	144	197	36·7	37·5	78·7
6	196	145	36·8	38·5	78·9
7	256	110	37·0	38·6	81·0
8	324	88	37·1	38·8	81·9
9	399	71	37·5	39·0	82·5

110 pixels to about 71 pixels for a sphere model with a 95-pixel radius displayed at 512 × 512 resolution. Because at certain resolutions perception of goodness of the forms does not increase, using the extra CPU time required to draw the images may not be worthwhile. In summary, evaluating the trade-offs in terms of the display requirements and subjective ratings of the form provides an indication of the kinds of displays which are adequate to produce good forms. Increasing the resolution or pixel sizes beyond certain limits may not provide corresponding increases in the perception of 'goodness' of the display objects.

Three-dimensional perception for CAD

Many of the objects designed using a CAD system are made to appear three-dimensional. The main difficulty in displaying these items effectively is that the three-dimensional objects must be displayed on a two-dimensional surface. This can be accomplished by providing depth cues to the operators. In visual perception, many depth cues have been identified. Some of these have been applied to CAD systems.

The perceptual depth cues can be divided into monocular and binocular cues. The monocular cues are those which can be viewed by one eye and, thus, could be represented on a two-dimensional surface. The binocular cues are those which need to be viewed by both eyes and, thus, are dependent on the existence of the third dimension when viewing. Murch (1973) identifies the following monocular depth perception cues. First, size is an indication of depth in that if two objects are considered to be roughly the same size then the smaller one appearing on a two-dimensional surface will be perceived to be further away than the larger one.

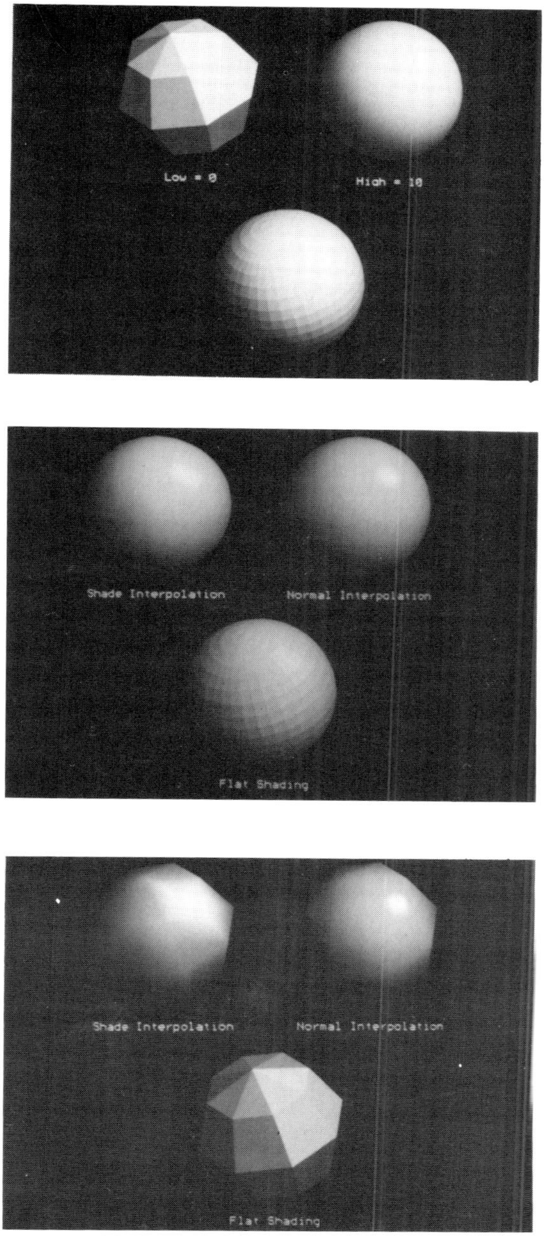

Figure 6.2. Examples of the 27 images which were composed of differing numbers of polygons using different graphics techniques (from Atherton and Caporeal, 1985, courtesy P. R. Atherton).

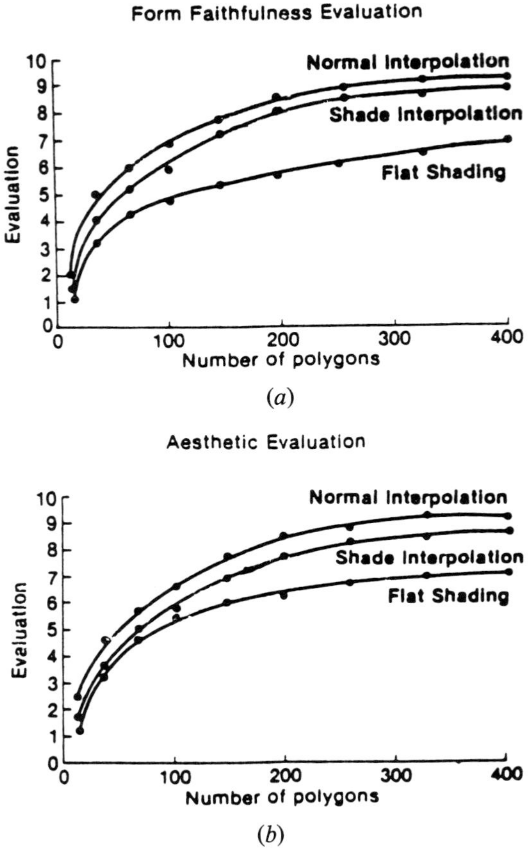

Figure 6.3. Graphs of the mean responses to the 'goodness' of the image for (a) form faithfulness, and (b) aesthetic evaluation across the number of polygons (from Atherton and Caporeal, 1985, courtesy P. R. Atherton).

Second, interposition is a cue in that if one object partially covers a second object the blocked object is perceived to be behind and beyond the blocking object. Third, the linear perspective cue of depth depends on the fact that as distance increases, parallel objects appear to converge. Fourth, contrast, clarity and brightness together provide depth cues in that the nearer objects appear to be sharper and more distinct and the further objects appear to be duller. Fifth, the shadow cast by an object provides some cues to the relative position of objects. Sixth, in texture gradient the texture of a detailed surface becomes finer as the distance increases. Finally, for motion parallax objects in motion appear to be moving at different velocities depending on their distance. Objects which are far away appear to move slower than objects which are closer.

The binocular cues provide the depth perception—stereopsis—commonly associated with three-dimensional viewing. The binocular cue of depth is dependent on the separation of the eyes. For close objects, the visual patterns on the two eyes will be offset from each other and slightly different. This is usually referred to as the disparity of the object and accounts for the stereoscopic perception of depth. As objects are further away, the disparity between the objects on the two eyes will not be as large.

Several techniques for CAD have been developed to take advantage of the monocular depth cues so that objects displayed on a two-dimensional surface can appear to be three-dimensional. One technique which is used is the elimination of hidden lines or hidden surfaces. In this case, lines or portions of lines and surfaces which would normally be behind objects are not shown. This technique uses the depth cue of interposition to indicate three dimensions. A second technique used is linear perspective where parallel lines are displayed to converge at their vanishing points. A third technique, kinetic depth effect, is related to the depth cue of motion parallax, relying on the motion of the object relative to the viewer's position to indicate a sense of depth. When an object is rotated about a vertical axis the lines close to the viewer move more slowly than those far away. A fourth technique, the use of intensity cues, relies on the depth cues of contrast, clarity and brightness. The intensity of lines is modulated so that lines further away are less intense than the close lines. Foley and Van Dam (1984) point out that as the complexity of the displayed image increases, the effectiveness of this depth technique decreases. Finally, artificial texturing uses the depth cue of texture to convey three dimensions. The density of objects can be changed depending upon the distance of the object.

Other means are available to create realistic three-dimensional images not necessarily related to the monocular cues of depth listed above. In particular, depth clipping is used in some CAD systems by cutting a plane through the object being displayed. By varying this back-clipping plane, the operator can dynamically display depth information. In general, ease of visualization for a CAD drawing relates directly to the projection and type of graphic feature used (Groover and Zimmers, 1984). Orthographic views are less comprehensible than isometric views, especially for depth relationships. In addition, perspective views which include color or animation result in the best visualization capability (Figure 6.4).

The advantages and disadvantages for the two types of modelling, wire-frame or solid, discussed in Chapter 2 can be considered in terms of ease of depth perception. One problem with wire-frame modelling is hidden line removal on complex images so that the lines defining the edges of an object remain visible, which could result in an image with multiple geometric interpretations (Groover and Zimmers, 1984) because operators use the interposition depth cue to assume lines further away and behind a surface should be hidden. The depth cue of shadowing is not possible for wire-frame modelling, and nor is the depth cue of texture gradient. Size, linear perspective, motion parallax, contrast, clarity and brightness could all be provided as depth cues for wire-frame modelling. Solid

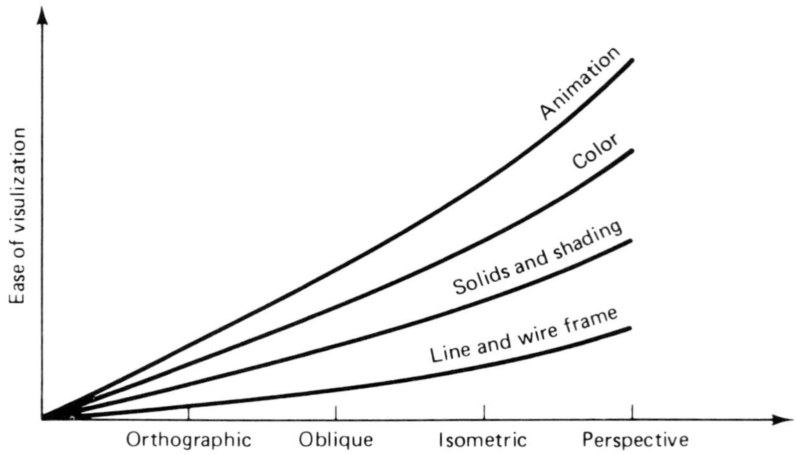

Figure 6.4. Ease of visualization for various views of an object across various projections (from Groover and Zimmers, 1984, courtesy Prentice-Hall).

modelling uses interposition as a depth cue and, thus, is useful for clarifying figures. In fact, all of the monocular depth cues can be incorporated in solid modelling: size, linear perspective, motion parallax, texture gradient, shadowing, contrast, clarity, and brightness.

6.4. Spatial representations and reasoning

After the visual information has been sensed and the perception of the objects continued, the visual or spatial information is manipulated based upon the requirement of the task. An important part of cognitive psychological research has been to understand the spatial representation of visual information and then how that information is used to make decisions, solve problems, or more generally, to reason. Spatial representations can be defined as descriptions which characterize three-dimensional entities or collections of entities whereas spatial reasoning can be defined as the ability to make inferences based on the information contained within a spatial representation (Perricone, 1983). Spatial reasoning is dependent upon the physical elements of illumination, geometry, reflectivity and image formation, as well as aspects of figure recognition and understanding (Besl and Jain, 1985). Theories have been constructed to capture the manifestations of spatial representations in human performance, and will be discussed below. A particular kind of spatial reasoning, figure rotation, will be discussed in terms of its implications for the representation of spatial information in memory. These aspects of spatial reasoning have important implications for the design of CAD workstations, understanding the CAD operator's reasoning, and the training of CAD operators.

Theoretical orientations for spatial representations

Pinker (1981) has proposed a structurally based theory of visuospatial cognition. According to Pinker, visual images and percepts are represented within a three-dimensional array of cells which receive input both from the eyes and from long-term memory. Each cell within this array represents a particular depth along a particular line of sight. The activation of a cell corresponds to representing the presence of a visible surface at the location of the visual space to which the cell corresponds. These cells are dually addressable by their coordinates via a fixed viewer-centered and a movable world-centered Cartesian coordinate system. The world-centered system corresponds to the real world view. A satisfactory explanation of how the human mind can accomplish certain aspects of mental image generation, three-dimensional mental transformations, and top-down and/or bottom-up pattern recognition is possible through translations between the viewer- and world-centered coordinate systems.

Kosslyn (1981) has focused on both the structure and functions of spatial representations. Structures embody the basic spatial information and are based on an active memory medium termed the visual buffer. The visual buffer is the foundation for mental images and is composed of parts of observed objects and scenes rather than the points of a surface as in Pinker's (1981) theory. Processes can be utilized to manipulate the structural information. The functioning of the processes can be compared to the modularity of a computer program in that sub-routines can be used to carry out operators which occur regularly. Kosslyn proposes that the processes of spatial reasoning are composed of four classes: image generation, maintenance, transformation, and generation.

Bajcsy and Joshi (1978) have views similar to Kosslyn's in that they too see the mind's ability to represent and process spatial information as being due to a combination of procedural and structural spatial knowledge. Bajcsy and Joshi, however, do not view them as separate but as a single structure. In other words, the procedural knowledge is an explicit part of the spatial representation. They postulate that the primitive units of a spatial representation are the characteristic features inherent in an object or scene such as corners, edges, lines, concavity and planes. The procedures are tests that can determine whether an object is, for example, round or elongated. Once these features and objects are identified, they are combined into a group or structure which can be represented by a heir-archical network with nodes representing features or objects and the relationships between nodes representing the part/whole information. As an example, consider the three levels for a representation of a car: at the highest level is the concept of the car; the car consists of the lower level of a chassis, doors and wheels; and at the third level, the wheels consist of the tires, rims and bolts. When perceiving and processing visual information, the human would consider where the features were placed in this hierarchy by using the available processes.

Recently, there has been an increasing interest in creating CAD systems with the capability to perform spatial reasoning to extract features from a figure or scene and perform the necessary spatial reasoning processes for high-level analysis. Lee and Fu (1982, 1983) have designed a computer vision system which mirrors some of the aspects of human spatial processing. This system is capable of three-dimensional object recognition using a single image. It attempts to extract edges in target regions and classify the edges as belonging to a parallelogram, an ellipse, a skewed-symmetric arc, or a corner. Other computer vision systems have been developed based upon human spatial reasoning; many are described in Winston (1975). From a CAD point of view, the computer vision systems are not only interesting as indicators of the reasoning that a computer could perform on an object, but they are interesting also in what they indicate about the representation of objects in a digitized form, much as would appear on a CAD screen, and which features of the objects are needed for computer identification. These important features could also be vital for CAD operator perception of the objects. As an example, Waltz (1975) found that providing shadows from a hypothetical light source helped the computer to differentiate between objects. Shadows could also be helpful for CAD operators to differentiate between figures.

The psychology of figure rotation

The ability to internally visualize the three-dimensional structure of a part or figure is one of the most important mental characteristics of good designers. An important question from a cognitive point of view for the CAD designer is the form of that internal or mental representation of an object. The internal form of the representation has implications for the kinds of mental transformations which can be carried out on it. To differentiate between theories on the form of the representation, a mental rotation task has been studied in several psychological experiments. In the mental rotation task, the experiment participant is required to mentally rotate an object to compare it to a reference object. The time and accuracy to perform this task has been studied when manipulating several variables such as the complexity of the figure or the amount of rotation of the object.

Two theories have been postulated for the form of the underlying representation of an object. One theory, the imagery or analog model, states that people can represent visual information in memory through images. These images bear a one-to-one correspondence to the physical representation of the object. The other theory, the propositional theory, states that visual information in memory is transformed into propositions. A proposition is the smallest unit of knowledge that can stand as a separate assertion. Although propositions have been hypothesized to occur in many forms, Kintsch (1974) represents each proposition as a list containing a relation (i.e., a verb) followed by an ordered list of arguments (i.e., the relations between the verbs).

These two theories make different predictions about how visual information is internally manipulated (see Table 6.3 for a summary). As a simple example of these different predictions, consider the following. The analog representation is

Table 6.3. Summary of analog and propositional predictions for the mental rotation task (from Barfield, 1986).

Variable	Analog model	Propositional model
Mental rotation process	During mental rotation the figure passes through a trajectory of intermediate states, analogous to an external rotation.	Discrete, feature-by-feature process.
Underlying representation	One-to-one correspondence between points on real object and points of mental representation of object.	Propositional network structures represent the relationships between figure components.
Rate of rotation	Independent of figure complexity.	Related to complexity of object.

best exemplified by the kinds of manipulations which can be made on physical objects. Rotating a piece of paper on the desk by moving it with the hands would be similar to the mental rotation of that piece of paper in the memory. On the desk, a piece of paper with complex drawings and a blank piece of paper could both be rotated in the same amount of time. The corresponding assumption for mental rotation would be that the complexity of the figure being rotated would have no effect on the time to rotate. On the other hand, a propositional representation is being exemplified by a computer program which manipulates information. Each proposition corresponds to information which must be coded in the program. To use the same example of rotation for a computer program, each item represented in the code would have to be transformed for the whole 'paper' to be rotated. In this case, the fewer the propositions, the faster the program and vice versa. The complexity of the figure being rotated would have an effect on the time to mentally rotate it if the representation of an object is similar to this computer program.

Kosslyn and Pomerantz (1977) summarize the differences between the two theories. They state the following for the analog theory assumptions.

> An image is a spatial representation like that underlying the experience of seeing an object during visual perception. Only a finite processing capacity (limited by the rate at which images may be constructed and the rate at which they fade) is available for constructing and representing images. Images once constructed are 'wholes' for representing all salient features of an object.

They state the following for the propositional theory assumptions.

> Information in memory is represented by networks of propositions. Only a limited number of propositions can be entered into active memory at one time. Networks may be accessed by a specified ordered search which scans node by node. Networks can be constructed so that any desired spatial relation can be represented.

The mental rotation task can differentiate between these two theories.

In a mental rotation task, the experimental participant is provided with a figure in either two dimensions or three dimensions. When the experimental trial begins, the participant is provided with another figure which is either a rotated version of the first figure or a rotated mirror image of the first. If the first figure is a rotated version of the second, one button is hit and if it is a rotated mirror image of the second, a different button is hit for the response. Time and accuracy are measured. Two important manipulations which have been performed to differentiate between the theories are manipulations on the amount of rotation and the figure complexity.

Shepard and Metzler (1971) used pairs of three-dimensional block figures in their experiment. The pairs differed in the amount of angular disparity between them and, thus, the amount they had to be mentally rotated to make the comparison. They found that the time to mentally rotate was a linear function of the amount of angular separation between the two figures. Cooper and Shepard (1973) performed a similar experiment on two-dimensional stimuli and found similar results. Both experiments support the analog theory in that the mental task is a close correlate to the physical task of rotation. The experimental results indicate that the participants mentally rotate an image of the first figure and then decide on a visual basis whether the two figures are the same.

Cooper and Podgorny (1976) investigated the effects of figure complexity on the time to mentally transform rotated or mirror-image figures. Two-dimensional figures, with variable numbers of angles or points as a measure of complexity, were used in the experiment. They found that the time to perform mental rotation tasks was statistically independent from the complexity of the figure. This experiment provided support for the analog theory over the propositional theory. One could always argue, however, that the figures used in the experiment were not difficult enough to find differences between complexity.

Yuille and Steiger (1982) performed a similar experiment to Cooper and Podgorny except that they used three-dimensional block figures similar to those of Shepard and Metzler (1971). The results of the mental transformations indicated that angular disparity had less of an effect on time to rotate for complex figures than for simple ones. Yuille and Steiger (1982) proposed that people use different strategies depending on the complexity of the figure. If the figure is fairly simple, they will use all the features to solve the task. If the figure is fairly complex, too much information must be temporarily retained in memory and the person must reduce the number of components attended to or perform poorly.

Barfield (Barfield and Salvendy, 1985; Barfield, 1986) performed a similar experiment to Yuille and Steiger (1982) using wire-frame modelling on a high-resolution CAD system. The experimental participants memorized the graphics figures and were then asked to answer questions concerning a rotated version of the same figure. They were asked to indicate if the displayed figure was rotated either in depth or in the picture plane, whether the figure was rotated in *x*, *y* or *z* axes, and to indicate the angle of rotation. The complexity of the figures had effects on axes of rotation and the angle of rotation but not on the depth/picture plane question. For all three questions, the rotation needed had statistically significant effects on the time to perform the task.

The results from the Barfield experiment indicated that performance did not fit neatly into one of the theoretical frameworks to the exclusion of the other. The effect of angle disparity on the time to answer all three questions and the lack of an effect of complexity on the depth/picture plane question would seem to indicate that the analog theory was appropriate to explain the data. The effects of complexity on the other two questions would seem to indicate that a propositional theory is appropriate to account for the data. A hybrid model for the mental rotation task appears to be the most appropriate to explain the data. For simple levels of figure complexity people mentally rotate the figure in an analog manner into congruence with the stored version of the memorized test figure. As figure complexity increases, people seem to perform the task by a feature-by-feature analysis. Some of the experimental participants, in verbal reports to the experimenter, indicated that this is indeed the strategy they used. As an example, one of the participants said, "as figures became more complex, I keyed on specific parts and rotated them separately."

Another interesting result from the Barfield experiments was a quantification of the amount of information transmitted by the CAD operator as a function of the complexity of the figure. If the operator is viewed as an information channel, then the percent of information transfer refers to the amount of information in the original stimulus which is retained in the response after passing through the human information processor. Table 6.4 provides this percent of information transfer for simple, moderate and complex figures. As can be seen from the table, moderately complex figures have the least percentage of information transmitted. These results again fit in with the hybrid model. For the simple figures, the experimental participants were probably using the analog model by mentally rotating the figure with relative ease. For the complex figures, the experimental participants were probably performing feature comparisons which would be relatively easy because the complex figures have more features to choose from. For the moderate figures, neither method was optimal for the task so performance suffered.

The results from the experiments on mental rotation of figures has implications for CAD tasks. In particular, the results provide predictions for when CAD designers can perform transformations mentally and when the CAD system

Table 6.4. Percent information transmitted as a function of the complexity of the figure (from Barfield, 1986).

Figure complexity	Axes of rotation (%)	Angles of rotation (%)
Simple	29	42
Moderate	22	14
Complex	57	54

would be needed to display these transformations. If the figures are relatively simple, CAD operators would not need to physically transform the objects on the screen to 'look' at them in different locations or orientations. These transformations could be done mentally on visual images similar to the predictions from the analog theory. If the figures are relatively complex, however, CAD operators could perform some mental transformations on individual features of the object and not on the whole object. This could have important implications for the kinds of errors which are made. Working on individual features in memory means that the integrity of the object is destroyed and the features may be placed back together incorrectly. The operator's memory could not be relied on in this case and the objects should be physically rotated on the screen. For simple figures the integrity of the object could be maintained and the features would remain in the same relationships after mental transformations.

These results also could have an implication on the training of CAD operators. When training, the information provided to the operator should be in the same form as it will be represented in memory. If represented by an analog theory, the information should be presented as integrated wholes. If represented by a propositional theory, the information should be presented in terms of the features which compose the whole object.

6.5. *Decision making*

The CAD designer must make many decisions when designing. What is the best layout? How will one component interact with another component? Is this device structurally sound? These kinds of decisions occur in the cognitive stage of the information processing model of Figure 6.1. Human decision making has been studied quite extensively in the laboratory where the optimal decisions are known and the human's deviation from optimality can be measured and categorized. Many of the deviations from optimality have then been verified in natural settings. The consistent deviations from optimality which may have an effect on CAD tasks are presented below. Knowing these deviations can help to prevent them in the future or suggest design possibilities for reducing them. Decision making can be divided into three categories (Wickens, 1984): prediction, choice, and diagnosis. Since CAD tasks will most likely only make use of choice and diagnosis decision making, these latter two categories will be discussed separately.

In choice decision making, the human must formulate two hypotheses and then gather evidence to determine which of the two is supported. An example for a CAD task would be the choice of whether to design a single integrated piece, which is strong and could be expensive, or to design the piece in separate parts, which would be weaker but cheaper. The methods which are used to make decisions can be compared to mathematical models which provide a yardstick of optimality. For choice decisions, the mathematical models used for comparison are statistical inference and Bayes' Theorem. Statistical inference is used in other situations to determine if one sample is statistically different from another sample. Similarly for decision making, people sample data for two different hypotheses to determine if one is different, or better, than the other. Bayes' Theorem can be represented by the following equation:

$$\frac{P(H_1 \mid D)}{P(H_2 \mid D)} = \frac{P(H_1)}{P(H_2)} \times \frac{P(D \mid H_1)}{P(D \mid H_1)}$$

In the equation, H_1 represents one hypothesis, H_2 represents the alternative hypothesis, and D represents the observation of a particular datum. The fraction to the left of the equals sign represents the odds in favor of a particular hypothesis; the two fractions on the right represent the prior odds and the likelihood ratio. As an example of how a decision would be represented by Bayes' Theorem, again consider the decision of designing an object as an integrated piece or as separate parts. The hypotheses can be stated as the probability of failing (H_2) or not failing (H_1). The datum in one case would be the design on the screen of an integrated object. The decision maker would then have to divide the number of times that an integrated piece did not fail by the number of times that it did fail. This number would then be multiplied by the likelihood ratio of the probability of it not failing given the particular design divided by the probability of it failing given the particular design. These odds could then be compared to the odds for a piece designed in separate parts. Non-optimality can be evaluated by comparing decisions of the operator to these optimal decisions based upon complete information for the statistical inference or Bayes' Theorem.

Non-optimality for choice decisions occurs especially when the human is required to sample data presented sequentially. In a CAD task, this could occur if the operator scans an object only looking at parts of it instead of the whole object. A common occurrence, anchoring, occurs when humans give undue weight to data sampled early in the sequence (Tversky and Kahneman, 1974). Humans are also conservative in that the prior probabilities are not adjusted as much as they should be, according to Bayes' Theorem, after each sampling of information. Another phenomenon, related to attentional overload discussed earlier, is that as the number of sources of information increases above two, humans do not necessarily make better decisions (Dawes and Corrigan, 1974; Dawes, 1979; Schroeder and Benbassat, 1975). Humans usually seek more information than they can handle, end up filtering out several sources of information, and pay the most attention to the most salient bits of information.

In diagnosis, the decision maker must consider several hypotheses to determine the cause of a problem. Diagnosis can occur when the designer tries to correct a wrong design. The decisions which are made can then be compared to the optimal solutions generated from Bayes' Theorem. Diagnosis is similar in many ways to choice decision making. Anchoring can occur in that humans tend to seek information that confirms the chosen hypothesis and ignore information which disproves the hypothesis (Mynatt *et al.*, 1977; Schustack and Sternberg,

1981; Wason and Johnson-Laird, 1972). Also similar to choice decision making is that a human has difficulty in maintaining more than three hypotheses in memory at once (Mehle, 1982; Rasmussen, 1981). This is related to the μ parameter from Table 6.1. The most valid hypothesis for the failure could be eliminated at an early stage. In addition, diagnosis deviates from Bayes' Theorem in terms of availability, representativeness and reliability. For availability, humans tend to support hypotheses with instances, such as the most recent occurrence, which can be easily recalled from memory. For representativeness, humans tend to compare the observed symptoms to those generated by the hypothesis to determine how representative the observed symptoms are. This is a good strategy except that the prior probabilities of an outcome are not considered as they should be according to Bayes' Theorem. As an example, a good match could be found between symptoms and hypothesized symptoms yet the problem may be a relatively rare event and should thus be deemphasized. Humans often do not take into account the reliability, such as reliability based upon sample size, of the data (Tversky and Kahneman, 1971, 1974). When a decision is made by choosing a hypothesis, the human is usually too overconfident that all possible diagnostic hypotheses have been entertained (Mehle, 1982).

Many of the non-optimal behaviors exhibited by humans can be attributed to heuristics or rules-of-thumb which are built up by making decisions in natural environments. In many cases, these heuristics are useful. In other cases, however, they can cause problems.

Several solutions can be offered from non-optimal decision making. In the design of decision aids, the designer must be careful that the aid does not increase the workload of the task so much so that fewer hypotheses or less data are considered in the decision. The decision may be worse, therefore, than if no decision aid were available. An easy solution to many of these decision making problems would seem to be to have much information, such as prior probabilities of occurrence of diagnosed problems and reliability of the data, available to the operator. To access this information, the operator would then have to interact with the computer which would require attentional resources and thus increase workload. Many of the solutions to non-optimal decision making, therefore, should be based upon decreasing, or at least not increasing, the workload of the operator.

Many of the problems of choice decisions can be handled through the use of integrated display of information. In an integrated display, several sources of information are displayed simultaneously instead of either sequentially or in different areas on the display. Integrated displays have the advantage that they remove the sequential nature of the evidence so that anchoring and recency effects are eliminated. They also have the advantage of affording equal salience between sources of information. Recall that, as the human becomes overloaded, only the most salient information makes it through the perceptual filter. With integrated displays, more than two information sources can be attended to. Methods for integration of information can be found in Goodstein (1981) and Berg (1983).

Integrated displays could also be useful for diagnosis decisions. Similar to choice decision making, they would help to eliminate the anchoring and overload problems that can occur for these kinds of decisions. In addition, decisions can be made more optimal by allowing the operator to determine the prior probabilities of events and the reliability of the data which is received. This method has the potential problem, however, that it may increase the workload of the operator without increasing decision effectiveness.

6.6. *Problem solving*

The design process for CAD offers many problems which must be solved. Modelling problem solving is helpful in understanding this process. A recent model of problem solving for computer tasks is the GOMS model. GOMS was developed by Card *et al.* (1983) based upon the earlier work by Newell and Simon (1972) on human problem solving. GOMS stands for Goals, Operations, Methods and Selection rules, which is descriptive of how the model works. GOMS has been applied extensively to the use of text editors but is also applicable to interaction with a CAD system. The purpose of the GOMS model is to predict performance based upon the particular CAD system and to analyze the task according to the input to the system and the plans and actions for carrying out the task or solving problems presented by the task. It has the capability to provide accurate time estimates of tasks for different systems and to understand the operator's problem solving behavior and expertise.

Card *et al.* (1983) have analyzed a CAD VLSI circuit task in the context of the GOMS model. The experimenters tested one expert CAD operator who had a year's experience with the system and around 300 hours practice on the system. The particular task tested was to modify an existing design; this task took about 40 minutes. Data were collected by keeping a time record of each input on all input devices and the coordinates of the input if appropriate. Videotape was taken of the operator and the screen during the task. Using this example will provide a description of how the model has been used and how it can be used in the future. For GOMS, each problem solving task can be broken down according to goals, operations, methods and selection rules.

The operations are the range of responses the operator has available to use at any point in the interaction with the CAD system. For the CAD system studied by Card *et al.* (1983) the operations can be categorized into four types: P for changing the physical location of pointing devices, K for marking and drawing, H for key presses, and M for mental operations for carrying these out. The pointing device used by the CAD system is a mouse which can be used to point to locations for the design or to point to items on the menu display. The drawing (the K operation) can be performed by either pushing the appropriate button on the mouse for marking the beginning of a line and drawing that line; a keyset can be used to indicate the kind of drawing to be carried out (Flashes move from one level of the circuit to another and Rectangle will draw a rectangle); and key presses (the *H* operation) can be used to center the cursor and use a particular function key for tasks. The operations are at the lowest level for the occurrence of actions which are either discrete movements or mental actions.

For the methods, the operations can be combined to carry out higher level commands. Each command uses a method which specifies how the operations can be strung together. Table 6.5 lists the 17 commands which were used for the CAD task studied by Card *et al.* Each command can be composed of two to seven operations. As an example, the method for drawing a rectangle is to think about the action (*M* operation), hit a button corresponding to a Rectangle on the keyset (*K* operation), move the mouse to the desired location for one end of the rectangle (*P* operation), hit a button on the mouse to display a mark of this location on the screen (*K* operation), move the mouse to another location for the other end of the rectangle (*P* operation), and hit a button on the mouse for drawing the rectangle (*K* operation). A command, in this case, is not a single operation but is a combination of several.

A CAD design task can be considered to be an overall problem which must be solved by the operator. Solving the problem involves breaking the task into subproblems and then solving each of these to obtain the overall solution. The methods and the corresponding operations must be combined, by using selection rules, to solve the subproblems. An overall map of the solution can be constructed by dividing the task into goals and subgoals. By analyzing the behavior of the operator through the actions, videotapes and verbal protocols (having the operator tell the experimenter the mental operations at each point in the problem solution), the goal structure can be analyzed. This goal structure can be divided into four different levels. Starting from the highest conceptual level and moving to the lowest levels, they are: the overall goal; phases which represent the division of the goal into subgoals; unit tasks, which is a further division of the subgoals; and events which correspond to the commands to satisfy the unit tasks. Each phase, unit task and event can be analyzed and labeled by analyzing the time record of the CAD task especially considering the pauses which occur. These pauses indicate that the operator may be moving on to another event, unit task or phase.

In analyzing the CAD task, Card *et al.* (1983) assumed that all keystrokes which occurred within 0·3 second of each other could be considered as one of the commands listed in Table 6.5. The pauses longer than 0·3 seconds but less than 5 seconds were hypothesized to be pauses between unit tasks. Any pauses longer than this, up to 80 seconds in the tasks analyzed, were considered to be pauses between phases. The data could be analyzed by computer to categorize these goal levels and some corrections by the experimenters had to be made depending on the verbal protocols of the CAD operator.

The unit tasks and phases are summarized in Table 6.6 along with the average times and ranges (CV) for performing each unit task. The unit tasks were composed of four different types and the phases could be divided into three kinds. The draw tasks were used to create new circuit elements to the layout. The alter

Table 6.5. Commands and operations used in a CAD circuit design task (from Card et al., *1983).*

Command	Operations needed for execution
Drawing Commands:	
(draw) Line 2 (2 end points)	P[location] K[MARK] P [location] K[DRAW]
(draw) Line 1 (1 end point)	P[location] K[DRAW]
(draw) Flash	M K[FLASH] P[location] K[DRAW]
(draw) Rectangle	M K[RECTANGLE] P[location] K[MARK] P[location] K[DRAW]
(create) Label	P[location] K[MARK] H[keyboard] M 6K[CONTROL I string] M K [ESC] H[mouse/keyset]
Parameter Changing Commands:	
(change) Layer	P[menu] K[MARK]
(change) Width (of line)	H[keyboard] M 3K[CONTROL W number] M K[ESC] H [mouse/keyset]
Deletion Commands:	
Delete (element)	P[element] K[DELETE]
Undo (last deletion)	H[keyboard] K[U] H[mouse]
Transformation Commands:	
Move (elements)	H[keyboard] M 2K[MM] H[mouse] 4(P[location] K[MARK]) K[ESC] P[location] K[MARK] P[location] K[MARK] H[keyset]
Copy (elements)	H[keyboard] M 2K[MC] H[mouse] 4(P[location] K[MARK]) K[ESC] P[location] K[MARK] P[location] K[MARK] H[keyset]
Stretch (element)	H[keyboard] M 2K[MS] H[mouse/keyset] P[element] K[MARK] P[edge] K[MARK] P[location] K[MARK]
Display Control Commands:	
Center (drawing)	M K[CENTER] P[location] K[MARK]
(change) Magnification	H[keyboard] M 2K[F|G digit] H[mouse/keyset]
Redraw (window)	H[keyboard] M K[R] H[mouse/keyset]
Dimensioning Commands:	
(measure) Distance	2(P[location] K[MARK])
(measure) Size	4(P[location] K[MARK])

tasks were used to move circuit elements or change their configurations. The dimension tasks were used to measure the dimensions of substructures, the distances between circuit elements, or the alignment of elements. The check tasks were used to check for connectivity or look for VLSI design rule violations. The four unit tasks were combined into three phase structures. The transcription phase lasted for about 14 minutes and was used by the operator to transcribe the layout of the circuit from the hand sketch into the CAD system. The vertical compression phase lasted about seven minutes and was used to compress the

Table 6.6. Times and ranges for execution of phases and unit-tasks (from Card et al., *1983).*

Unit-task type	Transcription phase (*n*) M ± CV (s)	Vertical compression phase (*n*) M ± CV (s)	Horizontal compression phase (*n*) M ± CV (s)	All phases (*n*) M ± CV (s)
Draw tasks	(28) 23·1 ± 0·36	(1) 19·0	(5) 11·6 ± 0·50	(34) 21·3 ± 0·42
Alter tasks	(7) 18·6 ± 0·69	(16) 20·1 ± 0·31	(31) 19·4 ± 0·72	(54) 19·5 ± 0·61
Dimension tasks	(1) 9·0	(1) 9·0	(8) 8·1 ± 0·66	(10) 8·0 ± 0·60
Check tasks	(2) 32·5	(2) 34·5	(4) 42·8 ± 0·66	(8) 38·1 ± 0·59
All tasks	(38) 22·3 ± 0·46	(20) 21·0 ± 0·45	(48) 18·6 ± 0·86	(106) 20·4 ± 0·64

circuit vertically by moving substructures around to make them fit more closely. The horizontal compression phase lasted about 15 minutes and was used to compress the circuit horizontally.

By dividing the task into basic components, GOMS can predict the times for those components when they recombine for other tasks. Card *et al.* (1983) found that GOMS could predict the times to execute all commands in the experimental session within 16%. The predicted time to execute all the commands was 1192 seconds from the GOMS model and the observed time was 1028 seconds from the CAD operator. The discrepancy between the two times was hypothesized to be due to the fact that the CAD operator was an expert and required less time for the mental operation (*M*) than expected.

The analysis of the problem-solving behavior of the CAD operator and the corresponding goal structures through the GOMS model has several possible applications. Testing operators and determining the average times for performing basic tasks which could be combined into other CAD design tasks would certainly be useful data. Overall goal structures could be obtained for other design problems and time predictions could be determined for finishing them. Also, alternative CAD workstation designs could be analyzed to determine which CAD would be faster and easier to use than another CAD. This analysis could also be used in training CAD operators. Expert CAD operators could be compared to novice CAD operators in terms of the goal structures for each. If the novice is not using the same kinds of structures, methods or operations, the comparison would show this clearly and suggest how help could be given to allow the novice to act more like the expert. The novice may not be aware that a shorter sequence of operations could satisfy the same command, Finally, this method has the potential to identify levels of expertise. Card *et al.* (1983) found that the expert CAD operator they tested devoted 96% of the time to physical operations and only 4% to the mental operations. Novices would have to think about what they were doing and, thus, would devote more time to mental operations.

6.7. *Response execution*

The last stage in the human information processing model of Figure 6.1 is response. Several kinds of responses can occur: for example, the stylus can be moved to a different position on the digitizing tablet; the CAD operator may look at a different part of the display; or help may be requested from someone else if a problem cannot be solved. The easiest response to quantify is the discrete movement of the hand or stylus to another position. This movement time is represented by Fitts' (1954) Law and was introduced in the previous section on information processing.

As presented in the previous section, Fitts' Law is represented by the equation:

$$\tau_{pos} = I_M \ln (2A/W)$$

where τ_{pos} is the total movement time, I_M corresponds to the time to correct a movement, A is the amplitude of the movement, and W is the width of the target. Recall that I_M was estimated to be 63 ms/bit. Fitts' Law shows the trade-off which occurs between speed and accuracy. Accuracy is represented by the width of the target (W). The speed of the movement can be fast if the accuracy does not have to be high. On the other hand, speed would have to be reduced if the accuracy is increased.

Table 6.7. Predicted movement times for various amplitudes and widths from Fitts' Law.

Amplitude (A) (cm)	Width (W) (c)	Predicted movement time (τ_{pos}) (ms)
1	1	44
10	1	189
20	1	261
30	1	276
10	10	44
20	10	87
30	10	113
40	10	131
20	20	44
30	20	69
40	20	87
20	30	18
30	30	44
40	30	62
30	40	25
40	40	44

As an example of how Fitts' Law can be applied to CAD tasks, consider the design of a menu overlay on the digitizing tablet. The times to move the stylus from one menu item to another can be predicted by Fitts' Law. Having these time predictions would then allow for the consideration of optimal menu layout designs. An important consideration is the amplitude of the movement from one item to another. Another important consideration is the size of the area for a menu item which can be touched by the stylus. Table 6.7 provides the predicted movement time for Fitts' Law for several widths and amplitudes. The values from the Table show clearly the trade-offs between speed and size of the space for the menu item. It may be optimal to have the frequently used items large and the lesser used items smaller. But having many large spaces for menu items would increase the needed amplitude for movements from one item to another.

Part III

THE MANAGEMENT OF CAD

Chapter 7
Introduction to the management of CAD

7.1. Why is management of CAD so important?

Previous chapters have described some of the benefits to the engineering design process that can be expected with CAD. Vendors claim that these changes will yield phenomenal 'bottom-line' improvements including 10-fold productivity increases, quantum leaps in innovativeness of designs, and increased manufacturability of drawings. Yet, if CAD's benefits are so phenomenal, why are there not more companies with CAD? In a 1982 survey of a nationally representative sample of manufacturing firms, only 10% were found to use CAD at all (Majchrzak *et al.*, 1986). In a survey of Michigan auto suppliers, Jacobs (1985) found the adoption rate to be only slightly higher (24%). Moreover, when CAD is adopted, actual productivity gains often do not approach the full spectrum of expected gains. Efficiency may increase but at the cost of high CAD operator turnover. Drawings may be more quickly produced, but not be more innovative or manufacturable. Hall (1984) describes a Fortune 500 electronics company which, after two years using a CAD system, had only achieved a 2-fold improvement over manually-drawn electronics schematic. Orr (1985) estimates that of the 15 000 CAD systems installed in the world as of 1985, only about 1 000 are actually used for their original purpose—design. The rest are used as nothing more than electronic drawing boards, a use described in previous chapters as barely scratching the surface of CAD's potential. With such relatively primitive uses of CAD, it is no wonder that small productivity gains like those of Hall (1984) have been reported.

Not only are there few firms using CAD, and those with CAD are under-utilizing it, there are also countless companies that have tried CAD and failed. Down (1985) cites an example of an automobile design group which is still complaining about their CAD system after several years. Their complaints include the following: the system fails to achieve the expected uses; people do not like using the system; and problems experienced in implementing the system have been used by workers to fuel their lack of faith in management's ability to do anything right.

Implementation failures are certainly not the prerogative of CAD technology. Clausen (1979) describes an example of a firm discontinuing its installation of a computer-based information system (CBIS) after five years of planning had been undertaken—an investment that could not be recouped. Dickson *et al.* (1980) described an MIS (Management Information System) that was so poorly implemented into the Minneapolis Post Office that the system was removed. Prior to removal, the system had been plagued with transaction errors, physical sabotage, data falsification and union resistance. In fact, failures have become so common that Henry Lucas, a noted researcher of CBISs, has commented: "During the past decade, organizations have developed large numbers of CBISs. Unfortunately, many of these systems must be classified as failures. Some systems have been withdrawn because they have proved unworkable, and others continue to operate though no one uses their output" (Lucas, 1975 a, p. vii).

These failures raise a question of pressing concern to managers and CAD researchers: why are these failures occurring? Without adequately addressing this question, proponents of CAD may find themselves in the same predicament as operations researchers did a decade ago—no matter how good the model is, it is not used (Ackoff, 1967; Bostrom and Heinen, 1977).

Some possible reasons for the problems experienced in CAD implementation have been suggested by research to date. In a 1981 survey of 34 engineering firms using CAD, Senker (1984, p. 227) found that the three barriers to utilization of CAD were:

1. Industrial relations problems
2. Supplier failure to deliver adequate software
3. Managerial inefficiency (described as management tasks inadequately carried out, such as delaying the appointment of a CAD manager)

In another study on potential reasons for CAD failures, Schaffitzel and Kersten (1985) examined the experiences of 20 medium-sized German firms. They found that a decisive factor in less successful implementations of CAD systems was the failure to restructure and redesign the existing organization as CAD is first introduced. Rowe (1985), who examined a failed implementation of a computerized stock control system, found that while management searched for technical reasons to account for the failure, most technical factors were in practice human and organizational problems. Finally, Heath and Gower (1986) describe results of numerous pilot studies conducted in the United Kingdom to ascertain the importance of management skills in the implementation of CBISs. The researchers found that management skills were required to overcome several important problems inherent in implementing new technology. Some of these problems included insufficient personal commitment, unreliable systems, and insufficient technical support.*

These findings of research and case studies have led to such conclusions as the following: "The success of information systems has been too narrowly defined in

*A reason for lack of implementation of CAD is of course its applicability to the production process. Some machine tool shops, for example, may not use CAD because their production process is not sufficiently repetitive to warrant 'automation' (Jacobs, 1986).

the past; only technical criteria have been considered . . . .Concentration on the technical aspects of systems and a tendency to overlook organizational behavior problems and users are the reasons most information systems have failed" (Lucas, 1975 a, p.2). And more pointedly for CAD systems: "The effectivity of CAD/CAM processes introduced into technical design areas depends as much or more on human factors, i.e., attitudes, fears, recognition incentives, compatible machine/user interfaces, etc., as it does on the capabilities of the equipment selected" (Hamilton and Sheehan, 1982, p.5).

For these reasons, then, the management of new technologies, especially management of the social and organizational issues involved in the installation of a CAD system, is an essential part of an understanding of how to derive optimal benefits from CAD.

7.2. *If management of these issues is so important, why are they ignored?*

While it can be argued that there are a few researchers and managers who recognize the importance of managing social and organizational issues that arise when adopting CAD, research findings indicate that most implementation efforts ignore these issues. In a series of case studies on the implementation of information technologies, Walton and Vittori (1983) found that while managers generally appreciate the fact that new technology will probably have organizational side-effects, there is little or no managerial effort to predict the nature of the side-effects. In a survey of 55 workgroups implementing office automation, the primary concerns of managers were the hardware/software issues, not employees' attitudes, skills, behavior, outcomes, or organizational impacts (Gutek *et al.*, 1984).

Why is the management of social and organizational issues given such little attention during implementation? Based on their interviews with managers, Walton and Vittori (1983) suggest that actual organizational side effects are rarely understood by managers. They found also that such side effects are rarely systematically assessed, thus perpetuating the ignorance. Moreover, Tapscott (1982) found in his review of the literature that "there is little understanding of the human element of 'people issues' of office automation" (p. 28). Finally, Johnson *et al.* (1985), based on interviews with managers in 194 organizations, report that managers see social issues as problems to be overcome for which solutions are left to chance. The managers fail to recognize two points: that these social issues may actually offer opportunities for adaptation of the new equipment and that solutions exist that can be systematically applied to overcome the social 'problems'.

The research cited above suggests that the management of social and organizational issues involved in implementing new technology is ignored because the issues are not understood by managers. They lack knowledge about the impact of computer-assisted technologies on the social and organizational factors in a firm. In addition, they lack an understanding of the impact of social and organizational factors on the successful implementation of computerized technology. In all fairness to managers, however, there is much that is not yet understood about the role of social and organizational factors in implementing new technology. Thus, in an effort to combat such knowledge gaps, Part III will review research evidence on the role of social and organizational factors when CAD is installed. With such a review, areas where sufficient knowledge exists for management prescriptions can be more clearly distinguished from areas still needing research.

7.3. What is meant by social and organizational factors?

Social and organizational factors involved in the installation of new technologies such as CAD include issues typically examined under the rubric of human resource management, organizational behavior and organizational design. Topics include job design, personnel selection and training, leadership, work motivation, authority systems, structural designs, performance measurement and corporate philosophy. As will be described in Part III, research has shown that many of these factors affect, or can be affected by, the installation of CAD.

Three ways in which social and organizational factors can be affected by, or affect, technological change are described. First described is the way in which social factors are *altered by* new technology, as when a job is redesigned or new skills are needed to optimally use the new technology. With CAD, for example, a drafter's job may need to be redesigned to allow the drafter to optimally utilize new information arriving from multiple sources. This role of social and organizational factors is referred to here as the *consequences of CAD*.

Second, those social factors *affecting* an employee's willingness and ability to adapt to new technology will be described. Such factors might include a situation where coworkers discourage an employee from learning new equipment. With CAD, for example, workers may initially resist training because they fear the effects of CAD on their future jobs. This role of social and organizational factors is referred to here as those factors affecting the *resistance of individuals to CAD*.

A final set of social and organizational factors that will be described includes those factors involved in the *implementation process*, such as when training is appropriately provided and advance planning is undertaken. With CAD, for example, success may be more likely when follow-up training is offered as users adjust to the new system.

These three roles of social and organizational factors—as consequences, as determinants of individuals' adjustment and as parameters of the implementation process—do not exhaust all social and organizational issues involved in CAD installations. However, they cover many of the relevant topics. Moreover, the categories are not necessarily mutually exclusive; a variable that encourages individuals' adjustment to CAD may also be important in the implementation process.

Nevertheless, these roles will help to distinguish and focus the range of empirical research relating to social and organizational issues in technological change. As such, a more organized exploration of that research and interpretation for concise management implications can be achieved.

7.4. *Variations in the use of CAD*

As described in previous chapters, CAD systems can take a variety of different forms—from complex sophisticated workstations to a simple CRT. CAD systems can also be used for a variety of different purposes. A CAD system might be used in the engineering department of one organization solely as a mechanism for providing efficient storage of designs. In another organization, the system may be used exclusively by the manufacturing department to develop prototypes and prepare tapes for computer-numerical control machine tools. In a third organization, the system may be used primarily by design engineers to perform tasks previously done by drafters.

As CAD is currently implemented, these variations abound. For example, in Jacobs' (1985) survey of Michigan auto suppliers, the distribution of work performed by CAD was *bi*-modal. Thirty-eight percent of the firms used CAD for less than 10% of their work activities while another quarter used CAD for 70% or more of their operations. Thus, given the status quo, it is inappropriate to adopt a singular concept of a CAD system, and the social and organizational factors pertaining to it.

To discuss the impact of CAD on social and organizational variables, however, a concept of the features of the system being examined must be advanced. As with the other chapters in this book, the following three chapters focus on the concept of what CAD *can* do, and not just how it has been used in most firms today. Thus, the concept of CAD advanced here is one in which CAD achieves its potential to modify the traditional engineering design process. Such a system is one in which CAD is the main design tool for research and engineering facilities. Such a system has terminals distributed throughout manufacturing, design engineering and drafting, with the terminals sufficiently compatible to interface. Such a system is used by both drafters and engineers (with job titles altered to describe new responsibilities). Finally, such a system may or may not provide manufacturing specifications or control computerized manufacturing equipment; this use is referred to as Computerized-Integrated Manufacturing (CIM) and not CAD. While few firms have implemented CAD to the extent described by this concept, such a concept has been widely acclaimed as the CAD of the future (e.g., Orr, 1985; Pitou, 1981).

In studying the management of CAD, then, social and organizational issues pertaining to such a far-reaching concept of CAD will be explored. For example, in this concept of CAD, the system becomes a communication device. As such, the ways in which CAD affects users' communication patterns are described.

In sum, variations in the use of CAD will be recognized throughout Part III.* However, there is a bias here toward the far-reaching implications of a CAD system which achieves its full potential in an organization.

7.5. The research to be reviewed

In Part III, research evidence pertaining to each of the three roles of social and organizational factors will be reviewed. In reviewing the research literature on the topic, the massive body of speculative pontifications have been overlooked, leaving case studies, surveys, and the occasional experiment as the basis for our conclusions.

In undertaking such a review, the reader must be forewarned that research focused specifically on the management of social and organizational factors involved in CAD is sparse. Therefore, extrapolation from research on technologies similar to CAD, such as the broader range of information technologies, is necessary. CAD shares numerous features with such other information technologies as Decision Support Systems (DSS), Office Automation (OA), Computer-Based Information Systems (CBIS), and Management Information Systems (MIS). These technologies all serve as communication devices, automating routine clerical tasks and facilitating editing and flexibility. They are used primarily (though not exclusively) with white-collar or knowledge workers. They can be implemented at a variety of levels of sophistication—from an electronic drawing board or sophisticated typewriter to an integrative multifunction communication link and expert system. Since all these technologies are produced in a growing marketplace, they also share a rapid rate of technological obsolescence.

Despite these similarities with information technologies, CAD is sufficiently different to raise caution in generalizing from research on information technology. Unlike CBISs, CAD does not supplement an organizationally perfected work process such as payroll. In fact CAD and CAE are replacing a process that to some extent is still a form of art. For example, finite element analysts were recently asked to predict the vibration properties of a simple part (Ewins, 1985 cited in Kay, 1985). The results of the survey showed a very large scatter in the analysts' responses. If experts cannot agree, the process being computerized by CAD is hardly as straightforward as the better-defined processes supplemented by information technologies. Moreover, CAD is different because, unlike DSSs or OA systems, CAD's installation in bounded subareas of a company can only serve as an interim solution (Pitou, 1981). If CAD is to achieve its intended benefits, it must affect a multidisciplinary, multifunctional, cross-departmental process. Such far-reaching effects make the implementation of CAD far more

*Variations in which CAD is used on the manufacturing floor by skilled trades personnel are not discussed since the issues are similar to those of CAM technologies and beyond the scope of this book.

complex and thus revolutionary than implementation of an information technology (Burks, 1984). As such, CAD may necessitate an introductory process much longer than that of information technologies. In Schaffitzel and Kersten's (1985) study of 20 companies implementing CAD, for example, they found that the introduction of CAD took several years. In contrast, while some information technologies may take equally as long, most are bought and installed within a year.

These differences between CAD and other information technologies do not suggest that we cannot learn about CAD from these other technologies. Rather, the differences suggest that CAD may be more difficult to implement and therefore the management of social and organizational issues are of even greater importance than with information technologies. Therefore, findings from research on information technologies provide a conservative assessment of the role of social and organizational factors in CAD installation.

7.6. Organization of Part III

The following chapters in Part III are divided by the three roles of social and organizational factors: Consequences, Adjustment to New Technology, and Implementation. At the beginning of each chapter, major issues about these roles are introduced and categories of social and organizational variables are identified. For each category of variables, expectations from the speculative literature about potential effects of the variables are described; these expectations are followed with a review of the research evidence. For the reader not interested in descriptions of research, summaries are provided of the relevant research findings for each category of variables. Finally, each chapter closes with conclusions from the research about implications for managing CAD.

Chapter 8
Social and organizational consequences of CAD

8.1. Introduction

This chapter will describe research pertaining to the social and organizational consequences of CAD. First, major categories of consequences are distinguished and described. Then, for each category, expectations about specific consequences of CAD are presented and research evidence reviewed. The chapter closes with conclusions about the current and future effects of CAD on social and organizational variables.

Practitioners of organizational development and proponents of open systems theory propose that a change in the technology of an organization creates change in other aspects of the organization—the social and organizational aspects. For example, in a model by Harold Leavitt (1964), technological change is expected to affect the structure of the organization (i.e., the communication and authority system), the tasks or jobs done, and the people (i.e., their numbers, skills, attitudes and activities) (see Figure 8.1). In this section, these social and organizational consequences of technological change, particularly as they relate to change from manual drafting to CAD, are described.

To understand the social and organizational consequences of new CAD technologies, it is necessary to remind the reader of the precise nature of the technological change occurring as a result of implementing CAD. As described in earlier chapters, some of the more popularly mentioned design changes resulting from CAD include:

Increased standardization in drawings and graphic symbols.
Less design time spent on routine work.
More analysis and integration of parts into designs of complete systems.
More design information from more constituents.

With these design process changes, social and organizational factors are expected to be affected. If such social factors are not appropriately managed, expected benefits of the design changes may not be achieved.

Two major categories of social and organizational factors are described that may be changed by the implementation of CAD and that may affect whether design process changes brought about by CAD yield CAD's expected benefits.

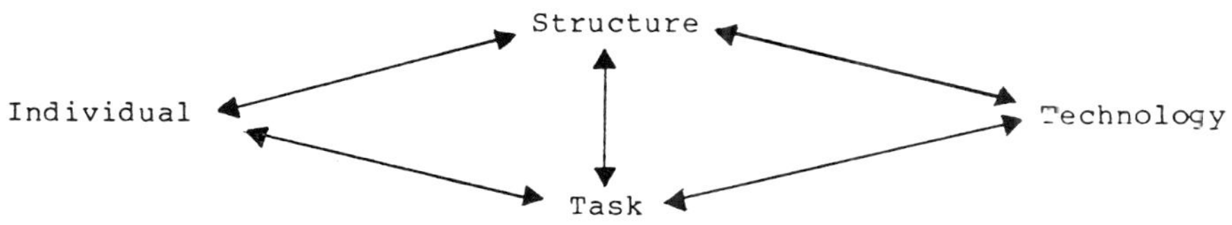

Figure 8.1. A conceptual model of organizational change (from Leavitt (1964), courtesy John Wiley & Sons).

These factors include: (*a*) aspects of the workplace; and (*b*) reactions of individuals in the workplace.

Workplace factors refer to the various ways in which CAD will alter the job (i.e., activities, skill requirements, etc.), the structure of the work environment (i.e., the way decisions are made), procedures (i.e., how formalized they are), and personnel policies. For example, CAD is able to complete routine design activities in less time than with manual drafting. This capability will only yield more innovative designs, however, if the job contents of engineers and drafters are concurrently changed to allow more time for non-routine activities, more unpredictability in job tasks, and more emphasis on the management of this extra time. If the quicker completion of routine tasks results in jobs that involve more rather than less routine tasks, the benefits of enhanced innovation will probably go unrealized. Therefore, workplace factors are conceived not only as possibly changing with CAD, but as intervening by either enhancing or negating the impact of design process changes on increased productivity.

The second category of social and organizational factors affected by CAD is the reactions of individuals to their jobs with CAD. Individuals' reactions to their jobs with CAD are important for a number of reasons. First, individuals' evaluations of their jobs are important determinants of the level of effort they put into their jobs (Hackman and Oldham, 1975; Vroom, 1964) and their overall adjustment to technological change (Lucas, 1975 a). Second, individuals' reactions to their jobs are important determinants of other individuals' reactions (Griffin *et al.*, 1984; Salancik and Pfeffer, 1977). That is, negative evaluations of a few can create negative evaluations among many. Individuals' reactions also serve as a barometer of the status of workplace changes; i.e., unhappiness among CAD users about the level of decision-making authority may signify the degree to which non-routine activities have been over-managed. Finally, individuals' reactions to their jobs with CAD are important because they may actually negate the positive effects of changes to the workplace. For example, CAD may necessitate working with others (e.g., manufacturing, drafting) more often. If this need is negatively valued by workers (e.g., designers preferring not to work with manufacturing personnel), an increased interchange with others will occur less willingly if at all. Therefore, reactions of individuals to their jobs with CAD are also expected to intervene by either enhancing or negating the impact of design process changes on increased productivity.

This distinction between changes to the workplace and changes to the individual is similar to a distinction made by Richard Walton on the primary and secondary effects of information technology (Walton and Vittori, 1983). Primary effects are depicted here as those workplace changes resulting from CAD implementation. By affecting the design process, CAD may have the potential to alter everything about the way the design process is carried out. As a result of these changes to the workplace, secondary effects on individuals may result. A job that is made more routine by CAD-induced design process changes is undoubtedly evaluated by individuals as worse than a job with no change in its routine. A conceptual framework is presented in Figure 8.2 for understanding social and organizational consequences of CAD. As depicted in this framework, a causal sequence will be explored in the literature whereby individuals' reactions are analyzed within the context of workplace changes resulting from CAD.

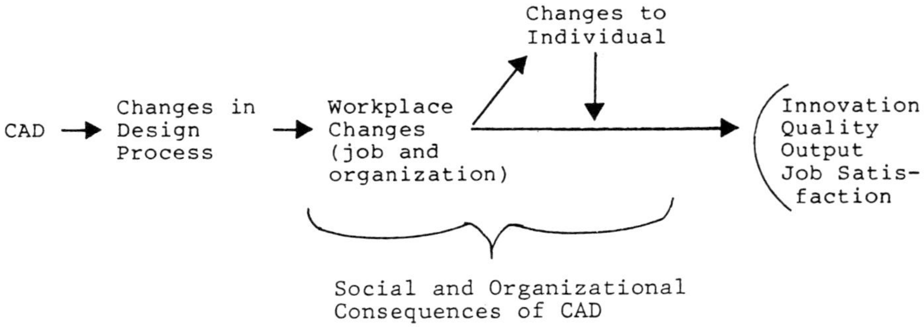

Figure 8.2. The impact of CAD on productivity.

Prior to reviewing literature on the social and organizational consequences of implementing CAD, expectations about the likely workplace effects of CAD and individuals' reactions to those effects are described. These expectations are based on theories from related fields as well as CAD-related speculation. Next, research on the effects of similar technologies are discussed, and finally, results of the few studies that address these issues directly with CAD are described. By proceeding in this manner, an effort is made to summarize what the empirical literature to date tells us about consequences of CAD.

8.2. *Workplace changes resulting from CAD*

Workplace consequences of changes in the design process induced by CAD can be categorized according to four main descriptors of the workplace:

1. Job tasks.
2. Organizational procedures.

3. Organizational structure.
4. Miscellaneous workplace aspects such as workforce size, performance monitoring, etc.

The effect of CAD on job tasks

Job tasks refer to the scope, range, content and routinity of the activities that individuals normally do in their jobs. Given the fact that design process changes will result in less time to complete routine activities, one expectation of a change to the job is the elimination (or at least reduction) of routine activities (Barlini, 1981) from some jobs. Another expectation commonly expressed is that some jobs will be downgraded such that even greater increases in routinity are seen. For example, with CAD, one might hypothesize that drafters' jobs may become more menial (as drafters simply input designers' work), with engineers experiencing the enhanced innovation on their jobs. Or, conversely, one may hypothesize that design engineers' jobs become *more* routine as their responsibilities usurp those of displaced drafters.

In addition to changes in the routinity of the job, the CAD-induced integration in the design process can be expected to exert other changes as well. Interdependence among drafting, design engineering, and manufacturing is expected to increase (Krouse, 1982) as designers and drafters must contend with more and difficult facets of the design process than ever before. No longer can the designer prepare a design with only minimal concern for its manufacturability. Moreover, this change in interdependence is expected to be reciprocal as well. Traditionally, the workflow of the design process has been conducted in a sequential fashion from design engineering to drafting to manufacturing. With CAD, input from others can or should occur at all steps in the process to optimize the design. As a result, the form as well as the extent of the interdependence is expected to change.

As interdependence increases, and some jobs become less routine (?), the skill levels of jobs involved with a CAD system are expected to increase as well (Eaton, 1985). For example, predictions have been made of the need for increased system knowledge, a broader knowledge of manufacturing, and an ability to think in abstract and conceptual models and problem-solving schema (Poitou, 1981).

A fiinal change to jobs that could be expected with the implementation of CAD includes a change in the way people communicate with each other. Research on performance of R&D groups has found that informal (Epton, 1981) and formal (Pelz and Andrews, 1976) person-to-person communication are key determinants of the performance of R&D personnel. Moreover, in an American Society of Civil Engineers 1976 survey, 85% of the members reported engaging in management type tasks, generically, and verbally communicating with others, in specific. Clearly, the role that communication plays in design work is important.

Not only is communication itself important in design work, but the pattern of communication determines to some extent how well R&D personnel perform. In Tushman's (1979, 1982) research on communication in R&D units, he found that performance was higher with complex non-routine tasks when the R&D unit communicated in a decentralized rather than centralized pattern, i.e., everyone talking to everyone without a central person coordinating the communications. He found that these groups were better able to handle the uncertainties inherent in non-routine tasks.

While decentralized communication may be effective for some tasks, other research has found communication among and between decentralized groups to be filled with pitfalls and difficulties. Allen's (1971) research found that physically separated group members (a common result of decentralization) is a key factor inhibiting communication. Tushman (1977), in a literature review, found decentralized communication to be difficult because people bring to the group their own idiosyncratic norms, language, values, time frames and coding schemes.

As these communication difficulties are so inhibiting to performance, the effect of CAD on R&D communication is an important issue. It may be that CAD exacerbates these difficulties if its implementation results in an even greater decentralization of design staff. That is, the constraints imposed by manual drafting and non-integrated CRTs may have prevented project teams from being too large, too multidisciplinary, and too scattered for optimally sharing, altering and experimenting with new designs. With CAD, the ease and speed of transmitting and altering designs means that earlier constraints are obsolete. This new technological capability may then promote the opportunity to further decentralize project teams and design work. In so doing, these changes may lead to more communication problems, and thus negate the positive effects of decentralization. CAD may also impair communication because it may promote less face-to-face verbal exchange—a mode of communication essential to R&D performance (Epton, 1981). For example, in research on coordination modes within organizations, Van de Ven *et al.* (1976) found that as task interdependence increases (an expected workplace change with CAD), coordination becomes more group-to-group rather than face-to-face. Yet face-to-face communication is important for R&D innovation (Pelz and Andrews, 1976). Will this consequence of CAD then harm the innovative design process? CAD's capabilities may inadvertently inhibit rather than facilitate innovation.

In contrast to hypothesizing CAD as a negative force on R&D communication, it is possible to hypothesize that CAD is a mechanism for overcoming traditional difficulties in communication. Allen's (1971) research found that the extent of communication among engineering colleagues was influenced more by the engineer's perception of the amount of effort it took to speak to colleagues than by the perceived benefits of the interchange. Therefore, CAD may facilitate communication simply because it makes it dramatically easier to communicate. Drawings can be instantly shared with others, messages left at the discretion of the sender, and complex information exchanged without ever leaving the desk or picking up a phone.

To summarize, the non-empirical literature proposes that CAD would change job tasks in the following ways: eliminate routine activities from some jobs, downgrade jobs of others, increase interdependence of the workflow, increase skill requirements of jobs, and either facilitate or inhibit the traditional communication process among design staff. A review of research studies testing these propositions follows.

Review of information technology research

Information technology research provides some data to indicate how a technology such as CAD may alter the activities of the job (i.e., routinity, interdependence, skill requirements). Bjorn-Andersen and his associates (1979) studied five banks in four European countries implementing computerized information systems to complete such tasks as account balancing, filing and customer information requests. The researchers retrospectively surveyed 379 users, developers and managers of the new system, and asked questions about personal background, perceptions of self and others, job satisfaction, and changes to work content of self and others. One of their key findings was that for the clerks working with the CBISs, job tasks changed in the following ways: routinity increased, discretion over errors increased, opportunity to choose work methods and sequence of tasks decreased, and the number (not variety) of tasks increased.

Gutek (1982) undertook a time series analysis of the adjustment of a secretary and a manager to a computerized managerial workstation. She assessed job satisfaction, self-esteem, system satisfaction, and work content prior to equipment installation, through stable use of the equipment and to its later removal. She found that the system created no changes to the secretary's or manager's jobs in terms of the distribution of work activities performed.

Whisler (1970) conducted a study of 18 life insurance companies using CBISs. He found that implementation of the CBIS increased the amount of interdependence among jobs as control became tighter and more precise. As a result, there was an increase in perceptions among individuals about the significance of their job in affecting more people. However, he found a decreased degree of interpersonal communication as clerks worked alone more often.

Mann and Williams (1960) conducted a classic case study of a change-over from a manual to CBIS accounting system in an electric light and power company. The researchers noted that the CBIS increased the need for coordination, eliminated routine and minor decision-making tasks, decreased autonomy to set work pace (because of the integrated work process), and changed jobs such that specialized tasks previously performed in separate sections were now done as stations by one person.

Stewart (1971) examined ten case studies of effects of CBISs on managers. She found that the CBIS forced managers to be more concerned about the objectives and methods of work performed by subordinates.

Finally, in reviewing six studies of 93 organizations implementing CBISs, Sanders (1968) concluded that computer usage had not yielded much (if any) upgrading of average requirements of jobs since both menial and high level non-supervisory jobs were changed.

In summary, these few studies on the effect of information technologies on job activities suggest, first of all, that as predicted from the speculative literature, interdependence among people and units increases with the implementation of information technology. Second, in terms of the technological impact on the content, routinity and skill-level of the job, no single pattern emerges. It appears that the amount of routinity in jobs with new technology will depend less on the technology and more on other factors such as the level in the organization at which the job is located. At lower-level positions such as clerks (or drafters), there may be an increased routinity by having less opportunity to choose work methods and task sequences and less control over work pace. At higher-level positions such as managers (or engineers), the technological change may decrease routinity. Across all levels, skill requirements associated with the new technology will stay about the same. In addition, these findings suggest that consequences of new information technology on job content are not technologically determined and will vary with the organization, industry and the detailed practices that accompany the new equipment (c.f., Bikson *et al.*, 1983; Iacono and Kling, 1986).

While this literature suggests that job content is not technologically determined, research studies are too sparse for confident conclusions. However, there is substantially more research on the changes in communication activities that one could expect with CAD. Substantial research has been done to date on computer conferencing, a technology with communication capabilities similar to those of an integrated, interfacing CAD system.

Kerr and Hiltz (1982), in a review of studies on computer-mediated communication, found that the technology increased users' choice of when to communicate, the speed of interaction, ability to join groups more freely, the explicitness of communication, and the number of social participations—hardly negative impacts on communication.

In an open-ended survey of 100 users of an office automation/electronic mail system, Edwards (1978) found that the system changed communication patterns in the following ways: it promoted instant communication, allowed for remote management, encouraged joint collaboration, discounted distance, enhanced the amount of communication, and decreased the use of the telephone.

Hiltz (1984) conducted a longitudinal survey study of the impact of an electronic information exchange system on 150 scientists and engineers. She found that the system did not usurp face-to-face communications; in fact, on-line communication stimulated the use of other communication modes. Rice and Case (1983) had similar findings in their longitudinal survey of electronic mail users.

In a review of the telecommunications literature, Short *et al.* (1976) found that opinions could be changed more effectively by face-to-face communication than by written means. Therefore, the use of telecommunications was felt to have a detrimental effect on changing the opinions of others. Examining this relationship further indicated that computer conferencing was actually more effective for what were referred to as low social presence tasks, i.e., tasks where interpersonal relationships and personal qualities of the individual are less important. When communication tasks required high social presence, such as when individuals must attend to others' idiosyncratic reactions and feelings, mediums with low social presence such as computer conferencing created distortions from face-to-face communications. For CAD, the implication is that design engineers interested in persuading other personnel about the adequacy of a particular design solution may prefer to do so in person rather than by using CAD. Although CAD allows the other party to view the design at will, the design engineer using CAD does not have the ability to bring his or her social presence to bear on the discussion.

Undertaking further study of social presence, Rice (1984) concluded that social presence of a particular technology could be increased by providing the technology with a special emphasis on stylistic and persuasive interpersonal strategies. Until that is done, however, he recommends that computer and face-to-face interactions be mixed for different tasks and different phases in problem-solving. Since computer conferencing necessitates structured, delayed, written responses, he suggests that it is best used for the structuring, evaluation and documentation tasks of problem-solving. Face-to-face communication should then be used for conceptualizing, searching and implementing activities. However, Short *et al.* (1976) note that differences between media (computer versus face-to-face) tend to be eliminated for simple tasks. Thus, for routine problems, CAD is probably appropriate for all phases of problem-solving, saving Rice's recommendations for more complex design problems.

In summary, this research suggests that, as predicted from the non-empirical literature, communication patterns are affected by computer technology. On the positive side, computer technology:

1. Increases choices of when to communicate.
2. Increases speed and explicitness of communication.
3. Discounts the importance of distance as a barrier to communication.
4. Encourages or stimulates the use of other communication media, such as in-person.
5. Yields no performance decrements from face-to-face communication for a range of simple problems.

Despite these positive consequences, computerized technologies appear to have some disadvantages. For complex design problems, only certain problem-solving activities appear to be best done with the computer. Moreover, when persuasion is necessary, particularly when related to peer pressure, computers may not be as effective as other modes of communication.

Review of CAD research

Research on effects of information technologies on job tasks suggested that CAD would yield little average change in the routinity of job activities and skill requirements, would dramatically alter communication patterns, and would increase interdependence among jobs. Are these predictions borne out by the sparse literature specifically focused on CAD?

In a survey of 88 design engineers and drafters, some using CAD and some using manual methods, Majchrzak *et al.* (1985 a) found that, as expected, CAD increased the amount of coordination among people in the organization. However, contrary to expectations, CAD users did not perceive their jobs either to involve more reciprocal interdependence between the jobs or to be less routine and more unpredictable.

Norton (1981) surveyed managers and CAD operators regarding their use of CAD. He found that skill requirements of some jobs were increased, with senior designers making almost exclusively 'high-level' decisions such as conceptualizing and problem definition. In contrast, junior designers who typically made 'low-level' decisions such as detailing had those decisions taken over by CAD, reducing skill requirements even further. Despite this evidence of some deskilling, certain new skills were needed for all jobs: creativity, broad knowledge about manufacturing processes and the ability to respond quickly and accurately to design requirements.

Newton (1984) compared jobs of drafters using CAD to those using traditional methods. He found that there were no differences between the two groups on the amount of autonomy they perceived in their jobs, the number of environmental problems (e.g., lighting, comfort, privacy, etc.) encountered in their jobs, and the amount of social support they received from peers.

The American Institute for Design and Drafting (AIDD) conducted a survey of 24 organizational members in 1983 on CAD use. They found that indeed CAD demanded certain skills previously considered not nearly as important. These skills are listed in Table 8.1, and include, among the most important, communication, coordination and creativity.

Wingert *et al.* (1981) interviewed managers of 14 German companies in various stages of CAD implementation and found that jobs with CAD involved new and higher-level skills. New skills needed with CAD included the fluent use of symbols, ability to work by using information in different dimensions and planes, increased abstraction to manipulate programs and numbers rather than designs, the ability to develop personal strategies for problem-solving rather than using existing schema, and the ability to change from directly creating alternatives to selecting the best variant of solutions provided.

In a review of the human factors literature pertaining to CAD, Barfield *et al.* (1986) found several job-related changes. New problem-solving skills are needed by designers such as pattern recognition, knowledge of design rules and relationships, complex decision making and the ability to process large amounts of information quickly. Moreover, the work pace of a job increases with CAD because decision making is now paced by the computer, and not the person. Finally, the authors suggest that some familiarity with computers may be important. The absence of this skill in other studies suggests it is probably only needed when CAD operators are expected to take on programming tasks, a situation not encountered in many organizations.

Table 8.1. AIDD survey of qualifications of CAD operators.

Q: *When operators were selected, did you look for any particular qualifications?*

20—*yes* 4—*no*

Q: *If yes, would you please list some of these?*

There were many answers to this question, but the following is a list of the most mentioned qualifications:

1—interest
2—initiative
3—enthusiasm
4—innovation
5—good design drafting skills
6—adaptability to change
7—self-motivation
8—logic oriented
9—good hand/eye coordination
10—visualization of objects, views
11—good communication skills
12—good work habits

Q: *Can you now identify any common characteristics of the CAD operators and list them in a value order list?*

The answers to this question were almost the same as the answers to above. The ones listed were the most mentioned in the order written:

1—highly creative
2—drafting design experience
3—enthusiasm
4—interest in CAD
5—good work and communication skills

These qualifications seem to reflect what most managers find existent in the best operators.

Other observers with primarily qualitative information about changes to jobs with CAD offer their conclusions. Down (1985), based on years of experience selling CAD to R&E shops, concludes that a major change with CAD is the increased communication imposed on drafters. He points out that since drafters are accustomed to solitary work with their own board, job requirements that necessitate a high degree of people contact would be inherently stressful. Describing the experiences of implementing CAD at AT&T, Wondrasch (1985) found that engineers dealing with CAD needed increased knowledge about computer software. In addition, as boundaries of the product realization process are extended with CAD, experience with human resources and skills to mediate turf battles inherent in extending boundaries were needed. Finally, Eaton (1985), describing General Motors' experiences with implementing CAD, identified a number of new skills for the CAD engineer at GM. Listed in Table 8.2, these new

Table 8.2. General Motors qualifications for an engineer with CAD.

"All right, then, what will engineering grads need to bring with them to the (CAD) workplace in the nineties?

- Deeper training in systems analysis. An ability to think in terms of complete, complex systems. To relate specifics to the system as a whole. To engineer synergistic results.
- A greater understanding of how electronic, electrical and mechanical disciplines interweave in the real fabric of industry.
- Training in 3-D computer graphics as basic design instruments.
- Familiarity with data base concepts, plus practical working experience, particularly with the newer, more powerful relational data bases.
- Knowledge of machine intelligence fundamentals. After 20 years in infancy, this technology will approach adulthood in the 1990s.
- Solid background in mathematics and physics.
- Broader knowledge of the science and materials.
- In-school experience with modelling and simulation techniques. These are basic tools for today's and tomorrow's engineers.
- Practical experience with macro languages.
- More extensive background in business economics. They have to become part of the engineering thought process.
- Last, but most important, is a creative approach to engineering. Creativity requires seeing beyond the obvious. In our business, it's what leads to Fieros and Saturns."

Reproduced from "The automotive engineering workpace of the nineties" by R. J. Eaton, by permission of the Copyright Owner.

job requirements can be summarized as an increased capacity to conduct thought experiments, think in terms of complete systems and from multidisciplinary perspectives, and have knowledge of macro languages, machine intelligence, data base concepts and fundamentals of mathematics and science.

Summary of effects of CAD on job tasks

The studies described above are briefly summarized in Table 8.3. In total, the few studies of CAD consequences appear to support the view that job contents with CAD are not determined solely by technology. Nor will the increased interdependence and mutual sharing across departments and functions automatically occur with CAD. Other factors such as the production process, industry, existing organizational design and management philosophy (e.g., about optimal job designs of workers) appear to be more 'deterministic' of job content and interdependence. Thus, while lower-level positions such as drafters could experience increased routinity with CAD and design engineers experience the opposite, such experiences result more from organizational decisions than technological features. The

Table 8.3. Summary of quantitative research on changes to job with CAD (from Barfield et al., *1986).*

	Information Technology			CAD		
Job dimension	Author	Sample	Finding	Author	Sample	Finding
Routinity	Bjorn-Anderson *et al.* (1979)	Clerks	More routinity, more tasks	Norton (1981)	Operators and managers	Less routinity for designers; more routinity for operators
	Gutek (1982)	Secretaries and managers	No change	Newton (1984)	Operators	No change in autonomy
	Mann and Williams (1960)	Clerks	Fewer routine and minor decision-making tasks	Wingert *et al.* (1981)	Managers	Less routinity
				Majchrzak *et al.* (1985a)	Engineers and drafters	No change in predictability of job
Workflow	Whisler (1970)	Clerks	More interdependence	Majchrzak *et al.* (1985a)	Engineers and drafters	No change in degree of reciprocal interdependence
	Mann and Williams (1960)	Clerks	More need for coordination			
Communication	Whisler (1970)	Clerks	Less interpersonal communication	AIDD (1983)	Operators	More need for communication skills
	Kerr and Hiltz (1982)	Review	More options for communication	Majchrzak *et al.* (1985a)	Engineers and drafters	More use of coordination models
	Edwards (1978)	Professionals	Increased degree and options for communication			
	Hiltz (1978)	Engineers and scientists	More communication			
	Rice and Case (1983)	Professionals	More communication			
	Short *et al.* (1976) Rice (1984)	Review	Less persuasiveness			

implication then is that an organization desiring to maximize the job content of all its workers with CAD could do so. Drafters could do more of the routine engineering tasks (e.g., facilities planning), freeing up designers' time for creative problem solving.

While it does not appear to be the case that one set of CAD job specifications can be delimited, the CAD research does suggest that overall skill requirements of most jobs with CAD are increasing. The implementation of CAD necessitates that engineers have the abilities to conceptualize abstractly, develop problem-solving strategies, apply systemic perspectives and have the facility to use knowledge about human resources and manufacturing procedures. Assuming that an organization implementing CAD is committed to keeping its drafters, the system creates skill requirements for drafters that are somewhat different than those of engineers. CAD drafters will need to increase their abilities to communicate ideas in their CAD jobs, be more creative, and have the ability to develop personal schema for solving problems. Such skills make it feasible for the CAD drafter of the future to optimally contribute to the design process.

Finally, research on information technologies and CAD suggest that CAD increases communication. However, specific ways that CAD can affect communication patterns have not yet been assessed. If this increased amount of communication is indeed focused on problem-solving design work, then the important benefits of CAD would appear to be realized. If the increased communication focuses on conflict around turf battles and priorities, any positive outcomes will be minimal at best. Nevertheless, in the absence of research specifically focused on CAD, one can only assume that the predictions from computer conferencing research would apply; that is, an integrated CAD system will have its most positive consequences for the organ ization when used for those tasks not involving substantial attitude changes about designs. In addition, CAD will be most effectively used for those phases in the design process that focus on structuring how a design problem will be solved, eliciting comments on designs from others, evaluating alternative solutions, and documenting results. Initial conceptualization of the design problem, solicitation of initial alternative solutions, and persuading others of the merits of a particular design are still best left to face-to-face conversation, rather than using CAD as the communication device.

What implications do these results have for the development of job descriptions and personnel selection procedures with CAD? Given that studies of the effects of information technologies have found that consequences for a job depend on the job's level in the organization, the content of CAD users' jobs in the future will probably be differentiated by level also. Computervision (1980) predicts four levels of jobs working with CAD. These levels and Computervision's recommended job descriptions for each are listed in Table 8.4. Briefly summarized from lowest to highest, these jobs are CAD operator, senior CAD operator, CAD designer and CAD engineering assistant. Note that according to Computervision, traditional design engineers are not on this list since they are not expected to be using CAD directly. Other observers of CAD, such as Eaton (1985) after his GM

Table 8.4. Computervision job descriptions for CAD personnel.

CAD operator	Prepares and corrects input media for engineering masters and diagrams; occasional contact with designers only; requires knowledge of systems commands and engineering drawings; entry level.
CAD operator-senior	Does job of CAD operators, plus creates and maintains computer library; requires 1–2 years experience with CAD, engineering drawings and hardware.
CAD designer	AAS who performs design and documentation studies on CAD applications; requires knowledge of CAD and knowledge of design and engineering fundamentals; knowledge of manufacturing processes also required; not an engineer.
CAD engineering assistant	Produces final CAD outputs through various data plotting and management routines; high school education required.

Reproduced from the Computervision Corporate Management Seminar on CAD/CAM, by permission of the Copyright Owner.

experience, would include engineers as CAD users.

Examining Computervision's four levels suggests that, on the average, job descriptions will not change with CAD although individual tasks across jobs will be reshuffled. Moreover, extending the list to include design engineers would probably yield job descriptions of engineers producing initial sketches and ideas as before (whether or not on CAD). One of the few activities likely to be added to future job descriptions is the need to communicate and coordinate with others—a job requirement primarily different for lower levels in the CAD job hierarchy.

While job descriptions may not change across all jobs with CAD, personnel selection and training for CAD jobs will be different since a whole new range of skills are needed. While the specific skills will differ for different applications of CAD, at a minimum CAD users will need to be selected for, or trained in, conceptualizing, problem-solving, human relations, communications, broad-based manufacturing and engineering knowledge, and creativity. Because of this mix of skills, CAD operators are not necessarily chosen for their drafting skills. In fact Jacobs (1985) found that seniority (i.e., job knowledge) was of little importance in employers' decisions about the selection of CAD users. Thus, criteria independent of technical tool-based skills become important for the selection of CAD personnel. It is no wonder, then, that the AIDD survey (1983) suggested that an additional criteria for selecting CAD personnel should be their expressed interest in learning the new system.

Effect of CAD on organizational procedures

A second category of consequences of CAD implementation is the effect on organizational procedures. As described in earlier chapters, one design change expected with the use of CAD is the increased standardization of drawings and graphic symbols. If CAD indeed increases standardization, then it is to be expected that this increased standardization would be accompanied by an increased formalization of organizational policies and procedures governing the use of CAD (Abeln, 1981; Barlini, 1985; Benn, 1983; Groover and Zimmers, 1984). Such an increased formalization could take a variety of different forms from more specific policies about the steps to take in the design process to policies governing time at a workstation.

Review of information technology research

Four empirical studies have examined the impact of information technology on the formalization of procedures in organizations. Alter (1976) interviewed managers involved in the implementation of 56 decision support systems (DSS) and found that the DSSs helped managers negotiate across organizational units. The effectiveness of the negotiation was fostered by formalizing the mechanics of the communication process and by providing a common conceptual basis across managers for decision making. Managers also commented that consistent definitions and formats across different organizational units were important aids to communication and made it easier to assess the impact of decisions on different units and managers. Finally, since the formalization ensured that information was reported consistently and there were formal rules governing its appropriate use, there was an increased acceptance by managers that the information they used was 'objective'. Clearly, Alter found that information technology increased formalization and this increase had additional consequences to the organization—all of which appeared to be positively valued.

In her review of ten case studies of effects of CBISs on managers, Stewart (1971) found that CBISs did indeed result in an increased formalization. This formalization was expressed as an increased concern for the accuracy of data, and more attention to the systematization of procedures, which translated into an increased use of formal procedures to complete work.

Bjorn-Andersen and associates (1979) also found increased formalization when examining clerks' jobs. The researchers point out, however, that the organizations they studied appeared to increase formalization of work procedures for the express purpose of reducing the number of mistakes that any single clerk could make. An organization willing to allow mistakes and experimentation in order to avoid the increased monotony associated with such formalized jobs may not have formalized organizational procedures to the same extent as the organizations in this study.

Mann and Williams (1960) also studied the effect of a CBIS on organizational formalization. They found that the level of formalization in terms of the rules and regulations did increase by substituting these rules for individuals' decisions. They reported that this increased formalization stripped some employees of those decisions that were the principal reward of their job.

These studies on the impact of information technology on organizational formalization suggest that computer-based systems do increase the use of formalized procedures. Does this experience hold true for CAD?

Review of CAD research

Majchrzak *et al.* (1985 a) studied the impact of CAD on formalization as perceived by 33 CAD users. They found that among CAD users, the greater the time spent on CAD the more the users reported formalized procedures for doing the job, more standardized operating procedures to cover situations encountered on the jobs, and a greater specification of job duties.

In the AIDD (1983) survey of organizations implementing CAD, respondents were asked if the CAD system had any impact on existing drafting standards. Of the 26% of the respondents reporting some change, specific changes mentioned included changes to document release procedures, signatures on revised drawings and special designations in log books.

In a Bureau of National Affairs (1984) review of documentation on workplace effects of visual display terminals (VDTs), it was found that many unions and state laws suggested formalized procedures on the amount of time workers were expected to sit in front of a terminal each work day, frequency with which the amount of exposure to radiation should be assessed, and proper ergonomic design considerations.

Personal experience and qualitative case studies have also found that CAD changes formalization of organizational procedures. Down (1985), with his experience selling and installing CAD systems, has found that to obtain the most benefit from the system, the organization must formalize the method by which design work is done, i.e., the use, development and integration of data bases, as well as the use of common language and symbols. Because drafting standards are already formalized, they are not expected to change. Palitto (1984), in his case study of CAD implementation at Firestone, found that a mistake made in the implementation process was transferring the workload immediately from manual design to CAD without allotting sufficient time to formulate procedures and policies for CAD use.

Finally, Hall (1984) describes specific ways in which policies and procedures with CAD need to be formalized. He describes one case study of a Fortune 500 electronic company in which he was asked to identify why productivity gains had not been achieved with CAD. Hall found that one reason for inadequate gains was that the design work process had not been changed to be aligned with the new technology. Specifically, he found that a logical, formalized approach to drawing creation was not being used by drafters; there were no formalized procedures for using existing drawings; design engineers were giving schematics to drafters without any procedures for ensuring readability, accuracy and quick interpretation; and symbols used on CAD were personally tailored so that different users could not easily converse with one another. Hall's suggestions for policies and procedures needing formalization with CAD are summarized in Table 8.5.

Table 8.5. Policies and procedures to formalize for efficient CAD systems: summary of recommendations.

Use of line weight options to narrow down options from 100 now provided with CAD to only those eight normally used. This will make drawing creation and revision easier.

Consider only 5–10 of the 256 layers available on CAD and assign them to the various types of drafting entities used (e.g., dimensioning lines, cross-hatching, notes and labels). This will encourage finer data structures, facilitate drawing modifications and reduce waste of time.

Standardize letter height.

Specify procedures for naming files.

Create libraries of symbols as well as details, drawings, programming, and basic geometric shapes.

Formalize procedures for system operation including presetting system to standards as defaults, specifying file-naming method, checkoffs for approval, and requirements for final plot.

Formalize/delineate a best approach to creating a drawing and the best way to handle revisions so that everyone does it in the same way.

Reproduced from Hall (1984), by permission of the Copyright Owner.

Summary of the effects of CAD on organizational procedures

The quantitative research studies discussed above are briefly presented in Table 8.6. This review of the research on CAD and information technologies suggests that CAD does formalize previously unspecified design methods and procedures. Since communication across organizational units in R&D has traditionally been complicated by idiosyncratic norms, language and symbols, the increased formalization with CAD is likely to overcome this difficulty and thereby increase communication and efficiency. However, as suggested by Mann and Williams (1960) and Bjorn-Andersen *et al.* (1979), increased formalization may not be positively viewed by all. Reactions of individuals to increased formalization will be examined later in this Chapter.

The effect of CAD on organizational structure

A third category of consequences of the implementation of CAD is on an organization's structure. Structure refers to the set of formal and informal ways in which decisions are made and implemented in an organization. Three aspects of structure, and the consequences of CAD for them, are discussed here. The three aspects of structure are differentiation, integration and centralization of decision

Table 8.6. Summary of quantitative research on the impact of CAD on the formalization of procedures (from Barfield et al., *1986).*

Author	Sample	Finding
Information technology		
Alter (1976)	Managers	Formalized mechanics of communication process which provided common conceptual basis across departments.
Stewart (1971)	Managers	More use of formal procedures to complete work.
Bjorn-Andersen *et al.* (1979)	Clerks	More formalization of work procedures.
Mann and Williams (1960)	Clerks	More formalization of decisions rules.
CAD		
Majchrzak *et al.* (1985a)	Engineers and drafters	More formalization in job duties.
AIDD (1983)	Operators	More formal procedures for releases, signatures on drawings, and log books.

making. Each of these aspects is explained and followed by a discussion of expected effects of CAD on each.

The first aspect of structure is the way organizational units or departments are distinguished from each other (called *differentiation*). By examining the differentiation of an organization's structure, we can tell what decisions are important or complex enough in an organization to be made by separate groups of individuals. A small company may choose to differentiate its units in the way depicted in Figure 8.3 (*a*). In this organization, only decisions made by production and marketing are felt to be sufficiently different to warrant differentiation. A larger or different company may feel that many more differentiated units are necessary, and it may base differentiation on different operations or functions. A more differentiated organizational structure is depicted in Figure 8.3 (*b*).

A second aspect of organizational structure is the way differentiated units are integrated (called *integration*). If an organization is to function properly, for every two differentiated units there must be a way for decisions made by those two units to be coordinated in some fashion. The decisions may be coordinated by someone at the top of the organization, as depicted in Figure 8.4 (*a*). In this figure, there are no formal mechanisms to horizontally integrate what the operations and administrative vice-presidents do. Instead, they must report to the President to achieve such integration. In Figure 8.4 (*b*) a different integration pattern is presented: integration is achieved horizontally as well as vertically. That is, the vice-president of operations can coordinate directly with the vice-president of administration.

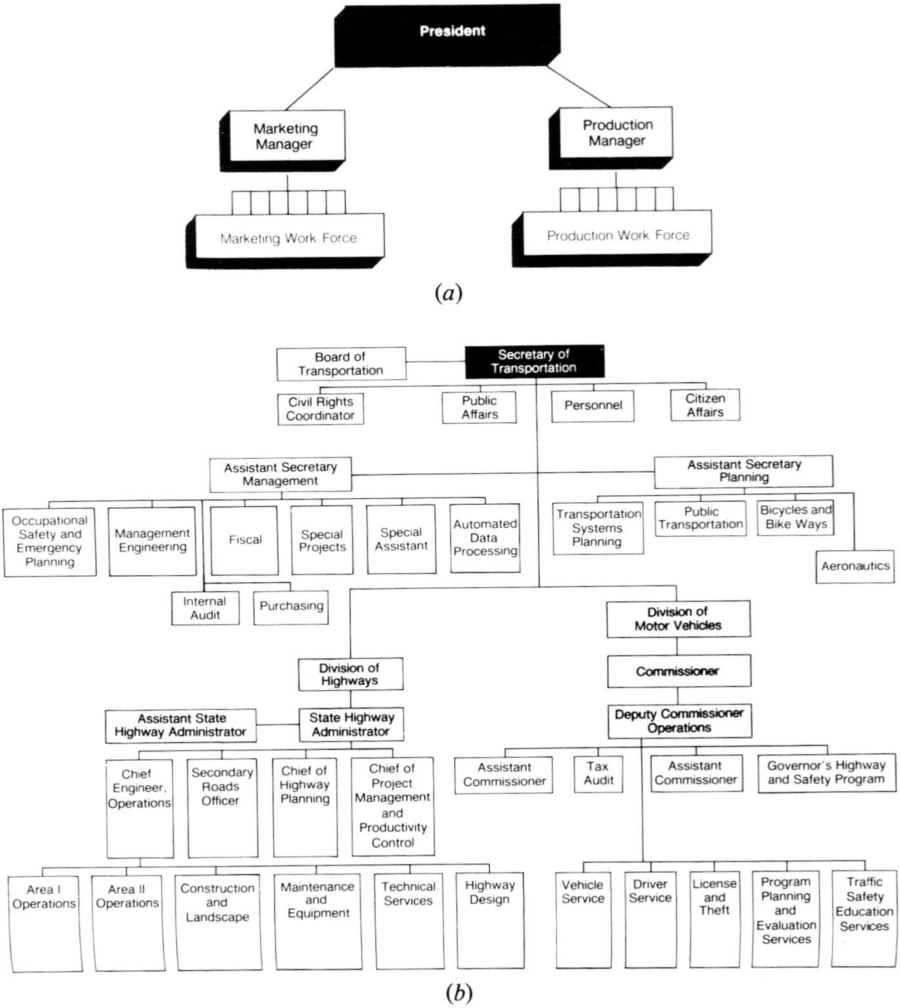

Figure 8.3. Examples of differentiation of organizational structure: (a) a less differentiated structure, and (b) a complex, highly differentiated structure (from Anderson (1984)).

Integration is important since differentiated units tend to develop their own goals, priorities, norms and modes of operation. By building mechanisms for integrating units into the structure, inherent conflicts between departments can be resolved. Otherwise, such commonly heard phrases as 'the right hand [e.g., marketing or engineering] doesn't know what the left hand [e.g., manufacturing] does' are heard. Common integrative mechanisms include dotted-line reporting

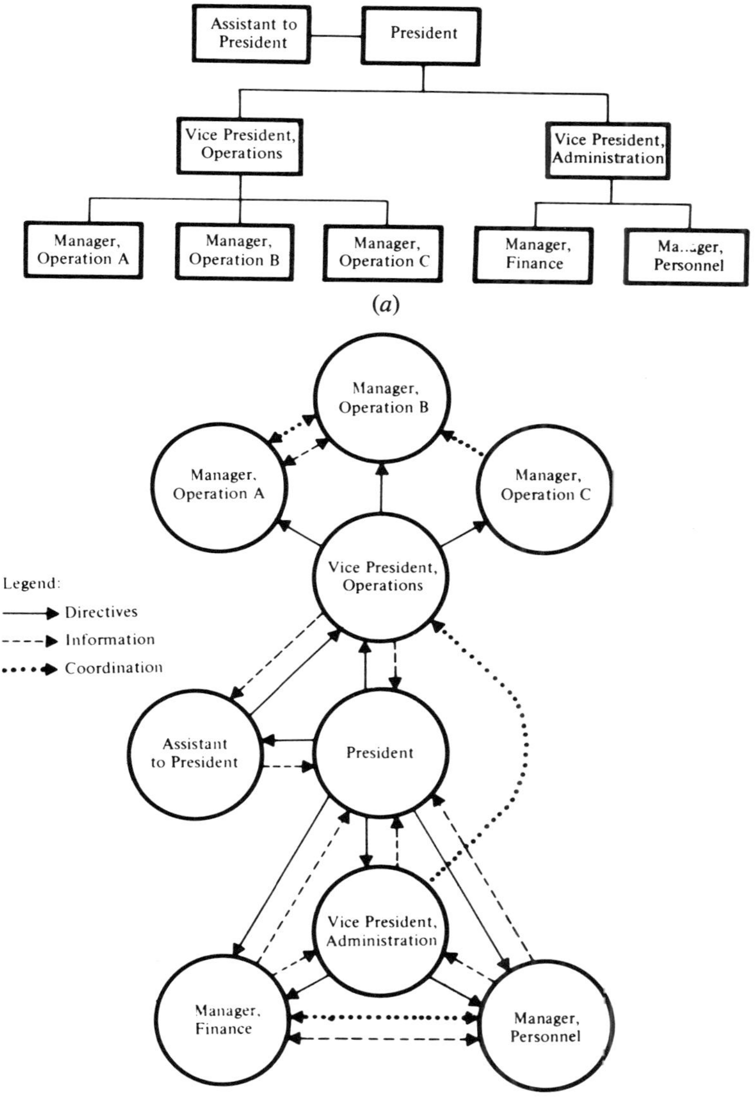

Figure 8.4. Examples of integration of organizational structure; (a) conventional integration, and (b) a systems approach to integration (from Tomeski and Lazarus, 1975, courtesy the Copyright Owner).

relationships such as those which exist in matrix-type organizations, coordinating or steering committees, individuals specifically designated as boundary-spanners (such as strategic planners or product expediters), and task forces.

A third aspect of organizational structure is the degree of *centralization of decision making* specified by the organization. Many different types of decisions (administrative, operations, procedural, strategic) can be centralized or decentralized; but most organizations follow a general pattern where most major decisions are either centralized or decentralized. Reexamining Figure 8.4 (*a*), one could envisage that most discretion on the job is not provided to anyone below those depicted on the chart; that is, strategic decisions or decisions about work procedures or scheduling are handled by the managers and not by subordinates working below them. In contrast, it may also be possible that this organization has adopted an essentially decentralized structure where managers are not the decision makers as much as the facilitators or coordinators for a consensus-development process with subordinates. Centralization is important since it determines who makes decisions in an organization about what. Thus, an organization that centralizes its CAD operations is signalling to its staff that only a centralized group of people can make decisions about CAD operations.

In sum, three characteristics of an organization's structure can be examined in terms of how they are affected by CAD: differentiation of units, integration between units, and centralization of decision making. From literature on organizational theory, several speculative propositions about specific changes to the structure resulting from the new technology can be postulated.

First, as concluded in the earlier sections of this Chapter, the implementation of new technologies such as CAD will yield increased communication and formalization. These changes can be expected to lead to a greater use of integrative and coordination mechanisms between units. For example, with the implementation of CAD, the use of committees as well as people serving in liaison capacities to help coordinate decision making across functional areas would be expected to increase.

Another prediction is that the more effective the integrative mechanisms, the less is the need to keep organizational units differentiated (Lawrence and Lorsch, 1967). For example, as CAD promotes integrative mechanisms for overcoming traditional barriers between design engineering and manufacturing, it is predicted that there will be less need to keep design and manufacturing separate and independent with their own goals, staff and priorities.

A third prediction is that with a decrease in the need for differentiation, the increased integration brought about by CAD is expected to encourage decentralization of decision making (Fry, 1982). For example, in a highly integrated CAD system, many decisions have been incorporated into the computer. To ensure an optimized design process, those decisions that are left to be made (e.g., definition of design problems) should most probably be made by those at the level most knowledgeable of the design process. Thus, managers with CAD systems will make fewer decisions themselves, allowing drafters and designers to innovate in only ways they know how. This new status quo would be manifested then as an increased decentralization of decision-making authority.

A fourth prediction about the effect of CAD on organizational structure stems from the Lawrence and Lorsch (1967) notion that units with different goals tend to become differentiated units. Thus, when CAD is installed, staff working with CAD may actually have very different goals and priorities and activities than staff continuing to work with manual drafting. For example, a CAD group may do more design modifications or plot presentations than a non-CAD group of designers and drafters. Organizations, therefore, may find themselves needing to differentiate between those working and not working on CAD—that is, create two subunits.

In sum, four predictions were derived from the theoretical literature:

1. CAD will increase the use of integrative mechanisms between different departments.
2. CAD will decrease the need to differentiate between different functions tied into the system (e.g., manufacturing and engineering).
3. CAD will decentralize decision-making authority over the design process to designers and drafters.
4. CAD will create a need to establish a differentiated unit of CAD users with goals, priorities and policies different from those of non-users.

Review of information technology research

A few studies on the consequences of information technologies have focused on the impact on organizational structure. Bjorn-Andersen *et al.* (1979) found that, as predicted, the implementation of CBISs created an increased need for integrative and coordination mechanisms. However, in terms of centralization of decision making, only decisions about data processing changed, with such decisions made by more centralized groups of people.

In Whisler's (1970) study of the implementation of CBISs, a complex effect was found on organizational structure. Specifically, those departments which greatly depended on other units to do their job, which focused primarily on problem solving rather than problem definition, and which worked under high time pressure, experienced more changes to the organizational structure with the CBIS than departments with inverse characteristics. It is interesting to note that engineering departments, to meet market conditions with or without CAD, have been predicted to become more like Whisler's first group of departments, i.e., high job interdependence, heavy focus on problem solving and high time pressure. The implication for CAD might then be that engineering units that become more responsive to market conditions are more likely to adaptively restructure their organization as CAD is implemented.

Both Mann and Williams (1960) and Sanders (1968) conducted case studies on the impact of CBISs on organizational structure. Mann and Williams found that the CBIS increased the need for coordination since the increased interdependence among units necessitated the need to have all decisions reviewed by all parts of the organization. Increased coordination was manifested as spending more time in meetings. In addition, there was more centralized control around procedures and new centers for coordination. Sanders' case study found that the CBIS increased decentralization of authority over how jobs were done. The researcher found that this decentralization was due, in part, to the fact that top management had greater trust in lower-level managers having the information to make decisions. This trust was coupled with the top managers' knowledge that, with the computer, they could monitor the basis on which lower-level decisions were made.

Pfeffer and Leblevici (1977) surveyed CEOs at 38 companies about their perceptions of differentiation and decentralization given different degrees of CBIS implementation. The researchers found that organizations with more employees using a CBIS had a greater number of different departments (i.e., increased differentiation) as well as more decisions made by lower-level staff (i.e., increased decentralization).

Finally, Ackoff (1967) reviewed the literature on implementation of MISs and found that a common assumption among system developers was that more communication between departments means better coordination of decisions and performance. However, in reviewing the research, he found that if performance measures between departments conflict with each other, communication between departments may hinder rather than facilitate organizational performance. Information that creates stalemates and undercutting is far worse than no information at all. Therefore, Ackoff concludes that the free flow of information without aligning cross-departmental goals should not be permitted.

In summary, this research on the impact of information technologies on organizational structure indicates that some of the predictions were borne out while others have no conclusive results. As predicted, information technology increases the use of integrative mechanisms, i.e., meetings, committees and coordinative procedures. The effect on the differentiation of units is far less clear. No studies mentioned finding less differentiation with computerization as expected, and only one study found that a new department of MIS was created. Moreover, effects on decentralization of decision-making authority are even less clear. One study found centralization to have increased, two found it to have decreased, and one found it to have stayed the same. Perhaps an explanation for these findings can be identified in Whisler's (1970) results where only certain departments displaying certain characteristics showed structural changes. Examining the generalizability of these findings specifically with CAD is the next step.

Review of CAD research

In one empirical study on CAD, Schaffitzel and Kersten (1985) studied the introduction of CAD systems in 20 German companies. They found that in the introductory phase, the restructuring and designing of the organization was a decisive factor in the success of the CAD implementation. More specifically, they suggest that this restructuring necessitated creating interfaces between design and manufacturing that were in addition to those interfaces naturally occurring via the drawing. One type of interface they recommend is the use of a centralized CAD department responsible for coordination activities—a change toward more differentiation.

In the Majchrzak *et al.* (1985 a) study of CAD users and non-users, the effect of CAD on decentralization of decision making was examined. Decentralization was examined in terms of the degree to which the respondent perceived that s/he could make job decisions without checking with a superior. Results indicated that the time users spent on a CAD system was not related to perceptions of increased decentralization.

In Palitto's (1984) case study of CAD implementation at Firestone, he found that the CAD system changed a narrowly focused unit (facility planning) into a service organization for electrical, civil and mechanical engineering. This group was eventually split off from the rest of drafting into two separate departments.

Delvac (1981) describes a case study of Sperry Corporation's CAD implementation in which the CAD system served as a primary stimulus for a move to place both the Design Engineering and Manufacturing Systems groups in the same facility. The two groups report to different directorates but the closer proximity, as an integrative mechanism, "has resulted in significant payback. Design engineering now develops geometric part descriptions which are accessed by Manufacturing without alteration for use in preparing the numerical control instructions required to operate our N/C Machine Tools" (p. 644).

Davine and Richards (1981) present another case study of the implementation of CAD, this time at a GE Ordnance Systems Division. They found that optimal use of CAD involved the effort of many functions (engineering, drafting, manufacturing, quality control, finance, etc.). Since most organizations are without a management entity to direct such a system, a typical problem arose which consisted of soliciting the voluntary cooperation across functions. To resolve this problem, a new integrative mechanism was established, called the CAD/CAM committee, which represented each function and established goals and priorities, as well as addressed system aspects requiring multi-functional agreements.

Finally, the AIDD (1983) survey also asked questions about organizational structure. Respondents were asked to list any positive or negative statements as guidelines for organizing a CAD department. One major guideline read as follows: "The CAD section or department should be operated as another 'community' within the company. It should be available to all personnel for learning its capabilities" (p. 12).

Summary of the effects of CAD on organizational structure

The quantitative studies described above are briefly presented in Table 3.7. As is apparent from the table, quantitative CAD research on this issue is sparse at best. However, it appears that CAD does affect an organization's structure. As predicted, implementation of CAD leads to an increased use of integrative mechanisms. Such mechanisms include matrix structures (Benn, 1983), committees,

Table 8.7. Summary of quantitative research on the impact of CAD on organizational structure (from Barfield et al., *1986).*

Author	Sample	Finding
Information technology		
Bjorn-Andersen *et al.* (1979)	Banks	More need for integrative mechanisms; more centralization of data processing decisions.
Whisler (1970)	Life insurance companies	More structural changes among highly interdependent, problem-solving, and time pressure departments.
Mann and Williams (1960)	Utility company	More meetings and centralized control over work procedures.
Sanders (1968)	Service	Decentralization of decision-making to lower-level managers.
Pfeffer and Leblevici (1977)	Variety	More differentiated departments and decentralization.
CAD		
Schaffitzel and Kersten (1985)	German companies	More use of structural interfaces between design and manufacturing.
Majchrzak *et al.* (1985a)	Engineers and drafters' perceptions	No relationship between CAD use and perceived decentralization.

and moving engineering and manufacturing into the same facility. Moreover, as predicted, several organizations found the need to create a new differentiated unit responsible for the new technology given the differing goals and priorities it demanded.

The precise effect of CAD on the degree of differentiation across all major units in the organization is unclear. This was not studied in any of the CAD research cited above and the information technology literature was unclear on this point. Apparently, whether or not the increased integration posed by CAD actually allows organizations to combine units (e.g., engineering and drafting or design and manufacturing) is probably more a function of the organization than it is of the technology itself.

Finally, the effect of CAD on centralization of decision-making authority cannot be resolved from the research. In the one study that tangentially touched on this topic, CAD users reported no change in centralization of decision making. However, given the uniqueness of this study and the lack of clarity in findings from information technologies, any conclusions are premature at best. Most probably the case is that suggested by Ellis (1984): that technology does not have a determining effect on the centralization or decentralization of all decisions. Instead, CAD increases options for organizations to centralize or decentralize, including the option to do both. Thus, organizations can, with CAD, control or centralize some information at the same time they decentralize other responsibilities to drafters and engineers. For example, with CAD, CAD operations and design standards may be centralized while selection of design team members or the determination of when a design is finalized could be left to the discretion of design staff. As with job content, the determination will probably be based more on management philosophy than on features of the CAD system.

Effect of CAD on miscellaneous aspects of the workplace

In addition to the three sets of consequences of CAD to the workplace that have been discussed thus far, five additional workplace characteristics can be identified as being potentially affected by CAD. These five have been identified because available empirical literature provides some evidence to test expectations. These five are:

1. Job displacement
2. Performance monitoring
3. Wages
4. Power
5. Career development

The effect of CAD on job displacement

Fears of job displacement with new technology have run rampant for years. Economists have predicted that lower-level employees (e.g., drafters) would suffer major unemployment. Are these fears based on empirical evidence as they apply to technologies such as CAD?

Three studies on information technologies discuss the effect of implementing information technologies on employment. Bjorn-Andersen *et al.* (1979) found no change in employment levels as the result of the implementation of a CBIS. In fact, the researchers found that to keep the technology functioning only a very small number of employees could be laid off and thus operating costs of the CBIS were dramatically underestimated.

Gutek *et al.* (1984), interviewed 250 users and managers implementing office automation. They found reductions in labor levels during the OA implementation period and beyond to be very slight. Of the 55 work groups represented in their sample, only 15% reported substantial reductions in staff with 51% reporting absolutely no change in staffing levels.

Finally, in a survey of 14 large employers each using over 1000 VDT terminals, the Bureau of National Affairs (1984) found little worker displacement.

Quantitative research on worker displacement resulting from CAD does not exist. However, case studies (Down, 1985; Majchrzak, 1985) find that drafters are not laid off with CAD. In fact, in its early stages of implementation, CAD creates an increased need for personnel able to input designs (e.g., drafters). Thus, rather than massive lay-offs, CAD implementation has been met with retraining.

The effect of CAD on performance monitoring

Computers have always generated fears about unobtrusive performance monitoring; that is, with CAD, upper management can now assess performance without either the knowledge or approval of subordinates.

In a survey of supervisors and users of CBISs, Kling (1978) found that while supervisors recognized that computers could be used to monitor employee activities without subordinate approval, few supervisors used it for that purpose. Reasons given included that (*a*) the supervisors already knew the performance of subordinates and did not need the additional information provided by the computer; and (*b*) the supervisors understood that the explicit use of the computers for performance monitoring would produce resentment and controversy among subordinates over the meaning of the data.

Johnson and associates (1985) studied the impact of word processing on 194 organizations and found only a few organizations using the computer to monitor performance. This finding was felt to be due in part to the fact that the performance measures provided by the word processor were constrained to counting output such as lines and pages typed. Other measures typically felt to be indicative of performance such as turnaround time, client satisfaction, etc., were not available on the system and thus needed to be assessed in more obtrusive ways.

Mann and Williams' (1960) case study of a CBIS implementation found that with the computer, individual responsibilities became more obvious and easier to evaluate since the tighter standards associated with increased formalization made errors more detectable.

Examining ten case studies of CBIS effects on management, Stewart (1971) found that use of the computer increased the possibilities of control by management but that this opportunity was not always exercised. BNA's survey of 14 organizations using VDTs had similar results: less than 50% measured worker productivity with the computer.

Finally, Bjorn-Andersen *et al.* (1979) found that the CBISs increased the degree of control that supervisors could exert since tasks were more formalized. Ironically, they report, those supervisors who understood the system did not use the computer for control; rather they relied more on personal control. Only those who did not understand the system very well tended to use it to monitor performance.

There is no research specifically focused on CAD. Yet these results suggest that CAD and similar information technologies will indeed increase the possibility of closer and unobtrusive performance monitoring, as feared. However, contrary to fears, the use of the computer for such monitoring is not deterministic; that is, management philosophy probably has more determining power on the use of computers for performance monitoring than technology. In addition, as people' tasks become more interdependent with CAD (as discussed earlier), an individual's own performance becomes less a function of individual than group activities. As a result, the notion of measuring individual-level performance is less meaningful. Therefore, group-level measures of performance, which probably cannot be assessed on CAD (such as client satisfaction with drawings or rapidity with which drawings move through the approval process), will be needed.

The effect of CAD on wages

Another fear with CAD is that management will perceive many jobs to be deskilled; thus, wages will be depressed in accordance to these perceptions. The one finding on this topic was obtained from the AIDD (1983) survey of organizations using CAD. In the survey, respondents were specifically asked if personnel selected internally to operate the CAD system were given a wage increase when they were assigned to CAD. Twenty-two of the 24 respondents reported no increase; nor were higher job classifications assigned. Therefore, while the survey did not explicitly ask if wages were decreased, the likely interpretation of such results is that there were no changes in wages at all. However, it should be noted that if, as discussed earlier on the impact of CAD on job tasks, CAD necessitates an increase in skills, there does not appear to be a salary increase concomitant with these new skills.

The effect of CAD on power

When an organizational change occurs, the question always arises as to whether or not there is a shift in power, both individual and departmental, in the organization. A few studies—none of which dealt with CAD specifically—have addressed the issue of power shifts in organizations implementing new information technologies.

Danziger *et al.* (1982) surveyed computer use among 500 city and county governments. With regard to power shifts, they found that no single group appeared to be a substantial beneficiary of power shifts. Most shifts that did occur conformed to the existing general structure in the organization; that is, if the government was mayor-controlled, the mayor increased his/her power with the computer while if the government was controlled by a city-manager, the power shifted toward the manager. But in no cases were power shifts substantial.

Kling (1980), citing a study by Bjorn-Andersen and Pederson (1977), found that power shifts occurred in the organization even when no such consequences appeared to have been intended. Moreover, shifts in power as perceived by the person did not always coincide with the perceptions of others. For example, plant managers implementing a computerized production scheduling system perceived that they had increased their power; however, peers perceived no such change. Production managers perceived they had lost power; and again peers perceived no such change.

Finally, Stewart (1971) in her ten case studies found that power shifts tended to occur only if the CBIS affected the relative importance of different departments. Otherwise, little change in power was observed.

These results suggest that the implementation of CAD will not necessarily cause a shift in power in the engineering/manufacturing organization, unless, as Stewart suggests, the relative importance of these units are affected. However, as Kling describes, power shifts may occur even when they are not intended. We must remember that power is a perceptual phenomenon—what others think is a change in power may not necessarily be agreed upon by all parties involved. For this reason alone, a concern about shifts in power—perceived or real—may become important as a consequence of CAD.

The effect of CAD on career development

A final miscellaneous workplace change expected when CAD is introduced in the workplace is a change in the career development pattern of drafters and design engineers. It has been speculated that a change is likely given the increased skill requirements of most jobs with CAD.

While again there are no studies specifically examining CAD, several studies on information technologies provide some clues of what the future may hold. Mann and Williams (1960) found that the CBIS affected career development by causing the organization to reassess its criteria for supervisory promotions. This was primarily due to the fact that technological change taxed the supervisors' combination of technical, administrative and human relations skills, and therefore provided an opportunity to assess how well supervisors do.

In Tapscott's (1982) review of office automation implementation, he found that office systems can provide a catalyst and a cause for changes in career development. Specifically, he found that new career paths were opened, such as secretaries or clerical staff being promoted to office managers or systems analysts. This opening of career paths was also found by Johnson *et al.* (1985) in her study of 194 organizations implementing word processing. Iacono and Kling (1985) describe a word processing clerk's career path which ended with the position of director of all administrative services. However, as Johnson *et al.* (1985) found, structured and approved career paths are not yet developed in most organizations. Promotion tends to be *ad hoc* and ill-planned.

In sum, if the results of these studies are any indication, CAD is likely to lead to the possibility of new career paths. For example, in one company implementing CAD, design engineers and drafters working with CAD have taken on such new jobs as internal CAD consultant, CAD training coordinator, systems specialist, and marketer of CAD services to other departments in the organization. However, while the possibility of new career paths exists with CAD, organizations may not take advantage of this opportunity. In one organization, CAD operators have even more dead-end careers than before since they are doing menial, non-engineering work in an engineering environment (Newton, 1986).

Summary of the effects of CAD on the workplace

This review of the literature on the impact of information and CAD technology in the workplace leads to several conclusions. First, CAD's consequences for the workplace are not all technologically determined. That is, many of the consequences of CAD are not as determined by the technology as other factors in the work context, such as management philosophy, the production process, market conditions, personnel policies, job design, worker morale and organization structure. Some of these workplace characteristics which will not necessarily change as a function of the implementation of a CAD system include:

1. Decentralization of authority to drafters and design engineers to make decisions about their work process.
2. Content and routineness of jobs.
3. Degree to which personnel from different functional areas involved in the complete design process work with each other in a mutually interdependent and supportive fashion to develop design solutions.
4. Use of the computer to monitor performance.
5. Power of different people in different departments.

For these workplace characteristics, then, the CAD implementor and researcher needs to look much more broadly at the entire organizational context in which CAD is installed. Decision-making authority will be centralized with CAD if management is opposed to granting discretion to lower levels or is particularly concerned about efficiency. Job content will change depending on whether the system is designed for the 'lowest common denominator' or for people to grow and evolve their own capabilities. The interdependence between engineering, drafting and manufacturing that is so greatly desired among CAD implementors of today will not result from implementing CAD. Barriers to interdependence (e.g., different rewards, languages, attitude, management support) must be identified and appropriately discouraged. Computer-based performance monitoring which is done without the consent of the subordinate is most likely to be done by managers now doing other kinds of unobtrusive, detailed monitoring. A manager who measures how long a drafter sits at his board as an indicator of hard work is likely to count the amount of time a terminal is logged on as an equivalent measure. More useful measures and monitoring procedures are likely to come only from more enlightened managers. Finally, the occurrence of power shifts is most likely when different departments lose or gain previously hard-earned power. Therefore, systems which are implemented such that relative power positions are presented need not result in unintended or inappropriate shifts in power.

The fact that the implementation of CAD does not directly create changes in these areas suggests that CAD can or should be used as part of a much more general business strategy for organizational growth. If the firm is attempting to gain a greater market share by producing less expensive parts, the implementation of CAD can be used as a catalyst for restructuring jobs and organizational design to meet this challenge. CAD will aid the process; alone it will not meet the need.

While some workplace characteristics are not determined primarily by the implementation of CAD technology, some very specific workplace effects attributable to CAD were identified from the research. These are:

1. Increased use of integrative devices.
2. Increased and different communication patterns on the job.
3. Increased skill requirements.
4. Increased formalization of work methods.
5. Possibility of alternative career paths for engineers and drafters.
6. No change in job displacement.
7. No change in wages.

Given knowledge of these workplace consequences, CAD implementors can now prepare their implementation plans accordingly. However, none of these changes will necessarily yield the positive benefits desired of CAD. Unless appropriately managed, they may not have any effect on the outcome whatsoever. For example, communication patterns will change to encourage more communication with more people, but if management actively discourages such communication, no increase in communication will be observed. Moreover, even if achieved, these workplace changes may not be accepted wholeheartedly by CAD users. It is this latter set of issues which is the focus of the remainder of this chapter.

8.3. Individuals' reactions to jobs with CAD

So far, this Chapter has focused on the consequences of CAD for the workplace. In the following, the effects of CAD implementation on individuals' reactions to the workplace are explored.

Individuals can evaluate their jobs in a number of ways: they can assess its challenge to them, the negative effect it has on their non-work life, or their contentment with it. Three such evaluations or reactions have been examined in the research literature as being affected by the implementation of such new technologies as CAD:

1. Perceived stress of the job.
2. Motivating potential of the job.
3. Satisfaction with the job.

The effect of CAD on the perceived stress of the job

One reaction individuals can have to their jobs with CAD is to report high or low levels of stress and pressure. In fact, a concern expressed by potential users of new technology is that the computer-pacing and restrictions imposed by the technology will increase the amount of stress the individual experiences on the job (see, for example, BNA, 1984). Research on the impact of information technology provides some insight into this potentially problematic reaction of workers.

Lucas (1975 a) studied the impact of information technologies in 16 organizations involving over 2000 users. He found that information overload created by the systems was a major stressor reported by the users.

In a similar vein to that of Lucas, Ackoff's (1967) review of the MIS literature found that two common assumptions made by system designers were that the greatest deficiency of managers is the lack of relevant information, and that managers will use information effectively when they obtain it. Ackoff then reviewed the data pertaining to these assumptions and found nonconfirmatory results. He found that managers are not lacking in relevant information; they already receive too much information as it is. Rather the greatest deficiency of managers is a lack of a filtering, evaluation and condensation system necessary to identify relevant over irrelevant information. Moreover, managers seldom use information effectively, especially for complex problems such as those involving probabilistic outcomes. Therefore, providing information alone is not sufficient, rather systems need to be designed to allow the filtering process to distinguish relevant from irrelevant information, as well as decision rules and performance feedback to identify mistakes made in solving complex problems. There is no reason to believe at this point that these issues have been considered in most MISs and CAD systems.

In her longitudinal study of 150 users of an electronic information exchange system, Hiltz (1984) also examined the impact of information overload. She found that, in terms of users' reactions to the system, "one serious adaptation problem for users was information overload" (p.147). Kling's (1978) survey of CBIS users also found reports of increased job pressure with increased computer use.

Finally, the Bjorn-Andersen *et al.* (1979) study of CBIS implementation found no uniform effect of the CBIS on workers' control over their work pace. If work pace and stress are related, this would imply that in their study, effects on stress were not conclusive.

The effect of CAD, specifically, on perceived stress has been examined in a few studies, summarized by Barfield *et al.* (1986). In their review, the authors conclude that stress increases due to the computer-paced nature of the CAD system. Newton (1984) also studied the effect of CAD on somatic complaints as manifestations of stress. In his survey of CAD and non-CAD drafters, Newton found very few differences between the groups concerning somatic complaints.

In summary, this review suggests that CAD is likely to lead to information overload. In addition, CAD will change traditionally self-paced jobs into jobs paced by the computer. While such changes to the job as information overload and reduced control over work pacing are likely to lead to increased stress, studies supporting this claim have not as yet been done.

The effect of CAD on the motivating potential of a job

The notion that the way people perceive aspects of their jobs helps to motivate them to work harder in their jobs has received widespread theoretical and research attention. Herzberg's (Herzberg *et al.*, 1959) two-factor theory of work motivation suggested that some aspects of the job (referred to as the intrinsic factors) serve as motivators for job encumbents. These factors include achievement, recognition, responsibility, advancement, the work itself, and the possibility of growth.

Developed in part from Herzberg's work, Hackman and Oldham's (1975) job characteristics model of worker motivation suggests that there are three critical psychological states that need to be present for an individual to be motivated to do well in the job: experienced meaningfulness of work, experienced responsibility for outcomes of work, and knowledge of the actual results of work activities. Each psychological state can be enhanced by different aspects of the job—in particular five specific aspects of the job are named as most likely to enhance the psychological states. These five are: skill variety; identity with a completed task; significance of the task on others; autonomy; and feedback from others and the job itself. The Hackman and Oldham model is depicted in Figure 8.5.

Note that these theories of work motivation, as well as others (e.g., Maslow, 1954; Vroom, 1964), rely primarily on people's perceptions of their jobs. While perceptions of jobs may have some basis in the actual job content, numerous factors other than the job content itself combine to influence people's perceptions (see, for example, Salancik and Pfeffer, 1977). Examples of factors that combine to influence perceptions of jobs include a person's prior expectations about the job, peers' evaluations of the job, and the person's view of the way the world should and does operate. As a result of these factors, perceptions of the job may or may not correspond to the actual job tasks performed. Therefore, while the review of the effect of CAD on job content described earlier showed few technologically determined effects, perceptions of the jobs may yield different results.

Given that perceptions and realities of jobs may differ, research on job perceptions of technology users were examined. From the Hackman and Oldham model described above, it was predicted that (*a*) the increased formalization found on the job as a result of CAD would yield perceptions of decreased autonomy on the job; (*b*) the increased skill requirements of CAD would yield perceptions of increased variety and possibilities of growth; and (*c*) the increased coordination

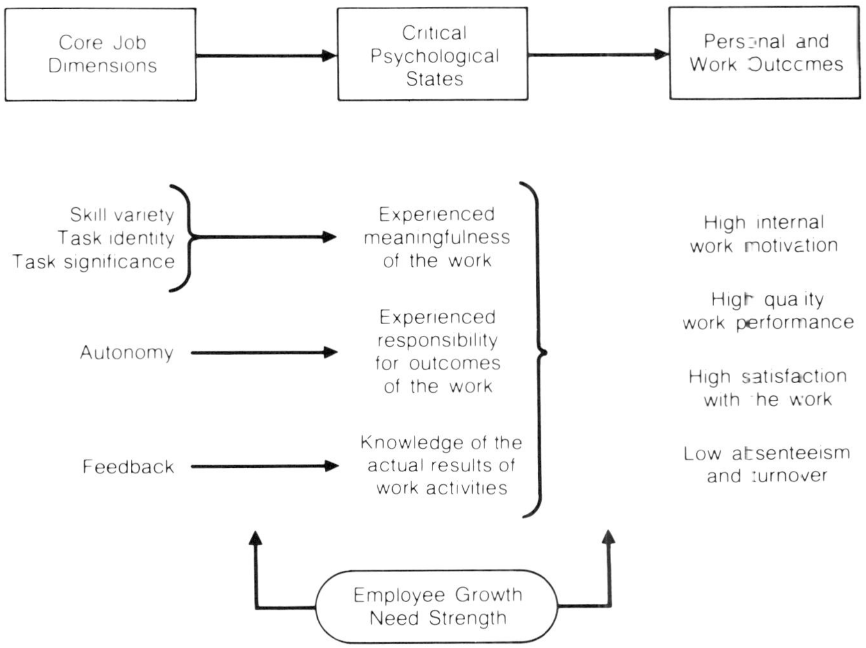

Figure 8.5. The Hackman and Oldham (1975) job characteristics model.

needed on the job with CAD would yield perceptions of increased feedback from others and increased feelings of responsibility over the finished products.

Several studies have examined the effect of information technology on perceptions of the job. Bjorn-Andersen *et al.* (1979) surveyed computer users about their perceptions of the changes to their job resulting from the CBISs. They found that many respondents claimed that perceptions of autonomy decreased; however, large numbers of respondents claimed that the computer system had no impact on most of the other 40 aspects of the job queried.

Dickson *et al.* (1980) studied the implementation failure of an MIS in a post office and found that a primary cause of the system's failure was that performance information was automatically measured by the system and was never fed back to employees. As a result of the new system, perceptions of adequate feedback on the job dramatically decreased.

Kling (1978) surveyed 1558 managers, analysts and clerks using CBISs. He found that most users perceived that the use of computers enlarged their jobs, i.e., increased those aspects of the jobs which are considered to motivate people to work harder. In contrast to Kling, Staehle (1982) surveyed 245 users of VDTs in 14 organizations and found that users did not believe that the VDT had enriched their work, contributed to work satisfaction, permitted freer organization of work, clarified the context of work, or increased the significance of work or recognition by colleagues.

Edwards' (1978) survey of 100 users of an office automation system found that the increased flexibility with changes provided by the system increased the user's sense of control or autonomy, as well as his/her identity with completing a finished document. Johnson *et al.* (1985), in a much larger study of office automation implementation, found similar results.

Finally, Gutek (1982) studied the adjustment over time of a secretary and a manager to a computerized managerial workstation. One of her major findings was that while the time actually needed for different job activities changed little, the system increased the secretary's evaluation of her work, such as the challenge, sense of accomplishment, and creativity provided by the job. The perceptions of the manager about his job changed very little.

Four CAD studies have focused more precisely on the effect of CAD users' perceptions of their jobs. In Majchrzak *et al.*'s (1985 a) survey of CAD users and non-users, the more time users spent on the CAD system, the less autonomy they perceived in their jobs. Moreover, CAD users indicated that they derived significantly more identity in completing an entire product when they used CAD than when they were using manual drafting boards; moreover their sense of identity was greater than that perceived by non-users. CAD also had an interesting effect on workers' perceived variety and possibilities of growth with the job. While all CAD users did not differ significantly from all non-users, for those CAD users whose jobs were less routine than non-users, variety and possibilities of growth were perceived to have increased. In other words, only when CAD created the desired workplace changes of decreased job routineness was CAD associated with enhanced perceptions of more motivating jobs.

Norton (1981) found similar results to those of Majchrzak *et al.* in his survey of CAD operators. He found that the effect of CAD on people's perceived ingenuity and care in designs were moderated by management; that is, to the extent that management provided for more autonomy and responsibility with CAD, ingenuity and care increased.

Johansson (1986) examined the implementation of CAD among designers in eight organizations. He found that work with CAD was judged as more interesting and meaningful. Newton (1984) found that perceived job autonomy did not differ for CAD users and non-users.

The literature on the impact of information technologies on people's perceptions is equivocal. In some studies, perception of the jobs decreased with technological implementation (c.f., Bjorn-Andersen *et al.*, 1979; Dickson *et al.*, 1980). In other studies, the perception that computers led to enlarged jobs was found (c.f., Edwards, 1978; Gutek, 1982; Johnson *et al.*, 1985; Kling, 1978), while in some studies no changes in perception were reported (c.f., Bjorn-Andersen *et al.*, 1979; Gutek, 1982). From research on CAD, it appears that the most likely explanation and prediction is that suggested by Norton (1981) and Majchrzak *et al.* (1985 a):

that perception of jobs will change only to the extent that some pertinent workplace changes take place. While clearly the workplace changes and perceptual changes need not be one-to-one (as Kling demonstrates), some positive workplace change must occur if any positive changes in job perceptions are to occur.

The effect of CAD on job satisfaction

Job satisfaction is affected by multiple factors. Such factors include not only the design or content of the job, but other organizational, personal and non-work variables as well. For example, a person may be dissatisfied not because his or her job is not intrinsically motivating, but because the pay does not seem to be commensurate with the effort exerted or because new financial strains at home necessitate a greater concern for financial compensation. Despite the multifaceted nature of job satisfaction determinants, there has been much speculation about the possible effects of such new technology as CAD on job satisfaction. Fears about reduced job satisfaction with CAD must therefore be examined.

Bjorn-Andersen *et al.* (1979) examined the impact of CBISs on job satisfaction and found no overall change attributable to the CBIS. They reasoned that changes in job satisfaction did not occur because the negative effects of the technology such as decreased autonomy were balanced by the positive effects such as decreased routinity.

Dickson *et al.* (1980) found that job satisfaction was decreased with the implementation of an MIS in a post office. Their rationale for this decrease was that those jobs perceived by the employees as high status because they were important in the information network had been eliminated as a result of the implementation effort. This act, more than the technology itself, seemed to cause the decrement in satisfaction.

Lucas (1979) conducted a longitudinal study of the implementation of a CBIS and found that the level of job satisfaction did not change as much as the dispersion among respondents of their job satisfaction scores. He reasoned that people's job satisfaction derives from a cost/benefit analysis of different elements of their job. Thus, when a new technology differentially affects people, each individual's job satisfaction might change, but with enough positive and negative changes, average job satisfaction across all people would stay the same.

Finally, just as Staehle (1982) found no changes in perceived job aspects attributable to VDTs, he also found no effect of VDTs on work satisfaction. Moreover, this author concluded that the degree of work satisfaction depended less on the VDT itself than on the VDT workplace.

Research on CAD reports similar results to those described above. Majchrzak *et al.* (1985a) found no differences between users and non-users in degree of job satisfaction. Newton (1984) found that CAD and non-CAD workers did not significantly differ in their job satisfaction. The BNA study of the effects of VDTs in the workplace (1984) found that dissatisfaction with VDTs reflected more the way in which the job was designed and technology implemented than the screen itself. Finally, Johansson's study (1986) of CAD designers found that increased job satisfaction was achieved not by CAD but by the increased productivity, creativity, quality of work, varied tasks and responsibility over work that resulted when some organizations implementing CAD induced such changes.

These findings from CAD and information technology research suggest that job satisfaction will not change specifically in response to the CAD technology. However, job satisfaction may change in response to the workplace changes resulting from CAD. For example, research has shown that R&D staff like autonomy in their jobs (Alestalo, 1979). Thus, if CAD decreases autonomy, job satisfaction will decrease. However, research also shows that a chief source of work satisfaction is the opportunity to engage in peer communication (Porter and Roberts, 1983). Thus, if CAD decreases autonomy but increases peer communication, as expected, the positive and negative effects will balance to yield no change in job satisfaction. Nevertheless, this balance should not be taken for granted, i.e., a poorly designed job will yield decreased job satisfaction whether or not CAD is implemented.

Summary of the effects of CAD on individuals' reactions to their jobs

Table 8.8 presents a summary of the studies described above. From the research, two findings are apparent concerning the effects of CAD on individuals' reactions to the job. First, CAD will probably increase individuals' perceived stress given the increased information they will obtain and the pacing of their job by the computer. Second, perceptions of users' jobs with CAD as well as their job satisfaction will probably be determined more by job design and other workplace factors than by the technology itself.

8.4. Conclusions

From this review of the literature on social and organizational consequences of CAD, several specific consequences were identified. CAD will yield:

1. Increased use of integrative devices.
2. Increased and different communication patterns on the job.
3. Increased skill requirements.
4. Increased formalization of work methods.
5. Opportunity to consider alternative career paths for drafters and designers.
5. More perceived stress.

Moreover, we also know that R&D staff will not react positively to the increased formalization, that the increased use of integrative devices will not necessarily create more interdependence among departments and across

Table 8.8. Summary of quantitative research on the impact of CAD on workers' job reactions.

	Information Technology			CAD		
Reaction	Author	Sample	Finding	Author	Sample	Finding
Stress	Lucas (1975a)	Users in service organization	Information overload	Barfield *et al.* (1986)	Review of human factors research	Increased stress
	Ackoff (1967)	Review of MIS research	Managers need system to filter and use information, not more information	Newton (1984)	CAD and non-CAD drafters	No change in somatic complaints
	Hiltz (1984)	Users of electronic mail	Information overload			
	Bjorn-Andersen *et al.* (1979)	Bank clerks	No change in work pace			
Job perceptions	Dickson *et al.* (1980)	Post office clerks	Decreased job feedback	Majchrzak *et al.* (1985a)	CAD users	Less autonomy, more identity; mediator role of workplace
	Kling (1978)	Government staff users	Enlarged jobs	Norton (1981)	CAD operators	Mediator role of management
	Staehle (1982)	Clerical VDU users	No change	Johansson (1986)	CAD designers	More meaningful work
	Edwards (1978) Johnson *et al.* (1985)	OA users	Increased autonomy and task identity	Newton (1984)	CAD and non-CAD drafters	No change in autonomy
	Gutek (1982)	OA manager and secretary	Increased secretary's perceptions; not managers			
Job satisfaction	Bjorn-Andersen *et al.* (1979)	Bank clerks	No change	Johansson (1986)	CAD designers	Mediator role of workplace
	Dickson *et al.* (1980)	Postal clerks	Decrease; mediator role of workplace	Newton (1984)	CAD and non-CAD drafters	No change
	Lucas (1979)	CBIS users	Increased dispersion, but no average change	Majchrzak *et al.* (1985a)	CAD users and non users	No change
	Staehle (1982)	VDT users	No change; mediator role of workplace			

functions, and that perceptions of the job, job satisfaction and workplace changes are more a function of management issues than of the technology itself.

Therefore, the importance of the management of CAD to achieve positive benefits from the technology cannot be overemphasized. Managerial mistakes early on in the design of the system can have irrevocable long-term consequences. Bjorn-Andersen *et al.* (1979) describe an excellent example of an important managerial decision inappropriately made. In their study of CBIS implementation, the researchers found that the computerization was originally brought into a bank to resolve difficulties of recruiting staff, labor turnover, absenteeism and inefficiencies. That is, since they could not get and keep the right people to do the work, they turned to the computer to replace the worker rather than turn to the organization to change it. In order to design a system that could replace workers, or at least keep personnel needs to a minimum, the system was

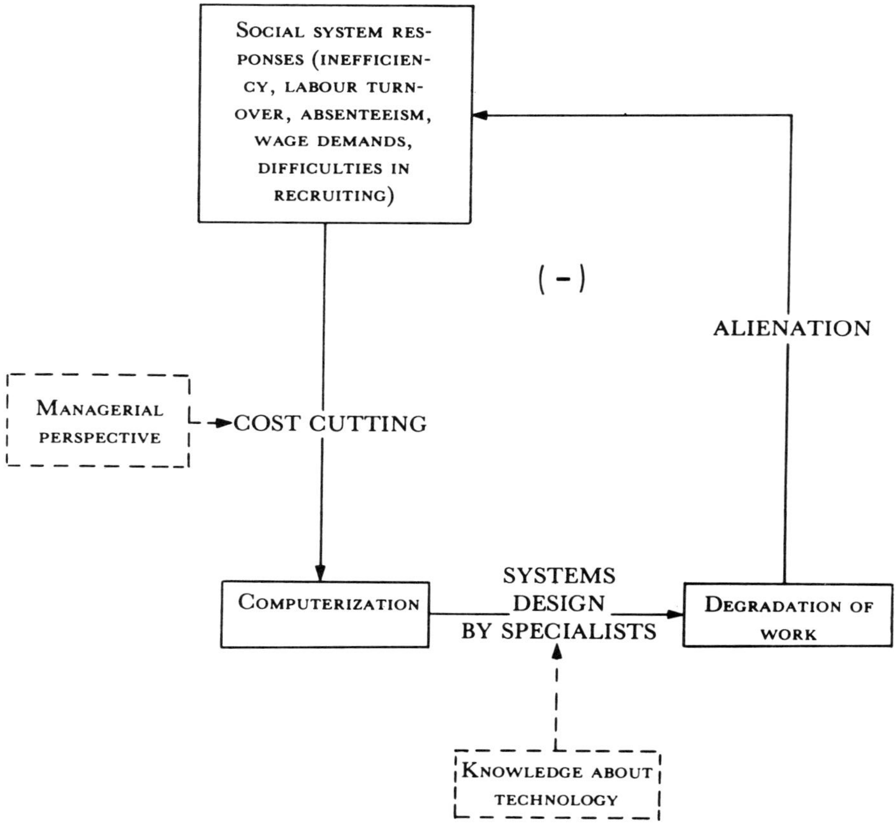

Figure 8.6. Consequences of continuing routinization of work (from Bjorn-Andersen et al. *(1979), courtesy Martinus Nijhoff).*

designed to have jobs that were as simple and routine as possible, such that the challenge people look for in their jobs was gone. Moreover, the needs to keep the computer on-line meant that nearly as many people were needed with the CBIS than before. Therefore, given that the system yielded jobs that were even less interesting than before, in an organization that was as poorly managed as before, and given that personnel needs were almost as great as before, the problems (turn-over, etc.) which were originally intended to be solved by the computer were not ameliorated. Thus, a cycling back effect as depicted by Figure 8.6 was experienced. Clearly, these failures could not be blamed on the CBIS!

In addition to the need to appropriately manage the CAD system to achieve positive consequences of CAD, management should be aware that CAD systems provide the opportunity to initiate organizational change not heretofore considered possible. In fact, in Stewart's (1971) case studies, she found that "The most striking impact from the use of computers was the way in which managers were stimulated to think about their policies or activities" (p. 220). Just as CAD can provide new options for *both* centralizing and decentralizing as described earlier, CAD also provides new options for structuring jobs and departments, and reinstituting management faith. However, this can only be accomplished if the implementation process is appropriately planned, and if people's resistance to change is well-understood. These are the issues to be turned to in the next chapters.

Chapter 9
Managing individuals' resistance to CAD

9.1. Introduction

The previous chapter discussed one way in which social and organizational factors need to be considered in the management of CAD. In this chapter, another role played by social and organizational factors will be explored. Here the focus is on the resistance (or adjustment) of those individuals in an organization expected to use new technology and the social and organizational factors that can be managed to reduce this resistance.

The chapter will proceed first with a discussion of the need for CAD managers and researchers to be concerned with resistance. Then several categories of factors that may affect individuals' resistance are introduced. For each factor, the relevant research is described accompanied by a discussion of the relative importance of that factor for reducing resistance. The chapter ends with conclusions from this review.

Resistance of individuals to technological change is an issue of much concern to managers (e.g., Gold, 1971; Zuboff, 1982). For example, Sanders (1968) provides a quote from a data processing manager whose company was discontinuing its use of an MIS: "Office support personnel failed to comply with detailed new procedures due to disinterest, and this is why EDP has not worked. We couldn't get these lamebrains to do what they were told to do" (p. 285).

Managers should be concerned about peoples' resistance to change for a variety of reasons. For one thing, resistance is a clear and open refusal to respond to managerial directives; when managers define their jobs as controllers and directors of subordinates' work, to resist sends a signal to everyone that the manager cannot do his or her job and the resister cannot adequately cope with authority.

A second reason why resistance to change is so serious for managers is that managers do not typically know how to deal with it. To resist a managers' program of action erodes the position and power of the manager. Unless the manager has other power bases available to him or her, such as expert or punishment power, and chooses to use it, the manager is left with few alternatives with which to handle the resistance.

Resistance to change is important for an additional reason as well: resistance has numerous and serious consequences to an organization. First, resistance creates employees who tend not be highly productive with that new technology. Such employees tend not to be motivated to perform to the prespecified levels of output. Given their low motivation, they are also unlikely to experiment with the new system to attain full benefits from the equipment. This lack of experimentation is particularly troublesome given Johnson *et al.*'s (1985) finding that an organization's innovative use of a system is dependent on the willingness of those employees using the system to make suggestions for new uses. Without such willingness, an organization is likely to be constrained to an unsophisticated system not well integrated with the organization. Finally, resistant employees may manifest their lack of motivation in destructive ways such as sabotaging the new technology. For example, Dickson *et al.* (1980) describe forms of sabotage to a new MIS that included deliberate errors in transactions, physical sabotage (e.g., paper clips in the machine) and data falsification.

A second consequence to the organization of resistant employees is that these employees are likely to learn only that which is minimally necessary to operate the new system. Acquiring a broader understanding of a new system as a whole and how it fits into the organization's strategy is rarely undertaken by the resistant employee. As a result, as even newer technology is installed, the resistant employee will be unable to adapt as well as the employee who acquired this broader knowledge.

A third consequence to the organization is the need to cope with difficult personnel problems. One such problem is encountered when resisting employees do not perform well, despite the fact that they actually performed quite well before the new technology was installed. Their low performance forces management into the uncomfortable situation of either terminating a previously well-liked and productive employee or allowing an unproductive, destructive employee to stay on the job. Either choice is likely to generate disconcerting reactions from fellow workers.

Another consequence to the organization is that resistant employees use an inordinate amount of time and attention of supervisors. For example, Mann and Williams (1960) describe the human resource challenges that supervisors had to cope with during an EDP implementation: keeping subordinates working on jobs that are to be phased-out, developing new job skills among workers, keeping ahead technically of subordinates, handling the problems in introducing white collar personnel to shiftwork, managing the continued overtime during implementation, and minimizing feelings of decreased productivity while system bugs are worked out. With all these morale problems, supervisory time is precious; using that time to convince resistant employees to adopt the new technology is not where supervisors are needed most.

A final consequence to the organization of resistant employees is the domino effect on other employees. An employee initially optimistic about a new technology is hard put to remain so if another employee continuously denigrates the new equipment. And as evidenced in the previous chapter on consequences of

CAD, management exerts substantial influence over how CAD affects jobs, such that jobs can be detrimentally affected by CAD if management wishes it to be so. Therefore, a negative employee may raise fears and concerns that only faith in management can overcome—a faith that may occasionally waver.

Given the importance of resistance to change for managers implementing new technology, it is essential that managers understand how best to manage (i.e., prevent, reduce) this resistance. Organizational development practioners and clinical psychologists have examined the broader category of resistance to general organizational change for many years. This literature (see, for example, Argyris, 1985; Bennis *et al.*, 1976; Goodman and Dean, 1983; Lewin, 1951; Zaltman *et al.*, 1973) has yielded several different perspectives on causes of resistance to change. These perspectives suggest that the following categories of factors may cause individual resistance (either alone or together):

1. Background of the employee.
2. Inadequate understanding of the organizational change.
3. Managerial barriers or lack of incentives to support the change.
4. Current job situation and how job is perceived to be affected by the change.

Individual background factors refer to such potential determinants of resistance as age, personality, job tenure and education. For example, a common proposition in the organizational development literature is that older workers are more likely to resist change than younger workers.

Inadequate knowledge, a second factor affecting resistance, refers to the proposition that people resist change because they do not understand it. If they understood it (typically through some partial exposure to the change), they would have less reason to fear it. For example, trying out a quality circle in one small work area allows other workers to evaluate the intervention, with positive evaluations likely to reduce resistance to the change.

Managerial barriers or lack of incentives is a third category of factors thought to arouse resistance to change. Such barriers might include management's selling of the change as a mechanism for replacing workers rather than enhancing their jobs.

The final set of factors identified in the organizational development literature as contributing to resistance to change are people's perceptions of their jobs—including both perceptions of their current job and their future job with the change. People who perceive that their current job is everything they want it to be and the organizational change will lessen their power, independence, recognition, or whatever, are more likely to resist change than those who do not perceive their current job as such.

With these four factors identified as causes of general resistance to change, hypotheses about the applicability of these factors as causing resistance to *technological* change can be raised and tested by a review of the empirical research. For example, older workers may be more likely to resist new technology than younger workers; partial advance exposure to a CAD terminal may make transition to CAD easier; managers that carry through with job protection promises as new technology is implemented may reduce resistance; and people who see that the new technology will make their jobs more interesting, challenging, etc., may indeed be more likely to accept the technology.

In addition to these four factors, two others may also be important factors contributing to resistance to technological change: system factors and implementation process factors. System factors describe characteristics of the new technology itself. For example, Saltman *et al.*'s research (1973) on predictors of an organization's decision to adopt innovations found that a primary set of predictors were aspects or attributes of the technology itself. Specifically, they found 19 attributes to be important, including risk, complexity, susceptibility to successive modification, and communicability of the technology. Thus, system factors may be important determinants of an individual's resistance to the new technology.

Implementation process factors, as the final set of potentially important contributors to resistance, concern how the implementation is handled. Training, the manner in which users are involved in the design of the new system, and the degree of preplanning are implementation factors. For example, Mumford (1969) found in her study of the implementation of EDP (Electronic Data Processing), systems that a primary variable in determining the attitudes of employees to technological change was the way in which the change was implemented.

To summarize, management of the resistance to technological change revolves around the ability to understand the factors contributing to it. Several factors can be identified as potentially influencing resistance. These are graphically depicted in Figure 9.1.

In this Chapter, empirical research will be reviewed to determine the extent to which these factors explain resistance to CAD and information technologies. While *a priori* expectations are that all the factors in Figure 9.1 are related to resistance, their degree of importance relative to other factors, and explicit predictions about how each factor affects resistance, is not clear at this point. We will need to turn to the empirical literature for this clarification. Finally, in this review all but one of the factors will be considered. The remaining factor—the implementation process—is sufficiently complex and multifaceted to warrant its own treatment in Chapter 10.

In the literature on technological change, individual resistance is measured in at least two ways—as attitudes about the new technology, and as the extent to which individuals actually use the new technology. Attitudes are typically assessed as people's satisfaction with the new system once it has been installed, or their satisfaction with their jobs when working with the new system. While satisfaction is a worthwhile measure in and of itself, if it is unrelated to use of the system, its utility as an indicator of resistance to change can be questioned. Several studies address this point. In Hiltz's (1984) study of an electronic mail system, professionals were asked prior to the system installation how much time they expected to spend on the system—a measure that could be interpreted as

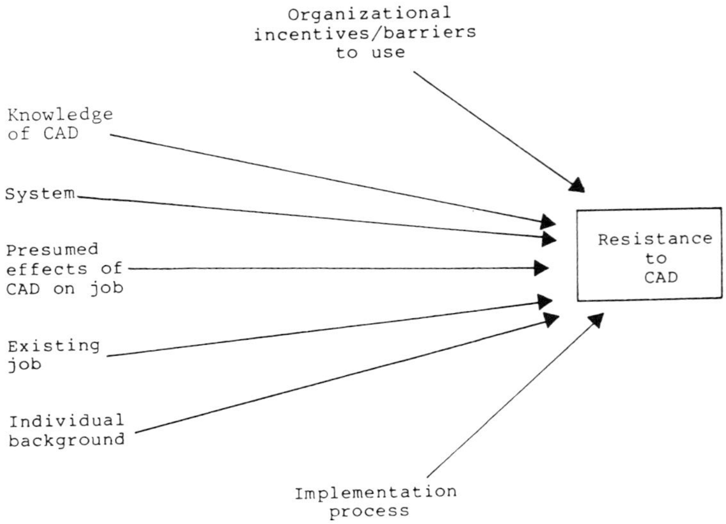

Figure 9.1. Social and organizational factors affecting individuals' adjustment to CAD.

pre-use attitudes about the system. She found that this measure correlated highly with actual system use. In their review of studies on computer-mediated communication systems, Kerr and Hiltz (1982) also found that pre-use expectations about the system were related to later measures of system use. Lucas' (1975b) study of a CBIS implementation reported similar findings. Finally, Swanson's (1974) study of the implementation of a computer-based retrieval system in engineering departments found that users' appreciation of the system (i.e., their perceived benefits of the system) were highly related to their use of the system. Clearly, these studies indicate that attitudes about a new technology are not only an important measure of resistance to change in their own right, but also validly predict inadequate use of the new system.

In addition to measuring resistance to technological change by attitudes, the extent and type of use of the new technology can serve as another measure. The applicability and interpretation of the extent of use of new technology as a measure of technological resistance necessarily varies with the degree of discretion a person has over the way—extent and method—he or she uses the new equipment. Drafters with no discretion over the amount of use can hardly have their resistance measured by how many hours they have logged onto the terminal. Moreover, Kling (1980) points out that those with discretion tend to use systems differently to those without discretion. For example, for those with discretion, the new system may be used to save the users' time, handle complex information, as a symbolic gesture to appear innovative, as a medium for playful work, or for political instrumentality.

Because workers have different degrees of discretion over using a new system, consequences of resistance may be manifested in different ways for these workers. For example, Eason *et al.* (1975) found that clerical workers who had to use a CBIS responded with frustration and loss of morale when they did not like the system; managers who had discretion simply did not use the system and thus suffered no morale loss or insisted on a human intermediary between them and the system. Therefore, the extent of use may have limited utility as a measure of resistance to technological change for certain types of workers. However, for those with less discretion, the *way* in which the system is used still tends to be somewhat motivational in nature and may thus indicate the degree of technological resistance being experienced. For example, although a drafter cannot choose *not* to use CAD, he or she can show a preference for manual drawing versus CAD when trying out new perspectives on drawings. Clearly the latter choice indicates someone who has adjusted quite well to the new system. Therefore it must be recognized that for those without discretion it is not the length of time in front of a terminal that determines ultimate adjustment, but the sophistication of use. With this in mind, let us now turn to empirical research on each of the five factors expected to contribute to people's adjustment or resistance to technological change.

9.2. System factors influencing resistance to change

Research on the implementation of information technologies identifies several technical system factors for individuals' adjustment to the technology. Alter (1976) interviewed managers implementing DSSs and found that systems technically able to provide useful information to managers bearing the burden of implementation are likely to be evaluated more positively.

Bikson *et al.* (1981) reviewed the literature on technological change for information technologies and identified several system variables likely to enhance people's evaluation of a new system: comprehensibility (ease with which the system can be understood, learned and used), divisibility (ease with which the system can be introduced in stages to avoid large-scale change), testability (ease with which the system can be tested provisionally and improved as needed), credibility (extent to which the system is espoused by eminent, authoritative and respected individuals), and compatibility of the system with users' established practices, norms and values.

Eason *et al.* (1975) surveyed 120 users of a CBIS and found that ease of system use and the extent to which the system fits with task needs was related to use of the system (for those with discretion over use) and satisfaction (for those without discretion over use).

Gutek *et al.* (1984), in their study of 55 work groups implementing office automation, found that inadequate system utilization was attributable to three variables: lack of access to equipment, problems with the system, and lack of adequate training to use the system. Their second variable is clearly a system factor.

Finally, in Rice *et al.*'s (1984) review of research on computer conferencing, several predictors of acceptance and use of computer conferencing systems were identified. Among these, access to the system was a key variable.

In the CAD literature, data are sparse. However, Barfield *et al.* (1986) reviewed the literature on human factors as they pertain to CAD systems and concluded that systems not technically designed as a "synergistic interaction of the user and CAD" are not likely to be used properly. In addition, Kay's (1985) experience with CAD at Hewlett-Packard led him to conclude that the use of CAD is limited to some extent by its difficulty of use—a system factor.

As briefly summarized in Table 9.1, this research indicates that the way in which the system is designed is related to resistance to the new system. A system designed to meet the users' physiological and job needs, and easily understand-
(1984) set out to identify factors that explained differences in amount of system

The relative importance of system factors

While system factors are clearly important, the question remains, how important are they? A few studies have addressed this question. In her longitudinal study of 150 users of an electronic mail system before and at two follow-up points, Hiltz (1984) set out to identify factors that explained differences in amount of system

Table 9.1. Summary of quantitative research on the relationship between system factors and individuals' resistance to change.

Author	System variable	Measure of resistance
Information technology		
Alter (1976)	Provision of relevant information	System evaluation
Bikson *et al.* (1981)	Comprehensibility, divisibility, testability, credibility, compatibility	System evaluation
Eason *et al.* (1975)	Ease of use; fit with task needs	System use and evaluation
Gutek *et al.* (1984)	Problems; system access	Inadequate system utilization
Rice *et al.* (1984)	Access to system	System acceptance and use
CAD		
Barfield *et al.* (1986)	Synergistic interaction of user and CAD	Improper use of CAD

use. She found that "motivations of participants and their location within a particular social context, *not* system characteristics, were the primary determinants of use, . . . assuming minimal criteria of ease of use and reliability are met" (p. 33). The motivations she refers to include the participants' anticipated value and level of use prior to the system actually being installed.

In their study of 55 workgroups implementing office automation systems, Bikson and Gutek (1983 b) compared the importance of system factors (such as functionality of the system) with non-system factors (such as work variety and the organization's orientation toward change) in predicting level of system use. The researchers found that system factors paled in comparison to non-system factors in predicting use. From this, they concluded that "the most critical problems in implementing information systems are not inherently technological ones. Instead, they involve characteristics of the organization and its implementation effort" (p. 19).

Cheney and Dickson (1982) surveyed 79 users across eight organizations prior to and after installation of a CBIS. They found that increased job satisfaction with the introduction of the CBIS was *not* affected by the technical sophistication of the system (i.e., a system that serves as an expert system rather than simply handles data faster); however, it *was* affected by the managerial sophistication of the organization's MIS department (i.e., a department that was user/service oriented rather than solely focused on system development).

Finally, Majchrzak (1985) examined the relative importance of system factors on the adjustment of CAD users (measured as job satisfaction and supervisory ratings of innovation and importance). Satisfaction with the system was found to have a significant influence, relative to work environment and organizational context, on job satisfaction only.

In order to be able to draw conclusions from these findings about the importance of system factors relative to other factors for predicting individuals' adjustment to technological change, one must remember that there have been no studies on CAD technologies which explicitly compare system factors to the other factors. Nevertheless, the relevant research suggests that system factors, though important, may serve primarily to set minimal criteria for reducing resistance. That is, if minimal criteria of system factors—in terms of understandability, relevance and use—are not met, the system factors will contribute to resistance. If minimal criteria are met, technical factors are less important than other factors in reducing resistance to technological change.

9.3. Individual background variables influencing resistance to change

A second set of factors potentially affecting resistance are individual background variables. Speculative literature on technological change has focused particularly on age as an important predictor of resistance. Therefore, the importance of age will be first examined, followed by an examination of other background variables.

Age

Numerous studies have attempted to determine if indeed the popular notion that older workers are more resistant to new technology is borne out by fact. Kaufman (1979) surveyed 404 engineers and examined three potential predictors of self-reported job and professional obsolescence: age, nature of work, and organizational climate. Conducting a path analysis of his cross-sectional data, he found that there was "no evidence to support the widespread belief that older engineers are more obsolescent" (p. 827).

Lucas (1975 b) surveyed 439 salesmen about a CBIS and found no consistent relationship between age and system use. Kerr and Hiltz's (1982) review of research on computer-mediated communication systems found that few studies included sufficient age ranges to assess relationships to resistance. Of the five studies with sufficient age ranges, three studies found age to be inversely related to use of a new system and two studies found no relationship. In her longitudinal study of adaptation to an electronic mail system, Hiltz (1984) examined the importance of motivations, system (i.e., ease of learning, friendliness of interface, quality of documentation), individual background, and management factors on predicting individuals' use of the system. She found that demographic characteristics of the individual such as age were not important predictors of use.

The relationship of age has also been examined specifically for users of CAD systems. Majchrzak's (1985) study of CAD users and non-users found age to be a relatively unimportant predictor for many non-users' fears of new technology. For users' satisfaction with the system, age contributed a significant part of the variance between individuals in adjustment when measured as job satisfaction but not when measured as performance. Moreover, the relationship was positive, i.e., older workers were more satisfied. This is the inverse of the predicted direction. Newton (1984) found that age did not predict job satisfaction with CAD, compared to other factors such as job control and social support. Finally, Delvac (1981) describes conclusions from his experience with CAD at Sperry Corporation that differ from those studies above. He concludes that older workers are less likely to adapt to CAD as easily as younger workers. However, to support his conclusion, he provided this explanation:

> Generally speaking, the age of the individual and how long he has done his job using conventional methods, will determine how quickly he adapts to the use of the graphic system. Some of our older employees seemed to be totally overwhelmed by the fact that they were interactively working with a computer and with the number of new techniques they were required to learn. Many felt that they could complete their jobs quicker using standard methods and could not be convinced that when they were familiar with the system their performance would significantly improve. Efforts to convince these individuals were abandoned

initially, and we concentrated on training the innovative people. We are now reintroducing many of these people to the system with significantly better results. It was necessary to first prove the value of the graphic system (p. 649).

Apparently, unknown to Delvac, his explanation suggests that age, in and of itself, was *not* an important explanation of resistance to CAD. Rather, many of the older workers, because they were already working very efficiently with the old system and had been rewarded for their productivity, were reluctant to change unless they knew that the new system would yield significantly better results. This alternative explanation to Delvac is supported by Tull (1984) in his discussion of CAD use at Lockheed-Georgia. Tull found that older workers tended to be harder to motivate initially because their extensive expertise in their jobs required the new system to be substantially better than their current way of working. However, Tull also found that, once trained, older workers tended to bring to the CAD system a work experience not found in younger workers and that this work experience helped them to recognize CAD's full potential.

In sum, these studies suggest that age is probably not directly related to resistance to technological change. The manager responsible for CAD implementation may find that older workers initially ask more questions than younger workers and are more likely to want some evidence that enhanced productivity will actually be achieved with the new technology over what could be expected if people just worked harder. This initial scepticism may not be so bad since it forces management to ensure that its technological choices for the company are appropriate. Furthermore, when more experienced workers are trained to use the system, they may be more likely to get the most from it.

Other individual background variables

Individual background characteristics other than age that might be related to resistance to change include gender, previous computer experience, personality and education. In Hiltz's (1984) study which found demographic characteristics to be unimportant predictors of actual system use, the demographic characteristics included (in addition to age) previous computer experience and gender. In the Kerr and Hiltz (1982) review of studies on computer-mediated communication systems, education, personality variables and previous experience with computers were not related to system use and system satisfaction. Lucas' (1975 b) study also found no consistent relationship between education and system use. In a study by Johnson *et al.* (1985) on the implementation of word processing in 194 organizations, numerous personality traits of users were examined as potential predictors of adaptation to the new system. These personality variables included playing computer games, seeking new ways to do things, seeking ways to solve problems, enjoying being a leader, and preferred communication style. None of these variables predicted adaptation.

In the CAD literature, only one study has quantitatively examined the importance of these other background variables on adjustment. A study by Majchrzak

(1985) examined the importance of education and a standard personality scale of resistance to change for predicting both the fears of non-users about CAD and the adjustment (job and system satisfaction) of CAD users. It was found that among non-users, educational level was highly related to the personality variable (those with more education had less resistant personalities). The two background characteristics were also related to non-users' fears about jobs with CAD such as reduced autonomy, variety, interaction opportunities and motivating potential. For example, those with more resistant personalities expressed more fears. Despite these significant bivariate relationships, the two background factors were not universally important for all non-users' fears when other predictive factors such as current job conditions were included. For example, these background characteristics accounted for 1% of the variance in drafters' perceived future autonomy of their jobs with CAD, while the current situation, such as the amount of interaction with peers, accounted for 33% of the variance. In contrast, the background variables accounted for 26% of the variance in engineers' fears about autonomy with CAD.

For CAD users in the Majchrzak study, the picture was slightly less complex. Education was not related to satisfaction with the system and job with CAD. The personality variable, however, was an important predictor of job satisfaction even when such job conditions as unpredictability and perceived autonomy were included.

In sum, research on the relationship between individual background variables (other than age) and individuals' adjustment to technological change has not been explored as yet to the depth that allows definitive conclusions. Only a few studies have examined any single background variable in the context of other variables; thus a consensus is lacking. However, a tentative conclusion which can be advanced is that there appears to be no consistent relationship between these individual characteristics and people's adjustment to technology.

Summary and relative importance of individual factors

The studies described above are briefly presented in Table 9.2. They suggest that simple bivariate statistics may indicate relationships between some background variables and resistance. However, comparing the direction of these relationships across studies or the importance of these relationships when other potential factors of resistance are taken into account suggests an alternative conclusion, namely: compared to other factors predicting resistance, the entire range of individual background characteristics may have only limited and attitude-specific effects.

9.4. Knowledge of technology as an influence on resistance to change

A third set of factors potentially affecting resistance is the amount of knowledge individuals have about the CAD system. Inadequate knowledge of new tech-

Table 9.2. Summary of quantitative research on the relationship between individual background factors and individuals' resistance to change.

Author	Background variable	Measure of resistance	Finding
Information Technology			
Kaufman (1979)	Age	Self-reported job obsolescence	No relationship
Lucas (1975b)	Age	System use	No relationship
Kerr and Hiltz (1982)	Age, education, personality, previous computer experience	System use and satisfaction not related	No conclusive relationship for age; other variables
Hiltz (1984)	Age, previous computer experience	System use	Unimportant predictors
Johnson *et al.* (1985)	Personality	Adaptation to system	No relationship
CAD			
Majchrzak *et al.* (1985a)	Age, eduction, openness to change	Nonusers' fears of CAD Users' job satisfaction and performance	Positive relationship of age and user satisfaction; complex (different relationships for different jobs and fears)
Newton (1983)	Age	Users' CAD satisfaction	No relationship

nology is expected to contribute to individuals' resistance to technological change in two ways. First, Lewin (1951) has proposed a model of the process people must move through to accept planned change. The model, which is generally accepted by organizational development practitioners, identifies the first stage of the process to be 'unfreezing', where an individual becomes convinced of the need for a change. Therefore, one way in which inadequate knowledge may contribute to resistance is when an individual has not been sufficiently educated about the system to be convinced of the need for the new technology. A second way in which inadequate knowledge may lead to resistance is that people may not be sufficiently exposed to the technology to feel comfortable about it and the changes it will have on their working lives. Each of these knowledge variables—about the need for the technology and exposure to it—may affect resistance independently of the other. Thus, empirical research pertaining to each of these variables are reviewed separately.

Recognition of the need for new technology

Dickson *et al.* (1980) interviewed 67 workers after the implementation of a new MIS in a post office. The researchers found that the provision of only minimal education about the need and purpose of the system was one factor affecting the negative reactions of employees to the new technology.

Alter's (1976) survey of managers implementing DSSs found that when the DSS was sold on how it outdid manual systems, rather than sold on some other basis, more positive attitudes toward the system were achieved.

Robey and Zeller (1978) examined variables distinguishing between an organizational unit rejecting a CBIS and a unit accepting and implementing it. They found that a major distinguishing variable was that the system was felt to be more urgent and important among adopters compared to non-adopters.

Bikson *et al.* (1981) reviewed the technological change literature as it pertains to information systems. They found that two key variables predicting adjustment were: perceptions of sufficient economic and social benefits of the system; and a clear recognition of a need for the system.

Hiltz and Turoff (1978) reviewed the literature on computer conferencing and found that "It is not enough to have the technological capability to design and use the system. There first must be an organizational need (that is, existing communication must be seen as severely inadequate for accomplishing an important task)" (p. 49).

In Hiltz's (1984) longitudinal study of adaptation to electronic mail, the anticipated value of the new system prior to system installation was a primary factor influencing individuals' motivation to use the system after its installation.

Finally, Rice *et al.* (1984) reviewed the literature on computerized communication and found that an individual's perceived need to communicate with others had a strong influence on the acceptance and use of a computer conferencing system.

These results suggest that recognition of a need for the specific technology purchased and not just recognition of the general need to adopt new technology is likely to reduce resistance to technological change. However, it should be noted that no studies have been done to date on this topic specifically for CAD.

Exposure to new technology

Technological resistance appears to be reduced when people recognize the need for that technology. Is resistance also reduced the more they are exposed to the system? Rice and Case (1983) surveyed 83 managers implementing electronic mail systems immediately after installation and several months later. One of the questions they were interested in was whether or not attitudes toward the system would improve as the participant became more exposed to the system, i.e., does comfort and understanding breed positive evaluations? Their findings from the survey indicated that the extent of system use did not affect people's reactions to the new system; that is, managers had achieved a stable set of attitudes about the computers' benefits immediately after installation and that these attitudes did not change after several months of use. Also, in a review of the literature on computer conferencing, Rice (1982) reported similar findings. However, according to his review, while increased use did not appear to enhance perceived benefits of the system, use did seem to be related to increased satisfaction and comfort with the new system.

Majchrzak (1985) studied the relationship between exposure to CAD (measured as the amount of training, use, and reading of articles on CAD) and fears about CAD among non-users. Increased exposure was only marginally correlated ($r = 0{\cdot}22$) with some of the fears. Majchrzak also studied the relationships between system satisfaction and exposure (measured as the amount of system use and time spent reading a CAD article) for CAD users. She found no significant relationship between exposure and system satisfaction.

To conclude whether or not exposure to the new technology is a contributing factor to resistance to change is premature on the basis of the available research. As is apparent from the summary in Table 9.3, data are sparse, especially for CAD. From the sparse research, however, it appears that the relationship between exposure and resistance is fairly complex and varies with the type of exposure and whether resistance is assessed among those not as yet using the system or those using the system.

The research suggests that among users actual system use may be related to increased system satisfaction although it is *not* related to increased perceived benefits. However, which is the chicken and which is the egg here? Does increased use lead individuals to justify their use by increasing their level of satisfaction with the system, or do people use the system because they are more satisfied with it? If the former interpretation is correct, then programs to enhance system exposure will help; otherwise, increased exposure may have limited utility for enhancing users' adjustment.

For non-users, resistance to technology constitutes fear of the unknown. Among this group of people, exposure unaccompanied by actual use of the system may not alleviate this fear. Reading an article or simply seeing a terminal may only raise more questions, rather than answer any. Clearly more research is needed here to help us identify when a little exposure may be useless, if not downright counter-productive.

The relative importance of knowledge factors

This review of research on knowledge factors indicates that recognition of need is related to individuals' adjustment to new technology while the role of exposure or system use is not at all clear. Given these findings, it is important to ascertain the extent to which knowledge is important relative to such other factors as management actions or job perceptions in explaining an individual's resistance.

Majchrzak (1985) conducted regression analyses on factors which might

Table 9.3. Summary of quantitative research on the relationship between knowledge factors and individuals' resistance to change.

Author	Background knowledge	Measure of resistance	Finding
Information Technology			
Dickson *et al.* (1980)	Education about need for MIS	System satisfaction	Positive relationship
Alter (1976)	Belief DSS outdoes manual system	System satisfaction	Positive relationship
Robey and Zeller (1978)	Belief in urgency and importance of system	Continued system use	Positive relationship
Bikson *et al.* (1981)	Perceived system benefits and need	Adjustment	Positive relationship
Hiltz and Turoff (1978)	Perceived need for specific system	Adjustment	Positive relationship
Hiltz (1984)	Anticipated value of system prior to use	System use	Positive relationship
Rice *et al.* (1984)	Perceived need to communicate with others; system use	Use of computer conferencing system; perceived system benefits; system satisfaction	Positive relationship between need and use, and system satisfaction
Rice and Case (1983)	System use	Attitudes about computers' benefits	No relationship
CAD			
Majchrzak (1985)	Amount of training, use, reading CAD article	Fears of CAD for nonusers; system satisfaction for users	Marginal relationships only

predict non-users' fears about CAD. She found that knowledge in terms of reading an article or obtaining a little training were relatively unimportant compared to other factors (current job perceptions) in predicting non-users' fears. For users, she examined the importance of these knowledge variables on job and system satisfaction. Knowledge was again not important compared to other factors (e.g., amount of participation in job decisions).

In the study done by Hiltz (1984) comparing multiple factors affecting use of an electronic mail system, it was found that the anticipated value of the system was one of the most important factors predicting its use. Knowledge in terms of understanding of the system prior to actual system use was not measured.

While these two studies hardly provide conclusive statements, they suggest an interesting set of tentative statements. First, for individuals to adjust to new technology, i.e., to keep resistance to technological change to a minimum, workers must understand the need for the new technology. Compared to other factors, and especially compared to the two factors discussed in this Chapter thus far (system factors and individual background factors), this recognition of need is a far more important determinant of adjustment. Thus, for example, Jacobs (1986) has found that in organizations where market conditions have made organizational survival a particularly pressing matter, there is little resistance to CAD when CAD users believe its use is directly related to their abilities to keep their jobs.

A second conclusion from this review is that the effect of knowledge in terms of actual use of the system may have little effect on non-users' resistance and may possibly have a meaningless and unimportant effect on users' attitudes. That is, initial attitudes tend to be fairly well-considered and do not necessarily change unless the system or circumstances change. More research is needed, of course.

9.5. Managerial barriers/incentives as influences on resistance to change

An individual's resistance to technological change may not only result from how much the individual believes the organization needs the new technology. There may also be important actions undertaken by management that inadvertently encourage resistance to the new technology. Four such actions are identified here.

Managerial competence

One set of actions may involve the competence of management to handle implementation. Two studies have addressed how individuals' perceptions of the competence of their management staff can influence their resistance to technological change. Collins and Moores (1983) surveyed clerical workers exposed to new computer technology in order to identify factors relating to workers' attitudes about the technological change. They found that the more that management was perceived to understand its role in the technological change process, the less fear and frustration was expressed about the technological change. In a similar vein, Dickson *et al.* (1980) studied factors affecting employees' negative reactions to a new MIS. They found that a major predictive factor was the previous failed attempts of management at implementing other technologies in the office. A management that 'has its act together' appears, then, to be an important incentive encouraging individuals to adjust to the technological change; just as a management that fails to instill such confidence creates a barrier to adjustment.

Job security

Another management barrier/incentive to resistance appears to revolve around job security promises. In the Dickson *et al.* (1980) study described above, the researchers found that another important factor influencing people's resistance was union opposition to the technological change, presumably due to that technology threatening job security. Johnson *et al.* (1985), in their study of the implementation of word-processing facilities, found that the more the technology was sold on the basis of control and labor reduction, the more the technology was resisted by the employees. Hamilton and Sheehan (1982) interviewed 81 CAD users and 14 managers at Rockwell on attitudes and experiences that were potentially related to CAD system utilization patterns. The researchers found that a key factor mentioned as helping to reduce psychological resistance to the CAD system was the assurance of job security. These findings then suggest that job security is an important issue in reducing resistance to change. A company that fails to provide job security assurances as the new technology is implemented may need to be prepared for the fact that it has created an incentive for more rather than less resistance.

Management support of system use

To promote individuals' adjustment to technological change, another management barrier/incentive appears to be managerial support (or lack thereof) for system use. As obvious as it sounds to say that if management wants to encourage system use, they should encourage system use, incentives to encourage such use are not always provided. Bikson *et al.* (1981), in their review of the literature on technological change pertaining to information technology, found that clear incentives to system use are indeed important determinants of adjustment. All too often, however, companies say they want the new equipment used but fail to provide either the time to learn how to use it or special recognition to those who go through the trouble of using it. In a similar vein, Hiltz (1984) found in her longitudinal study of adjustment to an electronic mail system that the existence of priorities in a job that do not conflict with system use was an important predictor of an individual's motivation to use the system. Thus, if management is intent on encouraging adjustment, restructuring jobs such that the new technology is integrated into the job tasks rather than simply a supplement to existing tasks is necessary.

Critical mass of users

A final management incentive that appears to affect resistance to technological change concerns management's efforts to create a critical mass of users. Bikson *et al.*'s (1981) review of information technology literature indicated that having enough other people using the system is important if resistance to the technology is to be overcome. Without enough users, those with optimistic attitudes towards the new system are too easily out-numbered. Barlini (1981) also identified critical mass as an important determinant of technological adjustment in his case study of a CAD implementation. Barlini recommends that the CAD system be implemented as an 'open' design system in which working stations are distributed throughout, favoring a wide use of the system. The more that people use the system and experience its benefits, the greater the constituency base supporting the new system, and the harder it is for resisting employees to remain resistant.

The relative importance of management factors

From this review, as briefly summarized in Table 9.4, there are at least four management barriers/incentives to other factors influencing resistance to techno-

There is little research, however, which explicitly compares the importance of management barriers/incentives to other factors influencing resistance to technological change. As a result, we cannot determine the relative importance of these variables compared to other factors such as individuals' recognition of the need for the new technology.

Nevertheless, it would appear from this review that management barriers and incentives at least have an important influence (although we don't know how

Table 9.4. Summary of quantitative research on the relationship between managerial factors and individuals' resistance to change.

Author	Management variable	Measure of resistance
Information technology		
Collins and Moores (1983)	Perception that management understands role in change process	Less fear and frustration
Dickson *et al.* (1980)	Previous failed attempts of management to implement new technologies; threaten job security	System dissatisfaction
Johnson *et al.* (1985)	Management selling technology on basis of labor reduction	"Resistance"
Bikson *et al.* (1981)	Clear incentives to system use; sufficient numbers of other users	System use
Hiltz (1984)	Priorities of job conflicting with system use	Reduced motivation to use system
CAD		
Hamilton and Sheehan (1982)	Assurance of job security	Reduction in "psychological" resistance

important) on technological resistance (provided, of course, that minimal system features are met). Therefore, to reduce or prevent resistance to CAD, management is well-advised to build up trust among subordinates in the way it handles the change process, ensure job security, show unequivocal encouragement to use CAD, have enough people on and involved with the system to exchange ideas and exert peer pressure, and provide support for continued use.

9.6. Perceptions of the current and future job as influences on resistance to change

A final set of factors potentially related to an individual's resistance to CAD is the set of perceptions the individual has about his or her current and future job. If workers expect the new technology to substantially alter their jobs in ways they dislike, or their current jobs are so highly valued that no change is desired, people are probably more likely to resist the new technology. The relationship between perceived job conditions and resistance is probably manifested in three ways.

Perceptions of users about their CAD jobs

A first way for the relationship to be manifested is among users. For people who have become users of the new technology, their satisfaction with their new job is probably related to their satisfaction with the new system. That is, if they like their new job with the new system, they are likely to be satisfied with the new system. Thus, resistance to CAD among users may be reduced by job redesigns that meet the needs of the users.

Bikson and Gutek (1983 b) examined the relationship of job conditions and system use and found that the more work variety there was in the job, the more likely it was that the office automation system would be used. Majchrzak (1985) also examined the relationship of job perceptions and system satisfaction among CAD users. She found that jobs perceived as having more positive interaction opportunities and feedback were related to system satisfaction. Finally, work by Anderson (Anderson *et al.*, 1985 a, b) found that the use of a hospital CBIS depended most directly on physicians' attitudes about the desirability of the system and its positive effects on the physicians' practices. These studies suggest the following tentative conclusions: (*a*) the more satisfied people are with their technologically-advanced jobs, the more they perceive their job with the new technology to be motivating; and (*b*) the more opportunity their jobs provide them to use the new technology in a variety of ways, the less likely they are to report dissatisfactions with the new system. Therefore, to encourage technological adjustment, redesigning jobs for motivation and variety will help.

Perceptions of non-users about their future CAD jobs

The relationship between job conditions and resistance can be manifested in ways other than that between users' perceptions and their system use. Job conditions may be related to resistance through the fears of non-users. That is, as non-users express concerns about changes to their jobs with the new technology, their resistance to the new technology will increase. A few studies have addressed this issue. Majchrzak (1985), in her analysis of CAD users and non-users, found that on all measured dimensions of their jobs, non-users feared that CAD would have negative effects on their jobs. Figure 9.2 depicts these results. These dimensions included job variety, significance, identification with a completed project, autonomy and feedback from others. These fears generalized across non-users in two sites in the same company as well as across engineers and drafters. Most interesting was that these fears were not corroborated by the experiences of CAD users. That is, CAD users reported that their jobs were not significantly different on these dimensions when compared to manual drafting. Thus, fears of jobs with CAD do exist among non-users, although they are unsupported by users.

Given that these fears exist, perceptions of non-users about how the new technology will affect themselves and their interests may have a major influence on the attitudes of employees to technological change. In her early review of technological change studies, Mumford (1969) found that, just as users' experiences with their new jobs are related to their degree of acceptance of the new technology, non-users' fears of the experiences with their future jobs are related to their resistance. Managers that fail to address these fears of non-users (through information, assurances, etc.) are not likely to be able successfully to alleviate the resistance (and remember, as discussed in the previous section, simply exposing them a little to the new technology may not be sufficient).

Perceptions of non-users about their current jobs

The relationship between job conditions and resistance can be manifested in a third way as well. It is possible that the conditions of the job existing prior to the new technology will affect people's likelihood to resist the new technology. Majchrzak (1985), in her study of CAD non-users, found that non-users' resistance (measured as perceived detrimental effects of the CAD system on their jobs) was predicted in part by the non-users' existing work environment. In particular, it was found that the more unpredictability existing in non-users' pre-CAD jobs, the more prepared they felt for the unpredictability likely to occur with CAD. Moreover, the more they coordinated with peers on their current job, the less fear they expressed about CAD. In addition, and perhaps most interesting, was that from here the findings diverged for the design engineer and drafter non-users. The findings, presented in Figure 9.3, suggest that drafting and engineering non-users fear CAD for very different reasons (although all job-related). For non-user drafters, less resistance to the new technology was reported for those who were

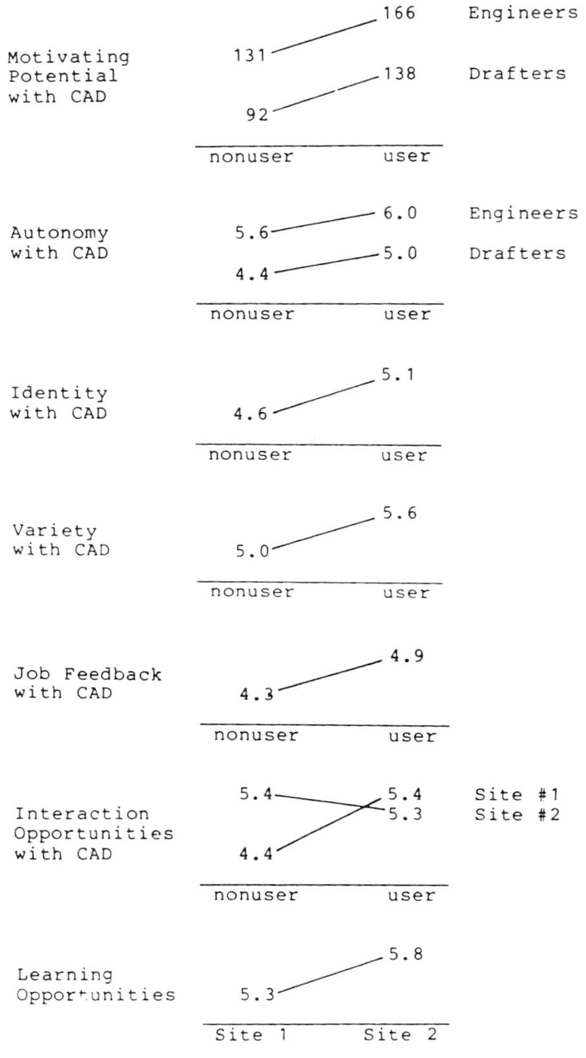

Figure 9.2. Fears of non-users (from Majchrzak, 1985).

more satisfied with their current jobs and who participated more in job decisions. In other words, drafters who feel they are well-managed and well-informed in their current job have confidence that the new technology will only enhance their well-being. Engineers on the other hand have a very different reaction. For non-user engineers, current job satisfaction and participation are not related to resistance. Rather, while engineers who use their peers to coordinate their work are less resistant, those that are currently in highly interdependent jobs express more fears

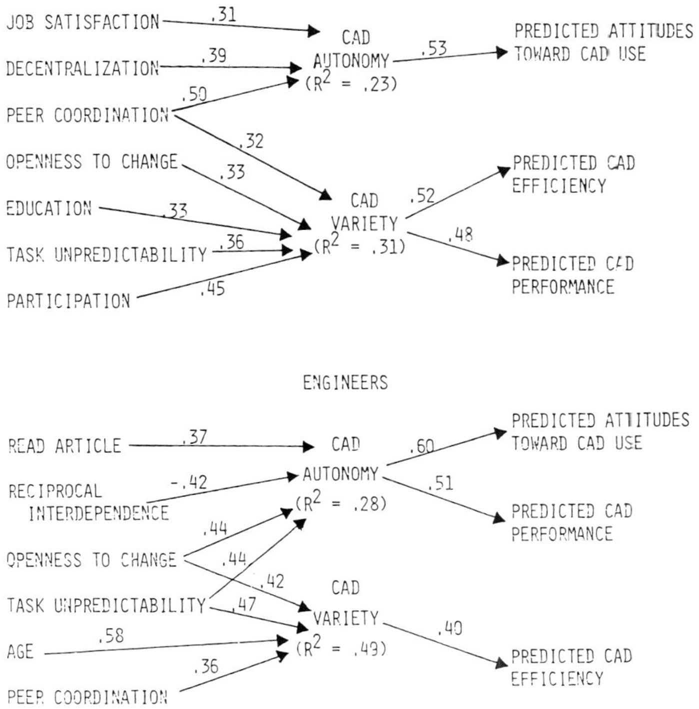

Figure 9.3. Regressions of non-users' fears about CAD (from Majchrzak, 1985).

about their future with CAD. In other words, engineers are focusing less on their own job satisfaction and more on how CAD will affect the way they work with others.

A possible interpretation of the Majchrzak findings is suggested by Alestalo's (1979) study of the influence patterns of 219 research teams of scientists and engineers. He found that autonomy in the workplace was a factor of primary importance to these professionals: the degree of autonomy experienced on the job in the scientific research process was related to productivity, creativity, outside recognition and number of publications. Thus, what may be happening with engineers is that they fear that CAD will remove the autonomy they enjoy so much in their jobs. Those engineers who are enjoying their current job as they work with others can only see CAD as negatively affecting their autonomy.

In addition to the Majchrzak (1985) study, researchers studying information technology also found that existing job conditions influenced resistance to change. Bjorn-Andersen *et al.* (1979) concluded from their study that clerks working on the most routine jobs tend not to be able to adjust to new technology as well as those working on less routine jobs. Dickson *et al.* (1980) found that an important factor predicting negative reactions of 67 workers to an MIS was the poor job conditions existing prior to installation. These conditions included the lack of information communication between workers and supervisors, advancement in the hierarchy by politics only, and low pay. Finally, in Mumford's (1969) review of studies on computer introduction, a variable having a major influence on attitudes of employees to technological change was the extent to which the organization met the personal needs and aspirations of staff prior to the implementation of new technology.

These studies thus suggest that there is a relationship between the conditions of the job that exist prior to the new technology and people's likelihood of resisting new technology. The precise form of this relationship is, however, unclear. It appears that unpredictable or non-routine 'pre-new technology' jobs help to reduce people's resistance to new technology. It also appears that the effect of other conditions of the pre-new technology job on resistance varies with the situation or the level in the organization. It may be that with lower-level workers (such as Dickson's postal clerks or Majchrzak's drafters), poor existing job conditions increase resistance to change, or the inverse, good existing job conditions provide the optimism that a technological change will yield a change for the better. For higher-level workers accustomed to little management interference, such as scientists and engineers, the advent of new technology appears to present the possibility of management meddling; thus, those already happy with their jobs are unlikely to welcome such involvement.

The relative importance of job perceptions

A final issue to consider in examining job conditions is their relative importance compared to other factors in contributing to resistance to technological change. In the Majchrzak (1985) study, she compared CAD knowledge variables, individual background variables, and current job conditions as factors influencing non-users' fears of new technology. In her regression analysis, the most important variables were the job condition variables, as described in the preceding pages. Robey and Zeller (1978) also conducted a study comparing the importance of different factors by distinguishing between plants accepting and rejecting the same computer information system in the same corporation. They found that of several factors examined as potentially discriminating between the adopting and non-adopting plants, two were the most important: staff in the adopting plant felt that (*a*) the system would have a more positive effect on the user's job (a job condition variable), and (*b*) that the system was more urgent and important (a recognition of need variable). These results suggest that indeed job condition factors are important, even with other factors considered, in influencing people's adjustment to technological change.

This review of job conditions—present and perceived future—suggests that job conditions are an important factor affecting technological resistance. However, the effect of existing work conditions, or the perceived effect of the technology on future jobs, are not likely alone to have a predictable, consistent effect on resistance. Rather, it appears that the effect of job conditions is likely to be a complex interaction between existing work conditions, perceived future effects and the perceived ability of management to pull off the change effectively.

9.7. *Conclusions*

This review of the research on factors predicting resistance to technological change originally proposed that five factors would be important: the system itself, the individuals' background, exposure to technology, managerial actions, and job conditions. Contrary to predictions, the review found that of these five factors, those exerting the most effect on resistance were the state of existing and future jobs, understanding the need for the new technology, and managerial actions constituting barriers and incentives for system use. Assuming that minimal technical features of the system are met (e.g., usability, relevance, comprehensibility), the effects of the technical features on resistance to technological change were much less important. Moreover, individual characteristics appear to have relatively unimportant effects on resistance. A table presented by Johnson *et al.* (1985) summarizing their work provides a depiction of the type of conclusions identified here (see Table 9.5).

It should be noted that certain relationships remain unclear at best. The precise importance and role of actual system use on technological adjustment is not clear. Given the positive relationship of coordination among peers for reducing resistance it may be that actual use of the new system is less important than who one speaks with about the system. Alternatively, it may be that a little knowledge goes a long way, or that a little knowledge is a dangerous thing indeed! Managerial barriers and incentives other than those identified here are also not clear. Moreover, studies comparing management actions to other factors have not been done. It may be found that, as with system factors, management barriers pale in comparison to other factors. Finally, the interactive effect of current and future jobs, while clearly important, is complex and not yet well described.

These results have several practical implications for managers struggling with the problem of resistance to technological change. First, ensure that minimal system features are met. Second, ensure that subordinate staff all down the chain of command understand the need for the specific new system selected. Third, do *not* assume that the provision of more knowledge will decrease resistance—the opposite may be true. Fourth, do *not* assume that older people are more resistant or cannot be turned to for help during the change process; however, expect their scepticism and be prepared with ready answers. Fifth, carry out—at the least—the four actions mentioned as management incentives for encouraging adjustment: provide recognition and reward for system use; implement enough technology and training to create a critical mass of users; ensure job security and mean it; and undertake those activities necessary to convey to subordinates that your managers understand their role in the implementation process and beyond.

Table 9.5. Factors predicting and failing to predict adaptation, from a study of 194 organizations implementing word processors, n = 645 users (from Johnson et al., *1985).*

Factors that DO predict adaptation
Training
- Helped me understand how word processors think
- Still learning new ways to use

Experimentation encouraged by organization
- Time to experiment
- Organization encourages adaptation
- Policies do not discourage

Communication
- Talk about adaptation with coworkers, supervisors, authors
- Participate in meetings where uses and procedures are discussed
- Received praise for adaptation from coworkers and supervisor

Participate in decision-making about
- Unit productivity
- Formatting procedures
- Training

Factors that DO NOT predict adaptation
Machine characteristics
- Reliability
- Ease of use
- Versatility

Personality features
- Play computer games
- Seek new ways to do things
- Seek ways to solve problems
- Enjoy being a leader
- Communicate directly with authors
- Prefer to communicate directly with authors
- Have friends elsewhere in the organization

Organizational Orientation
- Talk about organization's product
- Talk about group product
- Think tasks could be done better with WP

Participation in decision-making about
- Equipment choice
- Maintenance
- Personnel performance criteria

A sixth implication of these findings is that managers must analyze the existing jobs and expected future jobs of those to be affected by the new technology to determine if users and non-users have anything to fear. Lucas (1978) suggests that people react to new technology by conducting a cost-benefit analysis of the change to their jobs and lives when the technology is implemented with results determining how resistant they will be. Conducting such an analysis as a manager from the perspective of subordinates may provide important insights into how much resistance to expect and what factors may generate that resistance.

Seventh, remember that those who can voluntarily use new technology will manifest their resistance in different ways than those who have no discretion over use. Therefore, different measures to diagnose resistance, e.g., for engineers versus drafters, may be desired.

Finally, remember that resistance may not always be wrong (Bright, 1964). Healthy scepticism may be helpful, if not truly enlightening. For example, in Stewart's (1971) case studies of effects of computers on managers, she found that conflict between computer managers and user managers was not necessarily harmful; it provided a way of selecting between the views of the innovators and those of the more conservative managers. In one of her case studies, for instance, it was suggested that the senior manager who offered the most opposition to the computer provided a useful check on the enthusiasms of the computer department. Thus, in diagnosing resistance, note that one's own definition or interpretation of resistance may indicate your own resistance to feedback.

Chapter 10
Managing the implementation process

10.1. Introduction

As described in the previous Chapter, the manner in which a new organizational change is implemented is related to people's reluctance to accept the change. This Chapter describes key variables in the implementation process which encourage successful use of CAD. It begins with a general discussion of the importance of implementation variables and how research has defined successful use of new technology. Six categories of factors are then identified as potentially affecting the success of implementation. Research for each factor is then reviewed.

Several research studies confirm that the manner in which new technology is implemented is related to the successful utilization of the technology. Johnson and associates (1985) found word-processing operators expressing less resistance to the technological change than to poor implementation. Mumford (1969) found that a variable exerting a major influence on the attitudes of employees to technological change was the way in which the change was implemented. In the Bikson *et al.* (1981) literature review, implementation process variables were found to be related to the successful utilization of new technology. Such variables included key actors who support and champion the change, adaptive planning for both the organization and the technology, and user participation in the implementation. Finally, Mann and Williams (1960) found that poor implementation led to numerous morale problems faced by supervisors in managing their subordinates. In sum, the way implementation is managed appears to be important for achieving the full benefits of a new technology such as CAD.

In this section, empirical research on implementation will be reviewed to identify the important specific characteristics of the implementation process which are related to the successful utilization of technology. For purposes of clarification, it is important to note that 'success' in the implementation literature has been defined in three different ways.

First, successful implementation may be defined as the extent of organizational use of a new technology (what Bikson *et al.* (1981) refer to as the 'degree' of implementation). Thus, rather than a concern for how any one individual uses the new technology, as was the focus in Chapter 9, one definition of success used in implementation research focuses on the extent to which the organization as a whole uses the new technology. Measures of success in this sense may be machine-utilization time or the number of people using the new equipment.

A second definition of success in the implementation literature defines success as the extent to which technology is deployed to meet its original objectives (what Bikson *et al.* (1981) refer to as the 'fidelity' of implementation). An organization implementing CAD with the objective of increasing the innovativeness of its designs will be rated as having successfully implemented CAD only if more innovative designs are produced with CAD, and not simply if CAD terminals are in use 24 hours a day.

In many organizations, the objectives for the new technology are not at all clear. CAD may have been purchased to generally enhance the capabilities of the drafting or design department. While these are general goals for the new technology, they are not very specific. In such situations, Johnson *et al.* (1985) have suggested an alternative definition of success. Since general capability enhancement is desired rather than the achievement of any one objective, they recommend defining success as the sophistication of use of the new technology. For the word-processing equipment they studied, sophistication was measured as the extent to which the organization adapted and integrated word processing into the ongoing work process. They identified four levels of sophistication: low integration (where the word processing was used primarily as a typewriter); clockwork systems (where the emphasis in equipment use was on developing efficient procedures to reduce the number of keystrokes per document); expander systems (where centralized centers were developed to handle all word processing); and system-wide adaptation (where the systems were decentralized with operators responsible for the creative use of the systems).

The diversity of these definitions of successful implementation suggests that the way in which one defines success may depend on the technology being studied and the organization in which the technology is being implemented. Moreover, some of these definitions are clearly more stringent than others. For CAD, simply using terminals hardly seems to live up to the promises posed by vendors. Rather, measuring success based on the use of CAD to either meet specific objectives or to more generally enhance design capabilities seems a far more appropriate criterion. Therefore, in the following review of research special emphasis is given to studies that have examined variables related to the latter two definitions of successful implementation.

Countless variables that describe the implementation process have been suggested as potentially affecting success of the implementation effort. These variables can be grouped into six categories:

1. Organizational context of the implementation.
2. Top management involvement in the implementation.
3. User participation in implementation decisions.
4. Planning the implementation process.

5. Training.
6. Managing system developers to handle implementation.

These factors are graphically depicted in Figure 10.1. In the literature reviewed in the following pages, those variables within each of these six categories that have been found to be most important in increasing the success of CAD installations are identified.

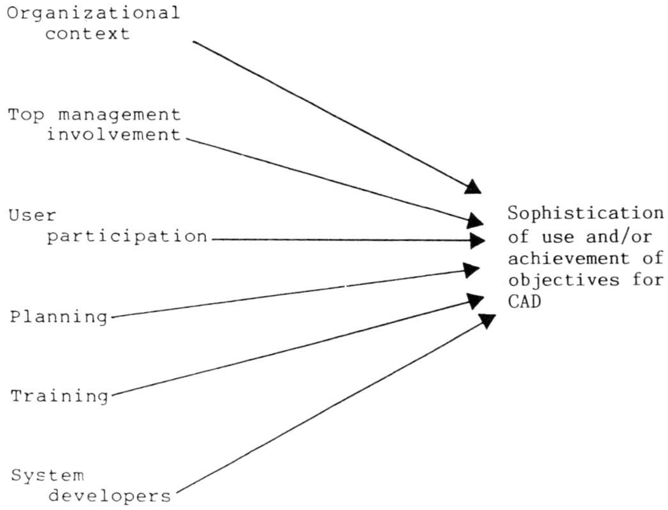

Figure 10.1. Factors related to the successful implementation of new technology.

10.2. The organizational context as it affects successful implementation

The context is the set of organizational goals and structure within which the implementation of the new technology will take place. Variables that describe the context include the organization's culture or orientation to change, the manner in which the organization is structured, the organization's rigidity, etc. In identifying contextual variables conducive to successful implementation, conclusions about organizational constraints that may prevent success can be derived. As such, a recognition of the limited role of factors in the implementation process may help to explain why some organizations never seem to successfully implement new technology.

Tomeski and Lazarus (1975) reviewed the information technology literature and identified how two alternative strategies to designing an organization may affect the way in which a CBIS is implemented. Depicted in Figure 10.2, they suggest that bureaucratic organizations (which are those that are more rigidly structured and departmentalized) are less likely to adopt revolutionary technological change than organic organizations (which are those that are characterized by more participative, informal and flexible structures). Extrapolating to CAD implementation, bureaucratic organizations, if they adopt CAD at all, are probably more likely to use it as a substitute for a drawing board, while organic organizations are more likely to use CAD to restructure the design process.

Bikson and Gutek (1983 b) also studied three organizational context variables in their survey: centralization of decision making, employee autonomy provided by the organization, and the organization's orientation toward change. The authors measured successful implementation as users' perceptions concerning the extent to which the new technology is integrated into their daily work. Of the three context variables, only one was found to be strongly related to successful implementation: the organization's orientation to change. More specifically, in those organizations where change is viewed as a positive, problem-solving and achievable goal, "white collar workers appeared to adapt more readily to innovative information systems" (p. 17).

In a survey of over 500 government municipalities adopting CBISs, Danziger *et al.* (1982) found that a variable related to how quickly government staff adopted a CBIS was the value orientation of the staff. An orientation focused more on consensus (i.e., participation) than partisan politics was more likely to adopt new technology quicker.

Johnson *et al.* (1985) also studied organizational context variables as potential predictors of the sophistication of use of word-processing equipment. The researchers found that more sophisticated use was associated with organizations in which management believed in flexible administrative rules and a reliance on employee self-discipline.

In one research study that addresses organizational context factors of CAD implementation, Jacobs (1986) found that a key variable constraining (or encouraging) implementation may be the particular industry of the organization. An organization which is in an industry with dependent supplier-customer relationships (e.g., automobile, government defense) may find the adoption of CAD to be essential for continuing contracts. Jacobs (1986) also found larger organizations more likely to adopt CAD (although Majchrzak *et al.*, 1985 b) found the relationship of size and CAD adoption to be much less clear). Although these few organizational variables may be related to adoption, simply adopting a CAD system does not guarantee its optimal utilization (from human resource as well as performance perspectives). Thus, while all organizations within a particular industry may adopt a new CAD system because they must, other aspects of their organizational context may constrain optimal use of that system.

Finally, there is substantial research on MIS implementations which attests to

Type of Organization	*Characteristics*	*Reactions to Change*	*Implications for Computerization*
Bureaucracy	• Rigidity • Formality • Departmentalized • Authoritarian • Imposed standards • Adherence to rules • Goals set by a few individuals • Rational man assumptions • Sanctions imposed	• Resists change • Slow to adjust to change • Difficulty in corresponding with environment	• Systems are likely to be unprogressive • Systems tend to perpetuate existing patterns • Computer use is likely to result in relatively marginal benefits
Organic	• Flexibility • Informality • Processes • Participative • Self-imposed standards • Personal initiative • Collective goals • Humanism • Motivation	• Adjustable to change • Induces desirable change • Easily corresponds with environment	• Modern, integrated systems are feasible • Dynamic systems tend to induce related changes in the organization • Computer use is prone to result in relatively significant benefits

Figure 10.2. Implications of organizational type for the implementation of computerization (from Tomeski and Lazarus, 1975, courtesy the Copyright Owner).

the important influence of political elements in an organization. This research suggests that managers implement MISs in ways that serve their own political motives (c.f., Kling and Iacono, 1984); to understand those motives is to understand how an organization's implementation activities will unfold.

The research briefly reviewed here suggests several tentative conclusions about how an organization's context may influence the way CAD is implemented. First, because of the penchant of bureaucratic organizations to avoid revolutionary change, such organizations are probably more likely to implement CAD as an electronic drafting device only. Second, organizations in particular industries may be more likely to adopt CAD, though not necessarily successfully implement it. Third, organizations with more positive attitudes about change are probably more likely to successfully implement CAD. Finally, organizational politics may determine *a priori* the success of an implementation effort.

With these conclusions, then, it appears that the importance of other factors in the implementation process (such as user or management involvement) is potentially constrained by the organizational context in which the implementation will take place. Thus, a bureaucratic organization negatively-oriented to change with political motives contrary to system optimization is likely to have implementation problems no matter how the other factors in the implementation process are managed. Managers implementing CAD in such organizations may be well-advised to be particularly cautious during implementation—so much so that delaying equipment installation until contextual factors are changed may be the wisest implementation decision.

10.3. The effect of top management involvement on successful implementation

In addition to organizational context, a second category of factors potentially affecting the implementation process concerns top management involvement. The need for top management support and involvement in implementing organizational change is such a well-accepted doctrine that it is almost folk-wisdom (e.g., Beer, 1980). Several studies on implementing technological change have also empirically documented the need for top management support.

In Sanders' (1968) case of the failure of a CBIS, he found that a reason for the failure was that the top management support vital to overcoming resistance to change was not obtained. Bikson *et al.* (1981) found that a key variable of the change process that enhances implementation of new technology is the presence of key actors (i.e., top managers) who support and champion the cause and use of the new technology. Ettlie and Rubenstein (1980), in their implementation study, found that while the importance of top management support was unquestioned, the acquisition of highly supportive attitudes about the new technology among this key group was much slower than expected. Finally, in the CAD literature, the AIDD survey of CAD users found that the most frequently mentioned advice provided by users was that "there should be a total commitment from company management to make the system work" (p. 11). This research suggests that not only is top management support important, but that this support needs to be obtained from the outset if implementation is to be successful.

While top management support is important, it is essential to ascertain how management should support the new technology, i.e., how should top management be involved in the implementation process and what support should top management provide to ensure successful implementation. Several studies provide suggestions on this issue.

Ettlie (1973) analyzed organizational data to understand the implementation process of organizations installing such production innovations as CAD. In this analysis, the author found that organizations were more successful in their implementation when their top management was more committed to the *concept* rather than the *hardware* of the new technology. That is, the involvement of top management in the general objectives and uses of the equipment rather than specific details of the hardware was necessary.

Three studies have found that while top management should focus more on the concept than the hardware, it needs to understand the new technology well enough to know how it fits into the work process. Johnson *et al.* (1985) found that more sophisticated equipment use was achieved in those organizations in which top management understood the technology, understood the system of human relationships in which work was done, and understood how word processing would affect the work process. Collins and Moores (1983) found that the more the workers perceived that management was willing to expend resources for the implementation process, the more they believed that the technological change would be successful. Ackoff (1967), in reviewing the literature on MIS implementation, found that a common assumption of system developers was that managers do not have to understand how an MIS works to manage and use it. Ackoff then reviewed the research and found that the data indicated the reverse; that is, incorrect judgments about equipment expenditures and optimizing system utilization result from a lack of understanding of the MIS.

Not only should top management be involved in both conceptualizing the technology and exploring how it fits into the organization, numerous studies suggest that top management should also be involved in the consensus-building process concerning system objectives. Mann and Williams (1960) examined this issue in their case study and found that a lack of consensus between managers of different departments regarding the understanding, intended use and priorities of the CBIS resulted in cross-departmental conflicts which slowed implementation. Kling's (1980) review found that the degree of consensus among top management over means and ends of the new technology determines in part whether new technology is used to make informed decisions or simply to rationalize already-made decisions.

This literature review of management involvement suggests several specific ways in which top management should be involved in the implementation of

CAD. First, top management must understand enough of the technology and the organization's business and workflow process to make reasonable judgments on how the technology fits in with the company's needs. In the words of one author:

> "Wittgenstein: Whereoft one does not understand, one should not speak.
> Hammer: Whereoft one does not understand, one should not automate."
> (Hammer, 1981; cited in Tapscott, 1982)

Second, top management needs to be involved in the implementation process primarily from a top-down perspective. That is, their focus needs to be on strategic concepts rather than the specific details of either the implementation or the technology. Too much involvement in operational decisions will remove the discretion needed by lower-level system developers as they adjust to the concerns of lower-level users of the system.

Third, top management must recognize a need to become involved not only in specifying objectives and uses, but in resolving the conflict likely to occur as objectives, priorities and uses are defined across departments and users. Interests of different departments and users are likely to be in conflict as strategic decisions are made, e.g., decisions about whether CAD should serve the needs of all designs, whether its output should feed directly to manufacturing tools, how CAD designs are approved, at what point in the design process should CAD designs be finalized and modifications halted, etc. Thus, an important role for top management is to resolve these conflicts as they arise—and preferably prior to full-scale implementation.

Finally, this research suggests that, upon agreement as to system strategy, priorities and use, this agreed-upon strategic direction should be communicated to employees affected by CAD. This is particularly important since people's perceptions of top management's role influence their optimism; thus, a strategic direction not communicated cannot combat employee pessimism. Moreover, technological change tends to disrupt people's lives in ways over which they have no control. Thus, as Mann and Williams (1960) found: "During much of the transition [to using a CBIS], the employees operated on faith: faith that the demands placed upon them would be rewarded in the future and faith in management's ability to effect the new change" (p. 235). Any communication that can help employees to maintain their faith is needed.

10.4. The effect of user participation on successful implementation

Not only does the organizational context and top management support affect the success of the implementation process, but user involvement in the implementation process itself appears to be important. Several studies from the CAD and information technology literature have identified the importance of user involvement.

In one such study, Clausen (1979) described a case of a computer system development that was stopped specifically because users were not involved in the initial decision concerning the purpose of the system.

In another study on the issue, Alter (1976) found that DSSs developed by technical people without the involvement of users was a primary factor "present in the history of almost every unsuccessful system in the sample" (p. 33): that is, of the 15 unsuccessful systems, 11 had not involved users, while 27 of the 31 successful systems had.

Johnson *et al.* (1985) also found that the participation of word-processing operators was important for enhancing the sophisticated use of the systems. The researchers examined this finding further and found that the most helpful form of this participation was soliciting involvement during regular meetings in which word-processing utilization was discussed.

Swanson (1974) had 37 managers of engineer departments complete questionnaires about computer-based retrieval systems used in the management of engineering projects. The researcher found that the number of questions system developers asked managers about system changes before the system was installed—a measure of *a priori* user involvement—was strongly related to the extent which the manager used the system.

Collins and Moores (1983) found that the more that users reported providing information to system personnel about their jobs and possible uses of the system, the less fear the users had about the technological change and the greater their perceptions of the success of the change effort.

In a study cited by Lucas (1975 a), Dickson and Powers (1973) found that the participation of operating management in the system design, their approval of specifications and their continued project review were associated with high levels of user satisfaction.

Finally, the AIDD survey of CAD users also identified user involvement as an important variable in successful implementation. In response to a question soliciting advice for organizing a CAD department, a comment provided by several respondents was "Select personnel that have a strong interest in the system and involve them in the department development" (p. 12).

These results suggest that user involvement is important for user satisfaction with the system, individual use of the system and organizational optimization of the system. Given the consensus in the literature on the importance of user involvement, a naive observer would assume that users are indeed involved in the implementation process. Yet the data indicate otherwise.

In their study, Bjorn-Andersen *et al.* (1979) surveyed different groups of people about their level of involvement in system development and implementation. The researchers found that computer manufacturers played a key role as programs were developed and fixed, users were little involved, top managers were involved only in the initial investment decision, and systems analysts and programmers were the most involved. In the authors' words: "it can be seen that in all five [organizations studied], user involvement was small or non-existent and user needs were specified either by bank top management or by the systems designers" (p. 330). Danziger *et al.* (1982) provide corroborative evidence in their survey of 3000 users of CBISs in over 500 local and city governments. They found that the quality of involvement of users with the data processing department was often unsatisfactory. For example, 37% of the users found the use of technical language by computer staff to be confusing, and reported that computer staff were more interested in the computer's capabilities than in solving users' problems. Finally, BNA (1984) surveyed 14 employers, each using over 1000 VDTs, and found that while 13 of the 14 employers informed employees prior to installation, the notice was typically less than three months and employee suggestions were not solicited.

These results suggest that while the involvement of users seems, at least in the literature, to be empirically supportable as aiding the success rate of technological implementation, users are not generally involved. Why aren't more users involved in the implementation process?

In the Danziger *et al.* (1982) study of government users of CBISs, the reason why user participation is so poor may be the way in which the gap between developers and users is bridged. Developers who find it difficult to communicate to users or solicit information in a way that leaves users feeling inadequately involved discourage user participation.

Bjorn-Andersen *et al.* (1979) suggest, based primarily on qualitative evidence, that the lack of user involvement is not due to a lack of management desire. They quote a French computer manager as saying: "It is not a good thing for the computer staff to work out problems alone. There should be more contact between the computer staff and the users" (p. 330). Given that the desire and perceived need for user involvement is there, the authors suggest that the reasons for the lack of user involvement seemed to be "due to ignorance on the part of the designers of how best to involve users, and to an absence of pressure from users to be involved" (p. 330).

Bostrom and Heinen (1977) reviewed the literature on MIS implementation failures and found that the lack of user involvement may be in part due to a choice made by the users themselves. If participation is perceived by users as undertaken by management for the express purpose of gaining acceptance rather than collaborative problem-solving, users will balk at such an involvement. This perception tends to be fueled by system developers who rarely allow users to actually accept responsibility for the success of the system; responsibility and thus credit and blame are typically in the hands of the developer. The authors suggest that users may also choose not to participate because of the time needed to make reasonable judgments. For example, in a survey of 2000 managers, the authors found that 80% of the managers wanted to influence the design of the MIS but were unwilling to invest the time.

In her longitudinal survey of 150 users of an electronic information exchange system, Hiltz (1984) also found users to be partly to blame for the lack of user involvement. She found that the more hours users spent on the system, the more features of the system they used. From this finding, she concludes that users may not be involved because they cannot tell the system developer what they need prior to using the technology.

Finally, Johnson *et al.* (1985) found that the lack of user participation was attributable to both managers and users. Managers were found to underestimate the capability of low-level staff to generate new ideas and applications of equipment and thus involved them only minimally in system development. Moreover, operators were found to not necessarily want participation in all types of decisions. Rather, they preferred involvement in decisions about training, but cared little about involvement in equipment choice.

The above studies about user involvement suggest several reasons why users are not as involved in the implementation process as the literature would recommend. These reasons are attributable equally to the users themselves, to managers of the users, and to the system developers. First, users are not more involved because they do not want to invest the time to learn the system. Thus, they want involvement only if their participation is truly problem-solving and only on those issues that matter to them and they can understand (such as training). Second, users are not more involved because system developers find it difficult to work with users. This difficulty is due in part to language barriers and in part to differences in focus. Finally, users are not more involved because managers fail to recognize how much users can offer to the implementation and system development process. Thus, missing is the level and type of encouragement necessary from the management staff if users are to become more involved.

These findings paint a rather bleak picture of the current state and future for user involvement. Yet, as the literature described at the beginning of this section indicates, user involvement is essential for successful implementation. Thus, three recommendations are suggested for enhancing the level and quality of user involvement.

The first recommendation for enhancing user involvement (by Hedberg, cited in Bostrom and Heinen, 1977) suggests that design decisions can be broken into two types: strategic (which estimates limits and objectives for the system) and technical (which works within the strategic guidelines to develop specific software and hardware options). Given the level of technical knowledge necessary to become involved in technical decisions, and given users' adversity to spending such time, Hedberg recommends that users be involved in the strategic decisions only, leaving technical decisions for the system developers to solve. Thus, users can feel involved in setting guidelines on issues about which they personally have concerns and in a way in which their involvement is productive.

A second recommendation for enhancing user involvement stems from Hiltz's (1984) finding that users' needs change as they become familiar with a new system. Due to this finding, Hiltz suggests that the typical approach to involving users, i.e., one-shot interviews conducted prior to system development and installment, is wrong. Rather, "an evolutionary design approach" in which continuous problem-solving discussion with users on a range of issues from software development to training would provide both a more knowledgeable involvement of users and the sense of continued improvement necessary to maintain a lengthy and changing implementation process. In support of this notion, the AIDD survey of CAD users found that a suggestion offered by several users for organizing a CAD department was providing time for people to work out system development problems on a continuous basis.

A final recommendation for enhancing user involvement revolves around the management of system developers. Clearly, something is wrong when system developers cannot speak the users' language or leave users with the impression that developers are concerned less with system use than computer hardware. Thus efforts must be made to identify ways to appropriately manage the system developers to help overcome the chasm between developers and users. The issue of how to manage system developers is dealt with in detail as the sixth and final factor of implementation process variables affecting successful implementations.

10.5. The effect of planning on successful implementation

Another category of factors that may affect the chances of a successful implementation of CAD is the way in which the implementation process is planned. How do implementers of new technology currently plan for implementation? In a recent study surveying managers of engineering firms using CAD, Senker (1984) found that managers reported four errors in the implementation planning process when CAD was installed:

1. The time needed to achieve effective functioning was under-estimated.
2. The utilization rate likely to be achieved with CAD was over-estimated.
3. The need to make adaptive adjustments was under-estimated.
4. The tasks involved in securing labor acceptance of change were under-estimated.

Palitto, in his description of Firestone's experience with CAD (1984), found similar errors in planning. Firestone's staff admitted that they had transferred the workload immediately from manual to CAD without allotting sufficient time for training, building a data base, formulating procedures and policies, and learning to use the system. Finally, Johnson *et al.* (1985), in their study of almost 200 organizations implementing word processing, found that the planning process for the implementation was characterized in virtually all organizations by little initial consciousness of how social factors are related to technical factors.

These findings suggest that organizational planning for the implementation of new technology is fraught with errors. Such errors include the under-estimation of the time, resources and need for organizational adaptation to the new technology, as well as an ignorance of the role of social and organizational issues in the implementation process. Thus, it would appear that organizations would benefit from a greater emphasis on careful planning of the implementation process.

However, how important is careful planning to successful implementation?

Support for the importance of careful planning prior to and during implementation is derived from a study by Ettlie (1973) who conducted a secondary analysis of organizations implementing production innovations. Ettlie found that organizations which successfully implemented their new technologies were more likely to have carefully planned for integration of the new processes into the existing workflow. Careful planning appears to be particularly important for such new information technologies as CAD. For example, in an empirical study of the introduction of CAD systems in 20 German companies, Schaffitzel and Kersten (1985) found that the duration of CAD introduction lasted for several years. Moreover, Mann and Williams (1960), in their case study of CBIS introduction, found that the scope of preplanning preceding the decision to install the CBIS determined whether changes to the organization were procedurally minor or structurally major. Thus, with CAD the opportunities for organizational changes are so great and the duration of the implementation and adjustment period so long, that the need for careful planning which keeps estimation errors to a minimum seems particularly important.

Given the importance of careful planning for implementation of CAD, what types of plans are particularly necessary to enhance the likelihood of a successful implementation? Johnson *et al.*'s (1985) research suggests that the approach taken by management to the implementation planning process is an important consideration. In their study, they found that the more management was willing to allow implementation to be an orchestrated, evolutionary process shaped by conflicts and negotiation, the more sophisticated the eventual use of the system. Thus, plans that are too tightly drawn in advance may not serve the best interests of the organization. Moreover, as Tapscott (1982) found in his research, "rational plans tend to be counter-political, [and thus such] plans are not implemented" (p. 29). Yet this need to allow evolution in the planning process must be coupled with the need for definition and objectives. CAD users responding to the AIDD survey (1983) offered this recommendation: "Organize a plan for implementation of the CAD system into your organization and set definite goals to reach with time frames on each" (p. 12).

Also to be included in the implementation plans is an explicit delineation of specific phases of the implementation process. David (1981) proposes eight distinct phases in the implementation of a successful CAD system. These phases are listed in Table 10.1. Of particular note in this list is that actual installation of the new terminals is the last step—completed only after substantial planning has been undertaken.

To David's list, other steps could be added as a follow-on. While installation may indeed be the last step of *initial* implementation, it should certainly not be the final step if an evolutionary approach to implementation and a long-term strategy to adaptation of the organization to the system is adopted. Therefore, an important step to add to this list is what is commonly referred to in the organizational development literature as the 'refreezing' phase of implementation. Refreezing refers to the set of activities involved in stabilizing the organization at a

Table 10.1. Implementation phases of a successful system.

- Analysis of current design process
- Study possibilities offered by CAD
- Define design process for CAD given user needs and desired integration
- Define functional specifications for CAD given design process
- Feasibility study of prototype
- Detailed definitions for new procedures and system
- Investment plan
- Installation

Reproduced from David (1981), by permission of Copyright Owner.

new equilibrium to maintain and continue the integration of the new technology with the organization. Such activities may take the form of developing new norms of behavior or rules, or providing continued reinforcement for use of the new system. A quote from Tapscott's (1982) research illustrates the need for refreezing activities: "A company was able to 'unfreeze' an office and successfully introduce a system. But they did not know how to institutionalize the change, or 'refreeze' the new system. They did not know that a system is most vulnerable once it is running. The system failed" (p. 29).

To prepare implementation plans as detailed and extensive as that recommended here, a framework for interrelating the various aspects under consideration in the implementation plans is necessary. Encarnacao (1983) provides such a framework, as presented in Figure 10.3. Through this framework, he suggests that implementation plans be concerned with several types of interfaces:

1. The interface between design requirements, design characteristics and the CAD architecture. Developing plans around this interface will yield a new model of the engineering design process with CAD.
2. The interface between the environment and the system (CAD architecture). Plans for this interface would match the system to the needs of the organization for control, complex data handling, flexibility, etc.
3. The interface between operator requirements, operator and job characteristics and operator dialogue. Plans resolving this interface would deal with issues of user and system response time, error types and rates, and data transfer times and rates.
4. Finally, the interface between the system, dialogue and performance assessments must be considered.

Using a framework such as that suggested by Encarnacao can help to ensure that such essential information as time line, personnel, task definitions, company procedures, management expectations, etc. is included in the implementation

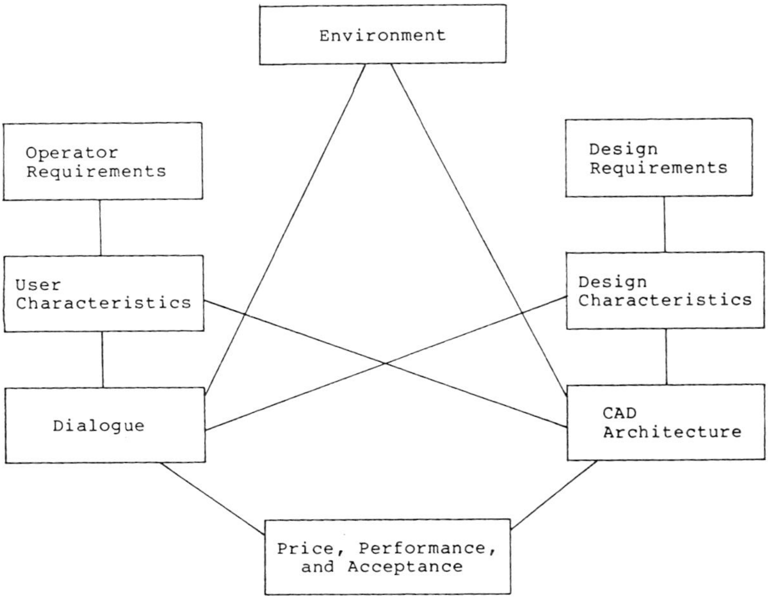

Figure 10.3. A conceptual framework for developing CAD implementation plans (from Encarnacao (1983), courtesy North-Holland Publishing Co.).

plans. Also, as Burks (1984) points out, an examination of these interfaces often yields non-CAD-related benefits such as identifying workflow bottlenecks and obsolete design standards.

In summary, an examination of the research on the set of variables related to planning for implementation suggests that implementation planning is indeed important for successful utilization of CAD. However, organizations are not giving planning the attention or time these processes deserve. An enhanced concern for social and organizational issues as they relate to the technical features of the system, as well as allowing for evolutionary but systematic change to occur as organizations learn to adapt to the new technology, is needed.

10.6. The effect of training on successful implementation

Numerous studies have emphasized the importance of training for enhancing the likelihood of successful implementation. The study by Bikson and Gutek (1983 a; Gutek *et al.*, 1984) found that one of the reasons why office automation was not fully utilized in most work groups was the lack of adequate training to use the system. Moreover, they found that 33% of the variance in managerial satisfaction with learning support and 21% of the variance in perceived incorporation of the computer into ongoing office activity was accounted for by four training variables.

Other studies have also identified the importance of training for successful implementation. Johnson *et al.*'s (1985) study of word-processing implementation in almost 200 organizations found that the more time users spent learning new ways to use the system, the more sophisticated the organizational use of the system. Staehle (1982) surveyed 245 users of VDTs in 14 organizations and found that the amount of training provided to new users concerning the functioning of the VDT had a positive effect on users' work satisfaction. In Sanders' (1968) case study of an implementation failure of a CBIS, one of the reasons identified for failure was that the data processing manager did a poor job of personnel preparation. Finally, Lazear in a 1984 *Computer Graphics World* article reminds us how important training is for CAD implementors in particular. Lazear estimates that in the USA alone there is a need to train 100 000 drafters and engineers in CAD over the next few years at an average cost of $10 000 per trainee. This cost includes the direct and indirect expense for instructor and student labor, supplies, use of a CAD terminal and the cost of less productive output. "This means the United States faces a staggering expenditure of $1 billion in training costs alone" (p. 49).

In summary, training of CAD users is important because it is related to job satisfaction of users, success of new systems, and sophisticated integration of systems into the organization's workflow. Moreover, concern for training is essential given the huge numbers of people and expenditures to be incurred over the next decade or so as CAD is adopted more and more widely.

Given the importance of training, however, is it given sufficient attention in organizations implementing new technology today? Six studies deal with this issue. A recent Harbor Research Group (Boston, MA) survey of CAD implementors found that the biggest single problem mentioned by CAD users was education and training (Wagner, 1985). In a recent study by Jacobs (1985), 202 Michigan auto suppliers responded to a mailed questionnaire on training for CAD. Jacobs found that there was generally a lack of an organized approach to training. Seventy-two percent of the firms with CAD used informal on-the-job training only; neither apprenticeships nor more formal training programs were provided. In addition, a full 40% of the firms had no training coordinator, with virtually all firms using vendor training and private training companies as the most popular source of training.

Majchrzak *et al.* (1985 b) surveyed a national probability sample of manufacturing firms and found that for those firms using CAD, few (19%) offered CAD training. Hamilton and Sheehan (1982) also interviewed CAD users (81 users at Rockwell) and found that one of the implementation problems most commonly mentioned by users was the lack of adequate training. Moreover, users complained that management failed to support any training or learning inefficiencies inherent in adjusting to a new system.

In their study of office automation implementors, Bikson and Gutek (1983 a) found that virtually all employees were dissatisfied with the focus of training, reporting it as too narrow. Moreover, they found little organizational attention to continuation of learning beyond initial training, an activity that over 90% of the employees judged to be necessary and the availability of which was significantly related to employee satisfaction.

In summary, then, users perceive training as it currently exists in organizations implementing new information technologies and CAD as inadequate. What is it about CAD training programs that are inadequate and how can they be improved?

To analyze existing training programs, it is helpful to conceive of training as consisting of two stages: initial training and continued or follow-on training. Initial training occurs when the individual is selected and may typically consist of sending the individual away to take a vendor training course. Follow-on training may take the form of advanced training classes offered by the vendor, or in-house seminars on more advanced commands or system problems that arise after installation. Understanding useful characteristics of each stage of training will help to develop a more complete training program.

Initial training in organizations implementing new technology today takes many diverse forms; however, there are some communalities. The AIDD survey of CAD users reported that most CAD training is initially done on-site by the CAD manufacturer. As more users are selected later on, training is handled by the firm itself, modelled after the vendor training. Jacobs (1985), in his survey of CAD training in Michigan firms, found a similar heavy reliance on vendors as a source of initial training. So did Majchrzak *et al.* (1985 b) in their survey of a national probability sample of manufacturing plants. In the Bikson and Gutek (1983 a) survey of office automation users, they found that the most common form of training was individual on-the-job training (a finding similar to that of Jacobs). They also found that employees reported that written manuals were of little value for initial training, that training was too narrowly focused, and that most employees had to turn to other users for assistance beyond the first days of training.

The state of existing initial training therefore seems to be one of a fairly narrow focus on specific terminal functions, little customization of vendor training for specific organizational work processes, and with most training done informally on the job with heavy reliance on peers. Is this the best type of training that can be offered? Several studies suggest that substantial improvements in our existing training programs can be made.

Tapscott (1982), in reviewing failures of implementation in office automation systems, found that "vendors install standard products in customer environments. The large body of failure literature indicates that such an approach has not and will not enable the successful implementation of integrated office systems"

(p. 31). He offers several reasons for a need not to rely on vendors: the vendor cannot understand all the different needs of the different subgroups; a training program appropriate at one point in time may not be appropriate later, given the dynamic nature of organizations; vendors tend to ignore human problems in the training and change process; and vendors tend to be poor at adapting to user requirements because they start with a solution in search of a problem. Tull (1984) extends Tapscott's conclusions to the CAD environment. With his experience of implementing training programs for CAD users, Tull observes that vendor training only provides a minimal level of system indoctrination; without customizing training to address the company's specific operating procedures, he states, the major benefits of CAD are difficult to achieve.

While vendors' training packages should not be used to substitute for in-house initial training programs, Ettlie and Rubenstein (1980) have found a special purpose for vendors. In their longitudinal study of automation projects, they found that successful implementation efforts were characterized by the vendors modelling the appropriate behavior for technology use and trouble-shooting for the organizations. From this finding, the authors recommend that the interaction between vendors and user personnel be exploited to facilitate the acquisition of new behaviors among users.

In addition to a new approach by vendors, initial training can benefit from a recognition of the type of training actually needed during the initial implementation period. Johnson *et al.* (1985) found that more sophisticated use of new systems was achieved when training gave a general education in concepts (e.g., work process) rather than a specific education in machine functions. The researchers also found that training which focused on learning new ways to use a system rather than simply more proficiently using specific functions yielded more sophisticated use of new systems by the organizations.

Tull (1984) also recommends a move away from the traditional training focused on specific machine operation. He points out that a shortcoming of most CAD training programs is that they teach operators how to draw on a VDT in a way analogous to manual drafting. Instead, operators must be trained to produce computer models that provide all the end-product information required by downstream users.

Training programs of the future should not only teach a broader range of skills than is currently taught, but should be directed toward a broader audience. Given the underestimates of management about the learning curve problem with CAD, a need to train design managers themselves in the basic use of CAD must be emphasized (Jacobs, 1985). Hamilton and Sheehan (1982) found that such training of design managers decreased resistance to change not only among the managers but among those working for them. Tull (1984) also suggests a familiarization course for managers. Such a course would explain how CAD will change managers' jobs, such as the changes to monitoring subordinates' work given new output cycles, and the changes to work scheduling and budgeting with CAD. Such a course can help managers to understand the frustrations of users in learning and adapting to the new system by exposing them, for example, to anxieties associated with slow response times. Tull suggests that such a course need not be longer than ten hours.

A final recommendation for improvements to initial training programs is offered by Hiltz's (1984) research. In her longitudinal study of the implementation of an electronic information exchange system, Hiltz found that the first sessions on the terminal were characterized by users expressing the need for feedback from others. One colorful example of such expression from one user was: "This is the first message of a wandering wordsmith caught in a time warp" (p. 95). This observation suggests that initial training programs need to incorporate extensive feedback as users become adapted to the new system. This need for feedback is corroborated by Holding (1986) in his recent review of the training literature. In his words: "Some feedback seems essential for acquiring a skill and many experiments have shown that successful learning is mediated by knowledge of results" (p. 32).

These studies lead to the following conclusions about characteristics important for future programs focused on helping users through their initial training period:

1. Customize training to organizations, decrease reliance on vendors to provide the training, and use real organizational examples during training sessions.
2. To facilitate customization of training not only within the organization but across individual users, conduct pre-training screening assessments.
3. Formalize training plans.
4. Help management to understand the learning curve.
5. Broaden training to include general concepts and system capabilities.
6. Broaden the audience of training to include those who are only indirectly involved in the new system.
7. Recognize that training will create anxiety and frustration; prepare management accordingly such that users do not feel unduly pressured to perform too early.
8. To reduce reliance on other users during the initial learning stages and thus increase the time spent on the system and not helping others, establish a user consultant with primary responsibilities to offer help to new users.

For a training program to lead to successful implementation of a new technology, not only must initial training be optimally designed, continued or follow-on training is also necessary to directly benefit the users and the organizations. Continuous learning or training appears to occur sporadically in organizations. Bikson and Gutek (1983 a) found that despite the fact that continuous learning was related to employee satisfaction, there was little organizational attention paid to continuous learning. Johnson *et al.* (1985) also found that the existence of continuous learning was related to a more sophisticated use of the new system; yet they too found little attention paid to continuous learning. Some continuous learning does appear to exist, however. The AIDD survey (1983) of CAD users found 16 of the 24 respondents reporting the conduct of continuous learning seminars or discussion sessions. Four topics for discussion at these sessions were mentioned: techniques and procedures, programming, software releases, and general discussions to improve quality or production.

Since continuous learning seems to appear only sporadically in some organizations, suggestions on improving those sessions seem appropriate. Based on his experience implementing CAD training programs, Tull (1984) suggests that trainees be returned to the instructor for problems after initial training has been completed and the trainee has had the opportunity to work on the job for a while. According to Holding's (1986) review of the training literature, trainees cannot be expected to learn very much in initial training sessions. This is because the trainees need practice to be able to absorb preliminary instructions. Holding goes so far as to say "overelaborate preliminary instructions before practice may not only fail to assist the trainee but may obstruct progress" (p. 14). Thus, by offering follow-on training, new problems that are encountered can be resolved, and more sophisticated commands can be introduced.

Another suggestion for improving continuous training comes from the case study of Firestone's experience with CAD (Palitto, 1984). In this case, it was found that biweekly meetings among users to discuss specific problems and ideas proved quite effective in keeping users and system developers informed of changes or the need for changes.

Another suggestion by Tull is that a hot-line be developed for operators to get immediate answers to questions after initial training. This suggestion is akin to that offered by Hiltz for initial training, but may prove particularly useful as users gain sufficient experience to try new system features and stretch their own capabilities.

Finally, Tull suggests that just as initial training should be provided to managers, the same managers should receive follow-up or continuous learning sessions. In this way, the managers can be kept informed of system evolution as well as the impact of such evolution on the way they need to manage their workforce.

In summary, this section on training variables has identified several characteristics of initial and continuous training that seem to be essential for successful implementation. Given the importance of training for such outcomes as job satisfaction and optimal system utilization, much education and emphasis on training is needed if the large numbers of drafters and engineers (100 000 alone in the USA) are to be ready to fully utilize CAD in the 1990s.

10.7. Managing system developers to effect successful implementation

The final factor to be reviewed in this Chapter as it affects successful implementation is the management of system developers. In a review of the literature on

MIS problems and failures, Bostrom and Heinen (1977) concluded that forces that influence technical design are not just the technology itself, but also the designer's knowledge, skills, values and assumptions about people and organizations. Moreover, in research described earlier, system developers have been found to be the main participants—if not determinants—not only of the system itself but also of the implementation process (Bjorn-Andersen *et al.*, 1979). Clearly, system developers are important players in implementation.

Because of their importance in the implementation process, the problems and limitations of system developers are particularly noteworthy. Bostrom and Heinen (1977), in their review of the MIS literature, identified several limitations of system developers: they don't think in a systemic fashion, being too narrowly focused on their own equipment; they tend to analyze situations and user needs from the top, ignoring the concerns of lower-level staff; they ignore non-rational and changing aspects of the organization in their system designs and implementation plans; and they know only a limited set of techniques for implementing change and handling resistance to change. Cougar and Zawacki (1978) surveyed 600 data processing professionals and 1000 non-data processing professionals and found a similarly negative limitation of data processing professionals: they had a negligible need to work with others—a job characteristic, needless to say, of great importance to optimal implementation.

Hedberg and Mumford (1975) surveyed 61 system designers of CBISs on questions which differentiated their attitudes towards others as either describing a Theory X or Theory Y style (Theory X assumes people are not intrinsically challenged by their jobs and are motivated primarily by money while Theory Y ascribes to the opposite tenets). The results of their survey indicated that system designers primarily ascribe to a model of man that most closely approximates that of Theory X. Thus, in designing a system, developers are assuming users do not want challenge in their jobs—a depiction that does not bode well for those users who must work with the system being designed.

Bjorn-Andersen *et al.* (1979) also surveyed system designers of CBISs. They found that the system designers reported few organizational constraints imposed on them by management concerning their alternatives for technical systems designs, yet they considered few and only minor alternatives to how their design might affect the work of others. The surveyed designers reported designing the system for those with the least training—an approach expected if they follow a Theory X model of man. The survey also found that the designers expressed little responsibility over the work design aspect of the system. Corroborating this evidence is Cougar and Zawacki's (1978) study which also found that data processing professionals feel less personally accountable for the outcomes of their work compared to other professionals.

This research on system designers does not paint a pretty picture. Tapscott (1982) portrays three roles for system designers in Figure 10.4. This research suggests that the designer as partner with the users is a dream not yet come true. Those developing CAD systems in the organization are apparently developing

Figure 10.4. The role of the designer (from Tapscott (1982), courtesy Plenum Press).

them for the Theory X worker. Moreover, system designers seem to be oblivious to the important role they play in matching the system to the user, job and organization.

These conclusions suggest the exceptional need to manage the system designer–user interface, since, apparently, system designers cannot be expected to appropriately manage the interface themselves. Several suggestions for managing this interface have been offered in the literature. Hiltz and Turoff (1978), based on a review of the literature on implementation of computer conferencing systems, suggest that an individual or team of individuals be appointed to manage the user–computer interface. Such a team or individual would serve as a central point of contact responsible for keeping files up-to-date, provide personal or telephone training and help, provide public relations to new users, and offer follow-up help and encouragement to new users. Of all these responsibilities, the authors suggest that the public relations function is the most important since it ensures that continued interest in the system is maintained.

Schaffitzel and Kersten (1985) found some support for the utility of a user–system interface in their research. They found such an interface to be a useful alternative to the typical approach of designers tiresomely questioning future users to identify incorrect development decisions. Finally, in research cited by Schultz and Sleven (1975), data processing managers' time alone can be useful in overcoming problems of the user–system interface. They found that the more time data processing managers spent in implementation, the more successful the implementation effort was perceived to be.

In addition to a need to manage the user–system interface, in some organizations a unit exists to specifically service the new technology implemented. We saw this creation of a unit specifically devoted to CAD work in the Firestone case (Palitto, 1984). When such units are created, an additional concern is the adequate management of such units. Several studies have documented the need, and offered specific suggestions, for managing such units.

Cheney and Dickson (1982), in their study of CBIS implementation, found that managers who took a user/service orientation toward managing their CBIS units were more likely to enhance job satisfaction among users than managers whose sole focus for their units was on system development.

Johnson *et al.* (1985) found that 'innovative' managers of word-processing units were more likely to be found in those organizations that had achieved a more sophisticated integration of their new technology with the organization. Innovative managers did five things: focused efforts on estimating a boundary for developing a miniculture to the unit; recruited respected members outside the unit as change agents to support the use of the new technology throughout the organization; focused unit work on a select number of core activities only; promoted innovation among unit members; and kept everyone inside and outside the unit informed in language they all understood.

Palitto's (1984) Firestone case found that the CAD unit managers went even a step further than just initiating a user/service orientation. Palitto found that along with the service orientation, a system to ensure customer satisfaction was developed by having all clients of the CAD units complete evaluation forms and unit coordinators check with clients to assess the satisfactory completion of unit work.

These observations suggest that not only is management of the user–system designer interface important, but, when a special technology unit exists, proper management of that unit is also essential.

10.8. Conclusions

This literature review offers several conclusions about important implementation variables. First, failures in implementation are caused by an interaction among multiple factors. Poor training alone will rarely be enough; rather poorly training only those directly involved in the new technology without asking for user involvement may prove much more fatal.

Second, the organizational context constrains the degree and success of implementation. Thus, for implementors who are in organizations that are primarily bureaucratic in nature and have managers with generally negative views toward change, they will find the going rough no matter how many correct implementation process principles are followed.

Third, top management must be involved in strategic and directional decision making. Top management must be kept away from the tactical or operational decisions; these decisions are best left to the negotiation and evolution inherent in the implementation process at lower levels in the organization.

Fourth, user participation should be managed for evolutionary problem-solving on setting directions, rather than solving specific technical problems. Valuable user time and frustration can be saved with such an approach.

Fifth, substantial planning prior to equipment installation is called for. Using systematic documentable frameworks that establish goals, timeliness and directions, yet allow for the evolution of solutions as conflicts on operational issues arise, is a strategy most likely to lead to successful implementation.

Sixth, more emphasis on training is essential. Training those only tangentially involved in the new technology as well as continuous follow-on courses are innovations that should be incorporated into future training programs.

Finally, since system designers tend to have a narrow, technical focus that ignores social and organizational issues involved in new technology implementation, system designers must be managed to enhance that interface—either directly, or through management of their own special unit.

Part IV

CONCLUSIONS

Chapter 11
Effective design and use of CAD

The previous parts of this book have concentrated on separate treatments of the technical, human–computer interaction, and management aspects in the design and use of CAD systems. The purpose of this final chapter is to integrate the research and topics which were discussed in these three separate parts. On the surface, these three parts appear to be totally different. Part I considered the technical aspects of CAD, discussing it from a machinery and computer viewpoint. Part III considered the managerial aspects of CAD focusing mainly on the people who will be affected by the implementation of CAD systems. Part II provided a bridge between these two areas focusing on both the equipment and the people who must interact with the computer. Below these surface considerations, however, discussions in all three parts ultimately have the same goal: the effective design and use of CAD systems.

Six criteria are frequently associated with the effective use of CAD systems. These criteria are listed in Table 11.1 and can be used to judge the effectiveness of the design and use of CAD systems. The last four criteria in the Table are objectives of a CAD system. The first two criteria are some of the means for achieving these objectives. For example, since CAD systems standardize the design process, design work can be done more efficiently. These measures are not necessarily comprehensive or exhaustive: in effect, several of these criteria are highly intercorrelated and others could probably be added to the list. These six do, however, provide a good method for summarizing the material presented in the previous chapters and for highlighting the contributions of each of the separate parts of the book. Each of these six criteria is discussed below along with topics from each part of the book.

11.1. Ease of use

In order for a CAD system to yield benefits to the organization, it must be easy to use. The criterion of ease of use refers to how well a system and workplace has been designed so that the learning time for the system is short, the system is forgiving of mistakes, and changes can be made easily to the designs. One means for achieving this ease of use is in the technical design of the CAD system. A designer

Table 11.1. A summary of technical, human-computer and management issues in the design and use of CAD systems.

Criterion	Technical issues	Human–computer issues	Management issues
Ease of use	Facilitates design changes	Design system for capabilities of user	Reduce resistance to change through incentives and training
Standardization	Use standardized symbol tables; use group technology concept	Ergonomic standards for workplace	Standardize work flow procedures while maintaining sufficient operator autonomy
Productivity	Integrate design, drafting, engineering analysis and manufacturing; use group technology concept	Reduce fatigue, stress, absenteeism	Develop organizational structures to enhance communication and encourage participation in system design
Effectiveness for conveying ideas	Provides ability to manipulate 3-D solid models for design, analysis and representation	Perceptual and cognitive aspects of 3-D manipulation	Train operators to design in 3-D with CAD
Creativity/ Innovation	Not applicable	By reducing attention to computer interaction, attentional resources are freed	Provide operators with time to experiment with system which yields creative uses of system
Quality of the design product	Facilitates conducting multiple tests and simulations before developing prototypes	Develop decision aids to make design choices	Reduce barriers to engineering–manufacturing interface

using a CAD system can change a design very easily; it is much easier to change a drawing using the graphics editor of a CAD system than to modify a manually done pencil-and-ink drawing.

Ease of use is also facilitated by the effective utilization of human–computer interaction methodologies. Ease of use can be reflected in the kinds of decisions which have to be made when designing the interface and choosing the interface appropriate for a particular task. As examples, several possible interface modes, such as menu displays, direct manipulation and keyboard commands are available, and the research has indicated the relative ease of each for specified purposes. Several possible input devices are available: some are better for drawing tasks and others are better for pointing tasks based on the time and accuracy required for various kinds of interface features.

Despite the above contributions to ease of use, CAD systems will not be utilized in industry unless management reduces the resistance to change. Such considerations include reducing managerial incentives for resistance, educating operators about CAD systems, and properly managing jobs so that change is viewed as an enhancement of an already good job situation.

11.2. Standardization

Standardization provides the opportunity for uniformity in design. With this uniformity, other benefits of CAD, such as increased productivity, can be achieved. Standardization is achieved technically in CAD operations through the use of group technology and standardized symbol tables. The use of group technology helps the designer to select standard parts or design features. Standard design symbols in the input process for CAD design forces the designer to standardize drawings for manufacturing.

From a human factors and management point of view, standardization of the workplace can be achieved in two ways. First, ergonomics and anthropometric data can help to standardize the CAD workplace design by providing recommendations for the preferred seat and table heights, the preferred illumination levels, and the correct sitting posture. Second, standardization can be achieved by formalizing the work and information flow among designers themselves and between designers and other segments of the organization. When formalizing the information and work flow, however, it is important that the operator's autonomy be retained to ensure job satisfaction upon the implementation of CAD.

11.3. Productivity

Increasing design productivity is clearly an important outcome of CAD systems. Productivity is defined as the ratio of inputs to outputs; a ratio frequently expressed in terms of output per man-hour. It has been reported that in comparison to conventional drawing, CAD can increase productivity from 3 : 1 to more than a 10 : 1 ratio; individual cases have been cited of 100-fold productivity improvements (Groover and Zimmers, 1985). Even higher productivity can be obtained by integrating design, drafting, engineering analysis and manufacturing. Through this integration, the same data base can be shared by all the engineering/manufacturing activities. Previously, paper drawings had to be sent between functional departments and the drawings had to be re-drawn to satisfy the desired format of each department. With the use of CAD, productivity is increased because time can be saved and errors can be reduced. The group technology concept can further improve the design productivity by classifying and coding parts and products. When designing new parts, existing similar parts can be retrieved as references. With group technology, many redundant designs can be avoided, thus preventing designers from "re-inventing the wheel".

Productivity is also increased when the principles of human–computer interaction are effectively implemented. For example, the effective design of CAD furniture, screen design, the physical environment and software help to reduce fatigue, stress and absenteeism. Since fatigue, stress and absenteeism are vital ingredients contributing to productivity, adhering to principles of effective human–computer interaction will help to enhance the designer's productivity with CAD.

In addition to technical and human–computer issues, productivity is increased with proper management. The appropriate involvement in system development of managers and CAD users helps to ensure a system designed to meet the users' needs as well as their ergonomic concerns. Finally, the development of new organizational structures for enhancing communication among parties within the CAD design function, as well as between those who use CAD in the design function and those in other functions within the organization, is most important if CAD operators' time is to be efficiently utilized.

11.4. Effectiveness

With manual drafting, the designer is constrained to representing and manipulating complex ideas in two dimensions. As such, important information is lost. Another criterion for judging the design and use of the CAD system is the effectiveness of the system for representing and conveying complex three-dimensional ideas. The technology of CAD provides unique opportunities in this area. CAD enhances the ability of designers to manipulate 3-D solid models in the design, analysis, and representation stages of design. For example, the rotation of objects in three dimensions provides an opportunity to look at the item to be designed from different directions. By viewing it from these multiple perspectives, additional information is conveyed to the designer than when merely looking on the object from one direction. The designer is also able to visualize the finished assembly design as well as inspect cut-off views.

Despite these possibilities with CAD, to benefit from the use of this technology, CAD operators must be trained in order to design in three dimensions. Moreover, the perceptual and cognitive aspects of design and manipulating objects in three dimensions must be understood. Research has been directed towards understanding the spatial representation in memory of the objects and the processes of spatial reasoning. Humans have the ability to mentally rotate simple figures in much the same way as a piece of paper can be manipulated by the hands to observe it in different orientations. For complex figures, however, humans break the figures into smaller parts and manipulate these parts separately. Understanding this spatial reasoning allows for an understanding of possible problems which may occur. If the operator manipulates objects feature by feature, errors could occur when recombining them into a whole.

11.5. Creativity

Creativity is frequently considered to be the most important aspect in design. Introducing CAD into the design process may actually decrease creativity by too much attention being given to the computer interaction instead of the creative aspects of design. Another criterion, therefore, for judging the effectiveness of the design and use of a CAD system is how creativity is maintained with its implementation.

The design process requires attentional resources for perception, cognitive processes and responses. Interacting with the computer will require the same limited attentional resources. If the computer interaction is difficult and complex, few resources will remain for the CAD operator to devote to the important creative design task. The attentional resources required for computer interaction tasks can be reduced by dividing subtasks between the available resource "pools", making the input and output compatible, and designing a system which is easy to learn so that the tasks become automatic for the operator.

By allowing the operator time to experiment with CAD systems, new, innovative and creative uses of the system will frequently result. The degree of creativity derived through this process is a function of the operator's innate creative ability.

11.6. Quality of design

A final criterion for judging the design and use of the CAD system is the quality of the design produced by CAD. The quality of design implies that the resulting product is reliable, durable, and easy to use. The technology of the CAD system provides the opportunity for rapidly evaluating and testing the quality of different design configurations through the use of computer simulation methodologies. Compared to designing with manual drafting, CAD designers are able to perform more testings on the CAD system before prototyping a product.

Quality of design can also be enhanced through the development and use of alphanumeric and/or graphic decision aids. Decision aids can, as an example, supply the operator with reliabilities of components of the piece by allowing access to a data base containing this and other information. Care must be taken in the design of these aids. Research on decision making has shown that people can only entertain a very limited number of decision hypotheses at any one time and too much information may actually make the decision worse than if no aid were given. Methods were considered for allowing decisions to be made better, and integrated information can be provided to the operator. The task can also be divided into smaller subunits so that each decision at each stage will allow the user to consider only a small number of hypotheses; further hypotheses can be considered at the next level.

While the considerations of the human factors and the use of advanced technology helps to enhance design quality, to achieve the quality designs promised by the CAD technology, a management system must be implemented which reduces the barriers to the engineering–manufacturing interface. Without such a reduction in the traditional barriers, the ability to produce designs that are both creative and manufacturable will be difficult to achieve.

11.7. Final remarks

In summary, the implementation of CAD can achieve multiple benefits to the organization and its employees. These benefits are possible with CAD, however, only if appropriate technical features are selected, the workstation is designed to enhance the human–computer interaction and the implementation of CAD is appropriately managed. Without consideration of these factors, CAD can create many more problems than it will solve. Many of the challenges are still in front of us.

References

Abeln, O. (1981), The economy of CAD systems. In J. Mermet (Ed.), *CAD in Medium Sized and Small Industries*. Amsterdam: North-Holland.

Ackoff, R. L. (1967), Management misinformation systems. *Management Science*, **14** (4), B147–B156.

AIDD CADD Committee (1983), *Survey of CAD system users*. Unpublished manuscript. Gretna, LA: American Institute for Design and Drafting.

Albert, A. E. (1982), The effect of graphic input devices on performance in a cursor positioning task. In *Proceedings of the Human Factors Society—26th Annual Meeting*, pp. 54–58. Santa Monica, CA: Human Factors Society.

Alestalo, M. (1979), Patterns of influence in research work: The problems of autonomy and democracy. *R&D Management*, **9**, 221–230.

Allen, T. J. (1971), How effective managers use information systems. *Harvard Business Review*, November–December.

Alter, S. L. (1976), How effective managers use information systems. *Harvard Business Review*, November–December.

Anderson, C. R. (1984), *Management: Skills, Functions, and Organizational Performance*. Dubuque, IA: Wm C. Brown.

Anderson, J. G., Jay, S. J. and Schweer, H. M. (1985a), Physician perceptions of the potential effects of computers on medical practice. In A. H. Levy, & B. T. Williams (Eds.), *Proceedings of the AAMSI Congress 85*, San Francisco, CA, May.

Anderson, J. G., Jay, S. J., Schweer, H. M. and Anderson, M. M. (1985b), Perceptions of the impact of computers on medical practice and physician use of a HIS. *Proceedings of 1985 Symposium on Computer Applications in Medical Care*, Baltimore, MD, November.

Anderson, J. R. (1980), *Cognitive Psychology and its Implications*. San Francisco: Freeman.

Argyris, C. (1985), *Strategy, Change, and Defensive Routines*. Boston: Pitman.

Artwick, B. A. (1984), *Applied Concepts in Microcomputer Graphics*. Englewood Cliffs, NJ: Prentice-Hall Inc.

Atherton, P. R. and Caporeal, L. R. (1985), A subjective judgement of polygon curved surface imagery. *Human Factors in Computing Systems, CHI '85 Conference Proceedings*, San Francisco, CA, April.

Baer, A., Eastman, C. and Henrion, E. (1979), Geometric modelling: a survey. *Computer Aided Design*, **11** (5), 253–272.

Bajcsy, R. and Joshi, A. K. (1978), The problem of naming shapes: vision–language interface. *Proceedings of TINLAP-2, Theoretical Issues in Natural Language Processing*, ACM, 157–161.

Barfield, W. (1986), Cognitive and perceptual aspects of three-dimensional rotations for computer aided design. Unpublished Ph.D. dissertation, School of Industrial Engineering, Purdue University.

Barfield, W. and Salvendy, G. (1985), Perceptual and cognitive aspects of three-dimensional rotations for computer aided design (CAD) systems. *Proceedings of the Human Factors Society—29th Annual Meeting*, Santa Monica, CA: Human Factors Society.

Barfield, W., Chang, T.-C., Majchrzak, A., Eberts, R. and Salvendy, G. (1986), Human factors in the design and use of CAD systems. In G. Salvendy (Ed.), *Handbook of Human Factors/Ergonomics*. New York: John Wiley.

Barlini, P. (1981), The SCM case: The experience undergone by a middle sized mechanical industry in the field of design and automation drawing systems. In J. Mermet (Ed.), *CAD in Medium Sized and Small Industries*. Amsterdam: North-Holland.

Barmack, J. E. and Sinaiko, H. W. (1966), Human factors problems in computer-generated graphic displays. Institute For Defense Analysis Research and Engineering Support Division, Contract SD-50, ARPA Assignment 15.

Barsky, B. A. (1984), A description and evaluation of various 3-D models. *IEEE Computer Graphics & Applications*, **4** (1), 38–52.

Beer, M. (1980), *Organization Changes and Development: A Systems View*. Santa Monica, CA: Goodyear.

Benn, J. A. (1983), CADCAM organizational charts and productivity. *Effective CADCAM*. Institute of Mechanical Engineering Conference Publications, 1983–7, June, London.

Bennett, J. S. and Englemore, R. S. (1979), SACON: A knowledge based consultant for structural analysis. *Proceedings of the Sixth International Joint Conference on Artificial Intelligence*, Tokyo.

Bennis, W. G., Benne, K. D., Chin, R. and Corey, K. E. (1976), *Planning of Change*. New York: Holt, Rinehart, & Winston.

Berg, C. R. (1983), Computer graphics displays: Windows for process control. *IEEE Computer Graphics and Applications*, **3** (2), 43–55.

Besl, P. J. and Jain, R. C. (1985), Three-dimensional object recognition. *Computing Surveys*, **17** (1), 75–145.

Bewley, W. L., Roberts, T. L., Schroit, D. and Verplank, W. L. (1983), Human factors testing in the design of Xerox's "Star" office workstation. In A. Janda (Ed.), *Human Factors in Computing Systems*, pp. 72–77. New York: Association of Computing Machinery.

Bezier, P. (1968), *How Renault Used Numerical Control for Body Design and Tooling*, SAE Paper 680010.

Bezier, P. (1972), *Numerical Control: Mathematics and Applications*. New York: John Wiley & Sons.

Bikson, T. K. and Gutek, B. A. (1983a), Training in automated offices: An empirical study of design and methods. *Proceedings of the IFAC/IFIP Joint International Conference on Training for Tomorrow*, Leiden, The Netherlands, June.

Bikson, T. K. and Gutek, B. A. (1983b), *Advanced office systems: an empirical look at utilization and satisfaction.* Unpublished manuscript (RAND Note for NSF), February.

Bikson, T. K., Gutek, B. A. and Mankin, D. A. (1981), *Implementation of Information Technologies in Office Settings: Review of Relevant Literature* (RAND Paper Series P-6697). Santa Monica, CA: RAND.

Billingsley, P. A. (1982), Navigation through hierarchical menu structures: does it help to have a map? *Proceedings of the Human Factors Society—26th Annual Meeting*, pp. 103–107. Santa Monica, CA: Human Factors Society.

Birmingham, W. P. and Siewiorek, D. P. (1984), MICON: a knowledge based single board computer designer. *Proceedings of 21st Design Automation Conference.*

Bjorn-Andersen, N., Hedberg, V., Mercer, D., Mumford, E. and Sole, A. (Eds.) (1979), *The Impact of Systems Change in Organizations*. Amsterdam: Sijthoff & Noordhoff.

BNA–Bureau of National Affairs (1984), *VDTs in the Workplace: A Study of the Effects on Employment* (BNA No. 45-LDSR-30). Washington, DC: BNA.

Bostrom, R. P. and Heinen, J. S. (1977), MIS problems and failures, Part I. *MIS Quarterly*, September, 17–32.

Bright, J. R. (1964), *Research, Development, and Technological Innovation* New York: Richard Irwin.

Broadbent, D. E. (1958), *Perception and Communications.* New York: Pergamon.

Brown, C. M., Burkleo, H. V., Mangelsdorf, J. E., Olsen, R. A. and Williams, A. R., Jr. (1980), *Human Factors Engineering Criteria for Information Processing Systems.* Sunnyvale, CA: Lockheed (1980).

Brown, C. R. and Schaum, D. L. (1980), User VDT parameters. In E. Grandjean and E. Vigliani (Eds.), *Ergonomic Aspects of Visual Display Terminals.* London: Taylor & Francis.

Brown, D. C. and Chandrasekaran, B. (1983), An approach to expert systems for mechanical design. *Proceedings of Trends and Applications 1983*, National Bureau of Standards, Gaithersburg, MD.

Brown, H., Tong, C. and Foyster, G. (1983), PALLADIO: An Exploratory Environment for Circuit Design, *IEEE Transactions, Computer.*

Burks, H. L. (1984), Formulating realistic expectations of CAD benefits. In R. M. Dunn and B. Herzog (Eds.), *CAD/CAM Management Strategies.* Pennsauken, NJ: Auerbach.

Bury, K. F., Boyle, J. M., Evey, R. J. and Neal, A. S. (1982), Windowing versus scrolling on a visual display terminal. *Human Factors*, **24**, 383–394.

Cakir, A., Reuter, H., von Schmude, L. and Armbruster, A. (1978), *Research on the Effects of Video Display Workplaces on the Physical and Psychological Function of Persons.* Bonn, FR Germany: Federal Ministry for Work and Social Order.

Cakir, A., Hart, D. J. and Stewart, T. F. M. (1979), *The VDT manual.* Darmstadt, FR Germany: IFRA.

Card, S. K., English, W. K. and Burr, B. J. (1978), Evaluation of mouse, rate-controlled isometric joystick, step keys, and text keys for text selection on a CRT. *Ergonomics*, **21,** 601–613.

Card, S. K., Moran, T. P. and Newell, A. (1983), *The Psychology of Human–Computer Interaction.* Hillsdale, NJ: Erlbaum.

Chang, T.-C. and Wysk, R. A. (1985), *An Introduction to Automated Process Planning Systems*. Englewood Cliffs, NJ: Prentice-Hall.

Cheney, P. H. and Dickson, G. W. (1982), Organizational characteristics and information systems: An exploratory investigation. *Academy of Management Journal*, **25** (1), 170–184.

Choi, B. K., Barash, M. M. and Anderson, D. C. (1984), Automatic recognition of machined surfaces from a 3D solid model. *CAD*, **16** (2), 81–86.

Clausen, H. (1979), Concepts and experiments with participative design approaches. In E. Grochla and N. Szyperski (Eds.), *Design and Implementation of Computer-Based Information Systems*. Amsterdam: Sijthoff & Noordhoff.

Collins, F. and Moores, T. (1983), Microprocessors in the office: A study of resistance to change. *Journal of Systems Management*, November, 17–21.

Computervision Corporation (1980), *Management seminar on CAD/CAM*. Unpublished document.

Cooper, L. A. and Podgorny, P. (1976), Mental transformations and visual comparison processes: effects of complexity and similarity. *Journal of Experimental Psychology: Human Perception and Performance*, **2,** 503–514.

Cooper, L. A. and Shepard, R. N. (1973), The time required to prepare for a rotated stimulus. *Memory and Cognition*, **1,** 246–250.

Cougar, J. D. and Zawacki, R. A. (1978), What motivates DP professionals. *Datamation*.

Cropper, A. G. and Evans, S. J. W. (1968), Ergonomics and computer display design. *The Computer Bulletin*, **20,** 369–384.

Cushman, W. H. (1984), Data-entry performance and operator preferences for various keyboard heights. In E. Grandjean (Ed.), *Ergonomics and Health in Modern Offices*, pp. 495–504. London: Taylor & Francis.

Danziger, J. N., Dutton, W. H., Kling, R. and Kraemer, K. (1982), *Computers and Politics*. New York: Columbia University Press.

David, B. (1981), Specification and implementation of an integrated CAD system: Methodology and examples. In J. Mermet (Ed.), *CAD in Medium Sized and Small Industries*. Amsterdam: North-Holland.

Davine, H. and Richards, B. (1981), CAD/CAM utilizing interactive graphics at GE. In J. Mermet (Ed.), *CAD in Medium Sized and Small Industries*. Amsterdam: North-Holland.

Davis, E. and Swezey, R. W. (1983), Human factors guidelines in computer graphics: a case study. *Human Factors*, **25,** 113–133.

Dawes, R. M. (1979), The robust beauty of improper linear models in decision making. *American Psychologist*, **34,** 571–582.

Dawes, R. M. and Corrigan, B. (1974), Linear models in decision making. *Psychological Bulletin*, **81,** 95–106.

DeJesus, E. J. and Callan, J. P. (1985), PEARL: a knowledge based expert assisted CAD tool. *Proceedings of the Second Conference on Artificial Intelligence Applications*, pp. 258–263, Miami Beach, FL, December.

Delvac, J. J. (1981), CAD/CAM implementation: A case history. In J. Mermet (Ed.), *CAD in Medium Sized and Small Industries*. Amsterdam: North-Holland.

Dickson, G. W., Simmons, J. K. and Anderson, J. C. (1980), Behavioral reactions to the introduction of MIS at the U.S. Post Office: Some empirical observations. In Sanders and Birkin (Eds.), *Computers and Management in a Changing Society*.

Doo, D. and Sabin, M. (1978), Behavior of recursive division surfaces near extraordinary points. *Computer Aided Design*, **10**, 356–360.

Douglas, S. A. and Moran, T. P. (1983), Learning text editor semantics by analogy. In A. Janda (Ed.), *Human Factors in Computing Systems*, pp. 207–211. New York: Association for Computing Machinery.

Down, E. (1985), Personal communication. December 2.

Duchnicky, R. L. and Kolers, P. A. (1983), Readability of text scrolled on visual display terminals as a function of window size. *Human Factors*, **25**, 683–692.

Dumais, S. T. and Landauer, T. K. (1981), Psychological investigations of natural terminology for command and query languages. In A. Badre and B. Shneiderman (Eds.), *Directions in Human/Computer Interaction*, pp. 95–109. Norwood, NJ: Ablex.

Dunnette, M. D. (1976), *Handbook of Industrial and Organizational Psychology*. Chicago, IL: Rand McNally.

Eason, K. D., Damodaran, L. and Stewart, T. F. (1975), Interface problems in man-computer interaction. In E. Mumford and H. Sackman (Eds.), *Human Choice and Computers*. New York: Elsevier.

Edwards, G. C. (1978), Organizational impacts of office automation. *Telecommunication Policy* (June), 128–136.

Ellis, P. (1984), Office planning and design: The impact of organizational change due to advanced information technology. *Behaviour and Information Technology*, **3** (3), 221–233.

Encarnacao, J. (1983), Interfaces of a CAD system with its application environment—requirements, conflicts, evaluation procedures. In K. Bo and F. M. Lillehagen (Eds.), *CAD Systems Framework*. Amsterdam: North-Holland.

Encarnacao, J. and Schlechtendahl, E. G. (1983), *Computer Aided Design*. Berlin: Springer-Verlag.

Engel, F. L. (1980), Information selection from visual display units. In E. Grandjean and E. Vigliani (Eds.), *Ergonomic Aspects of Visual Display Terminals*, pp. 121–125. London: Taylor & Francis.

Engel, S. E. and Granda, R. E. (1975), *Guidelines for Man/Display Interfaces*. Technical Report 00.2720, Poughkeepsie, NY: IBM, December.

English, W. K., Engelbart, D. C. and Berman, M. L. (1967), Display-selection techniques for text manipulation. *IEEE Transactions on Human Factors in Electronics*, **HFE-8**, 5–15.

Epton, S. R. (1981), Ten years of *R&D Management*—Some major themes: The role of communication in R&D. *R&D Management*, **11** (4), 165–170.

Ettlie, J. E. (1973), Technology transfer—from innovators to users. *Industrial Engineering*, **15**, 16–23.

Ettlie, J. E. and Rubenstein, A. H. (1980), Social learning theory and the implementation of production innovations. *Decision Sciences*, **11**, 648–668.

Faux, I. D. and Pratt, M. J. (1979), *Computational Geometry for Design and Manufacture*. Chichester: Ellis Horwood.

Fitts, P. M. (1954), The information capacity of the human motor system in controlling the amplitude of movement. *Journal of Experimental Psychology*, **47**, 381–391.

Foley, J. D. and Van Dam, A. (1984), *Fundamentals of Interactive Computer Graphics*. Menlo Park, CA: Addison-Wesley.

Frome, F. S. (1983), Incorporating the human factor in color CAD systems. *IEEE Proceedings of the 20th Design Automation Conference*, 189–195.

Frome, F. S., Levinson, J., Danielson, J. T. and Clavadetscher, J. E. (1979), Shifts in perception of size after adaptation to gratings, *Science*, **206,** *1327–1329.*

Frost, P. A. and Whitley, R. (1971), Communication patterns in a research laboratory. *R&D Management*, **1** (2), 71–79.

Fry, L. W. (1982), Technology-structure research: Three critical issues. *Academy of Management Journal*, **25** (3), 532–552.

Gade, P. A., Fields, A. F., Maisano, R. E., Marshall, C. F. (1981), Data entry performance as a function of method and instructional strategy. *Human Factors*, **23,** 199–210.

Gold, B. (1971), *Explorations in Managerial Economics*. New York: Basic Books.

Gomez, A. D., Wolfe, S. W., Davenport, E. W. and Calder, B. D. (1982), *LMDS: Lightweight Modular Display System*, NOSC Technical Report 767. San Diego, CA: Naval Ocean Systems Center.

Goodman, P. S. and Dean, J. W. (1983), Why productivity efforts fail. In W. L. French, C. H. Bell and R. A. Zawacki (Eds.), *Organizational Development*. Plano, TX: Business Publications.

Goodstein, L. P. (1981), Discriminative display support for process operators. In J. Rasmussen and W. B. Rouse (Eds.), *Human Detection and Diagnosis of Systems Failures*. New York: Plenum.

Gould, J. D. and Alfaro, L. (1983), Revising documents with text editors, handwriting recognition, and speech recognition systems. In *Proceedings of the Human Factors Society—27th Annual Meeting*, pp. 831–833. Santa Monica, CA: Human Factors Society.

Grandjean, E. (1979), *Ergonomical and Medical Aspects of Cathode Ray Tube Displays*. Zurich: Federal Institute of Technology.

Grandjean, E. (1986), Design of VDT workstations. In G. Salvendy (Ed.), *Handbook of Human Factors/Ergonomics*. New York: John Wiley & Sons.

Grandjean, E., Hünting, W. and Pidermann, M. (1983), VDT workstation design: preferred settings and their effects, *Human Factors*, **25,** 161–175.

Greenstein, J. S. and Arnaut, L. Y. (1986), Human factors aspects of manual computer input devices. In G. Salvendy (Ed.), *Handbook of Human Factors/Ergonomics*. New York: John Wiley & Sons.

Griffin, R., Youngblood, S., Bateman, T. and Wayne, S. (1984), *Objective and social environment forces as determinants of employee work perceptions and reactions*. Paper presented at the meeting of the Academy of Management, Boston, August.

Groover, M. P. and Zimmers, E. W. (1984), *CAD/CAM: Computer-Aided Design and Manufacturing*. Englewood Cliffs, NJ: Prentice-Hall.

Gunnarsson, E. and Östberg, O. (1977), *The Physical and Psychological Working Environment in a Terminal-based Computer Storage and Retrieval System*. Report 35. Stockholm: National Board of Occupational Safety and Health.

Gutek, B. A. (1982), Effects of office of the future technology on users: Results of a longitudinal field study. In G. Mensch and J. Niehaus (Eds.), *Work, Organizations, and Technological Change*. New York: Plenum Press.

Gutek, B. A., Bikson, T. K. and Mankin, D. (1984), Individual and organizational consequences of computer-based office information techniques. In S. Oskamp (Ed.), *Applied Social Psychology Annual*, **5,** 231–254.

Hackman, J. R. and Oldham, G. R. (1975), Development of the Job Diagnostic Survey. *Journal of Applied Psychology*, **60,** 159–70.

Hall, L. (1984), Policies and procedures for efficient CAD system use. In R. M. Dunn and B. Herzog (Eds.), *CAD/CAM Management Strategies*. Pennsauken, NJ: Auerbach.

Haller, R., Mutschler, H. and Voss, M. (1984), Comparison of input devices for correction of typing errors in office systems. In *Proceedings of the Interact '84 Conference, First IFIP Conference on Human–Computer Interaction*, pp. 218–223.

Hamilton, H. E. and Sheehan, D. F. (1982), *Human factors in CAD/CAM*. Paper presented at the meeting of the Society of Manufacturing Engineers, Los Angeles, March.

Hanratty, P. J. and Lowman, D. T. (1985), Fourth generation CAD/CAM. *Computer-Aided Engineering*, March.

Hayes-Roth, F., Waterman, D. A. and Lenat, D. B. (Eds.) (1983), *Building Expert Systems*. London: Addison-Wesley.

Heath, L. and Gower, J. (1986), *Management issues in information systems: Lessons from the UK Department of Trade and Industry pilot projects*. Paper presented at the International Scientific Conference on Work with Display Units, Stockholm, May.

Hedberg, B. and Mumford, E. (1975), Design of computer systems. In E. Mumford and H. Sackman (Eds.), *Human Choice and Computers*. New York: North-Holland.

van der Heiden, G. H., Bräuninger, U. and Grandjean, E. (1984), Ergonomic studies on computer-aided design. In E. Grandjean (Ed.), *Ergonomics and Health in Modern Offices*, pp. 119–128. London: Taylor & Francis.

van der Heiden, G. H. and Krueger, H. (1984), *Evaluation of Ergonomic Features of the Computer Vision Instaview Graphics Terminal*. Report of the Department of Ergonomics of the Swiss Federal Institute of Technology.

Helander, M. (1986), Design of visual displays. In G. Salvendy (Ed.), *Handbook of Human Factors/Ergonomics*. New York: John Wiley & Sons.

Henderson, M. R. and Anderson, D. C. (1984), Computer recognition and extraction of form features: a CAD/CAM link. *Computers in Industry*, **5,** 329–339.

Hensey, M. (1981), Communication for the effective management of design. In ASCE (Ed.), *Effective Management of Engineering Design*. New York: ASCE.

Herzberg, F., Mausner, B. and Snyderman, B. (1959), *The Motivation to Work*. New York: John Wiley & Sons.

Hiltz, S. R. (1984), *Online Communities*. Norwood, NJ: Ablex Publications.

Hiltz, S. R. and Turoff, M. (1978), *The Network Nation: Human Communication via Computers*. London: Addison-Wesley.

Holding, D. H. (1986), Concepts of training. In G. Salvendy (Ed.), *Handbook of Human Factors/Ergonomics*. New York: John Wiley & Sons.

Hultgren, G. and Knave, B. (1973), Contrast blinding and reflection disturbances in the office environment with display terminals. *Arbete Och Halsa*.

Hunt, W. and Voelcker, H. (1982), *An Exploratory Study of Automatic Verification of Programs for Numerically Controlled Machine Tools*, Technical Memorandum TM-34. Production Automation Project, College of Engineering and Applied Science, The University of Rochester, Rochester, NY.

Hünting, W., Läubli, T. and Grandjean, E. (1981), Postural and visual loads at VDT workstations, Part 1: constrained postures. *Ergonomics*, **24,** 933–944.

Iacono, S. and Kling, R. (1986), Changing office technologies and transformations of clerical jobs: A historical perspective. In R. Kraut (Ed.), *Technology and the Transformation of White Collar Work*. Hillsdale, NJ: Erlbaum.

Jacobs, J. (1985), *The training needs of Michigan auto suppliers: interim report*. Unpublished manuscript. Ann Arbor, MI: Industrial Technology Institute, September.

Jacobs, J. (1986), Personal correspondence. February 24.

Johansson, C. R. (1986), Design, implementation, and management of CAD/CAM systems. Paper presented at the International Scientific Conference on Work with Display Units, Stockholm, May.

Johnson, B. M. and Associates (1985), *Innovation in Office Systems Implementation*. (NSF Report No. 8110791). Oklahoma, OK: University of Oklahoma.

Journey, M. A. (1984), Summary of the ANSI virtual device interface and virtual device metafile. *Proceedings of Computer Graphics, 84 NCGA*, vol. II, pp. 535–538, Fairfax, VA.

Kahneman, D. (1973), *Attention and Effort*. Englewood Cliffs, NJ: Prentice-Hall.

Karat, J., McDonald, J. E. and Anderson, M. (1984), A comparison of selection techniques: Touch panel, mouse, and keyboard. In *Proceedings of the Interact '84 Conference, First IFIP Conference on Human-Computer Interaction*.

Kaufman, H. G. (1979), Technical obsolescence: Work and organizations are the key. *Engineering Education*, **69** (8), 826–830.

Kay, B. (1985), CAE–the move from tools to solutions. Paper presented at the Third National Conference on University Programs in CAEDM, Purdue University, July.

Kennedy, T. C. S. (1974), The design of interactive procedures for man–machine communication. *International Journal of Man–Machine Studies*, **6,** 309–334.

Kerr, E. B. and Hiltz, S. R. (1982), *Computer-mediated Communication Systems: Status and Evaluation*. New York: Academic Press.

Kintsch, W. (1974), *The Representation of Meaning in Memory*. Hillsdale, NJ: Erlbaum.

Kling, R. (1978), *The Impacts of computing on the work of managers, data analysts and clerks*. Unpublished manuscript. Department of Information and Computer Science, University of California at Irvine, November.

Kling, R. (1980), Social analyses of computing: theoretical perspectives in recent empirical research. *Computing Surveys*, **12** (1), 61–113.

Kling, R. and Iacono, S. (1984), The control of information systems development after implementation. *Communications of the Association for Computing Machinery*, **27** (12), 1218–1226.

Kosslyn, S. M. (1981), Research on mental imagery, some goals and directions. *Cognition*, **10,** 173–179

Kosslyn, S. M. and Pomerantz, J. R. (1977), Imagery, propositions, and the form of internal representations. *Cognitive Psychology*, **9,** 52–76.

Krouse, J. K. (1982), *What Every Engineer Should Know About CAD & CAM*. New York: Marcel Dekker.

Läubli, T. and Hünting, W. (1987), Gesundheitsprobleme bei ganztagiger Bildschirmarbeit an Beispiel der Flugreservationskontrolle. *Zeitschrift für Arbeitswissenshaft*, in press.

Läubli, T., Hünting, W. and Grandjean, E. (1981), Postural and visual loads at VDT workplaces. Part 2: Lighting conditions and visual impairments. *Ergonomics*, **24,** 933–944.

Lawrence, P. R. and Lorsch, J. W. (1967), Differentiation and integration in complex organizations. *Administrative Science Quarterly*, **12** (1), 1–47.

Lazear, T. (1984), The challenge of CAD training. *Computer Graphics World*, January, 49–50.

Leavitt, H. J. (1964), Applied organization change in industry: Structural, technical, and human approaches. In W. W. Cooper, H. J. Leavitt and M. W. Shelly (Eds.), *New Perspectives In Organization Research*. New York: John Wiley & Sons.

Lee, H.-C. and Fu, K.-S. (1982), A computer vision system for generating object descriptions. In *Proceedings of Pattern Recognition and Image Processing Conference*, pp. 466–472, Las Vegas, Nevada. IEEE, New York.

Lee, H.-C. and Fu, K.-S. (1983), Generating object decriptions for model retrieval, *IEEE Transactions on Pattern Analysis and Machine Intelligence*, PAMI-5, 5 (September), 462–471.

Lewin, K. (1951), *Field Theory in Social Science*. New York: Harper & Row.

Liebelt, L. S., McDonald, J. E., Stone, J. D. and Karat, J. (1982), The effect of organization on learning menu access. In *Proceedings of the Human Factors Society—26th Annual Meeting*, pp. 546–550. Santa Monica, CA: Human Factors Society.

Lucas, H. C. (1975a), *Why Information Systems Fail*. New York: Columbia University Press.

Lucas, H. C. (1975b), Performance and the use of an information system. *Management Science*, **21** (8), 908–919.

Lucas, H. C. (1978), Unsuccessful implementation: The case of a computer-based order entry system. *Decision Sciences*, **9**, 68–79.

Machover, C. (1984), Interactive computer graphics. *J. IEEE Computer*, October, 145–161.

Maeda, K., Hünting, W. and Grandjean, E. (1980), Localized fatigue in accounting-machine operators, *Journal of Occupational Medicine*, **22**, 810–816.

Majchrzak, A. (1985), Changes to work resulting from CAD. Paper presented at the conference of American Institute of Industrial Engineers, Chicago, December.

Majchrzak, A., Collins, P. and Mandeville, D. (1985a), A quantitative assessment of changes in work activities resulting from CAD. Paper presented at the meeting of the American Institute of Decision Sciences, Las Vegas, November.

Majchrzak, A., Nieva, V. F. and Newman, P. D. (1985b), *Computer-Automated Technological Innovation in Three Manufacturing Industries*. Final report submitted to NSF. Rockville, MD: Westat.

Majchrzak, A., Nieva, V. F. and Newman, P. D. (1986), A national probability survey of contemporary CAD/CAM adoption. In D. Davis (Ed.), *Implementing Advanced Technology*. San Francisco: Jossey Bass.

Mandal, A. C. (1982), The seated man: theories and realities. In *Proceedings of the Human Factors Society—26th Annual Meeting*, pp. 520–524. Santa Monica, CA: Human Factors Society.

Mann, F. C. and Williams, L. K. (1960), Observations on the dynamics of a change to electronic data-processing equipment. *Administrative Science Quarterly*, **5**, 217–256.

Maslow, A. H. (1954), *Motivation and Personality*. New York: Harper & Row.

Mayer, R. E. (1975), Different problem solving competencies established in learning computer programming with and without meaningful models. *Journal of Educational Psychology*, **67**, 725–734.

McCoy, K. F. (1983), Correcting misconceptions: What to say when the user is mistaken.

In A. Janda (Ed.), *Human Factors in Computing Systems*, pp. 197–201. New York: Association for Computing Machinery.

McDermott, J. (1983), R1: A rule-based configurer of computer systems, *Artificial Intelligence*, September 1983.

McLeod, P. (1977), A dual task response modality effect: Support for multiprocessor models of attention. *Quarterly Journal of Experimental Psychology*, **29**, 651–667.

Mehle, T. (1982), Hypothesis generation in an automobile malfunction inference task. *Acta Psychologica*, **52**, 87–116.

Miller, D. P. (1981), Depth/breadth tradeoff in hierarchical computer menus. In *Proceedings of the Human Factors Society—25th Annual Meeting*. Santa Monica, CA: Human Factors Society.

Miller, I. and Suther, T. W. (1981), Preferred height and angle setting of CRT and keyboard for a display station input task. In *Proceedings of the Human Factors Society—25th Annual Meeting*. Santa Monica, CA: Human Factors Society.

Mishkoff, H. C. (1985), *Understanding Artificial Intelligence*. Texas Instruments.

Mori, H., Mitsumoto, K., Fujita, T. and Goto, S. (1984), Knowledge-based VLSI routine system-WIREX. In *Proceedings of the International Conference on Fifth Generation Computer Systems*, 1984.

Moray, N. (1967), Where is attention limited? A survey and a model. *Acta Psychologica*, **27**, 84–92.

Mumford, E. (1969), Implementing EDP systems—A sociological perspective. *The Computer Bulletin* (January), 10–13.

Murch, G. M. (1973), *Visual and Auditory Perception*. Indianapolis, IN: Bobbs–Merrill.

Murray, W. E., Moss, C. E., Parr, W. H. and Cox, C. (1981), A radiation and industrial hygiene survey of video display terminal operations. *Human Factors*, **23**, 413–420.

Mynatt, C. R., Doherty, M. E. and Tweney, R. D. (1977), Confirmation bias in a simulated research environment: An experimental study of scientific inference. *Quarterly Journal of Experimental Psychology*, **29**, 85–95.

Nakaseko, M., Grandjean, E., Hünting, W. and Gierer, R. (1985), Studies on ergonomically designed alphanumeric keyboards. *Human Factors*, **27**, 175–187.

National Research Council (1986), Effective Utilization of Advanced Manufactory Technology. Washington DC: National Research Council.

Navon, D. and Gopher, D. (1979), On the economy of the human processing system. *Psychological Review*, **86**, 214–253.

Neal, A. S. and Darnell, M. J. (1984), Text-editing performance with partial-line, partial-page, and full-page displays. *Human Factors*, **26**, 431–441.

Newell, A. and Simon, H. A. (1972), *Human Problem Solving*. Englewood Cliffs, NJ: Prentice-Hall.

Newman, W. M. and Sproull, R. F. (1979), *Principles of Interactive Computer Graphics* (2nd Edition). New York: McGraw-Hill.

Newton, R. D. (1984), *Job satisfaction and somatic complaints among computer aided design drafters*. Ph.D. Dissertation, Claremont Graduate School, Claremont, CA.

Newton, R. D. (1986), Personal communication. March 7.

Norman, D. A. (1983), Some observations on mental models. In D. Gentner and A. L. Stevens (Eds.), *Mental Models*, pp. 7–14. Hillsdale, NJ: Erlbaum.

Norton, F. J. (1981), Interactive graphics and personnel selection. In J. Mermet (Ed.), *CAD in Medium Sized and Small Industries*. Amsterdam: North-Holland.

Orr, J. (1985), The merits of design automation. *Computer Graphics World*, January.

Palitto, R. C. (1984), Policies for system implementation and use: The Firestone Tire & Rubber Company case study. In R. M. Dunn and B. Herzog (Eds.), *CAD/CAM Management Strategies*. Pennsauken, NJ: Auerbach.

Pao, Y. C. (1984), *Elements of Computer-Aided Design and Manufacturing*. New York: John Wiley & Sons.

Pelz, D. C. and Andrews, F. M. (1976), *Scientists in Organizations: Productive Climates for R&D*. Ann Arbor, MI: Institute for Social Research.

Perricone, B. T. (1983), *Spatial Representation and Reasoning: A Critical Survey and Proposal, Representation and Processing of Spatial Knowledge*. Computer Science TR-1275, University of Maryland, May.

Pfeffer, J. and Leblebici, H. (1977), Information technology and organization structure. *Pacific Sociological Review*, **20** (2), 241–261.

Pinker, S. (1981), What spatial representation and language acquisition don't have in common. *Cognition*, **10,** 243–248.

Poitou, J. (1981), CAD and working conditions. In J. Mermet (Ed.), *CAD in Medium Sized and Small Industries*. Amsterdam: North-Holland.

Pollack, M., Hirschberg, J. and Webber, B. (1982), User participation in the reasoning processes of expert systems. In *Proceedings of the 1982 National Conference on Artificial Intelligence*. Pittsburgh, PA: AAAI.

Porter, L. W. and Roberts, K. H. (1983), Communication in organizations. In M. D. Dunnette (Ed.), *Handbook of Industrial/Organizational Psychology*. New York: John Wiley & Sons.

Ramsey, H. R. and Atwood, M. E. (1979), *Human Factors in Computer Systems: A Review of the Literature*. Report No. SAI-111-DEN, Englewood, CO: Science Applications Inc., September.

Rasdorf, W. J. (1985), Perspectives on knowledge in engineering design. *Proceedings of ASME Computers in Engineering Conference*, Vol. 2, pp. 249–253.

Rasmussen, J. (1981), Models of mental strategies in process control. In J. Rasmussen and W. B. Rouse (Eds.), *Human Detection and Diagnosis of System Failures*, pp. 241–258. New York: Plenum Press.

Requicha, A. A. G. (1980), Representations for rigid solids: theory, methods, and systems. *Computing Surveys*, **12** (4), 437–463.

Requicha, A. A. G. and Voelcker, H. B. (1982), Solid modelling: a historical summary and contemporary assessment. *IEEE Computer Graphics and Applications*, pp. 9–24, March.

Rice, R. E. (1982), Communication networking in computer-conferencing systems: a longitudinal study of group roles and system structure. In M. Burgoon (Ed.), *Communication Yearbook*, Beverly Hills, CA: Sage.

Rice, R. E. and Associates (1984), *The New Media: Communication, Research, and Technology*. Beverly Hills, CA: Sage.

Rice, R. E. and Case, D. (1983), Electronic message systems in the universe: Description of use and utility. *Journal of Communication*, **33** (1), 131–152.

Robertson, S. P. and Black, J. B. (1983), Planning units in text editing behavior. In A. Janda (Ed.), *Human Factors in Computing Systems*, pp. 217–221. New York: Association for Computing Machinery.

Robey, D. and Zeller, R. L. (1978), Factors affecting the success and failure of an information system for product quality. *Interfaces*, **8** (2), 70–75.

Robinson, C. P., Base, S. J. and Eberts, R. E. (1985), Eyes/ears; spatial/verbal: How should a cockpit talk to a pilot? In R. E. Eberts and C. G. Eberts (Eds.), *Trends in Human Factors/Ergonomics II*, pp. 51–58. Amsterdam: Elsevier.

Rock, I. (1973), *Perception and Orientation*. New York: Academic Press.

Rock, I., Halper, F. and Clayton, T. (1972), The perception and recognition of complex figures. *Cognitive Psychology*, **3,** 655–673.

Rogers, D. F. and Adams, A. J. (1976), *Mathematical Elements for Computer Graphics*. New York: McGraw-Hill.

Rousseau, D. M. (1979), Assessment of technology in organizations. *Academy of Management Review*, **4** (4), 531–542.

Rowe, C. J. (1985), Identifying causes of failure: A case study in computerized stock control. *Behaviour and Information Technology*, **4** (1), 63–72.

Rubin, T. and Marshall, C. J. (1982), Adjustable VDT workstations: can naive users achieve a human factors solution? International Conference on Man–Machine Systems, July, Manchester, England.

Rumelhart, D. E. and Norman, D. A. (1981), Analogical processes in learning. In J. R. Anderson (Ed.), *Cognitive Skills and Their Acquisition*, pp. 335–359. Hillsdale, NJ: Erlbaum.

Rupp, B., 1984, *Human Factors of Workstations with Visual Displays*. San José, CA: IBM.

Salancik, G. R. and Pfeffer, J. (1977), An examination of need-satisfaction models of job attitudes. *Administrative Science Quarterly*, **22,** 427–456.

Salvendy, G. (Ed.) (1982), *Handbook of Industrial Engineering*. New York: John Wiley & Sons.

Salvendy, G. (Ed.) (1984), *Human–Computer Interaction*. Amsterdam: Elsevier.

Salvendy, G. (Ed.) (1986), *Handbook of Human Factors/Ergonomics*. New York: John Wiley & Sons.

Salvendy, G. and Knight, J. (1982), Psychomotor work capabilities. In G. Salvendy (Ed.), *Handbook of Industrial Engineering*. New York: John Wiley & Sons.

Salvendy, G. and Smith, M. J. (Eds.) (1981), *Machine Pacing and Occupational Stress*. London: Taylor & Francis.

Sanders, D. H. (1968), *Computers in Business*. New York: McGraw-Hill.

Scapin, D. L. (1981), Computer commands in restricted natural language: Some aspects of memory and experience. *Human Factors*, **23,** 365–375.

Schaffer, G. (1980), Computer graphics goes to work. *American Machinist*, July, 149–194.

Schaffitzel, W. and Kersten, U. (1985), Introducing CAD systems: problems and the role of user-developer communication in their solution. *Behaviour and Information Technology*, **4** (1), 47–61.

Schneider, W. and Eberts, R. E. (1980), *Automatic Processing and the Utilization of Two Features*. Technical Report No. 8008. Champaign, IL: University of Illinois Human Attention Research Laboratory.

Schneider, W. and Fisk, A. D. (1982), Concurrent automatic and controlled visual search: Can processing occur without resource cost? *Journal of Experimental Psychology: Learning, Memory, and Cognition*, **8,** 261–278.

Schneider, W. and Shiffrin, R. M. (1977), Controlled and automatic human information processing: I. Detection, search, and attention. *Psychological Review*, **84,** 1–66.

Schroeder, R. G. and Benbassat, D. (1975), An experimental evaluation of the relationship of uncertainty to information used by decision makers. *Decision Sciences*, **6,** 556–567.

Schultz, R. L. and Slevin, D. P. (Eds.) (1975), *Implementing OR/MS*. New York: Elsevier.

Schustack, M. W. and Sternberg, R. J. (1981), Evaluation of evidence in causal inference. *Journal of Experimental Psychology: General*, **110**, 101–120.

Senker, P. (1984), Implications of CAD/CAM for management. *OMEGA, International Journal of Management Science*, **12** (3), 225–231.

Shepard, R. N. and Metzler, J. (1971), Mental rotation of three-dimensional objects. *Science*, **171**, 701–703.

Shneiderman, B. (1980), *Software Psychology*. Cambridge, MA: Winthrop.

Shneiderman, B. (1982), Systems message design: Guidelines and experimental results. In A. Badre and B. Shneiderman (Eds.), *Directions in Human/Computer Interaction*, pp. 55–78. Norwood, NJ: Ablex.

Short, J., Williams, E. and Christie, B. (1976), *The Social Psychology of Telecommunications*. New York: John Wiley & Sons.

Shurtleff, D. A. (1980), *How to Make Displays Legible*. La Mirada, CA: Human Interface Design.

Simon, J. R. (1969), Reaction toward the source of stimulus. *Journal of Experimental Psychology*, **81**, 174–176.

Small, D. W. and Weldon, L. J. (1983), An experimental comparison of natural and structured query languages. *Human Factors*, **25**, 253–263.

Smith, B. M. (1983), IGES: A key to CAD/CAM systems integration. *IEEE Computer Graphics and Applications*, pp. 78–83, November.

Smith, M. J., Cohen, B. G. F. and Stammerjohn, L. W. (1981), An investigation of health complaints and job stress in video display operations. *Human Factors*, **23**, 387–400.

Staehle, W. H. (1982), Technology and organizational change in office work: The case of the VDU. In G. Mensch and R. J. Niehaus (Eds.), *Work, Organizations, and Technological Change*. New York: Plenum Press.

Staley, S. M., Henderson, M. R. and Anderson, D. C. (1983), Using syntactic pattern recognition to extract feature information from a solid geometric data base. *Computers in Mechanical Engineering*, 61–66.

Stammerjohn, L. W., Smith, M. J. and Cohen, B. G. F. (1981), Evaluation of work station design factors in VDT operations. *Human Factors*, **23**, 401–412.

Steiger, J. H. and Yuille, J. C. (1983), Long-term memory and mental rotation. *Canadian Journal of Psychology*, **37**, 367–389.

Stewart, R. (1971), *How Computers Affect Management*. London: Macmillan.

Stover, R. (1984), *An Analysis of CAD/CAM Applications*. New York: Prentice-Hall.

Struckman-Johnson, D. L., Swierenga, S. J. and Shieh, K. (1984), *Alternative Cursor Control Devices: An Empirical Comparison Using a Text Editing Task*, Final Report: Task II.2. Vermillion, SD: University of South Dakota, Human Factors Laboratory.

Suther, T. W. and McTyre, J. H. (1982), Effect on operator performance at thin profile keyboard slopes of 5, 10, 15, and 25 degrees. *Proceedings of the Human Factors Society—26th Annual Meeting*, pp. 430–434. Santa Monica, CA: Human Factors Society.

Sutherland, I. E. (1963), SKETCHPAD. In *Proceedings of AFIPS*, **23**.

Swanson, E. B. (1974), MIS's: appreciation and involvement. *Management Science*, **21**, 178–188.

Swierenga, S. J. and Struckman-Johnson, D. L. (1984), *Alternative Cursor Control Devices: An Empirical Comparison Using a Tracking Task*, Final Report: Task

II.3. Vermillion, SD: University of South Dakota, Human Factors Laboratory.

Switchenko, D. M. (1985), In defense of the traditional (non-icon) interface: a position based on a selective review of the literature. In R. E. Eberts and C. G. Eberts (Eds.), *Trends in Ergonomics/Human Factors II*. Amsterdam: Elsevier.

Tapscott, D. (1982), *Office Automation: A User-Driven Method*. New York: Plenum Press.

Teitelbaum, R. C. and Granda, R. E. (1983), The effects of positional constancy on searching menus for information. In A. Janda (Ed.), *Human Factors in Computing Systems*, pp. 150–153. New York: Association for Computing Machinery.

Tirupatikumara, S. R. (1985), *Artificial intelligence techniques in facilities layout planning–The development of an expert system*. Unpublished Ph.D. thesis, School of Industrial Engineering, Purdue University, West Lafayette, IN.

Tomeski, E. A. and Lazarus, H. (1975), *People-oriented Computer Systems: The Computer in Crisis*. New York: Van Nostrand Reinhold.

Trowbridge, M. H. and Cason, H. (1932), An experimental study of Thorndike's theory of learning. *Journal of General Psychology*, **7**, 245–258.

Tull, K. (1984), Planning an in-house CAD/CAM training program. In R. M. Dunn and B. Herzog (Eds.), *CAD/CAM Management Strategies*. Pennsauken, NJ: Auerbach.

Tullis, T. S. (1981), An evaluation of alphanumeric, graphic, and color information displays. *Human Factors*, **23**, 541–550.

Tushman, M. L. (1977), Special boundary roles in the innovation process. *American Sociological Quarterly*, **22**, 587–605.

Tushman, M. L. (1978), Work characteristics and subunit communication structure: a contingency analysis. *American Sociological Quarterly*, **24**, 82–98.

Tushman, M. L. (1982), Managing communication networks in R&D laboratories. In M. L. Tushman and Moore (Eds.), *Readings in the Management of Innovation*. Boston, MA: Pitman.

Tversky, A. and Kahneman, D. (1974), Judgment under uncertainty: heuristics and biases. *Science*, **185**, 1124–1131.

Vaghul, M., Dixon, J. R., Zinsmeister, G. E. and Simmons, M. K. (1985), Expert systems in a CAD environment: injection molding part design as an example. *Proceedings ASME Computers in Engineering Conference*, **2**, pp. 77–82, Boston, MA, August.

Van de Ven, A. H., Delbecq, A. L. and Koenig, R. (1976), Determinants of coordination modes within organizations. *American Sociological Review*, **41**, 322–338.

Vroom, V. H. (1964), *Work and Motivation*. New York: John Wiley & Sons.

Wagner, P. (1985), New directions in mechanical engineering. *Computer Graphics World*, March, 34.

Walsh, V. and Baker, A. (1972), Project management and communication patterns in industrial research. *R&D Management*, **2** (3), 103–109.

Walton, R. E. (1982), Social choice in the development of advanced information technology. *Technology in Sociology*, **4**, 41–49.

Walton, R. E. and Vittori, W. (1983), New information technology: Organizational problem or opportunity. *Office: Technology & People*, **1**, 249–273.

Waltz, D. (1975), Understanding line drawings of scenes with shadows. In P. H. Winston (Ed.), *The Psychology of Computer Vision*, pp. 19–91. New York: McGraw-Hill.

Wason, P. C. and Johnson-Laird, P. N. (1972), *The Psychology of Reasoning: Structure and Content*. London: Batsford.

Weber, A., Sancin, E. and Grandjean, E. (1984), The effects of various keyboard heights on EMG and physical discomfort. In E. Grandjean (Ed.), *Ergonomics and Health in Modern Offices*, pp. 477–483. London: Taylor & Francis.

Whisler, T. L. (1970), *Information Technology and Organizational Change*. Belmont, CA: Wadsworth.

Whitfield, D., Ball, R. G. and Bird, J. M. (1983), Some comparisons of on-display and off-display touch input devices for interaction with computer generated displays. *Ergonomics*, **26**, 1033–1053.

Wickens, C. D. (1980), The structure of attentional resources. In R. Nickerson (Ed.), *Attention and Performance VIII*, pp. 239–257. Hillsdale, NJ: Erlbaum.

Wickens, C. D. (1984), *Engineering Psychology and Human Performance*. Columbus, OH: Merrill.

Wickens, C. D., Sandry, D. and Vidulich, M. (1983), Compatibility and resource competition between modalities of input, central processing, and output: testing a model of complex task performance. *Human Factors*, **25**, 227–248.

Wingert, B., Rader, M. and Riehm, U. (1981), Changes in working skills in the fields of design caused by use of computers. In J. Mermet (Ed.), *CAD in Medium Sized and Small Industries*. Amsterday: North-Holland.

Winston, P. H. (Ed.) (1975), *The Psychology of Computer Vision*. New York: McGraw-Hill.

Wixon, D., Whiteside, J., Good, M. and Jones, S. (1983), Building a user-defined interface. In A. Janda (Ed.), *Human Factors of Computer Systems*, pp. 24–27. New York: Association for Computing Machinery.

Wondrasch, P. J. (1985), Engineering for the 1990's. Paper presented at the Third National Conference on University Programs in CAEDM, Purdue University, July.

Yoshiura, H., Fujimura, K. and Kunii, T. L. (1984), Top-down construction of 3-D mechanical object shapes from engineering drawings. *Computer*, 32–39.

Yuille, J. C. and Steiger, J. H. (1982), Nonholistic processing in mental rotation: some suggestive evidence. *Perception and Psychophysics*, **31**, 201–209.

Zaltman, Duncan and Holbek (1973), *Innovations and Organizations*. New York: John Wiley & Sons.

Zuboff, S. (1982), New worlds of computer mediated work. *Harvard Business Review*, **60** (5), 142–152.

Zwaga, H. J. G. and Duijnhouwer, F. (1984), The influence of a fixed background in a VDU display on the efficiency of colour and shape coding. *Proceedings of the Human Factors Society—28th Annual Meeting*, pp. 331–335. Santa Monica, CA: The Human Factors Society.

Index